DOING PHILOSOPHY

DOING *PHIL*

Thomas Ellis Katen

Community College of Philadelphia
Philadelphia, Pennsylvania

OSOPHY

PRENTICE-HALL, INC., Englewood Cliffs, New Jersey

DOING PHILOSOPHY *by Thomas Ellis Katen*

© 1973 by PRENTICE-HALL, INC.
Englewood Cliffs, New Jersey

ISBN: 0-13-217570-3

Library of Congress Catalog Card Number: 72-6362

Printed in the United States of America
10 9 8 7 6 5 4 3

PRENTICE-HALL INTERNATIONAL, INC., *London*
PRENTICE-HALL OF AUSTRALIA, PTY. LTD., *Sydney*
PRENTICE-HALL OF CANADA, LTD., *Toronto*
PRENTICE-HALL OF INDIA PRIVATE LIMITED, *New Delhi*
PRENTICE-HALL OF JAPAN, INC., *Tokyo*

TO MY MOTHER AND FATHER

*Men of Athens, I honour and love you; but I
shall obey God rather than you, and while
I have life and strength I shall never cease from
the practice and teaching of philosophy, exhort-
ing anyone whom I meet and saying to him
after my manner: You my friend . . . are you
not ashamed of heaping up the greatest amount
of money and honour and reputation, and caring
so little about wisdom and truth and the greatest
improvement of the soul. . . .*

SOCRATES, *Apology*

*He said: Who then are the true philosophers?
Those, I said, who are lovers of the vision of
truth.*

PLATO, *The Republic*

Contents

THE WORK
OF THE PHILOSOPHER II

4 What Should We Do? Ethics

5 A Little Reflection on Some Big Questions

6 The Role of Philosophy in the Space Age

THE PERSECUTION AND DEATH
OF THE PHILOSOPHER **III**

Preface

When Your Cup Runneth Over—Empty Your Cup

Nan-in, Japanese master of Zen Buddhism, received a university professor who wished to learn Zen. The professor was most serious about his interest in Zen and was eager to commence his search for enlightenment, but Nan-in, a simple man, bade the professor relax, and gave him a cup of tea. Nan-in poured so much in the cup that it began to run over. The professor was a bit piqued and informed his Oriental host that his cup of tea was overflowing.

"Like this cup," Nan-in explained to him, "you are full of your own opinions and speculations. How can I show you Zen unless you first empty your cup."[1]

We are all full of our own opinions and speculations, our own prejudices and built-in hostilities. How can we ever be shown philosophy unless we

---

[1] *Zen Flesh, Zen Bones,* compiled by Paul Reps (Garden City, N.Y.: Doubleday & Company, Inc., 1961), p. 5.

first empty our cups? Philosophy should not be a mere pouring of more facts into our already overflowing cups of information. Philosophy should be a means of helping us to empty our brimming cups. When we do so we may become filled with the true delight of honest understanding; thus we may come to be filled with wisdom.

In my own case I took up the study of philosophy because I wanted to get out of the unremitting rain of unreflected-upon information one tends to be drenched with in so many areas of learning. I earnestly believed the study of philosophy did not involve merely the attainment of better information but helped one in becoming a better person. That was important to me. Philosophy more than other domains of knowledge provided the opportunity not just to gather information but also to reflect upon its meaning, and thus to really understand it. Furthermore, philosophy leads one beyond examination of specific factual matters to a consideration of the meaning of life itself, and one hopes that this will help one to become a bit wiser. It seemed to me that in struggling with the big questions of philosophy, a person could become a little bigger himself. In this age of mechanization, specialization, and immense complexity, there is a need for simple wisdom and for the philosophical activity of raising basic questions about matters that vitally affect us. Philosophy is not the hopelessly technical and recondite subject many take it to be. Rather, it is an often impassioned examination of all things that concern human beings. This is what philosophy meant to Socrates, in whose life we find embodied the very spirit of philosophy. Socrates wrote his philosophy not in musty tomes but in the streets of Athens where he was always to be found engaging in vital discourse with his fellow man. For Socrates, wisdom was not so much a matter of *having* a philosophy as it was of *doing* philosophy. The important thing to him was actively and critically *searching* for truth and justice rather than resting on a set of theoretical assumptions or ideas about man and the universe. For Socrates philosophy did not mean removing oneself from the world to meditate upon it; it meant getting involved in life, and ceaselessly and carefully examining every facet of existence.

Taking our cue from Socrates, we should understand philosophy as a process of diligently and constantly taking stock of ourselves and our universe. We cannot acquire philosophy by reading a textbook or by familiarizing ourselves with the views of philosophers; we have to live it and to love it. In this way philosophy becomes something we find ourselves naturally experiencing in everything we do. In living philosophy a person is always deeply exploring things—to understand them on a fundamental rather than on a superficial level. Philosophy means reflective examination not merely of technical philosophical issues but of *everything*. Thus we may say philosophy is the most relevant of studies, for anyone who "philosophizes" about his work, instead of just taking its assumptions for granted, will be a better doctor, lawyer, scientist, educator, actor, politician, economist, as well as a better person.

Not only can philosophy be far more relevant than most people think, but it can even be more interesting. One day a bright, bearded student complained to me that his philosophy course really turned him off. I have always thought it unfortunate that so many students seem to conceive of themselves like light bulbs to be turned on or off, but I did get this student's point, which simply was that his course in philosophy was boring. My feeling is that, of all subjects, philosophy is the last one that should be boring. Philosophy can and should be a fascinating field to wander through and wonder about. The study of philosophy can lead us to new discoveries and insights about ourselves and the world. If we really get into philosophy, it will get into us, for there is great power in ideas—power that can move men and nations and even worlds. There is also great pleasure in struggling with and gaining mastery over such ideas.

In any case, we should not forget that behind the great philosophical ideas are flesh-and-blood human beings in whose lives there is much drama. Philosophers are men whose lives are not simply built of the immaterial stuff of abstract wisdom, and one may well find oneself moved to laughter and tears by the drama of their lives. There is much humor in the lives of men such as Diogenes, Thomas Aquinas, Immanual Kant, and Bertrand Russell. According to conventional standards philosophers often behave in strange ways and they also have some strange ideas. There are not only many amusing incidents in the lives of the philosophers but there are also humorous possibilities in the development of philosophical ideas and problems. Although philosophy deals with matters that are quite profound, there can be fun in it. However, behind the fun in philosophy, there is a seriousness that mankind requires if it is to understand and cope with its deepest problems.

I decided to teach philosophy because I believed it concerned matters most important to men, and I wanted to help others become aware of this.

My first full-time teaching position was at a small liberal arts college situated in a small town that afforded many quick passages to woods and open spaces. I looked forward to this position because it would provide the opportunity to be close to nature as well as to my students. To me philosophy was very exciting. It meant wisdom, drama, intellectual discovery, and human communication. I was tremendously enthusiastic about the prospect of bringing the wisdom of philosophy to my students. But upon arriving at my new job, I found that students were less than enthusiastic about the prospects of receiving the wisdom of philosophy. My sense of a philosophical mission was slightly shaken when I overheard one student say to another that he had to take the "lousy philosophy course." The other student informed him he already had the course and it was a "drag." This student elaborated saying his teacher was always talking about how acceptance of death could confer meaning on life and then he added, "but all he ever did was bore us all to death." The philosophy course I was going to teach was a required course, and students felt a great hostility toward it. There were very negative vibrations. I began to envision placards reading "Philosopher Go Home."

It seemed to me that these students were turned off to philosophy because it was presented to them as a remote and irrelevant field of study involving endless arguments over hair-splitting details that only professional philosophers could find interesting. That was not what I thought philosophy was about at all, and it seemed to me that if I could present my case in such a way as to help students see that philosophy deals with issues that "hit them where they live," they would not be inclined to say "Philosopher go home." I wanted to bring philosophy home to them, not to have them send me home with my philosophy.

I like to flatter myself with the thought that over the course of my years of teaching philosophy I have experienced a lot of joy in doing philosophy with my students and friends and have always tried to bring philosophy out of the classroom and into life. A few years ago I came to feel that I would like to try translating my approach to philosophy into the form of a book. I have tried to cover technical material in my classes in such a manner that my students and I could experience philosophy not simply as an intellectual matter but as a human and personal affair. If something of this approach can come across in this book, those who read it may not only gain some information about the business of philosophy but may be moved a little by the spirit of philosophy.

It is not for information that we turn to philosophy but for ideas and concepts that serve to hold and give shape to what we know from other fields of knowledge. In the pages that follow philosophy is presented in this light—as a field of study that impinges on all facets of life. Toward this end the material in this book is divided into three main parts. The first and third are rather slim, and the second provides the major part of the bulk. I have found that both scholars and average people widely assume the philosopher to be most impractical. Particularly in an age of science and great change in which people demand practical results, philosophy more than ever seems to be irrelevant. Thus in the first part of this book, a brief look is taken at the life of the philosopher with a view to showing how impractical, eccentric, and even comical he is at times. But this may be more because he is truly irreverent than irrelevant, or because he renounces the ordinary run of pleasing consequences in order to discover truth. It is the *life* dedicated to truth which often motivates the *work* of the philosopher.

In this book our main concern is with the *work* of the philosopher, and this has mainly been achieved in the basic fields of *epistemology* (what we might loosely call the study of knowledge), *metaphysics* (the study of reality or Being), and *ethics* (the study of what is good or right), and what such terms may mean. Alongside ethics and under the heading of axiology or value theory, the study of *aesthetics*—the philosophy of art or beauty—and *logic*—the tool the philosopher uses or reflects upon to do his work—constitute an important aspect of the philosopher's work. However, in this book, which primarily aims at introducing the reader to philosophy, we do not get into the areas of aesthetics and logic. The assumption is that one would do better to examine these subjects separately after one has come to terms with some of the hard core problems in the very basic fields of epistemology, metaphysics, and ethics. The examination of the philosophies and problems of these latter fields constitutes the second part or core of this book.

Having briefly looked at the life of the philosopher and more extensively at his work, finally and briefly we look at the death of the philosopher. What some may see as the foolish life of philosophers issues in work that, while it may be regarded as impractical by matter-of-fact people, is of practical value to cause the martyrdom of the philosopher. The work of the philosopher should be and often is a dedication to truth, and it is the truth that frees one. In a world so thoroughly rooted in power as ours, the price exacted for freedom has often been sacrifice of personal safety, liberty, and even life itself. That philosophers have been persecuted at critical moments in history provides testimony to their relevance to those in power. In discussing this tragic finale we will consider the philosopher in broad and nontechnical terms as the lover of wisdom—which is what philosophy is—rather than merely as a professional or academic figure.

Thus the book will be unfolded as follows:

Part   I.   The Life of the Philosopher
Part II.   The Work of the Philosopher
Part III.   The Persecution and Death of the Philosopher

It is hoped that as a result of this endeavor the student will not feel merely that he has acquired some more information, but that he has acquired more vision and will feel some friendship toward philosophy and perhaps, the author.

I wish to express my deepest appreciation and gratitude to Steve Allen for his contribution of a very excellent and keenly perceptive introduction, and I think it should be noted that since this most relevant material was contributed with what seemed the speed of light, one would not have guessed this multi-talented man was at the time involved in so many other activities and projects.

My special thanks also to Monroe Beardsley of Temple University and Charles W. Mason of the University of Delaware for reading the manuscript and offering many valuable suggestions.

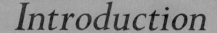

Introduction

by Steve Allen

A fundamental axiom of the free-enterprise economy is: you can't sell the customer unless you first pull him into the store. Even as regards absolute necessities it is considered necessary to present what is required in the most favorable light possible.

On a more rational planet it should not prove necessary to sugar-coat any intellectual pills. On this one, however, countless factors of media inevitably affect the reception of message. Perhaps for a few years after Gutenberg's invention of the press the unadorned reality of type on paper was sufficient to transfix the literate. Except for a fortunate few, however, the fascination with the bare thing-in-itself did not historically persist. To keep readers interested, publishers and educators resorted to various forms of printing type, to richly colored book-covers, to illustration, and other appeals to the senses.

At the present moment keeping young people acutely interested in the educative process is nothing less than a matter of the survival of our total culture. This seems now generally acknowledged as regards children of pre-school and primary-grade ages. The entire thrust of the new approach to basic education, in fact, involves approaching the student's mind through as many physical channels as possible so that the brain will be better enabled to retain important impressions. It is no longer considered enough, for example, to tell a child that one-third and one-third and one-third add up to a whole. We now reinforce the abstract message with three pie-slices of brightly colored wood which, when placed together, form a full circle.

Today the mind of man is assailed by an enormous amount of raw material, particularly in our large urban centers. People, objects, sounds, lights, colors, movement, dangers, pleasures, pressures of all kinds compete on the stage of our attention. Perhaps in a cloistered monastery concentration on dry and weighty texts might still be easily accomplished. And there are some, of a naturally scholarly bent, who apparently contrive to get a good education regardless of the physical environment. In the 1970's, however, particularly in the context of the experience of the American young, the distractions are of such an order that, if the vitally important message of philosophy is to really *reach* us, it must employ means specifically chosen because they are competitive in the present sensory context.

It has been said that war is far too important a matter to be left to the generals. Just so philosophy is far too important to be left to the philosophers, or even to those few students who are by nature inclined to a strong interest in such matters. For in the difficult world that now presses in upon all of us we greatly handicap ourselves if we face dangerous and puzzling questions unarmed by some degree of familiarity with thousands of years of philosophical speculation and debate.

This is not to say that to know what to do about problems of war and peace, nuclear disarmament, urban unrest, social injustice and race tensions we need only refer to Thomas Aquinas, John Locke, or Bertrand Russell. But it *is* to say that a reasoned and scholarly approach to the difficulties that perplex us is far preferable to the emotion-laden prescriptions of, say, either the Minutemen of the Right or the Weathermen of the Left. Most Americans rule out the appeal to naked violence that presently arises from the inflamed passions of both the Nazis and Fascists and the Revolutionary Marxists. But on what grounds, for precisely what reasons, do we regard such appeals as counter-productive? This question *can* be answered within the context of philosophy—those branches of it dealing with morals and politics.

Are all wars unjust? Was the Second World War justified but the Viet-namese War unjustified? Is capital punishment civilized? Thomas Aquinas thought it was perfectly proper to burn heretics alive. Today no philosopher would agree with him.

Are you frustrated by the "stubborness" of those with whom you argue? Is there then a proper technique of argument? What is *logic*? Are men really more logical than women? These are only a few of the many thousands of timely, where-it's-at questions that philosophy deals with. The reality, then, is clear enough. But how do you get young people interested in it?

In far too many cases, you don't; the average citizen is a philosophical illiterate. But it need not be so and along comes Thomas Katen to dramatize the point and to offer an attractive solution.

That he unashamedly "popularizes" philosophy in this entertaining book is evident. The important thing is he carries the trick off successfully. His success, I would think, is rooted in his motivation, which is a simple *love* for the field to which he has devoted his life.

Philosophy itself is, of course, the love of wisdom, and love implies joy.

"Having experienced a lot of joy doing philosophy with my students and friends," Katen has explained, "and always having tried to bring philosophy out of the classroom and into life, I came to feel I would like to try to translate this approach which had been so enriching to me and many of my students into the form of a book. . . . If something of this approach can come across in this book, those who read it may not only gain some information about the business of philosophy, but be moved a little by the spirit of it."

As a humorist, I found myself attracted by Katen's zest for his assignment.

"There is much humor in the lives of men such as Diogenes, Thomas Aquinas, Voltaire, Kant, and Bertrand Russell," and he says "there are many humorous possibilities in the development of philosophical ideas and problems. . . . Behind the fun in philosophy, however, there is a seriousness that mankind requires to understand and cope with its deepest problems."

What I believe Katen will achieve by his revolutionary approach to subject matter that too many young people regard as not only serious but dull is to demonstrate that the shape of today's world has been largely *determined* by philosophy. The systems of ideas with which all major philosophers have been concerned have had practical consequences that affect all of us. The awe-inspiring conflict between East and West on our planet is not merely a confrontation between large states in the historic sense; it is a conflict of philosophies. Not to understand both our own and that of our Marxist opponents is folly since it means playing a dangerous game without taking the trouble to learn the rules.

Once, hearing a teen-ager say that he did not like jazz music but did like rock-and-roll, I explained to him that rock is merely a subdivision of jazz, that it grew out of jazz. The same young man might today say that he is interested in Marx but has no interest in philosophy. Since Marx was a political philosopher the assertion is senseless.

Man today wants to understand himself, his fellow-man, his earthly environment, the realm of outer space, the mysteries of time, matter, nature, God. There are no more important questions. Thomas Katen demonstrates in this lively, seemingly irreverent outline, that there are no more interesting questions either.

PART I

THE
LIFE
OF
THE
PHILOSOPHER

I

On Digging
Deep Thought

Fools Who Thither Turn Their Blinking Eyes

The great and profound German philosopher Martin Heidegger once wrote:

> ... *"existence"* ... *designates a mode of Being; specifically, the Being of those beings who stand open for the openness of Being in which they stand, standing it.*

One may not be able to stand, let alone understand, such a philosophical pronouncement, and often as one goes further in the tomes of Heidegger he may feel deeper in a mire of obscurity:

> *The proposition "man alone exists" does not mean by any means that man alone is a real being. ... The proposition "man exists" means: man is that being whose Being is distinguished by the open-standing standing-in in the unconcealedness of Being, from Being, in Being.*[1]

[1] Martin Heidegger, "The Way Back into the Ground of Metaphysics," in *Existential-*

We lose a lot of prospective philosophy students from such talk. If an ordinary person went about talking like Heidegger, people would think he had lost his mind. Sometimes when philosophers talk this way they are even believed to be great minds. The trouble is that many persons believe philosophers are such great minds that the things they think about have nothing to do with the problems ordinary people are concerned about. Many people think philosophers make highly profound statements, but they do not think philosophers make any sense. And there are some who think philosophers make profound nonsense. Samuel Butler claimed that engaging in philosophy is like stirring mud, and a contemporary philosopher, Herbert Feigl, has complained that philosophy is the disease of which it should be the cure. Voltaire observed that when he who hears doesn't know what he who speaks means, and when he who speaks doesn't even know what he himself means, then that is philosophy. And he hadn't even read that statement by Heidegger!

It was once remarked that no thought is so absurd that some philosopher has not thought of it. After one philosopher convinces you by the most careful logical demonstration that nothing in the entire universe can ever move, another will meticulously establish that everything in the universe is always moving. If that doesn't mix you up enough there will always be a philosopher around to prove to you that you do not exist—by which time you probably don't even care to. Then there will be the philosopher who will argue with perfect logic that nothing cannot be nothing, because it is something; after all, if nothing were not something, how could it be nothing? Still another philosopher will argue that what we see is not really there, and only what we cannot see is really there.

Modern man simply does not have time for eternity. He is in too much of a hurry to catch his train, to make a fast buck, or to make love. Somehow it does not provide him with great satisfaction to be informed that money and sex are only illusions, or that trains and automobiles do not really exist. Money and sex may be only illusions, but they seem to be very pleasant illusions to many people. Have you ever tried to tell an operator of a motor vehicle stuck in a traffic jam during rush hour on the freeway that cars do not exist? Indeed he might wish they were only illusions, but he is unpleasantly certain the cars do exist.

People do not want to be told, however convincingly, the world does not exist, because the world is too much a part of their experience for them to accept that; they want to be told how to exist in the world. People are confused; they want solutions. One student told me that trying to figure out some of those philosophical problems was enough "to drive you crazy."

We can describe the situation of modern philosophy in public relations terms by noting the philosopher just does not have a good image. Indeed, one very establishment-oriented philosophy chairman once said to me, "Tom, we have got to do something to jazz up the image of philosophy, or sociology and psychology will be getting all of the elective students." He

ism from Dostoevski to Sartre, ed. Walter Kaufmann (New York: Meridian Books, Inc., 1956), p. 214.

wasn't much of a philosopher, but he was correct in his recognition of the fact that many students seem to be turned off by philosophy. People do not want to struggle through metaphysics to understand their problems better when they can forget them by taking marijuana. For many students pot is preferable to Plato.

What such students do not realize is that they must go to pot because their life lacks the philosophical foundations a Plato or some other philosopher can supply. When a person, a society, or a civilization lacks adequate philosophical assumptions that can instill men and women with meaning and purpose, they will experience a sense of being lost, and will have to seek substitutes. As a matter of fact, Heidegger's philosophy makes great sense of our world and its problems, however difficult it may be to get into his teachings because he works on so profound and original a level that he cannot speak in simple and direct terms. Philosophers deal with ultimate questions and ultimate foundations, and that these foundations are the basis for the practical level of everyday life is remote and not easy to see. Thus what the philosopher reflects upon seems impractical and not relevant to people seeking quick answers to immediate questions. What is more, the philosopher seems to live upon a level as impractical as that upon which he thinks; the life that produces an up-in-the-clouds system of ideas is itself up in the clouds. Those who agree that no thought is so absurd that some philosopher has not thought of it, might also suppose that no life is so absurd that some philosopher has not lived it.

A secretary for a philosophy department remarked to me that when she thought of a philosopher, she thought of someone who was dead. She thought of a philosopher as a fossil. Her statement gives expression to what many people think of philosophers. They do not think of them as dynamic individuals in the living present but as sort of bumbling old men from the dead past. Philosophers may be thought of as having great minds but also as *being* absent-minded professors, eccentrics who devote their lives to *thinking* about things instead of *doing* things. It is not often realized that thinking may be the most important form of doing. Nonetheless, it must be granted philosophers do have their idiosyncrasies. For example, there was one philosopher who slept twelve hours a night instead of the usual eight, justifying it by explaining that he slept "slowly."

If one returns to the origins of Western philosophy, one will not have to wait long to discover some rather curious behavior. The first great philosopher in the Western world was Thales of Miletus. Thales was a very wise man, and one night while he walked about profoundly reflecting upon the stars, he fell right into a well, from which he had to be assisted by a village maiden. For some men that might have provided an excellent opportunity to become involved with the maiden. Thales, as many of the great philosophers, was so devoted to abstract ideas he did not have time for any concrete romance. Nietzsche said that a married philosopher is a comic character, and Thales certainly would not have seemed comic by Nietzsche's standards. His mother used to nag him about getting married, but he would always tell her that it was not yet time. When he became older she told him it must be time, but he answered that now it was too late.

Another great pre-Socratic, Heraclitus, was the famous philosopher of change, who maintained that all is war and strife. He, too, might be regarded as something of a strange character. The epithet applied to him by his contemporaries was "the dark" because it was said that he painted everything black. He did not have a friendly attitude toward his fellow citizens, and once recommended that everyone should hang himself. The only person Heraclitus thought much of was Bias in Priene, the son of Teutames, and the only reason Heraclitus liked him was because Bias once said that most men are wicked. He also scorned most philosophers and men of learning as well as ordinary individuals and commented that such men only serve to prove that much learning does not teach men to think.

If one wanted to discover the spirit of philosophy one could not do better than to look at the life of Socrates, yet in the painting of that beautiful life there are many comic strokes. In the first place, Socrates did not look like a tragic hero; there were those who thought he looked more like an old goat. Alcibiades claimed that Socrates resembled Maryas the Satyr. (A satyr is part goat and has the ability to start riots.) Aristophanes claimed that Socrates did not walk like a man so much as he strutted like a waterfowl. And so Socrates strutted about Athens, fouling up his fellow citizens with that lethal Socratic irony. He would go about so humbly asking people questions, and telling them he knew nothing, and after they answered him he would make them feel they knew even less than nothing. It was said of Socrates:

> that frequently owing to his vehemence in argument, men set upon him with their fists or tore his hair out; and that for the most part he was despised and laughed at, yet bore all his ill usage patiently. . . .[2]

Once when a young man asked Socrates if he should get married, Socrates replied that whatever he did, he would regret it. And when Socrates' wife told him he suffered unjustly, he answered that it would make no sense to suffer justly. His wife, Xanthippe, had the reputation of being a shrew, and it is said she once poured water on Socrates and on another occasion tore his coat off his back. Socrates, who was a great philosopher and wanted to show his resignation, said that he got married to prove he could endure any hardship.

Although Socrates was a great philosopher to the Athenians, at times he seemed more a great buffoon or a clown. Another philosophical personage of antiquity who seemed to abound in some of the qualities of the clown was Diogenes the Cynic. Diogenes came after the golden age of Athens, after the time of Socrates, in a period of much cynicism and disillusionment. And yet there was no shortage of mirth in this cynic. In Athens he went

[2] Demetrius of Byzantium's views, summed up by Diogenes Laertius, *Lives of Eminent Philosophers,* trans. R. D. Hicks (Cambridge, Mass.: Harvard University Press, 1925), I, 151.

about in the daylight holding a lantern to help in his search for an honest man. There is a story that Diogenes, who looked so assiduously for an honest man, was thrown out of his native city of Sinope because he was discovered to be a counterfeiter. He retaliated to being exiled by sentencing the people of Sinope to remain there without him. Diogenes excelled in a quality known in Yiddish as *chutzpah,* which can best be translated as colossal nerve. For example, when Alexander the Great, before whom everybody bowed down, pompously offered to grant Diogenes any favor, Diogenes told this imperious world conqueror to step back and get out of the sun. That's *chutzpah.* Once when Diogenes visited a man who had a magnificent house, the man, knowing Diogenes' reputation, asked him not to spit on anything of value. Thereupon Diogenes spat upon the man's face, indicating that it was of no value. Diogenes admired dogs very much, and so a rather wise type threw a bone at him—in response to which Diogenes urinated upon him. When Diogenes was taken captive by some pirates, he carried on so that they were eager to get rid of him. And when he was to be sold as a slave, Diogenes was far from being filled with fear; instead, he instructed prospective buyers to step up and buy a master. Diogenes never ceased being critical of doing things in conventional ways. He saw, for example, no need for a person to have a whole house to live in, and, true to his own principles, he himself lived in a tub.

As the ancient world faded out and the medieval world began to emerge, the emphasis of philosophy shifted from here to eternity. The interest of medieval philosophers, however, was not always so spiritual. An excellent case in point may be found in the life of Abélard. It was in Paris that the brilliant philosopher Abélard was introduced to Fulbert, a canon of Notre Dame. Deeply impressed with Abélard's reputation as a man of learning, Fulbert requested Abélard to tutor his lovely young niece Héloïse. Abélard accepted, and Fulbert was delighted until he found out how passionately Abélard was putting himself into the role of teacher. He kicked Abélard out, but Abélard and Héloïse did not stay apart long, and when they came together again their union proved to be more pregnant than ever, and so did Héloïse. Now Fulbert had some philosophical advice for philosopher Abélard: get married! Finally Abélard and Héloïse did get married, but Abélard told only Fulbert, for in that time it was accepted for a cleric such as Abélard to have a mistress and an illegitimate child, but not a legitimate wife. However, old Fulbert was more worried about Héloïse's reputation than Abélard's. His solution was simple: he had Abélard castrated. In the end Héloïse was sent to a convent. Then came those deeply moving and magnificent love letters from Héloïse to Abélard. These letters revealed Héloïse's wonderful devotion to Abélard and her inspiring and tender affection. One would imagine Abélard must have deeply moved Héloïse for her to have remained so dedicated in the face of immense opposition.

This story, unfortunately, has been questioned by historical scholars such as Orelli and Lalanne who have found inconsistencies in style and content to indicate that Héloïse could not have written those torrid love letters. Then who did write them? A scholar named Schmeidler developed the case that those masterful letters expressing such profound love for Abélard were written by Abélard to himself. Scholars have cast doubt upon the assumption Héloïse actually scribed those memorable letters, and in this era of cynicism of that which is romantic as well as philosophical, what was in reality inspiring love can be viewed in terms of superficial externals and debunked. Who knows? Perhaps it shall yet be exploited as an "X"-rated movie!

One of the truly great philosophers of the Middle Ages, St. Thomas Aquinas, was not interested in sex as Abélard was but was interested in food. St. Thomas was a rather corpulent man who generally had very little to say, and as a young man when he opened his mouth it was usually for the purpose of eating. But if Thomas did not talk much, he did think a great deal. This did not make his father very happy, for his father was Count Landulf—a descendant of the Lombard kings—and he wanted his son Thomas to become a man of influence and importance. If he could not get Thomas a position of distinction in the military or politics, there was still status in being an abbot or a bishop, and with Landulf's influence that would be easy to arrange. Then, in the midst of his grand plans for his son, Thomas nonchalantly strolled into the castle one day and informed his father that he had just become a member of the Begging Friars. Count Landulf's answer was to have his son locked up in a tower. But nothing seemed to swerve Thomas from his course of religious dedication. At this point the count decided that what man had been unable to achieve with Thomas, woman might. Thus a sensuous woman was sent to the room in which Thomas was being kept. He chased her out with a branding iron. Finally Thomas escaped and went to study with Albert the Great. Thomas still did not develop the habit of talking much and fellow students called him the "dumb ox," but when he did talk, his colleagues found that he was the wisest fox. He went on to become one of the great names in philosophy.

As the modern age began to dawn, the interest of men generally moved from eternity to here. Francis Bacon, a British philosopher with a very modern outlook, was almost exclusively preoccupied with the here and not at all interested in eternity. He is a good example of the fact that not all philosophers have disdained practical considerations, and in this he had numerous predecessors. Just to show how easy it would be for a philosopher to make money if he wanted to, Thales had figured out when it would be a good season for olives and then had rented all the oil presses; in this way he amassed a fortune. Plato's brilliant student Aristotle was also a rather down-to-earth philosopher. There was a time when intrigue surrounded him and he fell into trouble with the Athenians. Remembering that Socrates had been executed by the Athenians, Aristotle remarked he would not give the Athenians the chance to sin twice against philosophy—a sentiment whose beauty is not marred by the fact that he was probably less concerned with the Athenians sinning twice against philosophy than once against Aristotle.

Although Aristotle was known as master of those who know, Bacon felt Aristotle knew nothing. He wanted to replace Aristotle's method with a strictly experimental, inductive approach to all problems. Bacon felt that learning had been held back too long by the dead hand of Aristotle and so he dedicated himself to a new *advancement of learning.* He also dedicated himself to the advancement of himself. Bacon said that he was born to serve mankind, but his main interest was in serving himself, and he admitted that what he really sought was political power. In this direction, he got a nice helping hand from Lord Essex, a man who had the power Bacon lacked. Essex was friendly and generous to Bacon, constantly giving him help and even giving him an estate. Delighted that Essex got him so fine a house, Bacon next sought to enlist Essex's assistance in getting him a fine wife. The noble lady he desired, however, instead married Sir Edward Coke, a highly distinguished attorney. Undaunted by his failure as a marriage broker, Essex proved what a loyal friend he was by getting Bacon out of debtor's prison when the philosopher's careless spending habits landed him there. Indeed, whenever Bacon got into trouble, Essex was there to lend his assistance. Then came the time when Essex got into trouble himself with Queen Elizabeth. Essex was imprisoned, and now Bacon came to Essex's side just as Essex had always come to his aid. There, Bacon passionately and eloquently argued that Essex was not guilty of that which he was suspected of, but that he was really guilty of *treason.* Bacon had no use for Essex now that he was in jail and soon to be executed. Bacon had become single-mindedly interested in obtaining the highest legal office in England, the Lord Chancellorship. Undaunted by setback after setback, he continued to use flattery and trickery until he eventually schemed his way into that position. But when the great philosopher came to this honorable office, he brought dishonor to it. He was found guilty of taking bribes and was sent to the Tower. He was not kept in prison long, being released on the promise that he would keep away from Parliament and the courts of England. His later years were spent trying to discover a means of preserving the body after death by freezing. While working on this project he caught a chill and died.

To go from the British philosopher Francis Bacon to the Prussian philosopher Immanuel Kant is to go from the man of the world to the most misty clouds of living. The poet Heine said that a life history of Kant could not be written because Kant had neither life nor history. Kant was the very quintessence of the absent-minded professor. In the midst of a profound lecture his attention might be captured by a missing button on a student's coat and he would forget what he was talking about. On two occasions Kant thought about getting married, but he thought about it so long that one of the girls got married to someone else and the other left town. Kant said that when he had wanted to get married he did not have enough money for a wife and when he got enough money for a wife, he no longer had any need for one.

Kant was known for his punctuality and it is said that the people of his

Illustration by Lazlo Matulay from FIVE COMEDIES *by Aristophanes. Living Library Edition. Copyright © 1948 by The World Publishing Company. Reproduced by permission of The World Publishing Company. Socrates is shown as the object of ridicule, the man lost in the clouds, in Aristophanes' play,* The Clouds.

home town set their clocks by him. Once he met his match in an Englishman named Green. One day they were to meet for a drive, but Kant was a minute and a half late. Green absolutely refused to get together with so unpunctual a person and rode off by himself. Kant was not only a neurotic about punctuality but also a hypochondriac. He would never drink coffee because he harbored great fears about what the oil in it would do to him. And he would never talk while he was out for a walk because he was afraid he might contract an illness through his open mouth. What is more, he detested perspiration which, he thought, was the most disgusting thing in the world—except possibly the garter. He believed that garters could stop the circulation in one's legs. He also found sex to be rather disgusting and dangerous as well; he believed it could kill one from exhaustion.

Another great German philosopher was Arthur Schopenhauer. Like Kant, he too had his fears. He kept all his possessions well guarded so that no one could steal them. His main concern, however, was his health. He lived in virtual terror lest he be stricken by tuberculosis, small pox, cholera, or worst of all, by poisoned snuff. The obsession which practically drove him mad was that he would fall into a trance and get burried alive. This philosopher believed life was so wretched that he said if man were sane he would kill himself, and would not permit a barber to shave him for fear the razor might slip and cut his throat. Although Schopenhauer did not think life to be of much value, he found himself in very comfortable circumstances

toward the end of his life. Then this pessimist enjoyed every minute of the recognition he finally received.

Schopenhauer passionately hated what he saw as the two horrible evils in the world—noise and women. As much as he detested noise, however, he probably detested women even more. Once when a woman was annoying him, he caused her to fall down a flight of steps. Nevertheless, his detestation did not prevent him from causing one to become pregnant.

In his great disdain of women Arthur Schopenhauer certainly did not stand alone among philosophers. Most of the great philosophers did not marry, and many of them did not even have sexual relations. One might say the twentieth-century British philosopher Bertrand Russell made up for the history of philosophy in this area. He married four times and had his share of extramarital sex as well. Bertrand Russell did not get along well with his first wife, and so he decided he would have to get along without her. He was happy with his second wife Dora, and they shared highly enlightened ideas about sex. However, when Dora became enlightened about the fact that her husband's research work with Oxford student Marjorie Spence was not always academic, she suddenly became less open-minded about sex. She alleged that Bertrand was guilty of adultery. Russell did not think Dora was being fair, inasmuch as Dora had four children since she married Bertrand and he had given her only two. Indeed on one occasion, one of Dora's lovers moved in and lived with the Russells. Dora retorted she never had a love affair with a man until after Betrand had had one with a woman. This was becoming complicated, so they divorced—and Russell married the student.

All of Russell's troubles were, of course, not with women. Many were with the government. As a pacifist he actively opposed World War I, constantly bringing himself into conflict with the government until he was finally sentenced to prison. During the trial Russell was accused of claiming there were evil thoughts in the mind of the American government, Britain's ally. Russell denied this charge, pointing out that, on the contrary, he was certain there were no thoughts at all in the mind of the American government. Everyone laughed but the judge and Russell went to jail. They could lock Russell away, but never his sense of humor, as we can see from the following story related by Alan Wood:

> *Russell had a cell larger than usual, for which he had to pay a rent of 2s a week. One of his first acts was to go to the Governor of the prison ... and ask solemnly what the penalty was for falling behind with the rent, remarking that if it was eviction he would not pay a penny.*[3]

In his *Portraits from Memory*, Bertrand Russell has reminded us that when he entered prison he was asked what his religion was. To this he answered that he was an agnostic. His interrogator could not spell the word

[3] Alan Wood, Bertrand Russell, *The Passionate Skeptic* (New York: Simon and Schuster, Inc., 1958), p. 113.

and observed that it did not matter, since all religions believe in the same God anyhow.

Bertrand Russell, in the tradition of many great philosophers, dedicated his life to making this a better and saner world. Ironically, however, such dedication frequently leads philosophers into impractical activities and makes them seem a bit crazy to ordinary practical people. Bertrand Russell was a serious man earnestly seeking to make this a better world, but in doing so he helped to preserve the age-old image of the philosopher as an eccentric.

Historically, philosophers have developed grand conceptions designed to instruct us on how we should live. But how have they lived? In tubs and attics—and they have even gone into stoves to think! French philosopher René Descartes put himself in a stove to keep warm while he figured out if he existed. Benedict Spinoza retired to the attic and there remained to laugh and cry as he attentively observed spiders spinning their webs. Spinoza, the most unperturbable of men, became most perturbed when his landlady came in and cleaned away those spider webs. British philosopher Herbert Spencer hated government so much that he would not even trust it to carry his mail; so when he wrote a letter, he delivered it himself.

We have presented some highlights of the foibles of philosophers not to show that they are fools, but to exhibit the kind of behavior patterns that have given rise to the impression that philosophers are impractical, far-out characters. Some episodes in the lives of certain philosophers lend themselves to mockery, and they have been mocked for their lack of realism and for not keeping their feet solidly on the ground. Goethe's Faust referred to them as "fools who thither turn their blinking eyes." If we have focused on philosophers at times when they were turning from reality in this way, it is because we wanted to show that they are human beings who do have frailties and foibles. There is a tragic as well as a comic touch in the life of the philosopher. He is not a RAND Corporation "think-tank" bureaucrat; he is a flesh-and-blood human being who is likely to have many peculiarities. Indeed the peculiarities of philosophers often result from their being more concerned with finding the truth than with finding popular acceptance. We might say that he is too involved in digging deep thought to be concerned about surface conventionalities. Thus I think it is important not to overlook some of the oddities in the lives of the philosophers because they may tell us something about ourselves as well as about them. The philosopher may seem too far-out just because many of us are too far in—too caught up in daily activities and routines that are less humanly productive than they are productive of boredom, tensions, and hostilities; too caught up in bureaucratic red tape that threatens to strangle human living; too caught up in the pursuit of material possessions that leave us only with feelings of emptiness; too caught up in self-destructive pride in the effort to attain power. Much human effort involves a vast expenditure of energy for things people do not need. One significant value in doing philosophy is that it should help us understand what we really do need.

Throughout the industrial world today people are failing to find meaning in their existence. It seems not just that *specific* things are wrong but that there is something amiss with the basic assumptions of our way of life. It is not just that people are disturbed because they cannot get what they want, for they are as much disturbed when they do get what they thought they wanted. It is not just that in a world of affluence multitudes of people cannot get jobs; it is also that multitudes of people who do have jobs cannot find any satisfaction in them.

We live in a technological era in which getting things *done* has become a major value in itself. The problem is that much of our doing is not based upon an understanding of what our true needs may be. In this sense, our doings seem to be our undoing. *Doing* things is exalted and *thinking* tends to be disparaged. Too many fail to see that thinking itself is a form of doing —indeed it may be the most important kind of human activity. We would have a difficult if not impossible time in discovering *pure* action unrelated to some thinking, for the actions people take are invariably based upon some kind of ideas. The question we must confront concerns how good are the ideas upon which our actions are based, and this is why philosophy is always practical and relevant. It helps us evaluate our ideas, and in so doing it enables us to discover a stronger basis for our actions. Furthermore, without careful reflection, people can never be sure that their actions are their own in the sense that they themselves have chosen them; unexamined actions may be merely the results of conditioning influences, manipulation, or even brainwashing. If a person is not the creative source of his action—in the sense that his action is the result of his own will or his own ideas—then it may even be questioned whether he is really acting or really doing. To be assured of really doing something, one must pay less attention to external action and more attention to controlling oneself by actively resisting the conditioning influences that stimulate passive responses. In the Western world *doing* is too much identified with external activity, for in many cases the most active thing one can do is to sit and think—to meditate.

Descartes, the very opposite of an active man in the usual sense, put himself in a stove so he might quietly engage in thinking. He arrived at the formula "I think, therefore I am." This may seem to be a statement that could shock no one, and yet one will perhaps find no more revolutionary statement in modern history, for Descartes was demonstrating that the essence of all men is of the nature of thought. This being the case, it follows that all men can think for themselves and therefore can arrive at the truth for themselves. In proclaiming this, Descartes was decisively undermining the authoritarianism that had ruled men's lives over the millenia. Neither pope nor president nor the populace has the right to come to conclusions for an individual. What Descartes was saying was that any individual, if he will take the trouble to think, can arrive at the truth for himself. And if a person can think for himself, he can decide for himself. This really is the theoretical basis for democracy. It is a revolutionary understanding. As the French historian Jules Michelet observed, in putting forth the formula "I think, therefore I am," Descartes had lit a fuse which finally exploded in the French Revolution.

From the study of philosophy one should gain an understanding of the value of the contemplative life and the power of ideas. Philosophers may have their peculiarities and infirmities, and they may lack wealth and power, but this in no way diminishes the importance of their contribution to the world. Karl Marx declared that philosophers have always been thinking about the world, but that it was more important to change it. The shallowness of this view can be seen in the fact that what is truly important about Marx's own life is not the various radical activities in which he was involved, but his radical thinking about the world.

In our complex, technological age, simple thinking or conventional wisdom will not provide us with a basis for understanding our world and responding to its challenges in a creative way. Really doing philosophy, in the sense of critically and imaginatively examining the questions of existence, should make us better able to confront our great problems. If we understand philosophy as philosophizing—not as a passive retreat, but as something we creatively do—we should be able to better appreciate its relevance. Thus before we deal with the work of the philosopher, we should understand something about the meaning of philosophy as a dynamic activity.

There's a Zing in Philosophy

If we wanted very much to have someone get the feeling of what philosophy is, we could not do better than to get him involved with Socrates. The life of Socrates was a ceaseless examination aimed at getting to the truth. He questioned everything in an effort to find something. Socrates was not just concerned with *philosophy;* philosophy is a noun, static. Socrates was interested in *philosophizing*—a verb, an activity. Socrates reasoned that if men fail to use their minds, if they permit them to lie fallow, they are living unproductively. A man cannot live as a man without self-examination. Man has a capacity for reflection no other animal has, and if he fails to reflect, he fails to live fully as a man. To really reflect is to continue to raise questions in a systematic pattern until answers that will not work—of which the consequences lead to inconsistency and absurdity—are eliminated. Only by eliminating all of the intellectual deadwood will man arrive at the living truth. This is what Socrates' life was about, and it is to a very large degree what philosophy is about. He proclaimed that *the unexamined life is not worth living*. When a man stops examining, he closes his mind and his humanity, for he is no longer fulfilling his human capacities. As long as a man raises questions, he can never be totally dominated by anyone or any force outside of himself. Thus philosophy is inherently in opposition to totalitarianism. A person who can raise his own questions is one who can live his own life and therefore be free.

To understand Socrates is not to learn his ideas and be able to repeat them, but to be able to raise questions as he did. I mean really raise questions. This means asking questions about things that are so taken for granted that no one would normally think of questioning them. The art of questioning is a creative task. The Socratic method aims at getting one to raise questions and examine the implications of the answers so that one becomes more and more creative in asking questions. Soon one begins to doubt that which is taken to be certain, and not merely that which is taken to be certain by others but by oneself as well. It is extremely difficult to even think of questioning that of which one is himself convinced, but that is what philosophy involves, and ultimately it is the only way one can really be honest with oneself. It takes a great deal of courage.

It was Nietzsche who said that it is not important to have the courage of your convictions but the courage to attack your convictions. Anyone can have the courage to attack the convictions of others, but to attack one's own is really difficult. Anyone can have the courage of his convictions; Hitler or a fanatic could have the courage of his convictions, but what they could not have is the courage to attack—to question those convictions. A fanatic is not strong enough to question his convictions; doing so might cause him to fall apart. His convictions help hold him together. That is fine, but if they are wrong convictions they may be holding him together in the wrong way—for example, with hatred rather than love, or with prejudice rather than tolerance. His convictions may be leading him in the wrong direction. General Custer might really have believed he should attack the Indians, and he had the courage of his convictions, but it might have been better for him, his soldiers, and his country if he had had a few questions. The man who has the courage of his convictions but not the courage to attack his convictions does not have true courage, for the lack of courage to attack your convictions is to be afraid of what you might find in yourself. Real courage resides in the resolution to face oneself. Often it takes much less nerve to face grave physical danger than to really come to terms with the meaning of one's beliefs.

If a man or a society fails to look at itself, then it cannot know what it looks like, and there can be no true basis for improvement or for real development. Because it can correct a stagnant condition, philosophy is valuable to oneself and to society. It assists in locating flaws and thereby makes it possible to correct them. It is not possible to answer questions until they are raised. If the operating assumptions of a civilization are not examined, it is difficult for it to respond to its challenges, and hence its very survival is endangered.

It may seem good to be able to live the easy life, but to lead a good life is never easy. One Sunday while the brilliant Danish philosopher Sören Kierkegaard sat puffing upon his cigar, he looked around himself and thought about the world, and it occurred to him how life was being made easy by mankind's many benefactors. These benefactors had contributed all kinds of technical and mechanical wonders. Scientists and engineers provide ingenious inventions that contribute to the greater comfort of living. But Kierkegaard was a philosopher. What could he give mankind? Kierkegaard thought about that as he finished his cigar, and it occurred to him that he had nothing to offer. Then the great realization dawned upon him. A philosopher cannot really do anything to make life easier, but he need not despair, for there is something he can do for mankind. Of course he can help make life *harder!* This may hardly seem an exciting possibility. But when things become too easy, people grow flabby—not just physically but morally and intellectually as well. Socrates said he would be a gadfly, stinging people into thinking and not letting them relax upon the bed of uncomfortable ideas. People are too content to let sleeping dogmas lie, but the true philosopher cannot permit that. He must sting them out of their complacency and prepare them to come to terms with their challenges. The philosopher must disturb man to get him thinking.

It is *thinking* that is really the business of philosophy. It may be supposed that thinking is nothing special since everyone does it, but this is not true. Most people do not think—not in the sense that thinking is a methodologically critical analysis and a question of basic beliefs. It has been said that when most people say they are thinking, all they are doing is rearranging their prejudices. Real thinking involves precise examination of one's prejudices.

We may say that philosophical thinking involves two primary elements:

1. analytic;
2. synthetic.

What we call the analytic element of thinking is the essentially critical element. On the analytic level critical assessment is central. It involves a systematic questioning of all matters. Nothing is taken for granted. Thinking involves being critically skeptical of anything that cannot be proven.

Philosophical thinking is not purely skeptical, however. If it were, it would fall into nihilism. There is a constructive as well as a destructive side to philosophy. It may be essential to analyze away old systems of ideas that no longer have the power to serve man, but it is also necessary to construct new systems of ideas to meet his living needs. This is what we mean by saying there is also a *synthetic* side to philosophy.

To come to terms with the dynamic problems of life, men require fresh insights, new ideas, and, at certain junctures, a new basis for understanding and experiencing life. The philosopher can make a contribution here. If people gave birth to babies at the rate they give birth to ideas, not only would there not be a problem of over population, but there might not even be any population. Men need new ideas and new categories of thinking and even of experiencing the world.

The main technical fields of philosophy are epistemology, metaphysics, and axiology (or value theory). Although very technical problems are the concern of these formal areas of philosophy, behind the technicalities is always the activity of philosophizing, of raising fundamental questions, and of seeking fundamental answers concerning matters that do matter to human beings.

PART II

THE
WORK
OF
THE
PHILOSOPHER

2

What Do You Know?
Epistemology

How Do You Know That?
Introduction to Epistemological Problems

Epistemology comes from the Greek words, *episteme,* which means knowledge, and *logos,* which means science or study. Thus epistemology is the science of knowledge. It can tell us what we can know or we cannot know. One important thing we may come to know is how little we can really know. We may even learn that we cannot know anything. This may seem silly. Imagine a student taking a course in philosophy. His parents, proud of him, ask what he learned in philosophy. He informs them he learned that he does not know anything. His parents, not very impressed, inform him that they could have told him that already. Ah, but there is a great difference between not knowing anything and knowing that you do not really know anything. It is the difference between folly and wisdom. Of course we cannot really say we know nothing, because that would be something we would know. To know that one knows nothing is a contradiction like a square circle. One could never be a complete skeptic, for if he were he would have to be completely skeptical of his skepticism. It has been put quite adequately by Dr. Joseph A. Leighton, who lets us know:

Critical skepticism involves suspension of judgment on all problems. This form of skepticism was first formulated by Pyrrho, 365-275 B.C., and was further developed by Carneades, 215-130 B.C. Dogmatic skepticism is self-contradictory, for to say that it is impossible to know is to make a dogmatic statement which claims to be truth. . . . Its (dogmatic skepticism) standpoint is that we are not certain whether we know something or whether we can know nothing. Since we do not know whether we do know something or nothing, the only consistent attitude is that in which there is a suspension of all judgment. To be thoroughly consistent, the Pyrrhonic skeptic would have to hold that he was not certain whether we ought to suspend judgment. The skeptic, to be consistent in all respects, should add that he cannot know whether one ought to say that one ought to suspend judgment, and that one cannot know whether one cannot know whether one ought to say that one ought to suspend judgment and so on ad infinitum. . . .[1]

Of course when we say we do not know anything, we may mean not that we do not know anything at all, but that we will not be dogmatic— that we will entertain some doubts. At least we should not burn at the stake those who do not have the good sense to believe the same things we do. Remember throughout history men have been most ignorant of what they were most assured about. We owe thanks to Shakespeare for putting it so well:

But man, proud man,
Drest in a little brief authority,
Most ignorant of what he's most assured—
His glassy essence—like an angry ape,
Plays such fantastic tricks before high heaven
As make the angels weep.[2]

We may study epistemology to allow the angels to weep less. We have seen that it can be as much of a problem to know what we cannot know as to know what we can know. What can we know or what can we not know? What can we know about the earth or heavens, about the past or future, about ourselves or others?

If we knew the answers to questions such as these, we could live better. Certainly there are issues about which we have to have some variety of knowledge to get on. But what can we really know?

Suppose you are a red-blooded young man walking along the street when your eyes suddenly focus upon a really voluptuous and highly sensuous creature wearing a miniskirt that evokes a maxi-response. Here is this beautiful creature with lovely flowing long blond hair and most appealing measurements. She is simply sexy. You feel stimulated. Unpleasant

[1] Joseph A. Leighton, *The Field of Philosophy* (New York and London: Appleton-Century-Crofts, 1923), p. 52.

[2] William Shakespeare, *Measure for Measure,* Act II, scene 2.

as this may sound, it should be realized there could be an epistemological problem here that should be faced before this stimulating person is faced. The epistemological issue here concerns how you can *know* that this is a girl. To raise such an issue may seem absolutely preposterous. After all you know what a girl looks like. Sure, but maybe this is a campy guy, a pretty boy in drag. This person who has aroused you could be a female impersonator. Female impersonators look like girls. Sometimes they look more like girls than girls do themselves. It could all be a put on. That *woman* you see could even be George Sanders.[3]

The way things are going in these days of loss of identity, a male does not have to be a female impersonator to look like a female. We are witnessing in our midst the emergence of unisex, at least in fashion. Thus even without a put on we could be hard put to tell the difference. Who knows? The girl one chases could even be a New York cop. Rapists and mashers were fooled by New York City policemen, disguised as lovely ladies, and tried to sexually assault them. It must be rather disturbing to discover the girl of your heart's desire turns out to be a cop. These were hardened sex offenders trying to rape policemen in *chick's* clothing. They were pros and thus it was their business to obtain carnal knowledge of women. If they did not know, what hope is there for amateurs?

[3] Photograph courtesy of 20th Century-Fox Film Corporation, from "The Kremlin Letter."

Obviously appearance may not be a clue to reality. How could one come to know if one really is a female? There are physical tests. It's not what's up front that counts but what's underneath. There are anatomical differences that may be disguised by a clever transvestite. You might then ask the curvy creature who catches your interest to undress so that you might undertake a physical examination. You could walk up to the *apparent* girl and say, "Would you mind taking your clothes off in the interests of epistemological inquiry?" Assuming that this doesn't turn the person off, there still could be problems. What if the person turns out to be a female physically, but psychologically cannot bear to be a woman and feels she is a man. Which is she? It has been reported that transsexuals lament that they are women imprisoned in men's bodies or, as the case may be, that they are men trapped in women's bodies. What is the real sex of a person? It is not easy to know. Dr. Henry Benjamin informs us:

> *Modern researchers ... delving into "the riddle of sex" have actually produced—so far—more obscurity, more complexity. Instead of the conventional two sexes with their anatomical differences, there may be up to ten or more separate concepts and manifestations of sex and each could be of vital importance to the individual. Here are some of the kinds of sex I have in mind: chromosomal, genetic, anatomical, legal, gonadal, endocrine (hormonal), psychological, and—also the social sex, usually based on the sex of rearing.[4]*

Not only are there varying concepts of sex to confuse us, but there is confusion in any given concept itself. Dr. Benjamin notes, "Just as the anatomical sex is never entirely male or female (one must recall the existence of nipples in men and a rudimentary penis, the clitoris, in women), so is the endocrine sex 'mixed' to an even greater extent."[5] Everything seems to be mixed up; how can we know what is what? Testes and the male adrenals produce small amounts of estrogen (female hormone), whereas there is androgen (male hormone) in the ovaries and female adrenals. Dr. Benjamin says, "it can be said that, actually, we are all 'intersexes,' anatomically as well as endocrinologically."[6] Does this mean we cannot know the difference between a man and a woman? Well sure, we can know for most practical purposes. What emerges, however, is the consideration that what on "appearance" may seem simple and obvious and certain may in "reality" be very complex, not so obvious, and uncertain. If you regard this as merely an academic problem your attention should be called to the fact that in the Olympic Games held in Munich August 26 to September 10, 1972 a "hair test" was used to discover if women competing in the events were biologically female. That means 1200 women had to be tested to determine if they were females. In an article called "When Is a Girl a Boy?" it is explained, "Such tests are necessary, Olympic officials explain, because in the past nearly half of some world records established by women have been set

---

[4] Henry Benjamin, *The Transsexual Phenomenon* (New York: Ace Books, 1966), p. 13.

[5] *Ibid.*, p. 16.

[6] *Ibid.*

by hermaphrodites—women with both male and female sex characteristics." (Connecticut Walker, "When Is a Girl a Boy?" *Parade*, April 16, 1972, p. 14)

Not only may we not be able to know what a real live woman is, we also may not know what a real dead man is. How can we know when someone is dead? This question not only may have theoretical significance but may be of practical urgency. As New York's Chief Medical Examiner, Dr. Milton Halpern facetiously expressed it:

> *It has come to the point where no one dares to stretch out on a park bench for fear he'll find himself declared dead and turned into an organ donor.*[7]

Time was when the heart stopped beating and a person stopped breathing, he was considered dead. Now because of the possibilities of keeping a heart going with electrical stimulation and the lungs with respirators, the functioning of the brain has been made the key variable. Yet it is extremely touchy to determine when the brain goes for good. What is called a flat electroencephalogram—one revealing nil electrical activity by brain cells—should convince us that the brain is dead. However, there is a chilling danger even here. For under certain conditions of being chilled but not entirely dead, there can result a coma that would produce a flat electroencephalogram.

It is also possible for a person to be pronounced dead when in a state of suspended animation. There are bacteria that can remain in such a state and be revived after hundreds of millions of years. Now with the possibility of reviving patients by electrical shock, drugs, and heart massages the epistemological question of when a person can be regarded dead becomes increasingly urgent. Supposing a man somebody hates is stricken, and his heart stops. He is definitely dead to the world, but as a confident physician commences to revive him, his enemy shoots him in the heart. Should this be regarded as murder? But the man is dead. How can one be accused of murdering someone who is already dead? On the other hand if the person can be restored, then the possibility of life was taken from him by shooting him. Is he who has taken it to be let off free? This problem is really exacerbated by the fact we now live in the age of "cryonics," the era in which it is possible to store human beings in liquid nitrogen at $-197°$ C for indefinite periods. Such persons can be stored until some future age when a cure is discovered for whatever stopped their functioning, and then the hope is they can be revived and returned to happy healthy living. Dr. A. S. Parkes has defined death as "the state from which resuscitation of the body as a whole is impossible by currently known means."[8] But as the age of cryonics advances, we will have the known means, so there will be no death. Because we could always revive a person, he would just be sick and not dead. Questions concerning life and death in the light of these

[7] Barbara Yuncker, "Transplants: When Does a Person Die?" *New York Post*, Saturday, April 12, 1969, p. 29.

[8] Quoted in Robert Ettinger, *The Prospect of Immortality* (Garden City, N.Y.: Doubleday & Co., Inc., 1964), p. 93.

developments have a pressing legal significance. If there is no death, can there be murder?

Not only is determining when a person stops living a thorny problem with epistemological implications, but so is determining when he starts living. The astounding practical implications of this can be illustrated by reference to a shocking criminal case, *People v. Hayner*. The defendant was tried for murder, was convicted, and the case was appealed. His daughter had given birth to a baby, and he engaged in the unfatherly activity of pulling "the top of the baby's head off." The defendant himself admitted: "I deliberately killed that baby. I didn't want to bring any disgrace upon the family." At the sheriff's office the defendant made and swore to the following gruesome statement:

> As I pulled on the head, the skin came off from a portion of the skull on top of the head and some of the brains came out running on the bed. The baby started to cry just after being born. I then cut the umbilical cord from the mother, using a pair of shears. I then took the umbilical cord which was still attached to the baby, from the mother, and wound it tightly around the baby's neck for purpose of strangulation, drew it tightly, and the baby stopped crying.[9]

The defendant's wife and daughter appeared as witnesses for the State against him. The wife testified that her husband had been sleeping with their daughter for some time before she became pregnant. This provided a motive for the crime, and powerful evidence unfavorable to the defendant was amassed. It was found there was adequate emotion to have led him to commit the crime. Furthermore he had the opportunity to do it, and the dead body of the child was found just where he revealed he had buried it. In addition to this damning evidence the defendant confessed. Yet the decision was reversed, and he was found not guilty as charged. Why? There was this perplexing problem concerning when a child is born alive and when he is alive in the legal sense. How can we *know* when one is alive? The People, or the State, introduced compelling medical testimony that the child was born alive and that the cause of death was an external force that shut off the air supply to the lungs. The pathologist reported that the lungs were fully expanded and that there was an interstitial emphysema of the lungs. In other words there was a tearing of the wall sacs and escape of air into the connective tissue of the framework of the lung. Despite this evidence it was not shown there was hemorrhage in the wall sacs and connecting tissue of either lung. This was taken as the crucial test since bleeding naturally follows the rupture of a blood vessel in a living person. Expansion of the lungs was not decisive because even though the child may have been breathing, he might not have had a separate existence.

We can only say it is not an easy matter to know when one is born alive or becomes human, and the consequence can legally be enormous.

[9] *People v. Hayner*, Court of Appeals of New York, 1949, in Rollin M. Perkins, *Cases and Materials on Criminal Law and Procedure* (Brooklyn: The Foundation Press, Inc., 1952), p. 15.

Now we see it is exceedingly complicated to know when one is dead and when one is born alive, but what about those who believe they can know someone is still alive after he is found to be dead? Some heart patients, who were reported medically dead and afterward revived, were interviewed by two doctors at Tulane University Hospital. These persons had reached the state at which there was no heartbeat, no blood flow to the brain, and no pulse. However, they were later brought back to life. What is interesting is that during the period of their death, there was no sign of soul or mind; they were utterly unconscious; there was just one big blank. Does this mean we can know that when death does call, there is nothingness? In one play an entire village lost its faith because a man who had been revived had no memory of an afterlife. We should be aware of the epistemological difficulties of communicating with the living. What about with the dead? The Reverend James A. Pike has said that he spoke with his dead son. Is there any way of knowing if that sort of thing could happen? Today most parents cannot talk to their children when they are alive. Could they when they're dead?

Is it possible to attain knowledge about communicating with the dead? Many interesting attempts and experiments have been made to show that we can. How can we account for something such as the Chaffin case, the details of which are provided for us by J. Gaither Pratt, eminent parapsychology scholar.[10]

James P. Chaffin, a North Carolina farmer had four sons. In 1905 he made a will, formally witnessed and signed, leaving his farm to his third son Marshall and making no provision for the other sons. In 1921 Chaffin died, and Marshall collected his farm. In 1925 the second son, also named James P. Chaffin, began to have vivid dreams in which he saw his father appear at his bedside. After a while not only did his deceased father appear but he began to talk. He didn't just make small talk either. In fact, he told him of a second will to be found in his old overcoat. Before this time, no one had heard anything of a second will. After this exciting happening James went to his mother's house to look for the overcoat, only to discover that it had been given to his brother John. At brother John's he found the coat. Sewed into it was a little roll of paper, tied with a string, and written in his father's handwriting was: "Read the 27th Chapter of Genesis in my daddie's old Bible." He invited a witness who went with him to his mother's, and after an extensive search found the Bible. Turning to the 27th chapter of Genesis, James found the second will. It provided the property of the father was to be equally divided among all four children who were to take care of the mother. It was dated January 16, 1919. Now Marshall, who alone had inherited the farm according to the first and only publicly known will, had already died, but his wife, upon seeing the second will, admitted it was in the father's handwriting and did not contest it.

Now if the son did not communicate with his dead pappy, how did he

---

[10] J. Gaither Pratt, *Parapsychology* (Garden City, N.Y.: Doubleday & Co., Inc., 1964), pp. 196–201.

ever acquire knowledge of the existence of that will? Surely it was not something his father had told him about and which he had forgotten. It would not be likely for him to have forgotten something of that importance, particularly when the property was going to his brother. Besides, why would he suddenly remember in 1925, four years after the death of his father? Careful tests were taken to determine whether he might have had any subconscious knowledge that the will was in the Bible, and it was indicated that he did not. What are we to make of occurrences such as these? That they should be a mere matter of coincidence is most improbable. Can we say there is extrasensory perception, life after death, ghosts? What can we know?

If you think it is too difficult to talk with the dead, what about talking with people from other planets? George Adamski made a bundle of money telling us about his talks with saucer people from the planet Venus. In fact he got along so well with these outer-space people that they invited him to take a trip to the moon and he went. Soon a lot of people revealed having had personal contact with spacemen. In UFO circles they became known as "contactees." Now what these persons report is absolutely preposterous in scientific terms. Can things happen that are scientifically untenable?

All of the reports on flying saucers are not on a par with those of George Adamski. For example, what are we to make of the Ubatuba sighting? A flying disc exploded off the coast of Brazil in September 1957 and was sighted near the town of Ubatuba in the province of Sao Paulo. The UFO report was of special significance because there was physical evidence in the form of fragments from the disc to reinforce it. Spectographic analysis revealed the metallic fragments were magnesium of a high degree of purity. The density of one sample was found to be 1.866, which is of great importance, for had this been pure terrestial magnesium, the density should have been 1.741. What is at stake is clearly stated in the Condon Report, the so-called scientific study commissioned by the United States Air Force. "The metal was alleged to be of such extreme purity that it could not have been produced by earthly technology. For that reason this particular material has been widely acclaimed as a fragment of an exploded flying disc."[11] Now even this report, hostile toward the assumption of UFOs, contained the admission, "Although the Brazil fragment proved not to be pure, as claimed, the possibility remained that the material was unique."[12] Yet the report did conclude, "This project has found no physical evidence which, in itself, clearly indicates the existence in the atmosphere of vehicles of extraordinary nature."[13] That is a very careful statement. Yet a member of the project who was dismissed from it (not for reasons of qualifications) believes a different conclusion might be justified.

In 1968 a neutron activation analysis of the material was made at the

[11] *Scientific Study of Unidentified Flying Objects,* Dr. Edward U. Condon, Project Director (New York: Bantam Books, 1968), p. 94.

[12] *Ibid.,* p. 96.

[13] *Ibid.,* p. 97.

FBI laboratory in Washington, and its results are most interesting. The member dismissed from the project, Dr. Saunders, makes this eminently clear. He tells us that what the sample does not contain is really significant:

> *If the fragment were ultrapure terrestrial magnesium, one would expect to find one of four conditions existing:*
>
> — *... it might have contained aluminum or copper, or both. There was no aluminum and only a trace of copper.*
>
> —*if someone had made a serious effort to purify the sample, the element most difficult to remove would have been calcium. There was none.*
>
> —*if someone had done an unusually fine job of removing the calcium, he would almost certainly have done it using a quartz vessel. This would have introduced minute amounts of silicon into the sample. The FBI tests showed that no silicon was present.*
>
> —*if someone had used the best techniques available to purify magesium in 1968, he would have employed repeated sublimation of the metal under a very high vaccuum. A mercury-vapor pump would be required to produced this vacuum, resulting in mercury contamination of the product. There was no mercury in the Ubatuba sample.*[14]

In 1957, at the time of the Ubatuba sighting, the alloy did not seem to have been known on this planet, and thus it is reasonable to assume the world's metallurgists might not have been able to duplicate it at that time.

In the Ubatuba UFO story we have a script qualitatively different from stories such as those created by George Adamski, who claims to have taken a trip to the moon with his saucer pals. Yet does it prove anything? Rare things happen even on this earth. Perhaps the fragments found constitute one of those rare things. Then again, perhaps not. How do we decide? How do we weigh evidence? More important, how do we arrive at an understanding of what shall constitute evidence? *How do we know?*

Did you ever go anywhere and have an overwhelming feeling you have been there before, and yet you know you have not? You go into strange territory, and yet it is familiar. It is a very odd feeling. It is as if reality is something very indefinite. You actually feel you lived before in a distant historic epoch. This phenomenon is known as *déjà vu.* Freud thought that it represented a rejection of reality, but Jung believed that it involved a deeper finding of reality. Jung felt that it could be an enrichment of this life by experience from a parallel life in the past. The usual scientific explanation, however, is that *déjà vu* is an illusion of some sort, "a breakdown of the normal mechanism of recognition."[15] Some psychiatrists maintain it might result from remembering a dream that the dreamer had forgotten. One doctor even maintained that the *déjà vu* experience could be because of an inadequate functioning of the brain. On the other hand, if *déjà vu* is for

[14] David R. Saunders and R. Roger Harkins, *UFO's? YES!: Where the Condon Committee Went Wrong* (New York: New American Library, 1968), p. 173.

[15] D. J. West, *Psychical Research Today* (Baltimore: Penguin Books, Inc., 1962), p. 57.

real, then perhaps the functioning of that doctor's brain was inadequate. Can anyone *know* what this type of experience really means? A wild possibility is the suggestion that *déjà vu* is not a memory of what happened in the remote past, but a "memory" of what will happen in the future. Dr. Nandor Fodor, a friend of Freud, has some interesting observations in this regard:

> *I was told by a patient that when he was handcuffed in the last war as a prisoner, in a flash it came back to him that he had dreamed of the scene four years before but did not recall the dream until the event actually came to pass.*[16]

There is also the story of Fodor's nephew. He dreamt five or six times of being an army officer in Italy. In his dreams, one night while having dinner, he met an extremely beautiful woman who afterward appeared in a black nightgown. This was before the First World War. Then came the war, and his corps was the first to be sent to Italy. There he was having dinner on the terrace of a castle when the beautiful woman appeared. They seemed to know each other, though they had never met before. There was even a black nightgown. Fodor's nephew was astounded and could not understand how he could have dreamed something that would actually come true five years later. Did he "remember" the future? Fodor also cites the example of Jonathan Swift:

> *The two satellites of Mars were discovered by Professor Halle in 1877. Some 150 years before, Jonathan Swift wrote in Gulliver's Travels of the astronomers of Laputa: "They have discovered two small stars, or satellites which revolve round Mars. The inner one is three diameters distant from the center of the planet, the outer one five diameters; the first makes its revolution in ten hours, the second in twenty hours and a half." These figures, taken at the time as proof of Swift's ignorance of astronomy, show striking agreement with the findings of Professor Halle.*[17]

Is it possible there can be knowledge of events before they even happen? Is it not difficult enough to know of events that have already occurred without seeking it in advance of their occurrence? Indeed the very question of knowledge from the past poses sufficiently serious obstacles that there are many who regard the study of history as virtually hopeless. How can we know about the past? We cannot simulate laboratory conditions and conduct controlled experiments with respect to historic facts. If you doubt a conclusion of a physicist you can go to a lab and run an experiment to check it. What are you going to do if you doubt a statement of a historian? You cannot run back in time. Who can know what Jesus said or did? You cannot go back and ask him. The same holds true of Socrates. How do you know that Plato didn't create a dramatic hero, and that in reality Socrates

[16] Nandor Fodor, *Between Two Worlds* (New York: Paperback Library, 1967), p. 134.

[17] *Ibid.*, p. 135.

was a garrulous old fool? How can you know there really was a Socrates, a Jesus, or a Lao-tzu? Look what happened to poor St. Christopher. One day he is protecting travelers and the next day not only is he removed as a saint, but the Roman Catholic Church raises doubts he ever even existed.

Attainment of knowledge from the past is a most difficult enterprise. Voltaire once said that the only thing you can prove by history is that you can prove anything by history. If you read different historians you will end up with different histories. There is tremendous disagreement among qualified historians concerning what happened. If historians cannot agree about what happened, how can nonhistorians ever know? History is invariably written from some point of view, and does not that point of view prejudice the accounting of the facts? Indeed history is certainly not mere chronology; its data consists of the actions of men. But these must be interpreted, and who knows what the correct interpretation is? It seems that the great Greek historian Thucydides found Cleon so distasteful that his view of Cleon's role in history was distorted. If you read Carlyle on history, you will find enormous admiration for great men and see history made by heroes. If you read Wells, who hated heroes, you will get a perspective of history very different from that of Carlyle. If you read Tolstoy, you will find that great men do not matter. Is it possible, then, to know anything of the past? For example, what really happened at Pearl Harbor? Are we doomed to hopeless subjectivism, or can we be objective concerning the past? Can there be any reasonably certain knowledge about what happened in the past?

Historians cause trouble enough, but what of prophets who, not content to mix us up about the past, raise questions about knowledge of the future? It is important to distinguish between prediction and prophecy. To make a prediction one need not possess any special, extranormal power personally. All one need do is rely upon some established generalization, a hypothesis, a theory, or a law; in terms of this one can say that such and such might be expected to happen. One might thus predict that if litmus paper is put in acid, it will change color. In other words, prediction is based on an experimental or rational reason for presuming that such and such will occur. What is significant is the public character of prediction: because what is predicted is based on evidence, it can be checked by anyone with normal intelligence who understands the rules of scientific procedure. There is no trick or magic involved.

With prophecy, on the other hand, there need be no basis in experience nor in reason for saying what will happen. The basis, rather, is that the person who says what will happen possesses some special power. It is not for the prophet to reason why, but just to say what people will do or that they will die. In a 1956 edition of *Parade* magazine Jeane Dixon was reported to have said that the 1960 election would be won by a Democrat and that he would be shot in office. Did she know in advance, or was that a strange guess? Even if she did know, however, we could not rely on such prophecies, for we could not know she knew until it happened, and then it would be too late. Because prophecies are not based on rhyme or reason, no one can depend upon them. After all prophets have been wrong many times. There is an appropriate story from ancient Greece. There was this Greek who doubted the power of Poseidon, the mighty God of the Sea. And so a believer showed him offerings that had been given by those who, in time of great danger of shipwreck or drowning, prayed to Poseidon and were saved. The doubting Greek was then asked if he were convinced, but he answered that before he made up his mind, he would like to hear from those who were drowned. Unfortunately, in dealing with prophecy, those are precisely the ones we never hear from. This is not the case in science, for in science a negative instance or counter example will make us abandon a theory or hypothesis or, at least, reduce the probability of our prediction.

But these considerations do not mean there cannot be foreknowledge; they mean that it is almost impossible for us to know if a prophecy is foreknowledge or not because we cannot verify it in the way we can verify scientific predictions. Take the example of Nostradamus. Can his prophecies simply be disregarded? Born on December 14, 1503, Michael Nostradamus had amazing things to say about the future. In fact his sayings can be interpreted as foreseeing World War I, World War II, the French Maginot Line and its crumbling, and such instruments of modern war as bombs and submarines. He has been given credit for predicting the Spanish Civil War and the coming of Francisco Franco to power.[18] There are also quatrains about Hitler, whom Nostradamus refers to as "Hister," whose rise to power he appears to have foreseen.[19]

Of course, there are a lot of "ifs" with these prophecies. Prophecy often manages to get a lot of mileage out of subsequent broad interpretation. Can we say that many statements of Nostradamus were wild ramblings that we are now reading too much into? Or should we take him seriously? How are we to know? If we do take him seriously we have some problems coming up, for not only does he seem to have predicted the coming of Napoleon and Hitler but also of an even more terrible dictator whose time is still to come. He foresaw that the third dictator's bloody war would last twenty-seven years and that heretics would be enslaved and slain. And he told us that in 1999, a great King of Terror will come from the skies, and there will be games of death. That is a wild prophecy, but the disturbing thing is that if we look around us, we might come to just as frightening conclusions on the basis of evidence. In this age of nuclear weapons, space programs, and violence, perhaps Nostradamus was not too far off. What is more, followers of Nostradamus have themselves made some uncanny predictions just on the basis of understanding what he had to say. Shall we dismiss prophecy as a way of knowledge? Shall we accept science as a way of knowledge? What shall we do?

Regardless of the answers to these questions, the scientific attitude must include an open mind concerning all matters. Can there be such a thing as foreknowledge, and will it perhaps be more important than science? Can we know better by prophecy than by science? Obviously in terms of a sys-

[18] James Laver, *Nostradamus* (Harmondsworth, England: Penguin Books, Ltd., 1952), p. 223.
[19] *Ibid.*, p. 226.

tematic approach to understanding and controlling the world, the answer to these questions must be negative. But on the other hand if we could get good enough prophecies, we would perhaps not need our systematic knowledge, or we could even complement it with prophecy. What is at issue are the means by which we shall know.

What shall pass the test of knowledge? What shall flunk it? That is not a mere academic issue. At issue are many practical matters concerning our lives. Shall we admit to the realm of knowledge statements concerning psychic phenomena? In other words, is it possible in the nature of things that there can actually be knowledge of something beyond the empirical world? And is it possible to have knowledge of how we should live? Can we know man on the scientific basis on which we know nature? This is a very important question, for it raises the problem of whom we shall turn to in solving life's questions. Who can know what is best? How shall we make decisions concerning personal or social matters? Can individuals know on their own what is best for them, their nation, or the world, or must they turn to doctors, lawyers, theologians, politicians, or scientists? We act upon what we take to be our knowledge, and thus if we are mistaken, it is likely that our actions will be misguided. It is then crucial for man to find a sound basis for his beliefs.

In an important sense, answering such questions depends upon understanding the nature of knowledge. For example, if we are led to conclude that knowledge can only consist of what can be measured or verified by our senses, then we would simply rule out any claims to know ghosts, gods, a life after death, or anything else that depends on extrasensory perception, pure deductive reasoning, or intuition. Epistemological inquiry is relevant to most issues that matter to us, inasmuch as the question of the validity of knowledge can be found underlying all such issues. Many problems discussed in this chapter might seem to be simply empirical problems rather than epistemological problems. What we were seeking to show, however, is that all empirical problems have epistemological implications. Very frequently when people claim to *know* something, they do so because of their perceptions. But as we have seen, our perceptions may be misleading. Even upon detailed examination, they may be inadequate to provide us with knowledge. Is sense perception an adequate basis for knowledge? If so, under what conditions? If not, is there any adequate basis for knowledge?

It may be an empirical problem to determine whether death involves the functioning of the brain or the heart, but that this is the case illuminates the difficulty of setting criteria on the empirical level. This in turn raises the question of whether we can ever feel confident in assuming we have knowledge when dealing with empirical questions. There are thorny difficulties in locating an empirical ground of knowledge, and perhaps, as Plato and others have suggested, there can be no knowledge of empirical matters. It may also be that there is no ground beyond the empirical level upon which man can attain knowledge. If this is so, then we will have to do the best we can on the poor soil of empirical data. Perhaps we should have less stringent criteria for knowledge. Perhaps when we say that we *know,* all we can mean is that on the basis of probabilities we have *good reason to believe* that something is so, rather than that we are *certain* it is so. In any event it certainly appears that empirical matters are invariably intertwined with epistemological problems on some level. Thus we may say that to understand more completely the empirical problems with which we are constantly confronted, we will benefit from an examination of epistemology.

Basic matters facing the philosopher who investigates the area of epistemology involve the meaning and nature of knowledge, the limits of knowledge, and a consideration of what is basic to knowledge—experience, reason, a combination, or mystical intuition? It is with such questions as these that the great philosophers have wrestled, and through an understanding of them we may find greater understanding of our world. We shall now consider some of the basic epistemological philosophies, such as rationalism, empiricism, and Kantianism.

The Truth Within: Rationalism

During the fifteenth, sixteenth, and seventeenth centuries vast changes amounting to a fundamental intellectual transformation were taking place in the life of man. New vistas were opening everywhere. One of the most profound influences on the making of the modern mind was the creation and development of mathematical physics. As we have seen, at the vital center of the new science was a new method of attaining knowledge, and it is therefore no surprise that at this time the primary preoccupation of philosophy was with epistemology, or questions of the meaning and nature of knowledge.

There were two components to the new physics, a mathematical one and an empirical one. Corresponding to these two components of physics are two eternal tendencies in epistemology, which are known as *rationalism* and *empiricism.* The rationalist takes as the perfect model for human understanding the mathematical disciplines. To the rationalist experience may not always be the worst teacher, but it is certainly never the best. The most reliable and certain knowledge is not to be discovered merely by searching out in the world, but by exploring the mind and reasoning. What we perceive in the outer world is so often blemished by error that we must not assume we can merely add up observed facts to find indubitable truth. True knowledge lies not in the mute senseless world of experience alone, but exists in man. His task is often to reason it out. Man cannot discover the *most important* truths by looking in the world, as these ·may be innate in him. For example, how can it be ascertained that *all men* are *born free?* Empirically this cannot be shown. This truth, if it be one, must be self-evident, for freedom is not a tangible property we can observe in a newborn infant. Some infants may be born under a dictatorial regime and others in a democracy. Empirically, it cannot be proved all men are born free. If this can be known, it is a truth that does not emerge from experience, but is innate in man. Generally, to the rationalist true knowledge is not basically a product of experience but depends to a large degree upon the structure of the mind. It is thus *a priori,* or before experience. For the rationalist then, certain basic truths can be *deduced* and need not be built up inductively.

In answer to the rationalist's belief that there are certain fundamental principles or axioms man can know through reason, and that he can deduce certain other specific truths from these, the empiricist argues that the rationalist has gotten it backward. One cannot find factual truths by reasoning them out of oneself. Factual truth is a product of experimental inquiry. Truth about this world lies in this world, and one must empirically observe it if one seriously wishes to see it. Truth about the world is *a posteriori;* it comes only after experience.

In the rationalist tradition there were such great philosophers as Plato, St. Augustine, René Descartes, Benedict Spinoza, Gottfried Wilhelm von Leibniz, and G. W. F. Hegel. The big names in the empiricist tradition included such philosophical luminaries as Aristotle, St. Thomas, Sir Francis Bacon, Thomas Hobbes, John Locke, Bishop George Berkeley, David Hume, Jeremy Bentham, and John Stuart Mill.

Plato and Descartes provide us a most illuminating illustration of the rationalist approach to the understanding of knowledge.

PLATO

If two persons were walking along the street when it suddenly started pouring rain so that both were being drenched, and one said, "Let's make a run for it to get in out of this rain," I think you can safely bet he would think it very odd if the other person in a serious mood said, "But how do you know it's really raining?" That kind of question is not appreciated by practical-minded people. Suppose, however, that the second answered, "Are you crazy? I know it's raining because I *see* and *feel* it. Okay? Now can we get to hell out of the rain?" If the first man at that point persisted and said, "But how can you ask to get out of the rain when you haven't even *proved* it's raining yet?" the second would probably conclude that it was time to get his old friend some kind of psychological treatment. The point is that so deeply ingrained in our very mode of coming to terms with the world is the assumption that what we perceive we *know*—i.e., seeing is believing—that we would think one who doubted it was either out of his head or an eccentric philosopher. So deeply are we impressed by what we perceive that we naturally assume that knowledge is perception.

Plato did not assume this. However he did not merely postulate another basis for knowledge; indeed he took this natural assumption that knowledge is perception very seriously and, therefore, held it up to the most thorough logical examination. By discovering woeful inadequacies in what we take too easily for granted, Plato was led to a different view, his own philosophy of rationalism. Plato did not simply declare by a kind of divine fiat that there is a higher way of knowing than by perception. Plato started on the ground of perception, and only upon making the discovery that perception, like New York, might be a nice place to visit but nowhere to live, was he led upward to the heavens and the idea of *a priori* knowledge, or knowledge before experience.

Plato's method of analysis consisted in painstaking examination of the implications of a doctrine, such as the one that knowledge is perception, and a consideration of how tenable such implications are. Untenable consequences reflect unsound premises. Thus a fault not immediately visible in an assumption may turn up in an examination of its implications. In his various dialogues Plato discovered that the logical implications of the view that knowledge is perception are:

1. Truth is relative;
2. This is a universe of Becoming, of incessant change;
3. This is a universe of particular things.

These natural and logical consequences must be examined to evaluate the original idea.

In the Greek language the general term for perception is *aisthesis*. Frequently Plato used *aisthesis* to mean not only sensations but also the judgments which arose from them. To assume that *aisthesis* or perception was knowledge led to many difficulties. In Plato's dialogues, Socrates took something very basic to man, such as memory, and revealed the great problem of accounting for it—or making sense of it—on the assumption that knowledge is derived from the senses. For example, when we remember something we do not perceive it; yet if knowledge were perception, we could not say that we knew what we were actually remembering.

Now the young and impetuous Theatetus was as sure as can be that what cannot be perceived cannot exist. He boldly announced that knowledge is perception, but old Socrates had a thing or two to teach this young maverick on this score. Socrates had something to teach us all about what we can know through our senses. We find tremendous illumination in exploring the implications of this view with Socrates' guidance.

Then if whatever one perceives is knowledge, as Socrates observed, the dictum of Protagoras that truth is relative must be correct. The Sophist teaching that truth is relative goes back for its philosophical basis to a rather arrogant chap named Heraclitus, an early Greek philosopher. Heraclitus was a very perceptive individual who carefully observed the world and was impressed by the degree to which it was filled with contradictions. He was also taken by the way in which things were constantly being transformed into one another, and he arrived at the conclusion that opposites are identical. There is in everything its own opposite so that no hard and fast distinctions can be drawn in life. Night is ever drawing toward day, and day toward night; in every man there is something of woman and in every woman, something of man. Thus was formulated the principle the Greeks called *dissoi logoi*, or the idea that everything has two sides. Nothing is absolutely this or that. This doctrine was taken up by the Sophists and given practical application to everyday life. If nothing was absolutely so, then one could defend any position as well as any other. Thus the Sophist came to be one who could make the worst argument appear better. In a period of great social change in which there was not only considerable intellectual dispute but many legal suits, this skill was a crucial one; especially since the Greeks did not have lawyers, one had to defend oneself if charged with a crime or faced with a legal suit of any kind. That is why Sophism paid off at this time. The Sophists received money for teaching men how to defend themselves by clever reasoning.

The Sophists were so assured of the *dissoi logoi* doctrine that they even held there were two sides to the argument that there are two sides to everything. In this intellectual context all absolutes dissolved, and it was increasingly difficult to maintain with confidence that anything was so. From here it was only a small step to the teachings of the Sophist Gorgias, who maintained that nothing really was so. Gorgias arrived in Athens in 427 B.C. as the ambassador from his city, Leontini, in Sicily. By saying that nothing could be true, he went further than most Sophists who said that anything could be true. He claimed that *nothing exists,* and that if anything did exist nobody could really understand it anyhow, and that even if you could understand it you could not communicate it. For, what happens when you try to communicate? You have to use words, but words are only symbols, and a symbol is always different from that which it is supposed to refer to; and so we all get hung up on words. Thus we cannot communicate any knowledge. Besides, we cannot even begin to know an object until we observe it and then observations are never foolproof, and only a fool would think they were. Furthermore, everyone observes differently. The result is that we can never be confident that anything is knowledge or truth.

It has been said if there is no god, then man has to become his own god, and if there is no truth, then man would have to make his own truth. Socially, this period of ancient Greek history was one of great flux and mobility, involving increases in trade and discovery of diverse cultural patterns. A natural response to such an age is confusion, and at such a time one might well conclude that nothing can be known. Yet this principle is too untenable to live by, and a more satisfying position is the one at which Protagoras arrived when he declared that whatever works out for one is true for that one. Who can dispute it? If someone says he is deeply in love, and you have never experienced love, who are you to deny his experience? If someone says he knows God, who can know that he really does not? Thus did Protagoras of Abdera come to the *homo mensura,* or "man the measure," doctrine. This is the doctrine that man is the measure of all things, and truth is relative to each individual. There is a song that goes "Where it's at for you, it ain't necessarily at for me." Well, that is precisely what Protagoras said!

According to Protagoras, "man is the measure of all things" because what appears to a man is so, and what does not appear is not so. Truth is relative to each man. If a guy and girl are together, and she says that it is cold but he says that it is hot, who knows what it is? We could find out by getting a reading of the temperature. Suppose we take a Fahrenheit thermometer, and the mercury column shows below 32°—or freezing. Does this mean that if the guy says he is hot, he is not? Maybe what makes most people cold makes him hot. Or maybe the thermometer is wrong. In any event, all a thermometer can do is provide a measurement of what is generally accepted as hot or cold. What is hot to one will be cold to another. So he can be hot, whereas she is cold. Maybe she is turning him on and making him hot, and maybe he is turning her off and making her cold. Who knows? There is no absolute hotness or coldness. Thus everything seems relative not only for individuals but even for substances. A given quantity of heat will change the temperature of glycerine much more than that of an equal weight of water. Thus hotness is not the same for both. If a man goes to the doctor and complains of having a heart attack, the doctor may determine, upon giving him a physical examination, there is nothing wrong with him organically, that he has suffered no heart attack, and that it is all his nerves. Suppose, however, that a man goes to a doctor and tells him he has a terrible pain around his heart, and the doctor, upon examination, tells him that he does not have any pain. This would be time to get another doctor. If you feel pain, you have pain, and no one can know that better than you. Protagoras believed that this principle is applicable to everything. What you perceive is what *you know*. No one can really judge anyone else's perceptions.

Socrates did not agree. If each man is the best judge of his own perceptions, and all that we know we get from our perceptions, then what right did Protagoras have to go around teaching others? He was the one who claimed that his perceptions were no better than theirs; so what could he teach them? Worse yet he charged them money for doing something he himself said could not be done, as Socrates tried to make very clear:

> *I am charmed with his doctrine, that what appears is to each one, but I wonder that he did not begin his book on truth with a declaration that a pig or dog-faced baboon, or some other yet stranger monster which has sensation, is the measure of all things; then he might have shown a magnificent contempt for our opinion of him by informing us at the outset that while we were reverencing him like a God for his wisdom he was no better than a tadpole. . . . For if truth is only sensation . . . why, my friend, should Protagoras be preferred to the place of wisdom and instruction, and deserve to be well paid, and we poor ignoramuses have to go to him, if each one is the measure of his own wisdom?*[20]

Furthermore, if man is the measure of all things, then the man who asserts that Protagoras is wrong, is right according to the view of Protagoras himself. Plato, perhaps more fully than anyone else in history, understood that the relativist is the most absolutistic of men. The relativist denies there are any absolutes, and he does so *absolutely*. One cannot consistently maintain that truth is relative, because in the very process of doing so one is

---

[20] Plato, "Theatetus," in *Dialogues of Plato,* ed. Benjamin Jowett (New York: Random House, Inc., 1937), p. 163.

maintaining an absolute. What is more, if man were the measure of all things, then each man would have his own system of understanding based upon his own particular perceptions; thus everyone's system would be different, and no one would be able to understand anyone else. Indeed it would have been impossible for Protagoras to have communicated his view that everything is relative. Then Gorgias would be right. But people can and do in some sense understand one another. Plato knew that men do not inhabit a private world nor do they inhabit a world that is unintelligible. The fact is that man's world is one of meaning. What is a necessary precondition for intelligibility and meaningfulness? The answer is that it is nonrelative or absolute standards that alone make objective judgments possible.

Thus assuming that knowledge is perception leads to the view that truth is relative, Plato discovered that such a view is self-defeating and actually pointed the way to the absolute.

The doctrine that knowledge is perception is reflected upon adversely by its implication that truth is relative. What of the implication that reality is constantly changing, or "becoming"? Heraclitus held that nothing ever stands still and that everything is in a state of constant motion or change. If knowledge is perception, then it must follow that this is such a world as Heraclitus said it was, for things in the world of perception are always undergoing change. What we perceive is perishable and in a state of constant flux.

Plato had some interesting objections to this view. For anything to be capable of description, he agreed, it must be in a determinate condition. If everything were always changing, however, nothing would ever be determinate. Even language would be impossible. To use words is to put labels on things—to give them names, but this assumes things have a fixed nature to be named. If everything were caught up in a Heraclitean whirlpool of becoming or change, then everything would change before it could be described, named, or known. If everything were constantly changing, it would not be possible to distinguish one thing from another for things would be changing into one another. We could never even say that a thing was itself. Plato observed in "Cratylus" that if all were in a state of transition, knowledge itself would be in a state of change, and thus it would not be knowledge. The point Plato was getting at was that if there could be any knowledge, it would have to be of that which had a determinate condition and fixed nature. Since we do seem to know some things, it follows that all could not be changing.

In fact if all were always changing, there could not even be change, for change is an alteration, and we could never speak of things being altered unless there were some more or less permanent things in which we could see the alteration. If I say to someone that he has really changed, I mean that in certain ways he is different from what he used to be. This does not mean he is completely and entirely different. If he were, then he would not have changed; he would just be somebody else altogether. If we want to make any sense whenever we talk about change, we must assume something stable that is undergoing the change. Even the very organs of perception through which we come into contact with the changing world must be unchanging, or else sight might change into touch, and we would not know what was going on. There would be no way of knowing anything was changing unless we knew of a permanent frame of reference. Suppose some terrible Doctor Cyclops reduced us in size to a few inches. If at the same time God happened to be in a playful mood and changed everything in the world in direct proportion to that, then neither Cyclops nor we could ever detect we had been changed to just a few inches. Knowledge of change points beyond itself to permanence.

We can think about relations, abstractions, or ideas, but we cannot perceive them. People may pay taxes to the state, they may get marriage licenses from the state, and they may go to war and get killed for the state, but they cannot *see* the state. They can see particular individuals who represent the state, but the state itself no one ever perceives. We can only perceive individual things. Thus we assume they are most real. According to Plato, that is where we go wrong. He believed that careful observation of the world of physical particulars takes one beyond it.

We see two sticks of the same size and call them equal. Observing the empirical world leads to such ideas as equality, but those ideas are not empirical. Equality is an idea, but without such ideas we could not deal intelligibly with this world. To make sense of, or judgments about, imperfect physical things in this world, we require the reality of ideas (such as equality) that serve as standards. Ideas, such as equality, beauty, and goodness, are part of the reality of our existence, and without them we could not understand particulars.

Understanding never results from mere observation of particulars. Hippias believed he could explain the meaning of beauty to Socrates in terms of particulars, such as a lovely maiden, a fine horse, or even a well-designed pot. But mere observation of a beautiful girl, whatever sensations it may give us, certainly does not give us "understanding" of beauty. It gives us only an example of beauty, not the meaning of it. A girl can be beautiful, a horse can be beautiful, and a pot can be beautiful. Yet a girl who looked like a pot or a horse would not be beautiful. The point is that there must be something more general that makes different particular things beautiful. There must be a general quality on the basis of which a particular can be understood. We cannot understand reality without admitting the reality of universals. Thus Socrates asked Hippias to teach him what the beautiful itself is.

Suppose Venus were a planet on which the only life was female, and the women of Venus never saw or even heard of such a thing as a man. Then one day a woman of Venus hops a flying saucer to the earth. The saucer lands in a field on earth, the woman from Venus slinks out of it, and the first thing she sees is this earthling who happens to be of the male sex. Would she know what kind of being this is? She might say to herself, "What a queer looking woman!" She might even think this some sort of mutation. In any case she would not know how to properly identify this being or what to make of it. Now on the other hand, suppose she lands, meets a woman, and the woman explains to her the meaning of the idea of man. The woman from Venus, assuming the language barrier was broken, could understand this, and then when she saw a man for the first time, she would not be mystified but would know what he was. The story illustrates the idea that individuals or particular things do not give us knowledge. Knowledge results from generalizations, or what Plato called universals. Universals are thus far more important to understanding than particulars. The idea or the universal is not something that can be perceived; it is something that must be conceived. Universals have to be real because it is only on the basis of their existence that we can understand or know. If we are to penetrate reality, we must grasp the universal.

Thus by meticulously careful reasoning, Plato came upon an exciting discovery. He found that following the assumption that knowledge is perception leads to a world in which truth can only be relative, everything is in a state of change, and there are only physical particulars. In the very process of exploring such a world, however, one comes upon another world, one of absolutes, permanence, and universals. Since this world cannot be *known* by perception, we must reject the view that knowledge is perception.

Indeed the world of sense perception is inherently unstable and uncertain, and thus man can never have more than opinion—or what Plato called *doxa*—concerning it. At the lowest level of perceiving things all man has is *hearsay*. This kind of information is not even based directly on experience, but on rumor or gossip, which are only shadows, images, or reflections of the perceptible world. Natural science is based directly on experience and can give us more than hearsay. It can give us *belief*. It cannot, however, give us certainty because anything gotten from experience is by its very nature contingent. We so worship science in this Space Age that we have forgotten Plato's point, but it is as valid today as it was in his time. A more reliable type of knowledge is mathematics because it can provide us with certainty. Nonetheless, its conclusions are only hypothetical because the major axioms of mathematics were *postulated* and not actually proven. The philosopher, seeking to get to the heart of reality, cannot be satisfied with that which is only conditional or unproven. As Plato saw it, the highest kind of knowledge had to be absolute and to serve as an ultimate foundation upon which all else could depend. The mind that reaches this is *noesis*, or one of rational intuition, and it alone leads to knowledge or *episteme*.

Plato's theory of knowledge was revolutionary. Men who are seeking knowledge through perception are looking for it from the wrong angle, and therefore Plato claimed they must be *turned around*. Truth cannot be seen by the eyes of our body; it must be seen with the eyes of the mind. Plato believed that the mind begins to grow critical when the bodily eye fails. Those who understand by their senses are living in a cave, darkened by ignorance. They do not emerge from the womb into the light of life. There can be no knowledge of life in the cave where men are chained in the ignorance of perception. It is necessary to get out of the cave and see in the light of the sun, to reason, and to rise to the truth. Socrates did that, and the cave dwellers killed him. He had knowledge, and they only had opinion. He understood by dialectical reasoning, whereas they understood by their senses. We cannot account for knowledge, nor can men live in justice, if we assume that knowledge is *a posteriori*—derived from experience. Truth comes not from without, but from within, through reasoning. It is *a priori*, or attained before experience. Thus rationalism, rather than empiricism, must be the foundation for knowledge and truth and for the realization of human justice.

It seems natural to assume that knowledge is not born in us, but is acquired from experience. After all, if you had no experiences, what would you know? What could you know? In Plato's dialogue "Theatetus" it is suggested to Socrates that the mind is like an aviary, and at birth it is empty. As birds must come to the aviary from without, so must knowledge come to the mind.

What are the consequences of such a view? If the mind is empty at birth, then knowledge must result from a learning of new things through experience. To learn something new is to acquire knowledge, and we can only be sure that what we acquire is knowledge by *recognizing* it as such. Of course, it is possible to recognize something only if we have previously seen or experienced it. Conversely, whatever we have previously experienced cannot be new. Thus upon encountering anything, we can only know what it is if we have experienced it before or have a prior idea of it in terms of which we can identify it; otherwise it would be a mystery. This presents a problem. How could we ever learn anything new if knowledge is perception? To learn something is to recognize it as being true, but as we have already seen, what is new cannot be recognized. We only recognize what we already have had contact with. The doctrine that knowledge is perception implies that we know nothing innately, but learn everything we know new from experience. We cannot learn anything new from experience, since there would be no way of recognizing what we were experiencing for the first time; and therefore, we could never know anything. If a professor presumed to teach logic to a student, how could the student ever know that what was being taught was really logic and not something else? If the student did not already know logic, then the teacher could lie to him and tell him anything at all was logic. On the other hand, if the student already knew what logic was, what need would he have for the professor to teach him? And what a fraud the professor is. He is spending his life bringing knowledge to students of what they can only learn if they already know it. This is only a problem, of course, if we assume that knowledge is perception.

On the assumption that rationalism is an adequate theory of knowledge, the same problem simply does not arise. For rationalism assumes that knowledge is *a priori*, or in some sense inborn, and not primarily learned from experience. If in some sense the truth were not already inside of us, how could we recognize it outside? Look what happens when we forget something. There is still a sense in which we may say we know it. A person forgets a name. He is then provided with a list of names that might contain the forgotten one. He shakes his head in doubt and asserts that none of the names on the list is the right one. Yet for the life of him he cannot say what the name is. Now how can he be so unsure about what the name is, and yet, so sure of what it isn't? He can recognize the wrong names only if deep within himself in some sense he knows the right one.

The point is that we cannot understand the functioning of mental processes on the assumption that man's mind is like a sponge sopping in data from the world. There is always an *a priori* element in knowledge. When learning occurs, truth is being recalled from within. We say, "Ah, we can see that it is so," which we could not say unless we were so rationally structured as to be capable of recognizing rational truths. Plato knew that man could not merely be a physical organism that is bombarded by external stimuli; there had to be a soul to which experience made sense.

Plato dramatized his understanding of the learning process in a myth of reincarnation. He assumed that, in a previous existence, the soul had sight of the truth. Learning in this life is remembering the unclouded truth the soul knew in another existence. In the dialogue "Meno" Socrates taught geometry to an ignorant slave boy. As a result of carefully devised questions to evoke certain answers, Socrates elicited truth from the slave boy and so solved the difficult problem. Students think it is hard to recall answers from last night, but this poor slave boy had to remember them from the last life. The point at issue, however, is not reincarnation. Plato wisely understood that at times the truth could be most adequately expressed through myth, and in this case the purpose of the myth was not so much to defend reincarnation as the *a priori* character of knowledge. To Plato knowledge is a recollection or remembering, *anamnesis*. This idea is relevant to the teaching business in an exciting way, for it makes teaching a really dynamic, dialogic process. The teacher does not stick facts into someone, but works with the student to get him to bring forth the truth. No one can be a good teacher who does not respect those whom he presumes to teach. If one does not feel that truth is already in his students, only needing to be brought out or illuminated, then he puts himself in the role of a great intellectual benefactor who has to give to the students. No wonder they get so little. The word education comes from the Latin *educare,* to bring up, or *educere,* to draw out. To find the truth, one cannot merely look into books or into the world; one must look in his own soul. Today when Plato is certainly not in academic style, we presume we are making progress in education when we get great new modern classrooms, dormitories, high-powered scientific laboratories, teaching by television, every variety of visual aid, fast-reading clinics (so one can more quickly assimilate the mountain of worthless nonsense that is constantly being published and one does not have to waste time experiencing and loving great things to be read), and everything else that impoverishes the soul and makes education a factory for robot production.

Whatever else one might say of Plato, he gave us an understanding of knowledge according to which education would never be a process for making robots, but would always be a labor of love, a deeply human experience. He was deeply concerned that his intellectual search had led him to the truth that what was most real was beyond the material and the mechanical, and thus was not machinelike and could not be apprehended by perception. It had to be grasped by thought. Men really learn by human and spiritual instruction, not by mechanical devices or teaching machines. By reasoning together and experiencing loving companionship, two souls here and now may be led to a vision of eternal truth. Such was the rationalist commitment of Plato.

FROM PLATO TO DESCARTES

A basic assumption of rationalists is that the source of knowledge and truth is *a priori*, or before experience. Rationalism is a technical philosophical doctrine. Although it is not the same as having great confidence in reason, certainly there is an important relation between having confidence in reason and the development of rationalism, for great trust in reason will lead to the assumption that one can discover truth just by reasoning and without recourse to empirical research. This is the central idea of rationalism. Because truth is before experience, one must discover it by looking within and reasoning it out. The rationalist believes that only through the eyes of the *mind* could one see ultimate truth. The world could be accounted for only in terms of certain intelligible principles to which reason alone could penetrate. Thus there existed a harmony between logical thought and reality. Phillip Frank in his book *Philosophy of Science* provides an excellent illustration of this principle. Geometry, Frank points out, provides a model of a demonstrative system of necessary truths, and thus in seeking an intelligible explanation of reality, many philosophers have turned to geometry as a foundation. In geometry we start from certain axioms that are not proven but should be self-evident, and from these axioms the truth of theorems is reasoned. Frank observes, "The impression is given in the ordinary teaching of geometry that there is a certain harmony between what can be proved and what can be observed in experiment."[21] Frank gives the example of what can be accomplished starting with an ordinary triangle. Thus if we consider the following:

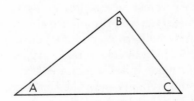

---

[21] Phillip Frank, *Philosophy of Science* (Englewood Cliffs, N.J.: Prentice-Hall, Inc., 1957), p. 52.

A + B + C = 180° in every triangle. The student is taught how to prove this. Starting with this triangle one can travel far. Frank observes, "If the quadrangle ABCD is divided by the diagonal BC into two triangles, and if in each of these triangles the sum of the angles is 180°, the sum of the four angles of the quadrangle is 360°."[22] For example:

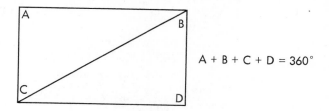

A + B + C + D = 360°

Given this, we can set the problem in which A, B, C, and D are all equal. That means that A = B = C = D. Each is a right angle, and so we have a rectangle:

Thus it becomes clear that, starting out with such a statement as the sum of the angles of a triangle is 180°, we can build rectangles. From such rational principles it is possible to derive empirical facts, and much can be built on that. Phillip Frank points out, "The existence of rectangles makes it possible to build a wall with bricks without gaps. Without rectangles we could not build in our usual way—our whole way of life would be different. We can see that the theorem about the sum of the angles in a triangle is very closely connected with our technical civilization."[23]

The point is that it seems we can do very practical things in the world of facts on the basis of general rational principles. This is why the rationalist believes that the use of reason is primary in understanding the world. The first great modern philosophers explicitly took a geometrical approach to philosophy. The fundamental example of those who did so are men such as Descartes and Spinoza.

René Descartes believed that mathematics was a universally applicable method, and that it was valid for all domains of human understanding. It

22 *Ibid.*, p. 53.
23 *Ibid.*, p. 54.

was Descartes himself who founded analytical geometry by showing how lines and figures could be replaced by algebraic symbols. He was firmly convinced that the philosopher could approach all problems, as the mathematician approached problems of his area of study. This very rational approach to the study of the universe led Descartes to break with the classical view of matter and to interpret it in rational terms. In the system of Plato and Aristotle, matter was understood as amorphous, irrational, and never an essential element of that which is. In opposition to this approach, Descartes conceived of matter as an independently existing substance that can be entirely understood by mind. Matter is that which is extended and, as such, can be dealt with by mathematical reasoning. Understanding matter as rational in this way opened the door to a mechanical interpretation of the physical universe, and this was of crucial importance for progress in the physical sciences. In this way rationalism planted seeds for the development of our scientific environment. Let us now consider the men who worked so systematically at developing the rationalist epistemology.

THE DOUBTS OF DESCARTES

What we might call the first explicitly modern statement of rationalism was formulated by René Descartes, the great French philosopher. During a freezing Bavarian winter Descartes, desiring to think in peace and in warmth, got himself into a stove and remained there all day, doubting all things in an effort to reach that which could not be doubted. Inside the stove he mediated upon such fundamental questions as whether or not man exists or if there is a physical world. Some might think he would have done better to have come out of the stove and taken a look.

Indeed the question itself seems silly. We all *know* we exist. "Know?"— or do we take it for granted? In what sense do we exist? Just what is our nature? Do we have a nature? You know you exist, but could you prove it? It is not an easy task. I find young men and women go all through high school, do a couple years in college, learn all sorts of things, and if you ask them to prove they exist, they become dumbfounded. What good is it to learn all of these things if you do not even know who you are, what you are, or worse yet, *if* you are? If a person seriously tries to show he does exist, he will usually start out with his senses. A person might say, "I know I exist because I can see myself."

> *"Sure you can, but did you ever see a stick immersed in water?"*
> *"Yes."*
> *"Well, how did it look?"*
> *"It looked bent."*
> *"Was it really bent? No, of course not! It was really straight."*
> *"Then isn't it possible you don't really see yourself, but that it just looks that way?"*
> *"No, I don't think so."*
> *"You saw the stick looking bent, but you say it really wasn't."*

"*Oh, that's different. If I feel the stick I can feel it is straight.*"

"*Well, come on, why should you suppose that what you feel with your hand
is more reliable than what you see with your own eyes*"

"*There are laws of physics which can explain this.*"

"*In other words, there are rational laws that can show there are not things
which you see with your own eyes. Interesting! It is possible the same could
be the case when you look at what you uncritically call yourself.*"

"*I guess so.*"

"*You can't be sure you exist, then, or if you do, what you are?*"

"*But look, I'm not just like the stick. In that case what I see and feel conflict.
But I not only can see myself, I can feel what I see.*"

"*You can feel yourself?*"

"*Yes, I can feel myself.*"

"*What does a self feel like?*"

"*What?*"

"*Well, I mean you may feel an arm or a leg, or a face, but that's specific.
What's a self? Is that like an arm or leg? Besides, you can feel things that
aren't there. During the war soldiers who had had their legs amputated without
being told afterward complained of feeling severe pain in their legs. So it is
possible to feel something that isn't there.*"

"*I guess so, but I certainly feel sure I see and feel myself.*"

"*You do dream, do you not?*"

"*Of course, I do.*"

"*Well, while you are dreaming you see and feel, don't you?*"

"*Yeah.*"

"*So, you see and feel things when you are dreaming, but at the time you
are not aware you are dreaming. So maybe, then, you're dreaming now, and
thus what you think is so is only a dream?*"

"*Yes. But wait. When I am dreaming all sorts of crazy things happen, and
then I wake up and live in a more orderly world which mostly seems bound by
laws of cause and effect. Once I had this great dream in which I was in bed
with this girl, and then I awakened and there was my wife. That's known as
the nightmare of reality.*"

"*Oh, but look here, that proves nothing. Maybe reality is crazy, there is no
such thing as an orderly world of cause and effect, and that is only a dream.
When you awaken is when all of the crazy things happen. How can you tell
when you go to bed and think you are starting to dream you are not really
waking up, and when you think you are waking up in the morning you are
starting to dream? The wild gal you dreamed of is real, and your wife was just
a nightmare. How can you really know the difference between dreaming and
being awake. You can't, because any distinction you offer may just be a part of
your dream.*"

"*It seems crazy.*"

"*Maybe what's real is crazy. When people suffer from illusions they are
quite certain what they perceive is real. Well, it isn't. Maybe this whole world
we fear may be blown up isn't even here to be blown up.*"

"*Well, at least that's one solution to civil defense problems.*"

"*It might be, but we can't even be sure about that.*"

"*Is there anything we can be sure about?*"

"What do you think?"

"Mathematics, that's something we can always be certain about. Even Einstein, who said we can never be sure about physical science, said we could be sure about mathematics. I remember reading him on that. We can always be certain that 3 + 7 = 10."

"Can we?"

"Sure."

"Well 3 + 7 = 10, and you are right it always does whenever we add it up, but what if all of us always add it up in the same way: wrong! Suppose there is something in the very nature of our calculation that deceives us. It is possible there is a Malin Genie *who is out to make fools of us . . ."*

"Wait—a Malin what?"

"A Malin Genie, a Great Deceiver, a devil, an evil God. What if this Malin Genie is sadistic, and with his perverted sense of humor really derives enormous pleasure out of making asses out of us, and tricks us every time we make additions? What if he systematically deceives us every time we add up any numbers? Every time we add up 3 and 7 he pulls our leg in exactly the same way, and so we keep thinking it's adding up to 10. But heaven only knows what it's really adding up to."

"Well, if it does I wish it would let us in on it. I'm beginning to think I don't know anything. But look, isn't that idea of a Great Devil ridiculous"

"Sure, and it is very very highly improbable, but it is possible, and that means we haven't accounted for all possibilities if we don't consider it. But if we do consider it, even though it is not likely, still it is possible, and thus we cannot be absolutely sure even about math."

"Well I'll be damned."

"I don't know."

"Who could know anything? It looks as if nothing can be known. I can't think of any way of showing we know anything."

"Well perhaps things are not so bad. Look what we have to try to do is doubt everything until we reach something we just can't doubt, and of that we can then be certain."

"Right. But it seems you've shown we can doubt everything."

"Not exactly. There is one thing we can't doubt. We can't doubt that we are doubting, for by doubting that we were doubting we would still be doubting. There's no getting away from it."

"No doubt about it."

"To doubt is to think. We can't doubt away doubt, nor think away thinking. Cogito ergo sum, I think: therefore I am. Thinking is going on, and thinking implies a thinker. So if I don't know anything else I know I am a being who thinks. I am a thinking substance. That cannot be doubted, and to know that is to really know something. From there we can go far."

"You've saved the world."

"Not yet, but that will come from proving my own existence."

Such doubts and questions as these were raised by René Descartes as he sat in his stove, and he finally came to his illumination that, since he could deny everything except that he was thinking, he had to be a thinking being. This may not seem very realistic: we start already thrown into the world and have to take that for granted. Descartes did not agree; he believed we could take nothing for granted. We have reason, and with it we can prove things, but he had to find out what we could prove. Some things we can be more sure of than others. What are they? Descartes had seen that tremendous strides were made in the field of mathematics. He wanted to find a method for philosophy that would yield as great certainty as could be attained in mathematics. He could only get to that certainty by doubting all until he could doubt no more.

This was not merely an intellectual exercise with Descartes; he was deadly serious. People have to have something to believe in or they go mad. What can one believe in? Descartes was looking for the most positive and absolute foundations. That is why he had to question everything. Anything that could not stand the test of his questioning could hardly be a foundation for living. What he believed he had found most indubitably was that man is a thinking substance, a soul. His very nature is that of thought. Thus he is a *res cogitans*, a thinking thing. This conclusion could not be doubted and could not be established by perception—by looking in the world. It could be established only by looking within, by reasoning. The truth that was ultimate was found within. Knowledge is, as Plato maintained, *a priori*.

Descartes found that the greatest certainty was the existence of the self as a thinking thing, but after reaching that certainty he could go beyond to other things. From the certainty of his own being Descartes had a foundation upon which he could build to the existence of God, other selves, and the rest of the world.

He reasoned that there must be a god as a natural implication of the knowledge of himself. He also came to see that he was a finite and imperfect being, but to see even his own "imperfection" required that he have the idea of perfection. Without it there would be no standard by which he could measure his imperfection. But where does an imperfect ordinary mortal get the idea of perfection? A man cannot even come to the conclusion he exists except in the imperfect act of doubting. The source of the idea of perfection must be that which is perfect, and that is God. Certainly this perfect being, God, must exist, because it would hardly make sense to attribute perfection to that which did not even exist. Descartes was going back to what is known as the *ontological argument* for the existence of God. This is a classical argument that because we have the idea of a perfect being there must be one, for if we admit that a being is perfect, we cannot deny that such a being exists. To do so would be to reveal an imperfection and thus to contradict ourselves. Descartes was certain he existed because he had proved it, but from his discovery that he was finite and imperfect, he concluded that he could not be the cause of his own existence. There had to be a perfect being who was the cause of his idea of perfection and of his existence.

Assuming he had grasped in an intuition the truth at the end of the chain of reasoning he was following, Descartes saw the way from himself and God to the world and other selves. As a thinking thing Descartes knew he existed, but only as a thinking thing. He did perceive a body and a world, but his perceptions could be deceptive. But he had also proved there was a perfect God. Would a perfect God let man be so deceived? No, that would not be the type of nasty trick a perfect One would pull. St. Paul had maintained God could be known *creatura mundi*, from that which he has created. Now God did not make man perfect; instead He gave him liberty and the power to make judgments. It is good to have such abilities, and yet, because of them one can err. This is perfectly consistent with the perfection of God. But for God to create man so that he *must* err and be deceived would be devilish. That is what that Malin Genie would do, but a good god would not. Thus Descartes concluded that his perceptions of his own body and a material world were, while open to error, not illusion.

In this way Descartes came to a position known in philosophy as dualism. He proved the reality of *res cogitans*, thinking substance, and from that he came to the assurance of *res extensa*, extended substance—body, or what we call the material world. Thus there are two basic components that go to make up reality; they are mind and matter, or spirit and body. The metaphysical significance of this is considerable and will be fully explored in connection with our discussion of metaphysics. Descartes started assuming he knew virtually nothing and ended up convinced he knew practically everything. Did he really prove as much as he thought?

Descartes's dualism appears to be a reasonable conclusion, inasmuch as there certainly do seem to be mental events and physical events. But it leaves unanswered one very important question: How can they be explained to *interact?* Descartes's own efforts to explain the interaction of mind and body proved to be a distinct failure, so that dualism gave rise to problems for which it could not provide a solution. A view known as *occasionalism* was formulated to deal with difficulties left unanswered by Descartes. A Dutch philosopher and follower of Descartes named Arnold Geulincx made the effort to logically account for the relation between mind and body. Geulincx retained Descartes's idea that mind and body are distinct, but he regarded them as so *distinct* as to be incapable of interaction. Mind and body *seem* to be casually related to one another; for example, I think I would like to go to a movie tonight, and so I take my body and go. Yet something of one nature cannot affect something of an entirely different nature, so Geulincx tried to come up with a way to explain the apparent relationship between mind and body. Suppose two clocks were so perfectly synchronized that when one pointed to a given hour, the other would strike the corresponding number of chimes. There is perfect accord and harmony between the two clocks so that they appear to be in interaction, and yet they are not. Maybe mind and body are like these two clocks; they seem to *interact,* and yet no evidence of interaction can be discovered. May it not be that mind and body do not really *interact,* but are perfectly synchronized like the clocks? Of course they could only be synchronized in this way by a supreme being. Thus Geulincx reasoned that God has so arranged reality that *on the occasion* of a given occurrence in the nervous system or the body, there emerges a given occurrence in the mind; and *on the occasion* of the will of mind, there arises a change in the nervous system or the body. This theory has been known as *occasionalism.*

Geulincx's occasionalist argument was very meticulously defended by the French philosopher Nicolas Malebranche (1638–1715). Philosophers like Geulincx and Malebranche explained the mind-body problem by introducing a harmony arranged by God. Here was a clearly religious solution to the problem, and yet, paradoxically, their ideas made a significant contribution to materialism, for in terms of this theory, matter (the body or material world) was rendered completely free from spiritual or mental influence. Descartes had clearly separated mind from body, soul from matter, thus making possible the formulation of an independent science of matter or physical science. With Descartes mind had influence over matter, but with the *occasionalists* even this was taken away. A complete and thorough rift opened up between mind and body.

A great German metaphysician came to a solution of the problem somewhat similar to the one developed by the occasionalists but with a basic difference. Gottfried Wilhelm von Leibniz (1646–1716) shared the view of the *occasionalists* that there cannot be *interaction*. If one wishes to tear down an idea, he cannot pull it apart with his hands, nor can he dynamite it. He can only take it apart logically. Similarly if someone wants to blow up a bridge, an idea will not do. In short there is simply no evidence of any actual direct *interaction* of mind and body. Leibniz, however, did not regard divine synchronization of the functioning of mind and body as tenable. He regarded it as more logical to remove the idea of body or matter altogether. Leibniz could not see how the conception of material substance could be defended. Since a substance is that which *exists in itself* and is independent, it cannot be divided, and yet extension or matter is divisible and thus cannot be of the nature of a substance. All substances, therefore, must be spiritual in nature. Yet all spiritual substances are of the same type. Thus Leibniz saw the universe as a hierarchically organized scheme of immaterial substances. There was a plurality of these which he called *monads,* and he explained their apparent interaction as a *preestablished harmony.* The monads do not actually interact, but they are so arranged that an occurrence with one is in exact harmony with an occurrence with another. This is possible because the universe is conceived as a harmonious system.

The problem with such theories as the occasionalism of Geulincx and Malebranche or the preestablished harmony of Leibniz is that, while they provide an account of why acts of mind and body seem to go together, they do so by introducing hypotheses that could in no way be verified. Is it harder to believe that mind and body somehow affect each other directly than to believe that somewhere from on high a supreme being is creating a beautiful orchestration of reality? Such a solution was far too stagey.

In its dualistic conclusion, Cartesian rationalism opened the door to one of the major problems of modern man—alienation. Attempts to close this door by talking about divine synchronization and preestablished harmony would not work because, for a man to really feel at harmony with life, reality has to be harmonious. That all is ultimately of one substance means there is no basis for alienation, and man can truly feel at home in the universe. Geulincx, Malebranche, and Leibniz could not gloss over Descartes's discovery that men, through their consciousness, are aware of their difference from that which is outside of them. In all dualist and pluralistic accounts of reality men are creatures alien to one another and to nature.

RATIONALISM AND THE AGE OF REASON

The rationalist epistemology was not just an attempt to show us how we can know but to show us how to live. The implications for the reasoned existence, based on a rationalist theory of knowledge, were particularly illuminated in the life and philosophy of Benedict Spinoza (1632–1677). So fully did Spinoza understand things by the deductive philosophy of rationalism that he patterned his entire philosophy on the model of geometry. Even problems of ethics were cast in a geometrical form. Instead of emotionally plunging into the waters of morality, Spinoza put himself to the task of conducting a fully reasoned analysis of ethics, actually formulating ethical axioms, definitions, and postulates. Yet, however dry and lifeless so formal an approach may appear, honest human feeling did dwell in Spinoza's house of geometry, and he did not get lost from life in the intricate system. Indeed Spinoza never lost sight of the underlying purpose of philosophy, which was not to get entangled in weaving a web of reason for it own sake, but to discover for man the best life one could live.

Spinoza came to the conclusion that the object to which one devoted himself with love determined whether or not one would find fulfillment in life. If one gives his love to things of the senses, he will sadly find they lack the staying power to confer any lasting happiness. Just as the understanding that man gains from his senses is unreliable and incapable of giving true knowledge, so the lowest kind of pleasure is that which comes from the senses and is incapable of blessing him with happiness. Spinoza was not an unrealistic rationalist. Like Plato in the ancient world, he felt the full force emotional drives had in moving men. However, men who allow themselves to be impelled by the need for money, sex, power, or fame, never satisfy their deepest human yearnings. Spinoza claimed that men pursue such values because of *inadequate ideas*. He anticipated Freud in showing that men were motivated and driven by passions that they could not understand and into which they lacked insight. Spinoza believed the remedy lay in bringing these deep unconscious strivings to self-consciousness. Men suffer deeply and are tormented by irrational fears and gnawing anxieties because they lack adequate ideas of what they need as men to sustain themselves. One who takes the narrow way of life and searches for sensual and purely physical pleasures misses the true joy of gaining a vision of life in its total perspective.

Thus while Spinoza was a very committed rationalist, he was not naïve about the power the senses exercised over man; it was just that he believed if man were to make a meaningful adjustment to reality, he would have to bring those emotions under the control of reason. As reason could provide man with a more reliable type of knowledge than the senses, so too could it make possible a better kind of life for him. The ultimate insight emerges from living the life of reason. The highest knowledge and human blessed-ness is gained through intuition, which enables man to see as God Himself sees. So man may transcend the very narrow confines of perceptual existence and attain vision of the highest beatitude.

One might believe that the rationalist vision of life has a blind spot to the suffering, misfortune, and tragedy of existence. Leibniz, who with Descartes and Spinoza rounds out the "big three" of continental rationalists, dealt with the question of evil. As we view this world, things may often seem to make little sense, and the world may seem to be filled with evil. Leibniz assured man not to worry because, though things might seem rather black, this is *the best of all possible worlds* in the final analysis. After all, God had a choice in creating this world; He could have created it differently, but since He did not, this one must be the best it could be. It would be inconceivable to think that God does not know how to make a world. That's His business! What do we know about creating worlds? He made this world, and if it was good enough for Him, then it should be good enough for us. If you do not believe in God, that is another matter, but if you do, then what Leibniz maintained is not unreasonable. Leibniz spoke of a *principle of sufficient reason*, the point of which is that however bad things may seem now, if we had sufficient knowledge, we would be able to see that things could not possibly be better. Leibniz believed there was a reason for everything, though we might not always be able to know what it was.

Thus we see that the rationalist philosophy, whether correct or incorrect, had enormously important implications for all domains of existence. Men—brilliant men—saw everything in the light of reason. The ultimate was reached with Hegel, who proclaimed that the real is rational, and the rational is real.

Of course, all of the developments in the Age of Reason and Enlighten-ment were by no means related to rationalism in epistemology. But the rationalist faith that committed men to seeking truth and knowledge through reason was the same or very similar to the rationalist faith that led men to assume that a rational approach to all life was possible. Here was the religion that came out of the church of modern science. As we have seen, there were two fundamental dimensions to modern science, a mathematical and an empirical. The rationalist faith was always more related to the mathematical aspect of modern science, and from it rationalism took the roots for its development. The mathematical aspect of science deals with man's effort to quantify reality. The physical aspect of science is quite another story. To what extent can there be success in quantifying the physical world? Empiricist philosophers showed that there were many difficulties inherent in the basic rationalist project of understanding knowl-edge. And in developing their ideas of what knowledge really is, the em-piricists found a much less rational universe than that envisioned in the rationalist philosophy. In many ways modern science has become the faith of modern man; in many ways modern science lacks the substance to be a meaningful basis on which man may live. Modern science, modern man, and civilization are foundering. Insight into the reason why can be afforded by examining the development of the empiricist epistemology.

The Truth Without: British Empiricism

The rationalists believed that by reason alone man could ascend to the highest truths. They believed that sense experience was misleading and unreliable. Through the looking glass of pure reason, they believed, man could gain vision of universal truths, and from these he could "deduce" particular truths. Great truths were believed to be hidden, not in the world of experience, but in the world of reason—the mind. The empiricists retorted that there was nothing in the mind of man save what experience put there, and thus induction, rather than deduction, was necessary to attain universal truth. One cannot start with generalizations; one must come to them as a result of observing phenomena and events in the world of experience. In the mordern world the first major assault and frontal attack upon rationalism and the most coherent and systematic defense of empiricism was launched by John Locke and developed by Bishop George Berkeley and David Hume.

JOHN LOCKE

The philosophy of empiricism was developed against a background of social and political unrest in seventeenth-century Britain when England was in the throes of immense industrial progress. In this context of social and scientific change, people were much caught up in the whirlwind of practical existence and sought practical solutions to their pressing problems. Men just did not have time for the eternal verities of rationalism. Merely probable knowledge about the workings of this world proved far more useful at this time than did certain knowledge of an eternal world, which itself was quite uncertain. Englishmen were involved in practical matters, and knowledge had to be a practical pursuit. A doctor could not learn to cure a patient by locking himself in a stove and meditating upon who exists, as Descartes had done. He would have to find some practical medical information, or it might turn out to be his patients who did not exist. This was a time of industrialization, of technical and economic progress, and there was a great demand for practical results. Greater emphasis was placed on knowledge that comes from experience rather than from pure reason. While many of the great rationalists were mathematically oriented, empiricists were generally more skilled in some practical pursuit.

One of the first significant formulations of empiricist philosophy in modern times was accomplished by John Locke, who himself had training in the empirical field of medicine. Locke prescribed experience as a much needed medicine for the understanding of knowledge and sought to demonstrate the utter inadequacy of the rationalist position that knowledge originates in innate ideas. In defending the thesis that there are inborn or innate ideas, the rationalists had contended that there are certain universally accepted principles. Locke categorically denied this. He observed that while rules of logic may be self-evident to those who have intellectual training, it is not the case that such rules are grasped automatically by those who are feebleminded or by very young children. With respect to the position there are universal moral laws, Locke suggested that a person had only to look beyond "the smoke of his chimney" to see its falsity.

The fact is that ideas seem to vary consistently with the level of individual or cultural experience, and therefore it is reasonable to conclude that they arise from experience. Descartes had claimed that the search for truth was a matter of *thinking* rather than of *experience*. He believed the road to absolute certainty had to be paved with systematic doubting. For this reason Descartes declared the necessity of starting with a clean slate by doubting everything. This is ironic because a basic point of Locke's was that the slate Descartes had started with was hardly clean. On the contrary it was contaminated with the mess of innate ideas or *a priori knowledge*. And so Dr. Locke prescribed some brainwashing to clean the slate of the idea of *a priori* knowledge. Locke was aware of no evidence that at birth the mind contained anything like innate ideas, and thus he concluded that it was a *tabula rasa,* or blank tablet. Knowledge is only possible when experience is written upon this blank tablet.

Thus instead of looking in to find truth, Locke insisted we must look out to the world. Knowledge is a consequence of our perception of that world. Basically, Locke argued, what is perceived—what is seen—must be presumed to be there. The view that what we perceive actually exists out there independently of us is known in epistemological theory as "realism." We must be careful not to confuse epistemological realism with the doctrine of realism in metaphysics or the school of realism in literature and the arts. Indeed one could go crazy trying to figure out which realism is real—or even which is which. For the present we will just rack our brains on the epistemological version.

Realism in epistemology is what would seem to be a very obvious truth. It is that the world we perceive out there is actually out there; it has *independent objective existence.* This hardly seems a momentously important proclamation, yet it is important because it is not so obvious as it may seem. A person might say, "Well, of course, I know it's there because I see it," but the question that arises concerns whether what we see is always actually there. Indeed is it ever there? The realist is not just saying that our perceptions are real, but he is also saying that the *objects* of our perception are real. What does it mean to make this distinction? It means although we may say that what we perceive is real, a question may still be raised whether it is real in a physical sense, objectively and independently of us, or whether its reality is dependent upon our perception. We look and see a tree. The tree is real, but what is the nature of its reality? Is it real as a physical object? Is it real as a spiritual entity? Or does its only reality lie in some combination of our percepts? The realist insists there is an objective physical world existing independently of us in the form in which we perceive it. The idealist may also claim there is an objective world existing independently of us, but he contends its nature is nonphysical. The idealist may also build the case that there is no objective world out there at all, for all of reality exists only in our perception of it.

Epistemological realism is the opposite of epistemological *idealism*. This idealism is the view that we can know only ideas and never know material objects. Thus we have no basis for inferring the reality of material objects. The realist, on the other hand, argues that it is possible to know physical objects, for they do exist independently of our perceiving them. Idealism may seem far less tenable than realism, and yet examination of realism will show there are some serious chinks in its epistemological armor. This should immediately become evident when we realize that it is almost impossible to develop an adequate case for a very basic form of realism known as *common sense realism*. (Because common sense realism assumes that things are just as they are presented to the senses, it is also known as *presentational* realism.) That this is the case has led to the formulation of a more sophisticated form of realism, which is called *representational realism*. One sometimes feels like asking if the real realism will please stand up.

Common sense realism is the position that what man directly perceives exists. Despite its name and the fact that it certainly seems to make sense, there are serious problems for this form of realism. One is that the same object perceived from varying angles will appear different. This is a problem because it suggests when we perceive things we do not get them purely as they are, but in a state altered by our perception and position. Thus it might seem more logical, as John Locke came to assume, to assert that when we perceive things we are not getting them directly but are getting a copy of them from our senses. Locke contended that the world is not directly *presented* to our senses, but is *represented* by them. Thus Locke's version of realism is known as *representational realism,* or the *copy theory* of knowledge. He believed, as do all realists, that an external world does exist independently of us. However when we look at it, we are not getting direct knowledge of it. Our senses do not put us in direct contact with the world, but only represent it to us, so that what we are getting is like a photograph or copy of it. This is because when we "see" a tree, for example, our seeing is only our mind interpreting what the light from the tree does to our eyes, and what we know, then, is not the tree itself. Similarly when we touch a tree and feel its hardness, all we are really experiencing directly is what is happening in our skin. We assume that the sensation of hardness *represents* what the tree is really like, but this is only an assumption.

A young lady is wandering through an open field, happily taking in the fresh country air and viewing the beautiful landscape. She is attired in a lovely red outfit, and suddenly she becomes concerned when she discovers that a bull is watching her. The bull starts to run toward her, an angry look in his eyes. She probably thinks that the bull doesn't like her because she is dressed in red, but he wouldn't even care if she was wearing yellow, green, or blue. He just does not like people strolling through his field; in fact he would hardly be interested in the color of their clothing since he cannot perceive colors. The outermost layer of the retina is composed of two kinds of cells called rods and cones; the rods are thin and the cones are thick.

These are the receptor cells; they receive the image the eye sees. It is by virtue of the cone cells that man distinguishes colors. Bulls, however, do not have cones and apparently do not perceive color distinctions. They have rods and perceive relative shades of light and darkness. This raises a most interesting consideration—that what we see does not depend simply upon what is out there but also upon what is in us. Indeed because of a retinal disparity in man, what we see is even dependent upon whether we see it with the right or left eye. Thus the stimulus pattern received from an object and transmitted to the left eye is different from that transmitted to the right. Just think if you were a fly and had five eyes of two different types, or if you had a thousand eyes as some insects do, things would look very differently than they do with your two eyes. The obvious conclusion then is that we do not come into direct contact with the world, but get it to us through our senses, which may affect or distort what it is really like. Thus it is difficult to maintain, as common sense realism does, that we are getting a direct presentation of the world.

The senses are rather unreliable witnesses to the truth. Instead of directly presenting us reality, the senses frequently present us illusion. Often people cannot see what there is to be seen right before their eyes, and yet at other times they see things that are not even there, as in the following case. Suppose a man drives his girl to a lonely spot, parks the car, lifts up the top of his convertible, and beholds the stars. He very romantically tells his girl how wonderful it is to be with her under the stars. The girl, who has had a course of astronomy and epistemology, observes that actually there may not even be any stars up there. "What?" the poor guy asks. He tells this girl that their romantic future may be written in those stars. She explains that those stars he thinks may govern their future may themselves be things of the past. She tells him the stars he now sees may already have been in a great war and have been blown out of existence. The guy says, indignantly, "But how can you say that? I'm looking at them now." She points out that when he gazes at the stars what he sees is not something in the present but from the past, something that might even have discontinued to exist by that time. The velocity of light is finite, and therefore it takes time—maybe millions upon millions of years in some cases—for the light of the star (which we see as the star) to reach our eyes here on earth. One does not see the star immediately, or to put it more pointedly, one does not see the star when he seems to be seeing it. Thus by the time he is seeing it, the actual star may no longer exist.

If the senses are the source of illusion and other error, can we be certain they do not always mislead us? And if we do become convinced there is some external reality to cause the perceptions we get, still upon analysis it cannot be maintained that reality is that to which we are given direct access by perception. Thus although John Locke believed that there had to be an external world as the cause of our perceptions, he was equally convinced that that external reality was not exactly what common sense believed it to be. Common sense realism assumes that there is nothing between the object and our perception of it. Locke, of course, did not believe that our perceptions could be caused by nothing, but he reasoned that the external reality that caused them was *represented* to us by our senses rather than directly *presented*. Standing between our ideas and the world is our perceptual apparatus. Thus we come to know objects of the world not directly but rather through our perceptions, or, as Locke would say, through our ideas of them.

In developing his theory of representative realism Locke followed philosophers Democritus, Hobbes, and Descartes, and scientists Galileo and Boyle, in drawing a distinction between two kinds of qualities—primary and secondary. *Primary qualities* are objective in that they inhere in objects themselves, whereas secondary qualities are subjective and are dependent upon our perception. The primary qualities are extension in space, number, shape, solidity, and motion. These qualities are an integral part of objects—inseparable from them. They form part of the objective structure of reality. What would be more preposterous than shape that did not belong to an object to give shape to? Imagine someone demanding to have a beautifully shaped ————. Someone asks him a beautifully shaped what, and he answers he just wants a shape in itself. We would think such a person mad. Thus shape is a primary quality. It is there in the object whether or not we perceive it. This is why Locke called primary qualities "real."

On the other hand, *secondary qualities*, such as color, taste, sound, or smell, are not as dependent on the objects as on us. When someone hits a drum, the air around it vibrates. That movement of the air is an objective fact; it would happen whether anyone were around or not. But it is not sound unless there is an ear there to respond to the vibration and interpret it as sound. In fact there are many vibrations in the air that are of too low or too high a frequency for us to hear them—like those made by radio waves and dog whistles—and we do not interpret these as sounds. Thus the existence of sound depends upon ears to hear it, whereas the movement of the vibration of the air does not depend upon being perceived. Color, taste, and smell are subjective, like sound; they depend upon and vary with the percipient, and therefore they are called secondary qualities.

The world is composed of objects that have primary qualities. But what are the objects? We have already seen that the primary qualities of extension, number, shape, solidity, and motion exist independently of our perception of them, but they do not exist independently of the objects of which they are the qualities. They just cannot be hard and square and heavy in themselves; they must be hard, heavy, square something. But what? And how can we know it? We can perceive all the qualities of a thing, but we do not perceive the thing itself. Say there is a hard, heavy, irregularly shaped object in front of us. We say it is a rock. We can perceive its hardness, its heaviness, its irregular shape, but can we perceive its "rockness"? Can we perceive the thing that has these qualities, as distinct from the qualities themselves? Locke presumed that logic demands one to conclude that there is something that binds these qualities together—that is, something of which they are the qualities. Yet he admitted that he did not know what it was. This "what" that we knew not, he called "substance." This substance is the substratum of the qualities; it is what the qualities are qualities of.

If one starts with the understanding that knowledge is perception, it logically follows that he should encounter more difficulties with such categories as primary and secondary qualities and such ideas as substance, than Locke did. Indeed if one is going to maintain this understanding, one may have to give up the world itself—that is, repudiate realism. Let us see how this works.

John Locke sought to demonstrate that all our knowledge is built up from our perceptions (the doctrine of empiricism). If this is true, we might then want to ask what our perceptions are built up from. What is it that we perceive? The man of common sense assumes we perceive exactly what is out there. Not exactly, reasoned Locke. To put it in television lingo, we may say that our perceptions do not give us a live play of reality; they give us only a replay of it, and in the process something may be lost. We want to know what is real, but because our senses stand between our minds and reality, we always get only a reproduction and never the original. Our senses do not give us a direct line to reality, but only a copy or report of it; and reports or copies are terribly susceptible to distortion.

The proverbial man of common sense believes that our senses lead us directly to reality, but it has become good sense to conclude that our senses very much mislead us. How far do they mislead us? John Locke, who saw that our senses fail to give us a *direct* vision of reality, was blind to the fact that our senses may give us a vision of what is not out there at all, never was there, never will be, and never could be—and even if it could be would be such that we could not know about it anyway. We may be able to show that things we experience with our senses invariably fall prey to distortion, but surely there must be things out there that are being distorted. Thus did John Locke reasonably conclude. That is why he quite logically arrived at the position that our senses do not give us *direct* contact with things in themselves out in the world, but rather provide us with a picture or copy of these things. This seems a sensible view of the function of our senses, but does it make sense? How could Locke have been so confident there was a world out there when he had said the source of all knowledge is perception. If *everything we know* comes from our perceptions, then it is beyond us to know where our perceptions come from. And yet Locke told us they came from physical objects. Locke's position that all knowledge is based on perception, on the one hand, and his position that there is a physical world out there, on the other hand, seems to be a case in which the right hand didn't know what the left was doing.

Let us consider the problem Locke had in the light of the following. The doorbell of a man named Mr. Smith rings and he, assuming that if the bell rings someone must be there, goes and opens the door. Sure enough, standing there is a wise old philosopher named Wisdom with long streaming silver hair. Wisdom says to Mr. Smith, "I have come to tell you that you are not really yourself." Mr. Smith asks, "Then who am I?" Wisdom informs him that he is just a copy of himself, that the real Mr. Smith is secreted away in the archives in Washington, D.C. and that he is only an imitation of this real Mr. Smith who is locked away in the archives and who embodies all of the characteristics and details of which the Mr. Smith at the door is a copy. Mr. Smith tells Wisdom that he must be putting him on. However Wisdom assures him he is really serious. Smith asks how this can be possible. Wisdom answers, "Cloning!" and then goes on to explain that scientists, by taking a single cell from a carrot or a frog, have succeeded in "growing" precise duplicates of the parent cell donor. Wisdom explains that the government, taking one small step for itself and a giant step for mankind, took the original Mr. Smith and extracted a body cell from him. The body cell, possessing forty-six chromosomes, fulfills all the requisite properties for making a complete person. Wisdom concludes, "And so they made you." Smith says, "God, I'm not real," and he faints. Wisdom disappears into the night.

Smith's father, Mr. Smith Sr., is much more concerned to get to the truth, for he fears he may die soon and does not wish to leave his fortune to a copy son. Smith Sr. hires a private detective named Jones to find Wisdom. Jones finds Wisdom in a cave seeking the inner essence of an onion, and brings him to the wealthy old Smith, who demands proof that the man he takes to be his son is a cloning job. What kind of proof does Smith Sr. want? He wants to see the alleged original so he can determine if he really is an exact model of which the man he now takes to be his son is only a copy. If Wisdom tells Smith he cannot see the original son because he is not only in the archives but in an iron mask, and no one can ever see him, there would be no reason to take the story of the cloning seriously because it would not only be unsubstantiated, but unsubstantiable. Of course, Smith might ask to see a picture, or for corroboration from responsible persons who might have seen the original son before he was put in the iron mask. If Wisdom's response is that no one ever saw the original son because he was always in an iron mask, Smith might doubt not only the story but Wisdom's sanity as well.

Wisdom's claim seems preposterous because, not being able to get a peek at the man inside the iron mask, he cannot know that the alleged copy Smith looks just like him and is only a duplicate. To determine that one thing is a copy of another, we have to be able to look at both so we can compare them. If the alleged original Smith can never be viewed, we have no way of determining that the alleged copy Smith looks just like him. Locke well understood that common sense realism did not really make sense, but his correction of that view perhaps made even less sense.

The common sensé, or naïve, *realist* maintains he has a direct line to reality, meaning by that the world out there. His position is that the world is *presented* directly to him through his senses.

John Locke saw this view was inadequate because standing between our minds and the world are our senses that may affect our view of it. Thus our senses do not present the world directly to us, but *represent* it to us, or give us a report of it. Locke's analysis, then, revealed to him that man is utterly dependent upon his perceptions for his knowledge, and these give a copy of the world.

The problem with Locke's representative realism should be obvious. Locke maintained that our perceptions give us a copy of an external world. Yet, since on Locke's own view, man is understood to be *bounded* by his perceptions, he has *no* independent access to the world beyond, which alone could provide him with a means of judging whether his perceptions are a copy of it. To conclude that our sense data are a copy of an *external* reality, it would be necessary to view both the copy and the original from a detached vantage point in order to compare them.

There is just one problem here: one cannot stand outside of his perceptions. One's perceptions are an inherent part of a person, and one views the world through the portals of one's senses. A man cannot get beyond those portals—at least not on the empiricist assumption that we cannot explain knowledge except in terms of our perceptions. Thus for one to know there is a world out there of which our perceptions are a copy would require one to stand outside of oneself, and that's not easy! Indeed on an empiricist view it is not even possible. Locke was saying that the only knowledge we can have is based on our perceptions and is not direct knowledge of an external world. And yet he held the position that there is an external world of which we can have indirect knowledge. There's the rub. If we cannot get directly to reality, there is no way to know what it is like in itself so that we can say our perceptions provide us with a copy of it. We are hopelessly locked up in the prison of our perceptions, and can never break out of them to compare them with any alleged external reality.

BISHOP BERKELEY

Bishop George Berkeley clearly understood the problem we have just outlined and choked Locke's theory on a cherry. Consider the composition of a cherry. It is soft to touch, has a red color, is tart to taste, and is round in shape. Our experience of a cherry is made up of many different perceptions —to wit, its softness, its redness, its tartness, and its roundness. None of these could exist in itself, and all *must* somehow be held together to provide us with the coherent object. What must underlie and hold together these particular perceptual qualities? What is that something Locke called *substance?* Today we understand that molecules underlie objects. We perceive sounds, colors, tastes, odors, and sights, but we do not perceive substance or molecules. Yet we are driven to conclude that the latter exists to make sense of the former. Locke reasoned the idea of substance was required to explain why particular perceptual qualities cohere to give a unified object. Bishop Berkeley did not buy that, any more than John Locke would have bought a bag of cherries that had no color or taste, and could not be seen or touched. Even had he been told he were getting the substance of the cherries, he would not have bought the bag. Indeed one can be sure that, apart from its qualities, Locke would not have found the substance of a cherry very substantial, and neither would anyone else. And so Berkeley did not consider the idea of substance very substantial! Material substance apart from perceptual qualities is utterly unknowable and should be unthinkable, Berkeley argued.

Thus Berkeley unequivocally denied there could be such a thing as material substance (that which underlies and gives coherence to perceptual qualities) that Locke called primary and secondary qualities. In fact, the good Bishop thought the idea of primary and secondary qualities a rather bad one. Locke and many scientists maintained objects are made of *primary qualities*—those that are objective and inherent in an object, such as its mathematical dimensions, its shape and solidity—and *secondary qualities*—those that are subjective and dependent upon the way in which they are perceived, such as colors and tastes. But Berkeley pointed out primary qualities are every bit as dependent upon our perceiving them as are secondary qualities. Could anyone know the shape or size of any object without seeing it or feeling it? Thus the shape of an object is just as dependent upon getting to it with our senses as is the color. Then why say one is subjective and the other is not? It seems that everything we come to know, primary as well as secondary qualities, we know through perception. This was the great realization of Bishop Berkeley. We know the stench of approaching New York from the Jersey side because we *smell* it, and we know the amorous scent of an exotic perfume worn by a beautiful woman because we take it in through our nostrils. We know a sumptuous steak is delicious because we taste it. We know a seascape is beautiful because we *see* it. We know a piece of music is profoundly moving because we *hear* it. We know something is hard or soft because we *touch* it. That's how it is. What we know we perceive. Berkeley did not believe we could know anything that we cannot perceive. Thus he was led to his classic conclusion that *to be is to be perceived, esse est percipi*. If nothing can be known except by being *perceived*, then we have no basis for saying anything exists that is not being perceived. The very being of an object, therefore, depends upon its being perceived. After all it is totally beyond us to claim that something exists if it is not being perceived. If no one is perceiving it, who is to say it exists?

The question has been posed as to whether a tree falling in a forest when no one was there would produce a sound. The common sense realist would certainly affirm there would be a sound, although no one would hear it. But if no one can hear it, then who can say there would be a sound? If no one were there, not only would the falling tree not make a sound, but there wouldn't even be a tree or a forest for it to fall in. After all since there is no way for us to get outside of our perceptions, there is no way to know there is anything outside of our perceptions. John Locke admitted that secondary qualities, such as a color or the taste of sweetness, could have no existence independently of us, and yet at the same time he declared that primary qualities can and do exist independently of our perceiving them. Berkeley regarded such a distinction as entirely untenable, for it would be just as inconceivable for an object to be completely devoid of any color as for an object to be completely devoid of tactual qualities. Both primary and secondary qualities are in the same bag, and that is the bag of our perceptions. Since all we know is securely tied in that bag, there is utterly no basis for asserting any reality outside of that bag. Thus we cannot say there are material objects, for we have no basis whatever for saying so. Berkeley, of course, did not deny that there are mountains, forests and streams, cottages, food, and a whole world of things. Rather he very logically affirmed that these exist for us only as *sense data*. Certainly we perceive objects, but these objects are not matter, or "substance": they are sense data. We have a perception of a house. Our perception is not matter, but a sense datum. All we know are sense data—seeing, feeling, hearing, tasting, and smelling. We do not know anything *causing* sense data—that is, we do not know there is a material world out there producing our sense data. How ironic it all is. Throughout the ages materialists have regarded the assertion that anything exists beyond matter as superstitious nonsense, for anything other than matter was held to be unknowable. And now it turns out to be *matter* that is unknowable; it turns out to be matter that is nonsense.

The common sense outlook assumes the existence of physical objects. However once it is realized that all we have are sense data and that no direct connection with any physical world is possible, it becomes obvious that there is no reason for affirming the existence of physical objects. It is not good sense to assert the existence of that which is unknowable and hence unprovable. It has always been the position of the materialist that he must be "tough-minded" and admit the existence of nothing he cannot prove by his senses, nothing beyond the material world. Thus the claim that a spiritual world exists seemed down right laughable to the materialists. Now Berkeley was showing that the joke was on the materialist. We never sense material objects. Our perceptions are certainly not composed of physical objects, and we know not what exists beyond our perceptions. Thus it is the existence of matter that is an absurdity.

Berkeley was being ruthlessly logical and seeking to follow what seemed to him entirely tenable premises to their inevitable conclusion. If all we can know are our perceptions, then there is nothing in the world that can provide a foundation for asserting there is a world beyond our perceptions. James Boswell, famous biographer of Dr. Johnson, was so impressed by Berkeley's reasoning that he remarked to Samuel Johnson that Berkeley could not be refuted. Dr. Johnson did not utter a word of response—that is, not with his tongue; instead, he answered with his foot. He gave a good kick to a stone, said "ouch," and disposed of Berkeley's theory by saying, "I refute it thus." Good show! After all, if a person's foot encounters stones the sensations received from them would seem to provide evidence there actually are such objects as stones out there. This would seem a natural conclusion to the person of common sense. Chelm, a town in Poland, in the first decade of this century had a population 90 percent of which were Jews, and it became very important in Jewish folklore and humor. From the rich tradition of stories about Chelmites are some precious ones on the philosophers of Chelm. The problem of illusions was known to be of deep concern to them. There is the story of the Chelmite philosopher who on a cold Sabbath afternoon was discussing the vanity of all things. He maintained to his fellow philosophers that all *things* were illusions and that nothing existed in any external reality beyond our senses. One of his colleagues was so shaken by this idea that he could not sleep that night. He got out of bed and paced up and down in his room, talking to himself. He said that it is true there are no physical things, and as he was saying this, he bumped into the stove, causing great pain to his shins. From that experience he concluded, "It looks like there really is a stove after all." Is there really a stone and is there really a stove? Did Dr. Johnson's foot and the Chelmite philosopher's shins prove what philosophical reasoning never could?

Was Berkeley refuting this? A brief moment's reflection will show he was not. Berkeley never denied that stones and stoves exist. What he affirmed was that they exist as *sense data,* not as *material objects.* Kicking a stone or stumbling into a stove means having a perception of a foot encountering a stone or of shins meeting a stove. Dr. Johnson would not have been pained by the stone had he not *perceived* it. Said Bishop Berkeley:

> *It is indeed an opinion strangely prevailing amongst men, that houses, mountains, rivers, and in a word all sensible objects, have an existence, natural or real, distinct from their being perceived by the understanding.*[24]

However widely this view may be held, Berkeley maintained, it involved a contradiction. It is a contradiction because what we perceive are our sensations, and things never exist unperceived.

> *Light and colors, heat and cold, extension and figures—in a word the things we see and feel—what are they but so many sensations ... or impressions on the sense? And is it possible to separate, even in thought, any of these from perception? ... Hence, as it is impossible for me to see or feel anything without an actual sensation of that thing, so it is impossible for me to conceive in my thoughts any sensible thing or object distinct from the sensation or perception of it.*[25]

In short, poor Dr. Johnson stubbed his toe on a perception and did not hurt Berkeley's theory at all.

All Johnson knew was that a stone had hurt his foot, but this does not at all imply that the stone was a material object. What it means is that he had the perception of a stone and of its hurting his foot, but a perception is an idea, not a material thing. Perceptions exist not as physical things but as ideas. Now although we cannot reason to the existence of material obects from our perceptions or ideas, we can and must reason to the existence of spirits or minds. For if there are ideas, must there not be minds that have them? Berkeley observed that no one could think of anything without having an idea of it. If perceptions or sensations of things are ideas and not physical things, they can exist only in minds. Thus the world is made of two sorts of realities: (1) *ideas* or *perceptions,* and (2) *spirits* or *minds.*

Berkeley's conclusion that reality can be entirely understood in terms of two types of entities, perceptions or ideas and minds, means that it is not possible to know anything exists beyond what our minds perceive. This view is known as *subjective idealism.* It is known as idealism because it affirms the existence of ideas, perceptions, and mind and denies the existence

---

[24] George Berkeley, *A Treatise Concerning the Principles of Human Knowledge,* ed. Chas. P. Krauth (Philadelphia: J. B. Lippincott and Co., 1874), pp. 195-96.
[25] *Ibid.,* pp. 196ff.

of matter. It is subjective in that it holds nothing exists except that which is perceived by the individual mind.

Berkeley's philosophy might seem to imply a rather fantastic scheme of things. For example, in his thinking it would seem to follow that if a group of people in a room were to go out of it, the room itself would go out of existence, as there would be no one to perceive it. To emphasize such a problem, however, is to miss the main thrust of Berkeley's philosophy. If all we can know is our perceptions, it follows we cannot know anything outside of our perceptions, such as physical objects. Now if we understand a room purely as a datum of our senses rather than as a physical object, it is not really a problem whether it exists or not when we are not about. Since the room will be there when it is being perceived, it can hardly matter whether or not it can be there when no one is there. We may *assume* the room is there when it is not being perceived by anyone, but since there can be no evidence for such a thesis, it cannot be said that we *know* the room is there. To assume something is just to suppose it is the case, but to know something is to be aware of what really is the case. It is important and may be crucial to distinguish between what we assume and what we know. It makes quite a difference whether we *assume* someone is guilty of a crime or *know* it. Indeed one of Berkeley's highly beneficial achievements consisted in his showing that we actually only assume many things we believe we know. We do not know there are material objects; we only assume them on the basis of inferences from what we perceive. It may seem there is nothing more obvious than the fact that we directly apprehend a world of material objects, and thus that we live in the type of universe in which matter reigns supreme, but Berkeley's analysis showed that we cannot *know* this. Berkeley zeroed in on the kind of conclusions it is legitimate for human beings to arrive at.

Indeed one can conclude nothing beyond one's senses. Can one say there is anything or anyone at all beyond the realm of his perceptions? Berkeley himself claimed we could not get beyond our perceptions to physical objects, and yet he claimed there were spiritual objects or minds— other selves. Of course we cannot perceive minds or the self, so how could Berkeley know that other minds or other selves existed? Was he being inconsistent? To be consistent, shouldn't he have held the philosophical position known as *solipsism?* Solipsism states that the individual can prove nothing to exist beyond himself; the term means "I alone exist," and we might describe it as a case of getting carried away with oneself. If one knows nothing but his own perceptions, he cannot know that anyone other than he himself exists. Logically this is a very compelling position—so much so, that the distinguished logician Christine Franklin wrote to Bertrand Russell, informing him she was a solipsist and advising him solipsism was so logically sound that she was surprised everyone was not a solipsist. This amazed Russell, who figured that if she were a committed logical solipsist, she would not write to anyone and would never think about whether or not everyone else were a solipsist, for she would know there was no one else to write to and no one else to be a solipsist. If the truest test of a philosophy is whether one can live with it, then Christine Franklin's statement may be a manifestation that one cannot live with solipsism. The inadequacy of solipsism is reflected in one's behavior and speech, and perhaps that should be accepted as an adequate refutation. It may be more important that Berkeley, who did not realize that he himself was treading on the quicksands of solipsism, was seeing into the development of a world view and the making of a more and more unlivable world.

That Berkeley himself did not understand the universe to be absurd is irrelevant. It was more significant that he, in following the empiricist's premise that all knowledge depends upon sense experience, did open the door to a senseless universe. As paradoxical as this may sound, the progress of science, which we think of as the height of rationality, actually brought with it a regression in rationality. One might say that as rational science flowered, the world increasingly seemed to become a kind of theater of the absurd. Early in the development of modern science Berkeley's analysis showed up some absurd possibilities of the scientific orientation of empiricism. Men still had a vision then of a solid, rational, and orderly universe functioning in accord with necessary mechanical laws. A rational man could feel at home in this world, and the universe seemed an extension of man's rationality; it was predictable and very much under man's control. Soon things would be getting out of control, and man would begin to realize that neither he nor his universe were very rational.

Physicists had always insisted that the tiny particles that make up atoms act in regular, uniform ways, but in 1932 Werner Heisenberg won the Nobel Prize for demonstrating that atomic activity was not as uniform as had been imagined. The randomness he found provided the basis for his quantum theory and his Principle of Indeterminacy. This meant that the idea of orderly causation was being replaced by one in which rational predictability failed to work. In mathematics it was discovered that even a simple elementary number theory resisted formalization; this was followed by the incompleteness theory that revealed some mathematical problems to be insoluble. Complementing this came the breaking of man's image as *homo sapiens,* or rational animal. Since then this seemingly irrational universe has seen the rise of existentialism, dehumanized modern art, dissonant music, and the theater of the absurd. It is a universe in which men experience great difficulty in finding meaning and feel alone and alienated. Communication fails and men feel less and less any true sense of togetherness in an overpopulated universe. Under such conditions men seem more and more to be pushed toward solipsism.

It is instructive to view the irrational tendencies in our era and the enthronement of the Absurd in relation to the philosophy of empiricism. The empiricist philosophy, based on the assumption that all knowledge results from sense experience, provides the perfect foundation for modern science. While empiricism is consonant with the modern *scientific* attitude, rationalism is more in accord with a metaphysical orientation. Of course science involves metaphysical problems, so there would be nothing inconsistent about a scientist's being a rationalist, but at the same time he is also at home with empiricism because his primary aim is to get to the empirical facts. The scientist looks at the world and tries to report what he finds, whereas the metaphysician often looks in himself and reasons about what *must* be. Throughout history when men looked for *first* causes beyond the world of experience to explain things, scientific progress was greatly impeded. It was only with a more empirical approach that science could become an important force to man. In the medieval period, theological and metaphysical ideas dominated and guided man, giving meaning and purpose to his life, but they did not give him the most accurate understanding of his world. When a concatenation of historic forces accumulated to make theological and metaphysical conceptions less relevant to life's practical problems, man had to find a new orientation that came to be provided by science. This meant getting away from concern with ultimate questions and causes and concentrating upon empirical ones at hand. Science conferred upon man great worldly profit, but its underlying philosophy of empiricism seemed to be a high price to pay for these gains in that it threw away man's soul and could not give him meaning and purpose. By emphasizing basic perceptions rather than airy speculation, empiricism *seemed* at first to put man on solid ground, and yet it has failed to give him real grounds for living. Thus Berkeley, although he was a bishop, developed a philosophy that in its *effect* (if not in its intent) deprived reality of solidity, shattered an orderly view of nature, loosened the foundations of certainty, and drew man in the direction of solipsism.

Of course Bishop Berkeley himself believed the assumptions of his empiricist philosophy were entirely consonant with an orderly and purposeful understanding of life. Although he could see no basis for assuming the existence of material substance, he did not take all substance out of life; indeed he reasoned that there had to be spiritual substance or one could not account for perceptions and ideas. (We do feel we have an inward experience of ourselves.) Berkeley also reasoned that we can have a certain experience of other people's lives. He did not maintain that there can be an immediate knowledge of the other person, but a mediate one was possible. You see, it's like this: I hear laughter. It's the kind of noise I produce when my risibilities are tickled. I hear sobbing. That's what I do when I am sad. As laughter and tears are related to my mind, when I perceive laughter and tears of others, I can infer that they must be related to another mind. The existence of others is thus established by analogy. Thus despite his empiricist position, Berkeley inferred the existence of other minds.

He, then, was not a solipsist. He could infer or prove, by analogy, the existence of others. But who wants inferred friends? The ancients understood the friend as a second self—one immediately grasped through affection. It's a fine world when, instead of knowing other humans by empathy *directly,* we have to deduce them and know them by analogy. By Berkeley's time, it seems that the cold barrier of logical inference—or deduction—was being placed between one self and the other, and we may say that man was on the road toward what David Riesman calls "the Lonely Crowd."

Berkeley did not understand his view of reality to imply a disorderly or absurd universe. It may seem absurd to suppose that if everyone vanishes from the forest, the forest itself will vanish, but the Bishop did not so suppose. All of us may vanish from the forests, but the forest will not vanish because it is still being perceived. By whom? Ronald Knox's limericks answer this question.

> There was a young man who said, "God
> Must think it exceedingly odd
>
> > If he finds that this tree
> > Continues to be
> When there's no one about in the Quad."

> ANSWER

> > Your astonishment is odd
> I am always about in the Quad.

> > And that's why the tree
> > Will continue to be,
> Since observed by

> > Yours faithfully,

> > > God

Bishop Berkeley said:

> all the choir of heaven and furniture of the earth, in a word all those bodies which compose the mighty frame of the world, have not any subsistence without a mind ... so long as they are not actually perceived by me, or do not exist in my mind or that of any other created spirit, they must either have no existence at all or else subsist in the mind of some external spirit. ...[26]

As Berkeley saw it, the mind of that external spirit was always about, and so things never would go out of existence. Bishop Berkeley used to trudge about, exploring the Cave of Dunmore in Ireland, wondrously admiring the petrified wood and salt crystals of the cave. He did not doubt it existed when no one was on earth to perceive it, for he understood that God was always around.

Thus God saves the continuous existence of the world for Berkeley's philosophy, but one might wonder if Berkeley's philosophy does as much for God. After all Berkeley did make a strong case that we cannot know anything except that which we perceive, and yet before he finished, he had us all knowing Him whom no one can perceive. If someone were to tell us that he talks to God or that God talks to him, we would immediately send him to a psychiatrist who would try to help him see that he is suffering from delusions. God is not a Being who is open to perception. Then how did Berkeley, who had so ingeniously established the incapacity of man to get beyond his perceptions, manage to leave the doors open to heaven?

Of course the answer to this question might not matter, for one might

[26] *Ibid*, p. 197.

ask what difference Berkeley's philosophy makes anyway. What does it matter whether we call the furniture of the universe by the name of sense data or matter? We will still sleep, eat, and drink. We will still perceive the same sexual organs when we make love and the same weapons when we make war. And if the room should cease to exist when no one is there to perceive it, no one would know or care. After all it would still be there when someone returned. Does matter matter? Our life would still be the same, but what is real would be called sense data instead of matter. A great discovery should result in vast changes in our living, and Berkeley made what would seem to be a fantastic discovery—that there is no real world out there—and yet it doesn't seem to make much difference to anyone. When Berkeley published his conclusions, no sensational headlines appeared in the world presses. This was almost embarrassing for people who believed in the importance of philosophy. People became panic-stricken and scurried about seeking shelter like frightened animals when Orson Welles broadcast a fictitious invasion from Mars in 1938, but when Berkeley seriously announced there was no physical world, people did not even seem to care.

Nothing was really changed by his philosophy. We still say Columbus discovered America, we still seek to make scientific discoveries, and we still make hydrogen bombs to blow up the world that is not out there. When all is said and done, it seems Berkeley has said a lot and done little. Why should men pay attention to his views, which do not seem to make any practical difference?

Yet because man's practical orientation to his experience would not be significantly altered by the establishment of Berkeley's philosophy, it does not follow that the theoretical consequences would not be of paramount significance. For example, even far-reaching scientific discoveries do not immediately affect one's immediate practical activities. The theory of Copernicus that this is a heliocentric (or sun-centered) universe rather than a geocentric (or earth-centered) one did not significantly alter man's immediate practical affairs, and centuries later people still say the sun rises and sets. It would certainly be carrying practicality to curious extremes, however, to contend that it makes no difference whether one assumes the nature of reality is spiritual or material. The material world has served to crush many human hopes. In viewing this as a materialistic universe, religion is seen as an illusion, and ideals not related to *material* progress are thought misguided. If this is a materialistic universe, man as part of it must view himself as a machine and cannot think of himself as having a soul. Thus man should mainly strive for physical pleasure, as spiritual goals can have no tangible value for him.

Furthermore a view that limits man's knowledge to that which he can perceive drastically curtails his capacity to understand his universe as orderly and meaningful and tends to lock man in himself. The scientific commitment to understand the world through sense experience has enriched man in empirical benefits, but it has left him poor in philosophic meaning and without any sense of human power in an era of fantastic empirical power. Thus, although it did not make headlines, Berkeley's philosophy is significant because it clearly reveals rather strange consequences to which the empiricist commitment may lead. Far from having no practical results, Berkeley's empiricism has resulted in a world view that fails to provide man with a feeling of roots in a rational and meaningful universe. A philosophical image of the universe does exercise great influence upon man's capacity to feel at home in it. And if man cannot find Berkeley's god —and to a considerable extent he cannot—then his world does become a rather empty and strange one. Thus it seems that Berkeley's philosophy does matter.

Perhaps there is no higher tribute to the practical importance of Berkeley's position than that an involved political activist and revolutionary as Lenin directed such vitriolic acerbity toward it. Berkeley's philosophy seemed to Lenin to provide such an excellent basis for capitalism that it was actually propaganda for it, because in denying material conditions, it downgraded the significance of economy. Furthermore, Lenin observed that the science of geology may be posed against Berkeley's philosophy, for geological research has established that the earth existed long before life evolved and before there was anyone to perceive it. Berkeley, of course, would not have had to doubt such geological findings; he would have maintained that the mind of God was always present to perceive the earth even before life evolved. However Lenin did not believe in God, nor could he see how Berkeley could establish His existence with the weak arguments he used; and of course Lenin, with his complete dedication to the philosophy of materialism, thought that any arguments for the existence of a supreme spiritual being were weak. Later philosophers, convinced by Berkeley's argument against the existence of a material world directly perceived out there, but not convinced by his arguments for the existence of God, had an answer for the objection that Lenin raised. Known as *phenomenalists,* these thinkers maintained that sense objects need not be perceived for us to say they exist just so long as they are *capable* of being perceived. Thus it may be said that the earth existed before life appeared on it (without saying there had to be a God above) as long as one understood that the earth's nature is such that *if* an observer were there, he would have been able to perceive it. The famous utilitarian and empiricist philosopher John Stuart Mill advocated such an explanation. Mill stated that physical objects are permanent possibilities of *sensation.* Where Berkeley had said that to be is to be perceived, Mill would say that to be is to be perceptible, whether or not any actual perception takes place. The tree will continue to be, not because God is always in the quad, but because the tree always has the possibility of being perceived when someone comes into the quad. Thus a physical object may be analyzed as consisting of percepts that are *actual* and *possible.* When we are there, it is actual and we perceive it, and when we are not there, the continuing possibility of sensation remains.

Even with this phenomenalist improvement, the empiricist philosophy may still seem to give us a world that is far too dependent upon our egos. Indeed the much celebrated death of God in the contemporary world may be attributed to the development of modern science, which is based on the egocentric philosophy of empiricism. Although religion may not be incompatible with science in philosophical terms, it seems that religion and science historically have turned out to be quite incompatible. As the new physics and the new biology were developed, God and spirituality were eliminated from nature, and nature came to be viewed purely as an empirical object. The divine was thus being removed from nature where it might touch and inspire us earthlings. Science was making God more remote, and so existentially God was already in critical condition and nearing the grave long before his death was announced in the nineteenth century. As science conferred great empirical power upon man, it made him feel less and less dependent upon divine power. It is often claimed than man may have been at the center of the universe in the pre-Copernican world and the sun-centered Copernican theory of the universe took him off center stage. But it was still *God's* world. In the era of modern science, however, it was more and more becoming man's world. In the effort to understand the world modern science starts with sense experience; then in Great Britain where the scientific and industrial revolutions were so influential, Bishop Berkeley showed that the world depends for its existence upon the mind of man. In this connection it is interesting to note that a most telling criticism of Berkeley, developed by the distinguished philosopher of realism R. B. Perry, is called the *"egocentric predicament."*

That something is not perceived does not in itself prove that something does not exist nor that it cannot be proved to exist by some other means. To say at the outset, as Berkeley did, that we can only know things exist when we perceive them is to render it impossible to prove they exist when we are not perceiving them. For if we start with the major premise that all things are dependent upon us, we cannot logically arrive at the conclusion anything exists independently of us. If we say we can only know an external world by being there, then it is impossible to *test* the possible existence of an external world when we are not there. Thus we become ensnared in the egocentric predicament that relates the existence of everything to one's own self. The whole universe becomes dependent upon one's little ego. I remember the time when a profound German professor, in response to a question about a book he had not even heard of, shocked his whole class by saying that if he hadn't heard of it, then it could not be important. Compared to what subjective idealism implies, this professor was being downright modest, for subjective idealism would say not only that the book wasn't important, but that it didn't exist! As Perry argues, all that Berkeley was justified in saying was that if no one is there, we cannot be *sure* if something exists; this is very different from concluding that *esse* depends upon *percipi,* or that the very existence of things is a consequence of their being perceived.

Thorny indeed were the difficulties in the philosophy of Bishop Berkeley; nonetheless, it must be conceded that he offered a brilliant analysis of the meaning and implications of the doctrine that explains knowledge in terms of sense experience. Indeed, had the brilliance of the Bishop been less luminous, the untenable aspects of empiricism might not have shown up so clearly. Starting at the beginning one might well have expected that empiricism would have led toward realism and the affirmation of an external world, as Locke had thought. It took Berkeley to show how empiricism impels us toward subjective idealism, and after him it took Hume to show how it finally mires us in skepticism. Berkeley's enormous philosophical fuel power enabled him to follow the idea that knowledge is based on sense perception from the firm ground upon which it began toward the increasingly shaky ground of skepticism.

A nagging problem with Berkeley's theory involves the difficulty of distinguishing between reality and illusion. When some one sees something that is not actually out there we say he is suffering from an illusion. But on Berkeley's theory how can anything ever be an illusion, inasmuch as seeing it is the only criterion of whether it is out there or not? Berkeley himself believed we could distinguish between reality and illusion in terms of how constant or vivid the perception is, yet illusions can often be rather vivid and constant. One is not particularly inspired with confidence in Berkeley's handling of the matter. I think it significant that empiricist *philosophy* leads to a predicament in which the distinction between reality and illusion becomes tenuous, for we are living in a world of empirical science in which we encounter mounting difficulties in distinguishing reality from illusion. Technological change takes place at such a dizzying pace that men lose their bearings, traditional thought and social patterns are upturned, and people cannot be sure of anything upon which to depend. People lack a feeling of personal substance and are vague about reality. In these electronic times when powerful mass communications media create a world for us in which we do not experience reality at first hand, in which we can be influenced beneath the level of consciousness, we are so engulfed in artificiality that it is not easy to know where illusion ends and reality begins. The arrangement of our sense data has become so dazzling and so structured that we are cut off from the substance of reality. *Philosophically,* the beginning of the expression of these tendencies may be observed in empiricism.

When we go from Bishop Berkeley to the next great British empiricist, David Hume, we go further in the direction of philosophical meaninglessness. The philosophical ground beneath modern science was fast eroding.

DAVID HUME

All the seeds that had been implanted in empiricist theories of knowledge and were abundantly watered by the philosophies of Locke and Berkeley came to full bloom in the teachings of David Hume (1711–1776). All the skeptical potentialities in empiricist philosophy became actualities in his teachings. The skeptical Scotsman Hume went to France and there labored to produce his *Treatise of Human Nature*. In this work he proudly believed he had given birth to ideas of truly philosophic greatness, but the book did not have a very successful life. Indeed Hume himself admitted that it fell stillborn from the press. Hume's philosophy was quite unpopular, in fact no one seemed to like it. Only one man appeared willing to befriend this philosophy, but he was a very influential man—the third Marquis of Annandale. Unfortunately, he was also a very crazy man. Hume received a letter from this lunatic, who wanted to engage him as a tutor in philosophy for three hundred pounds.

Thus Hume, this philosopher with seemingly strange ideas, went in the winter to Weldehall, the mad Marquis's large lonely mansion. Three courts had found the third Marquis of Annandale to be insane, and now the skeptic Hume was trying to teach him philosophy! Sometimes the Marquis would grab hold of Hume and cry for help, and at other times he would demand that Hume leave the room. He would rant and rave. What an atmosphere for instructing in philosophy! The mad Marquis was not the type of student who could contemplate eternal truths in silent meditation. In fact he liked to leap over the furniture and slide down the bannister. Sometimes he would suddenly jump forth and begin to laugh madly. Annandale's tour de force consisted in calling a servant and then hitting him on the head with a log when he arrived. With such a person Hume had to discourse on profound questions of philosophy.

There is something appropriate about Hume's domestic arrangements because if we can accept Hume's teachings, then we must accept the fact this is a wild world. Hume started out with the recognition that Locke and Berkeley were correct in asserting perceptions to be the source of our knowledge. Then he recognized that Berkeley was right in claiming Locke could have no knowledge of material substance or matter, but he believed Berkeley was wrong in asserting there was spiritual substance or mind. Hume was prepared to follow empiricism to its most logical conclusions, even though they might lead him to a most illogical world.

Philosophizing under the bright sun of Newtonian physics, David Hume was concerned that we remained so in the dark about understanding ourselves. Thus he set for himself the task of establishing a science of man. He wanted to study science to explain the principles of human nature. The method he advocated for this project was the *experimental method,* which meant there should be *careful* and *exact* experiments. Hume felt this work to be urgent because he believed that a science of human nature was not only important but basic. He reasoned that mathematics, natural philosophy (or what we would call physics), and natural religion presupposed a science of man because they all had to be understood and judged by man. Hume was after something big—the formulation of a complete system of the sciences, and this would mean a foundation for all human knowledge.

Hume wished to destroy what he regarded as the untenable assumption that there are different levels of knowledge. It was widely believed at the time that there was an ordinary kind of knowledge and a higher kind that may be called a metaphysical knowledge. The difficulty was that this higher knowledge was so high that it seemed beyond comprehension. Hume saw no valid basis for believing that there was any such knowledge. Its height gave it lofty pretensions, but it led to superstition rather than to human understanding.

Hume's analysis assured him there was but one kind of knowledge, and it could be divided into two classes. One division he called the knowledge of *Relations of Ideas* and the other, he called knowledge of *Matters of Fact*. *Relations of Ideas* involve all knowledge that is demonstratively certain owing to the very relations of the ideas themselves. An example of this type is supplied by mathematics. Truths of geometry are purely deductive and are not dependent upon any external facts. Truths of *Relations of Ideas* are what we call *formal* rather than *factual* truths; they are not determined by any external evidence but by *analysis* of the relations of the ideas. This type of truth is discovered easily because of our understanding that a necessary relation is one whose negation is not even conceivable. Thus it is not conceivable that $2 + 2$ can equal anything other than 4 once we know the meaning of numbers. Therefore, should we be informed that two dollars and two dollars make five dollars, we know that it cannot be true; we don't have to count *actual dollars* to find out. The point is that what Hume calls relations of ideas, or formal truths, are not matters of fact but of definition. We know $2 + 2$ *must* be 4 because we have so *defined* it, or set it up that way. We know the statement a mother is a female is true. Why? Simply because mother is *defined* as a *female* parent. We do not have to see; we just know by inspecting the relation of ideas. One cannot assert the opposite of that which is true by definition without getting a *contradiction*. Thus if one says "this person is a mother but is not a female," we know that this statement cannot be true. If, on the other hand, someone says, "This mother is the breadwinner and head of her house and has taken over the chores of her husband," we would have to see if this statement is true. The truth of this statement is not a *formal* question but a *matter of fact*. This type of truth can only be determined by observing conditions in the empirical world.

Hume convincingly argued that, whereas *certainty* can be attained in dealing with statements of *relations of ideas,* only *probability ratios* can be attained when dealing with statements concerning *matters of fact*. A statement of relation of ideas *must* be true because it is *defined* as such, and to assert its opposite is not possible for it would lead to contradiction. Suppose someone introduced you to a man named Oscar and said, "Oscar is Orville's uncle; and he is an interesting uncle because he has no nephews or nieces." You asked if the "uncle" was just an honorary title and were told that it was not. You would be forced to conclude Oscar is not an interesting uncle; he is an impossible uncle, for it is impossible for one to be an uncle and have no nephews or nieces, inasmuch as an uncle is *defined* as one who had a nephew or niece. As it is a contradiction to speak of a square circle, so it is a contradiction to speak of an uncle with no nephews or nieces. Thus if we know a man is an *uncle* we can be *certain* he has at least one nephew or niece. It is *necessarily* so. With matters of fact, however, it is never "necessarily so." Suppose we know that Oscar is a really great guy, and thus upon learning he is an uncle, we say, "Oscar will be a great uncle." That is a *matter of fact*. An Oscar is not one defined as being a great uncle, and thus to find out whether he is or not, we have to investigate what kind of uncle he actually is. Perhaps Oscar would would be good at many things, but he is not good at being an uncle. So it is with all matters of fact—we can never be sure.

We can be sure a man who *is* an uncle will have *as a minumum* one nephew or niece, but we cannot be sure there *will be any* uncles at all. There can be certainty and necessity in the worlds of logic and mathematics, but there is only probability in the world in which we have to live.

What Hume had accomplished with his *distinction* between *Relations of Ideas* and *Matters of Fact* was to show there can be no certainty or necessity regarding *Matters of Fact*, and only that can be necessary or the only thing of which we can be certain is that the assertion of the opposite of a *statement* will be a contradiction. This means there can only be certainty concerning relations of ideas but never concerning matters of fact. We may feel quite certain the sun will rise tomorrow, but the opposite possibility is not a contradiction, and therefore it is conceivable the sun might not rise tomorrow. It would indeed be an inconvenience for the sun not to rise tomorrow, but it would not be a contradiction! If we are counting on the sun's rising tomorrow, we need not fall into a state of dread for fear it might not because the *probability* is that it will; indeed we can assume with a very high degree of probability that it will and can act on such probability. But we can never be certain. That's the way it is! There is no certainty concerning any matters of existence.

Hume's empiricist analysis resulted in destroying much of the substance of reality. Not only did Hume mutilate metaphysical mansions, tear down theological terraces, and eradicate rational ethical edifices, but he also sacked the sanctuary of science, for even its assumptions came under his destructive attack.

Hume started where empiricists always start, with our perceptions. There is nothing we can know that we do not perceive. All our information comes from our senses. Where else? No one can show there is any *knowledge* that we have not gotten through our senses. Beginning with our perceptions, empiricists then build up a system of knowledge based thereon. Hume, a very logical empiricist, noticed they were building too much, far more than empiricist foundations were capable of supporting. Berkeley had shown that Locke built too much when he constructed a material world out of the building blocks of perception. But Berkeley clung to spiritual substance, and now Hume saw that if one were to be a consistent empiricist, spirit would have to go too. We no more can have a perception of the self than we can have one of matter. If it is true we cannot know physical objects, it is certainly no less true we cannot know spiritual objects, such as a self or mind. People feel quite certain there is such a thing as the self. But what is it? Indeed where is it? The idea of Self has been a favorite with metaphysicians, and it is also an idea acceptable to the man of common sense. Yet let one try to think of the "self" and see what he comes up with. When the person thinks of his self, he never thinks of any independent entity, but in fact he thinks just of some particular perceptions. There is no perception of a mind or a self as such, but when we think of our self, there are *perceptions* of feeling hot or cold, love or hatred, hunger or thirst, or pleasure or pain. As Hume put it:

> *There are some philosophers, who imagine we are every moment intimately conscious of what we call our Self; that we feel its existence; and are certain, beyond the evidence of a demonstration, both of its perfect identity and simplicity.*[27]

Hume saw only one problem with such philosophy, and that is that it goes contrary to experience. Is it not with most of us as it was with Hume?

> *For my part, when I enter most intimately into what I call* myself, *I always stumble on some particular perception or other, of heat or cold, light or shade, love or hatred, pain or pleasure. I never can catch myself at any time without a perception, and never can observe anything but the perception. When my perceptions are removed for anytime, as by sound sleep; so long am I insensible of myself, and may truly be said not to exist. And were all my perceptions removed by death, and could I neither think, nor feel, nor see, nor love, nor hate, after the dissolution of my body, I should be entirely annihilated. . . .*[28]

Hume concluded that if one looks into himself, he will not *see* a self; what one will find is a succession of experiences, of hoping, desiring, fearing, and loving! That is all there is. When one isn't experiencing, one isn't. Hume said he could not find that he had a self apart from particular perceptions. He admitted metaphysicians might suppose they had found the self, but he believed that the rest of mankind, like him, could only find their perceptions.

Careful analysis does indeed reveal the idea of the self to be a dubious one. What is the self? Does a person have any enduring identity? If he does, we may ask what it consists of. It could hardly be the body. Think of a person's body about a dozen years ago. How different it is today. Not only was its shape probably rearranged but all the cells it then contained would now be gone. Thus he would not only look different but he would even be different chemically; and his ideas would probably be different too. Then in what possible sense can one say he is the same person he was a dozen years ago? By virtue of what is he the same? One might say by memory. But suppose one suffers from amnesia and cannot remember his past. Would he be a different person from the one he was twelve years ago? If not, what would make him the same?

People say, "Not getting any younger, you know." And of course everyone knows that. It is a truism. No one gets younger, people just get older. Do they? What is it that gets older? If there is not self, can it be said one is getting older? How? *Who* is the "one" who is getting older? A man today has none of the cells he had when he was a boy, does not look, nor think the same. Then how in the world can he be said to be the same? What, if any, is the link of identity? If there is no link, must we not conclude the

[27] David Hume, *A Treatise of Human Nature,* ed. L. A. Selby-Bigge (Oxford: Clarendon Press, 1888), Bk. I, Sec. VI, p. 251.

[28] *Ibid.,* p. 252.

man is a different person than the boy was? What if an astute criminal, a student of David Hume, pulls off a great bank robbery and then disappears for twelve years? After that period he returns and is arrested; when he comes before the judge he pleads "not guilty." On what basis? Suppose there are many witnesses who identified him and there is other evidence against him, such as fingerprints. The judge asks him how he can plead innocent with these facts, and the man replies: "That evidence amounts to nothing, for it is against someone else, not me. You see, I am not the same person I was twelve years ago. All my bodily cells have been replaced, I no longer have the same ideas I had then, and I have in no way broken any laws since my body and ideas have so fully changed. And so, judge, if you convict me you will be sending an innocent man to jail, and you wouldn't want to do that, would you?"

Now the judge just might answer "sorry about that but I would." He might point out to this criminal that his fingerprints have remained the same. But is that fair? If all that remains of a man are his fingerprints, should we suppose the essence of the self is fingerprints? Is one's soul his fingerprints? There are persons who have no fingerprints. Should we say they have no souls? Twelve years pass after committing his crime before he gets caught, but in the meantime he has filed away his fingerprints, had his face lifted, and undergone a sex change operation at Johns Hopkins Hospital. Should such a person be found guilty of a crime committed twelve years earlier? Actually, a judge might take all these acts as even more incriminating. Is there any basis for doing so? If so, what is it?

As for Hume, he could not see that there was any enduring quality by which we could identify one as a self. He saw man as nothing but a bundle or collection of perceptions:

> *Our eyes cannot turn in their sockets without varying our perceptions ...
> nor is there any single power of the soul, which remains unalterably the
> same, perhaps for one moment. The mind is a kind of theater, where several
> perceptions successively make their appearance; pass, repass, glide away,
> and mingle in an infinite variety of postures and situations. There is properly
> no simplicity in it at one time, nor identify in different [times]. ...*[29]

Descartes believed man was a full being composed of body and soul; Platonists believed man was a soul imprisoned in a body; materialists believed man was all body and no soul; and then with Hume out went both body and soul! To Hume man was nothing but a *bundle of perceptions.*

Whether we can ultimately view man as *only* a bundle of perceptions may be open to serious questioning. Yet our own world should make clear to us that man *can be* a bundle of perceptions. Hume had understood a real possibility, the possibility of man so conditioned by his environment that he lives only as a *response to stimuli.* Hume understood man in terms of his perceptions and saw no basis for asserting the existence of any self to unify those perceptions. It is not a flattering image of man, and yet today

[29] *Ibid.,* p. 252.

the life of man presents a not very flattering picture. Fascism, communism, and the mass media of capitalism all treat men as bundles of perceptions to be gift-wrapped for their own purposes. In an environment of technical perfection and power in which there is overmechanization, overorganization, and overpopulation, men can be conditioned, brainwashed, and have their minds raped. Men are bombarded with so much artificial stimuli they fall into the habit of just responding to them. More and more men lose their inner character, their capacity to determine their own destinies; they become part of mass and group movements, not swimming their own course but just drifting with the currents. Our lives become increasingly determined by external stimuli. Those with great technical power at their disposal can ignore the notion that other people have *selves;* they tend to view men as bundles of perception, and this attitude seems to work for them. When dealing with bundles of perception it is not difficult to so arrange the stimuli to elicit the response desired. One lovely possibility is *subliminal perception.* People go to a drive-in theater and are deeply engrossed in watching a tender love scene; vicariously they may be living through it —at least those not making their own love scene—and then at that sensitive, beautiful moment, by means of tachistoscopes, flashed upon the screen for a millisecond or less, is such a moving message as "Eat Popcorn." These words are superimposed over the lovers' sweet and passionate kiss, and without the conscious awareness of the viewers are recorded by the optic nerve and delivered to the subconscious, which reacts to them. Comes the intermission, and people run out and buy popcorn. It doesn't take an ingeniously creative imagination to foresee the possibilities. As our technological capacities manifoldly increase, how difficult would it be to slip a subliminal message across the television sets of millions of viewers to vote for a given candidate?

The point is that the less men act from the center of their being, if there is such a thing, the more they behave as if they were bundles of perception. Although Hume's understanding of man may fail to do justice to human possibilities, nonetheless it does reveal a condition to which man may be reduced, and in our highly technological age of mass manipulation the human being may become the Humean being.

The doctrine that knowledge is perception has devastating consequences not only for the metaphysical idea of the self but also for the theological idea of God. If perception cannot give man knowledge of the self, no more can it give him knowledge of God. If all we know is that we perceive, it seems reasonable to conclude that God, who is of such a nature as not to be open to perception, simply is not or cannot be known. Hume did not develop this line of attack, but his extreme empiricism rejected all the traditional arguments for God's existence.

The reality we know through our senses really makes no sense. The senses cut us off from physical reality, do not give us a basis for knowing a self or God, and leave us without any rational basis for ethics. Hume concluded that we can have *feelings* about matters of morality, but we cannot use reason to make judgments in this area. Reason can show us what the consequences of our choices may be, but it cannot tell us what we should choose. As interpreted by Hume, this is a world without rhyme or reason, and his empiricist razor cut to the very quick of what men had assumed to be real and valid. In the age of reason and science it was not unfashionable for men to turn reason and science against religion, but Hume went much further, even turning against reason and such a fundamental scientific concept as the principle of causality.

What is the principle of causality? If a man takes a baseball and heaves it through the display window of a store, the owner of the store will unhesitatingly tell you what is involved in the principle of causality. The person who tossed the baseball is responsible for breaking the window and therefore must pay for it or go to jail. The idea of causality assumes that there is a necessary connection between two things or events and that one of these has the power to produce the other; this is called the *cause*, and that which is produced is called the *effect*. One of the earliest systematic analyses of causality was undertaken by Aristotle in ancient Greece. Common sense usually assumes a given cause always has a given effect. In the case of the broken display window, the assumption would be that the man who threw the ball was the cause, and the broken window was the effect. Aristotle, with his careful analytic study of problems, concluded that a single type of cause would not suffice to explain the bringing about of some effect. The term Aristotle used, which has been rendered into English as cause—the *aitia* —was appropriated from Athenian courts of law and implied following a definite plan by which nature could be understood. Aristotle claimed that to know is to know by causes. As he understood it, the task of physics was to learn the causes of physical change. He believed there were four types of causes, or four ways of explaining nature. To understand reality there are four basic questions we must raise, and in supplying answers to them we give statement to the four causes:

1. THE MATERIAL CAUSE—what something is *made* or *composed* of

2. THE FORMAL CAUSE—what something *is;* its *essence*

3. THE EFFICIENT CAUSE—what *brought* something *into existence*

4. THE FINAL CAUSE—what *purpose* something serves; its *Why*

For example, an act like the robbing of a bank could be explained in Aristotelian terms as follows:

THE MATERIAL CAUSE may be understood as the matter with which the bank vault was blown up—the dynamite or the constituents of which it is made.

THE FORMAL CAUSE may be understood as the essence of the robbery, the precise plan, formula, or pattern—including the idea of blowing up the vault with the dynamite—used to successfully carry out the robbery.

THE EFFICIENT CAUSE may be understood as the burglar who will carry out the robbery, blow up the vault, and run off with the money.

THE FINAL CAUSE may be understood as the purpose of the bank robbery, or what good it is to the bank robber—in this case, that it will give a poor deprived criminal enough money to live like a banker.

Aristotle's doctrine of causation held sway over men's minds and was invested with official status in the Western world from the ancient period to the Renaissance, but with the development of modern science and the establishment of experimental method as a means of achieving scientific progress, the Aristotelian view of causation lost its influence. Material cause is not understood in modern science as it was by Aristotle. Aristotle understood matter in a *metaphysical* sense; he viewed matter as the principle of particularity. Matter is that which shows that something of a given *nature* actually exists. The *form* of a thing reveals to us *what* it is and the *matter* reveals *that* it is. Modern science understands matter in a more empirical sense. Newton viewed matter physically rather than metaphysically; whereas the idea of Aristotle's material cause emerged from his understanding of matter, the modern notion of cause grew out of viewing matter in a purely physical sense. Newton described matter in terms of hard, massy, impenetrable, and movable particles, and it was in terms of their interaction that we could understand cause and effect. Of course as science advanced further, the very idea of cause itself was thrown into question.

Final cause proved no more consistent with the aims of modern science than material cause. The function of final cause was to raise the question of what good something was or what its purpose was. Experimentally oriented scientists denied that final cause could serve any meaningful scientific purpose. When Galileo wanted information about the way things move, he experimented by actually rolling balls down an inclined plane. He regarded such questions as *why* the balls rolled down the plane or what *good* it was for them to do so as completely irrelevant. Galileo believed the scientist's task consisted in *describing* how nature works and not in getting bogged down in theological, metaphysical, and moral questions.

Formal cause, or discovery of the essence of the thing, also eluded the grasp of the empirical scientist. Aristotle assumed invariable forms of essences could be found in nature. Particularly since the formulation of the theory of evolution, the idea of any fixed properties—or essences—that must belong to a given group has been discredited. Scientists work with empirical probabilities, not with necessary and essential forms.

Thus after the Renaissance, the idea of causality was limited to *efficient cause,* or that which brought something about. This was convenient because isolating an efficient cause, a factor or set of factors responsible for producing some thing or event, could be accomplished by observation and measurement. Thus understood, causality came to be regarded as indispensable to scientific inquiry. Universal causality was part of the scientific outlook in the era when mechanistic science was being firmly established. Our universe was viewed as a system in which things did not happen by chance, but by necessity, and in accord with mechanical laws. Everything that happened was necessarily connected in a great causal chain. Then David Hume came along and pulled apart all the links of the chain.

Hume was particularly concerned with the question of causality because he understood how important it was to mankind:

> *I have just now examined one of the most sublime questions in philosophy,* viz. that concerning the power and efficacy of causes; *where all the sciences seem so much interested.*[30]

Not only science but also common sense, as we have already indicated, assumes that cause and effect necessarily join together the things and events of the world. Thus the idea of cause and effect seemed to cry out for rigorous examination, and Hume certainly supplied it.

As we have seen, Hume distinguished between *relations of ideas* and matters of fact, making the point that there can be *necessary* truth concerning *relations of ideas,* but that these necessary truths have nothing to do with the world of facts; there can be no necessary truths concerning matters of fact, and we cannot be sure of the existence of anything beyond present sense perceptions and what we can remember. What is it, then, that allows us to depend on anything other than that which we are immediately perceiving? We can have confidence that certain things will happen in a given and orderly way, Hume answered, because of our belief in the principle of causality. Certain things have happened in a certain way, and certain things have gone together yesterday and today; thus we presume some necessary connection between them and count upon their happening and going together tomorrow. We resolve doubts we have about any matters of fact not immediately being perceived by using the causal principle.

Because it is so important, Hume believed that some questions had to be answered concerning the validity of the causal principle. We must ask how we come by knowledge of cause and effect. If we should watch someone playing billiards and observe one billiard ball hit another, which then rolled into one of the pockets on the billiard table, we would naturally assume that the hitting of the second ball by the first caused the second to be driven into the pocket. What else but the force imparted by the first ball could explain that the second ball rolled in the pocket? This is so evident even a philosopher should understand it. It seems nothing could be clearer than that in a pool game one ball's striking another is the *cause* of the other ball's movement. Hume wanted to know whether this is really so clear to reason, or is something we pick up from experience. Suppose you just landed from Mars, where, let's say, they have no pool tables, billiard balls, nor anything remotely similar. Suppose you are a rational Martian, but on Mars there are no collisions and you have never seen one. If you were then informed that one ball was going to be brought into contact with another, would it be clear to your reason that one would communicate movement to the other? It certainly would not. We cannot tell *in advance* of our experience what the effect of any cause will be. If our rational Martian knew nothing in advance about milk or bread, meat, lions or tigers, and men, he would not

[30] *Ibid.,* p. 156.

know after being acquainted with these that milk and bread would nourish men, but lions and tigers would not. That there is a cause and effect relationship between milk and babies is not something we can know in advance by reason; we learn it from experience. Thus the law of cause and effect is not something we understand from reason before experience, or *a priori*; it is something we learn *a posteriori*, or from our experience. In other words, cause and effect relationships are not relations of ideas; they are matters of fact. Cause is one thing and effect is quite another thing. The mind can never find the effect in the cause. Therefore, a cause and effect relationship is not something to be reasoned out in the mind but to be found out in the world.

The idea of cause and effect arises from learning, from conditioning. The idea of causality is built up from contiguity, succession, and constant conjunction. When things are close to one another, succeed one another, or are constantly conjoined, we come to believe there is a necessary link between them. We get into the habit of expecting certain things because we have experienced them in the past. We expect that when one billiard ball strikes another it will communicate motion to it because that is the way we have seen it happen in the past. We expect tomorrow will come because it always has in the past. But there is no guarantee it will happen that way in the future; we have no experience of the future and thus cannot possibly know what it will be like. Causality is not a principle of reason but a form of addiction: that the sun will rise tomorrow is something we believe because of habit, not because of rational necessity. Thus we hold tightly onto the principle of causality because experience has conditioned us to expect certain things to go together.

Oliver Hardy used to say to his masterful comedy partner Stan Laurel, "Now look at the mess you've gotten us into." Now look at the mess we have gotten ourselves into! We started out by feeling confident we could know about things out of the range of our experience by the principle of causality. If we did not have a good idea of what tomorrow would bring, we should have to cringe with fear, not knowing what dangers to expect. But because things have happened in a regular pattern in the past, we can expect them to happen that way in the future, assuming there must be a necessary bond between them. Although Hume did not himself use the term, this has come to be known as the *problem of induction*. We have every confidence the future will be like the past because our world is governed by cause and effect patterns that assure that it will be. Thus we can be sure about the world of experience that is not immediately present to our senses because of the law of cause and effect. But how can we be sure of this law? We can be sure of it because our past experience convinces us by habit that there is a law of cause and effect. It looks as if we've been had. We can be sure of our experiences because of cause and effect, and we can be sure of cause and effect because of our experience. We can also be sure that this is circular reasoning.

This type of reasoning may be regarded as a form of the fallacy *petitio principii,* which is the fallacy of begging the question, arguing in a circle, or seeking to prove the truth of one thing on the basis of another thing that itself stands in need of proof. The difficulty of arguing in a circle is that such a big hole exists in the middle of the circle. A person goes to the bank and applies for a ten thousand dollar loan. The bank president, Sam Molloch, asks him for collateral, but he replies he has no collateral. Mr. Molloch then requests a reference. He tells the president, "It's all right, Freddie Fink will vouch for me." Mr. Molloch, unimpressed, says, "Freddie Fink? I never heard of him, so he can't be a credit reference here." To that the man responds, "Oh, don't worry. Freddie Fink is 100 percent okay. I'll vouch for him." And so he doesn't get the money. The pattern involved is to prove A by reference to B, and then when B is questioned, to prove it by reference to A. According to Hume, it is just this kind of reasoning that is involved in the validity of experience and the validity of the principle of cause and effect.

Since the days of Aristotle, scientific explanation was assumed to be based on general laws. A very significant question, then, concerns how we can formulate those laws. General laws often involve terms that themselves cannot be verified in experience. This is one of the primary problems with the concept of causality, as David Hume made very clear.

All we can know are our perceptions. Empiricists belabor the point that whatever we suppose we know by other means, such as *intuition* or extra-sensory perception, fails to be reliable. Yet, as Hume observed, empirical science is willing to incorporate the idea of causality even though we have no perception of a bond linking a particular cause to a particular effect. To most people, the idea of cause and effect means that there are necessary connections in nature, which everyone talks about, but no one has ever seen. Hume observed that we see one event and see it followed by another, but we do not see any link connecting them. We do not have any empirical knowledge of this link or necessary connection; we only *infer* it. We observe a succession of events, but not any power or force binding them together. We perceive someone strike a match and then perceive flame, so we just naturally assume that some power in the match produces the flame. No one has ever seen that power however. In nature we find no powers or forces that necessarily engender certain effects.

In fact, it is a fallacy to assume that just because a second thing follows a first, the first thing is the cause of the second. This fallacy is technically known as the fallacy of *post hoc, ergo propter hoc*. It means, "after this, therefore on account of this." Someone is driving a car, and a black cat cuts across the street in front of him. He drives on a few more blocks and gets a flat tire. As he labors to repair the tire, there in the scorching sun, he says to himself, "That damn black cat!" Now it is a fallacy to assume that one has gotten a flat tire *because* a black cat crossed his path. Merely because one event follows another is not sufficient to establish that one is the cause of the other. Most people would say that before we can say one thing is the cause of another following it, it would have to be shown that there was a *relation* between the two. Hume tried to show that the relation between two events is never in the form of a necessary connecting link. According to Hume's position, it can never be asserted that a preceding event is *necessarily* related to a succeeding one; therefore, it would seem that Hume regarded all assertions of necessary causal relationships as examples of the *post hoc, ergo propter hoc* fallacy. Take this example: A young man, who has studied Hume in a philosophy course, is walking along the water-front late one night and chances to see a fierce-looking man stab another man in the heart with a long knife, pull the knife out, and run off into the night. A policeman a block away, not seeing this as clearly, runs to the observer and asks him if he saw that fierce creature kill the man now lying there in a pool of blood. The student, with utmost confidence, replies he did not. The police officer presses, "But you were standing within a few yards of them. You must have seen that man who ran off, plunge a knife into the other man's heart." The student answers, "Oh yes, of course, I did see the first man stick a knife into the second man's heart, but that's not what you asked me. You asked me if I saw him kill the other man, and that I didn't perceive." With a look of total amazement on his face the policeman says, "Don't be wise, or you'll be in a lot of trouble. If you saw him stab the man in the heart, you saw him kill the man." At that point the philosophy student pedantically shouts in the face of the policeman: "Post Hoc Ergo Propter Hoc!" The policeman, who does not understand Latin and certainly does not understand that he was guilty of a fallacy in his reasoning, concludes that the philosophy student must be drunk.

But if we think about the case carefully, how can we say sticking a knife in another's heart *causes* his death? No one *sees* it cause his death. Two distinct events can be seen, and nothing more. One event is the stabbing, and a second event is a person slouching, falling over, and dying. Most normal persons would say that is enough, but not Hume. All we can know about the stabbing incident is that there were two events happening right after another. We may want to connect these incidents by saying that one of them caused the other, but if we do so we must recognize that it is *we* who are making the connection: there is no connection in the facts themselves; there is only succession. You might ask then, if the knife didn't cause the man's death, what did? Hume would regard that as a bogus question. This man's dying may have been preceded by some other event like coronary occlusion, which may very often precede dying, but there is still no basis for asserting there is a connection between coronary occlusion and dying. One can only say they often happen together.

If one makes a study of physics textbooks, one will find that Hume's point was not lost on physicists. The word "cause" will almost never be found. Physicists realize the logical implausibility of asserting necessary links and so concentrate upon mathematical correlations. What about our courts where problems such as stabbings and shootings must be faced, and responsibility must be fixed? Could our law courts function properly without assuming the notion of cause? In law texts, one will even find such anti-Humean words as *necessary causation*. Let us consider a case involving causation with a view to deciding if a Humean approach to it is reasonable. Lewis shot Will Farrell in the abdomen.[31] Not only was the pain excrutiating

---

[31] *People v. Lewis*, 124 Cal. 551, 57 Pac. 470.

but Farrell's anger was immense. Suffering from a severed mesenteric artery, Farrell did not have much zest for life, and in fact death began to seem more and more attractive. Thus he made an interesting request of Lewis: "Shoot me again." Lewis, however, was not a very obliging gentleman and did not shoot him again. In fact, no one would accede to Farrell's request to assist him in ending it all. Instead, he was put to bed. Farrell then asked for a knife so he could cut something. Given the knife, he cut his throat and died. The question the court had to resolve was the cause of Farrell's death. On the face of it, it would seem rather clear that if a man cuts his own throat and dies, he has caused his own death. However, the court ruled that Farrell was not responsible for his own death. This was not because the judge was a Humean, denying the validity of cause. It was because he was stretching the *cause* to make it fit elsewhere. It was decided that Lewis was the *cause* of Farrell's death. How can this be? The legal doctrine covering this situation is embodied in the so-called *causa sine qua non* rule. This means that if an injury would not have occurred "but for" someone's wrongful act, the person who committed the wrongful act is responsible for the injury. It seemed logical in this particular case to assume that in the normal course of his activities Farrell would not have cut his throat. It was concluded that, *but for* the fact that Lewis shot him in the abdomen, Farrell would still have been around. Thus Lewis was adjudged to be the cause of Farrell's death although Farrell died only after he cut his own throat, and not when Lewis had shot him in the abdomen. This seems to show that the courts are far less skeptical about causality than Hume was; in fact our courts seem to be very certain about fixing cause.

Here is another case. A man raped a woman. She was so shocked by this and felt so disgraced that she went to a drugstore and bought poison; she then went to the hotel room she had stayed in with the man, took the poison, and died several days later. The rapist was held to be the cause of her death and was convicted for murder. It was reasoned that if he had not gotten her so distraught by raping her, she would not have taken poison; thus he was the cause.

Suppose you see the film *Bonnie and Clyde* and are so impressed that you decide to become a robber. You get your gun and drive to a gas station, and when the attendant comes and asks how much gas you want, you tell him you don't want gas, you want his money. You point your revolver at him. Frightened, the gas attendant makes a run for it, and hides himself behind a gas tank. You take a shot at him but, being a poor shot, you miss. Then, from inside the office, the manager of the station pulls out a rifle and shoots at you. He is not a good shot either and misses you, but by accident he hits his own employee. Not having wanted anyone to get killed, you get disgusted with the whole thing and drive off. Later the police arrest you. What are you charged with and what can you be convicted of? Who is guilty for the killing of the gas attendant? *You are!* It was held you were the *cause* of his death, even though you didn't shoot him. (Some people would even say that it is not the robber who is guilty but Warren Beatty, the man who made the movie. After all, if he hadn't made *Bonnie and Clyde*, then none of this would have happened. Does this seem far-fetched? Well, it is, but if we stop to think about it we can recognize that it is precisely this argument that is often used in defense of censorship.)

This is not a hypothetical case; it actually happened. Charles Frederick Moyer and William Paul Byron carried out a felonious invasion of a gas station owned by Earl Shank. Attacked by armed robbers, Mr. Shank opened fire. It seems one of the bullets fired hit his own employee Harvey Zebe, and Zebe died. Who was held to be the cause of Zebe's death? Moyer and Byron, who didn't shoot anyone. It was held:

> *Every burglar is a potential assassin and when his felonious purpose encounters human opposition his intent to steal becomes an intent to kill and any weapon he finds at hand becomes a weapon of murder."* Every robber or burglar knows that a likely later act in the chain of events he inaugurates will be the use of deadly force against him on the part of the selected victim. For whatever results follow from that natural and legal use of retaliating force, the felon must be held responsible.[32]

In this particular case Moyer and Byron had armed themselves with deadly weapons to carry out their plan to rob Shank, and their attack led to Shank's firing at them to protect himself, his employees, and property; the decision reached was that Moyer and Byron were responsible for the death of the man Shank shot.

> *In the case of* Taylor v. State, 41 Texas, Cr. R. 564, 55, S. W. 961, *which grew out of (a) train robbery, it was likewise held that the defendant was properly convicted of murder in the first degree. The court said in that case,* "The whole question here is one of causal connection. If the appellant here set in motion the cause which occasioned the death of deceased, we hold it to be a sound doctrine that he should be as culpable as if he had done the deed with his own hands.[33]

In what was called the Anarchists' Case, *Spies et al. v. People* (1887) 122 Ill. 1, 12 N.E., 865, 3 Am. Stat., 320, the decision was laid down:

> *That any act done by a party to an unlawful conspiracy, in furtherance of and naturally flowing from the common design, is the act of each and all of the conspirators, (1) even though the conspirator who did act cannot be identified: or (2) though the defendant may have been absent ... or was not anticipated, if the conspirators either did or ought to have anticipated the results, although they did not contemplate the means.[34]

In other words, if you are in a conspiracy you do not even have to be there when the person gets killed to be blamed, and this may hold even though in making the unlawful plans there was no intention to kill anyone.

[32] *Commonwealth v. Moyer,* Supreme Court of Pennsylvania, 1947, 357 Pa. 181, 53 A. 2d 736.

[33] Rollin M. Perkins, *Cases and Materials on Criminal Law* (Brooklyn: The Foundation Press, Inc., 1952), p. 316.

[34] *Ibid.,* p. 317.

A classic case on this notion of causality is the "Squib Case." The facts were as follows:

The defendant threw a lighted squib made of gunpowder from the street into the market house. A large concourse of people were assembled there. One Willis to prevent injury to himself and to the goods of one Yates, grasped the lighted squib and threw it across the market house where it fell upon one Ryal. The latter, to save his own goods from being injured, took up the lighted squib and threw it across the market house and struck the plaintiff in the face, putting out one of his eyes. . . .[35]

Ryal threw the squib that took out the plaintiff's eye. But Ryal was not judged to be the cause of the plaintiff's injury. The guilty party was the person who threw the squib into the market house. From thence it went to Willis, and from Willis to Yates, to Ryal, and to the injured party. In the court's eyes that looked like a causal chain, and since the defendant initiated the chain, he was responsible for all of the links.

If Hume strictly adhered to his own teachings, would he have to throw out much of our legal procedure? Would he say that a man never should be convicted of a crime because we can never say that he is the "cause" of the pernicious effects that followed his actions? Certainly not. Hume did not cast the idea of responsibility to the winds in formulating his causality argument. Causality had almost always been understood to mean that there are certain necessary links joining events or things. It was this idea that Hume wanted to strike down. Although he did not want us to understand things in terms of the existence of invariable sequence or necessary links, he did contend that we could understand them by the idea of regular succession. The distinguished British philosopher A. J. Ayer argues that by the statement "C causes E," it can only be understood to mean "*Whenever* C, then E." This, of course, is the sort of thing Hume was saying, and although it is a way of saying that the idea of causality is not valid, it is not a way of saying we must go about in fear that the sun will not rise tomorrow, nor does it mean we can never prosecute criminals. What it means is that we must adjust ourselves to live in terms of probability ratios, and that there cannot be a basis in certainty for anything we do. Hume showed that the empirical world is not a world of necessity, but a world of probability. After Hume, scientists came more and more to see that this is a world of contingency and that what happens is a matter of *probability*. Thus they began interpreting nature as statistics rather than as being subject to laws that can give us certainty.

What Hume was about was this: We find no necessary connections in nature. If we do not find any there, what makes us so sure they are there? We can answer in one word—habit! We get so used to seeing things go together that we assume they belong together, but this is just an assumption. Next time one turns up, the other may not! There are no invariable sequences in nature, but when we perceive things contiguous, constantly

[35] *Ibid.*

conjoined, succeeding one another with regularity, we infer that they go together. We cannot say they *must* go together; we can say they *probably* will, and we can act on these *probabilities*. If someone says, "Let's go swimming tomorrow," one need not answer, "I can't say, because there is a chance tomorrow won't even come." We can plan to go swimming because tomorrow will *probably* come. Of course, as our nuclear arsenals grow bigger and as pollution continues to engulf us and make this a poisoned planet, the probability of there being a tomorrow (especially a tomorrow that has water fit to swim in) may be diminishing.

We can live by probabilities, and we can safely act upon the basis of those probabilities that are highly confirmed. Hume's argument may not seem to really make much difference to us in our daily lives. We may well accept what is implied by his logic and readily grant that it would not be a *contradiction* for a speeding truck to crash into us and yet do us no damage. Still at the same time, none of us will be walking into the path of any oncoming trucks, and neither would Hume if he were still alive. We may never be able to be empirically certain about anything, but when the probabilities are high, we can for all practical purposes act as if we are certain.

Up to a point it may be said that Hume's arguments do not make much difference to our daily existence. Yet Hume's arguments are not entirely without significant practical effect. Science, which we *regard* as being a very practical enterprise giving us results that are certain, has had enormous effect on our lives. Ironically, while laymen imagine science to be one in which certainty is attained, most scientists have the view that there is nothing in the physical universe about which they can be certain. It was the giant of science Albert Einstein who expressed the view that insofar as anything could be known with certainty it could have nothing to do with the empirical world, and insofar as anything referred to the empirical world it could not be a matter of certainty. The fact is there could be great progress in science precisely because it did take assumptions such as those of Hume seriously. By banishing talk about causes from their research, scientists could explore many areas where older thinking in terms of causes would have imagined the question closed. By working on the assumption that only empirical probabilities can be attained rather than looking for some unattainable metaphysical certainty, scientists were enabled to get down to what makes the physical world work. Thus science made it possible for man to attain greater control over nature than he had achieved in all previous history.

Indeed the material effects of scientific thinking were of a staggering magnitude. So positive did the nature of the empirical world, built upon modern physical science, seem to be that it could not be seen that the underlying philosophical assumptions of science were somewhat negative. Modern science grew on an attitude extremely hostile to the idea of any kind of final purpose—god, or heaven—and yet its work made possible the development of what we might call a technological heaven. We live in a world in which it seems that technologically anything is possible. In such a climate it is not surprising that some men have come to look upon science and technology as gods to be worshipped. Yet it is becoming increasingly clear that real human fulfillment does not automatically emerge in a world filled with technological marvels. Men need more than knowledge of how to do things; they also need meaning and purpose. Even in a world of electronic wonders there is the need to wonder what things are all about and to ask the question of why things should be as they are. The substantial empirical world that resulted from the work of modern science may now seem to be teetering because the philosophical presuppositions of modern science are really quite unsubstantial. I believe a careful study of Hume's philosophy gives us a clear view of the infirm foundations of empirical scientific philosophy. The philosophy that lies at the base of modern science cannot give man the kind of answers he now seems to thirst for. And so in this glorious age of science, men everywhere feel they are living in a wasteland.

It may be said that Hume's empiricist approach to philosophy led him to an idea of reality depleted of material content, of spiritual foundation, of individual pattern, of necessary connection, and of moral meaning. If there is no law of cause and effect that guarantees things to happen in an orderly way, then there will be terrible insecurity, even though we can still act on probabilities.

This uncertainty, built into the framework of Hume's world, must seep into our lives at some point. We must come to live with contingency, grief, pain, suffering, and death. There must be something beyond to make endurable what men must face in this life. There must be some rational framework that can make sense of this world. Hume, however, saw the framework itself to be frail. This is the terrifying type of world in which men not only feel *fear* but also are racked by *anxiety*. When one is afraid, there is an *object* causing the fear; if the object causing the fear is removed, the fear is dissipated. In anxiety, however, the suffering is worse because there is no specific danger. The enemy is unseen, and therefore, there is little one can do but experience *angst,* or a terrible dread. A world in which there is no ultimate certainty breeds anxiety and gives rise to existentialist philosophers and such writers as Kafka. A Humean world is one in which *anything can happen,* or as Dostoyevski saw it, one in which all is permissible. In such a context all assurances of reason are of no avail, and men come to see little with the eyes of their minds and to rely to a great extent on blind emotion. Without rational foundations the world cannot be a reasonable place. Living at a time still thought to be the Age of Reason, Hume prophetically proclaimed that *reason only is and only ought to be the slave of the emotions.* One can interpret this statement in a very positive sense, taking it to mean that one should not permit the cold and dry intellect to dampen the warmth of his heart. However, this idea also has a very frightening meaning, for its suggests the possibility of unreasonable power dominating truth and of reason being enslaved by emotion.

In our own age the unprecedented growth of rational science has been accompanied by the creation of monstrously irrational power. We live in dangerously ironic times in which unreasonable myths are defended with the full arsenal of logic and reason. We have "think tanks" whose job is to find reasons to support decisions and plans of power. We think of intellectual giants, of great philosophers and scientists, not as men who are to give us direction and purpose, but as men who are to be directed by our narrow purposes. We respect Einsteins, Oppenheimers, and Paulings, not for their scientific genius, but for their skill in serving the needs of our power machinery. When Einstein used to criticize our politics, news editors would write that he might have been a great scientist but he did not know anything about politics; only they knew about politics because they were unhampered by reason. Rationality is no longer something to be used to lead us; it has become something to be used to serve our irrational needs. It is to be used to make our weapons of terror even more terrifying, to provide us with the means of chemical, biological, and radiological warfare, antiballistic missile systems and bigger bombs, but it is not to provide us with insight into goals of living. Indeed it seems to be used mainly to show us how to end living.

Engulfed in a world of gigantic power, reason becomes so dwarfed that it cannot be seen or heard. And when men cannot rule their destinies by reason, they fall prey to terrible frustration; and out of such frustration violence is born.

Our scientific civilization which rests much upon Humean assumptions, and is teetering. In an irrational world in which there is little that is substantial and little basis for order, men lose a sense of meaning and purpose in their lives. It is a frightening situation and we, who now live in a world balanced on terror rather than on reason, are pulled apart by it. In such a world people particularly feel insecure because they lack a metaphysics to make sense of their world. Hume contributed to the shipwrecking of metaphysical meaning. At the very end of his *An Enquiry Concerning Human Understanding*, Hume wrote:

> *If we take in our hand any volume; of divinity or school metaphysics, for instance; let us ask, does it contain any* abstract reasoning concerning quantity or number? *No.* Does it contain any experimental reasoning concerning matter of fact and existence? *No. Commit it then to the flames: for it can contain nothing but sophistry and illusion.*[36]

According to Hume, there could be no metaphysical basis to invest our lives with meaning or any rational foundations for life. Matters of value, of ethics and beauty, Hume claimed, were better felt than reasoned on, and he insisted that reason should be a slave of the emotions. Such were the only assurances the philosophy of empirical science, as understood by Hume, could give us. It is little to go on and leaves man without sound foundations. Hume knew it, knew it all too well. He knew the darkness of his own philosophy and found words to make it existentially clear:

[36] David Hume, *An Enquiry Concerning Human Understanding* (Chicago: Gateway Editions, Inc., 1956), p. 183.

*Where am I or what? From what causes do I derive my existence, and to
what condition shall I return? Whose favor should I court and whose anger
must I dread? What beings surround me? and on whom have I any influence,
or who have any influence on me? I am confounded with all these questions,
and begin to fancy myself in the most deplorable condition imaginable, in-
viron'd with deepest darkness, and utterly depriv'd of the use of every
member and faculty.*[37]

Hume was frightened by the possibilities of his own philosophy. Had
he squarely faced them, he might have become the first modern existentialist. Instead he took refuge from the meaning and implications of his
philosophy in a game of backgammon and became the precursor of logical
empiricism or logical positivism. Hume asserted:

*Most fortunately it happens, that since reason is incapable of dispelling these
clouds, nature herself suffices to that purpose, and cures me of this philosophical melancholy and delirium, either by relaxing this bent of mind, or
by some avocation, and lively impression of my senses, which obliterate all
these chimeras. I converse, and am merry with my friends; and when after
three or four hours of amusement, I would return to these speculations, they
appear so cold, and strained and ridiculous, that I cannot find in my heart
to enter into them any farther.*[38]

What meaning can a philosophy have for a man when he has to run
away and play backgammon just so he won't have to think about it! A philosophy should make sense of things and so should provide men with a
meaningful outlook. But the philosophy that emerged from modern science
was so senseless that one who looked it straight in the eyes, as Hume did,
was forced to run away and hide from it in superficial distractions. A meaningful philosophy enables man to put things together, to have a general
unified perspective, but in a fragmented world where things are coming
apart, philosophy too becomes enmeshed in the process of dissolution.
Contemporary philosophers, particularly in Anglo-American countries, view
philosophy as a trade rather than a mission, as a job *apart from* one's life
instead of *a part* of one's life.

This is a schizophrenic condition in which the life one lives as a philosopher becomes completely cut off from one's life in the everyday world.
Modern scientific man, feeling alienated, lost, cut off, cries out for unity,
but the cry is lost in the wilderness as there is no philosophy to provide it
for him. In a world seemingly endless in space and time, with the forces of
disintegration ever mounting and man often incapable of knowing himself
more than as a bundle of perceptions, he comes to feel hopelessly alone.
Man seems lost in the fog of modern existence, a feeling profoundly expressed by Herman Hesse in his poem "Fog." It was in this poem that
Hesse expressed the view that man is groping through fog and snow and
can feel no life but his own, that man can never really know others, and
thus everyone is alone.

[37] Hume, *Treatise, op. cit.*, p. 269.
[38] *Ibid.*

The empiricist's world is disconnected and empty and is a world man has great difficulty living in. With Descartes, the rationalists entered the modern period of history and philosophy, adopting a methodological approach that *started* off the enterprise of philosophy on a note of healthy skepticism. It was healthy because it used skepticism only as a means of attaining necessary truth. Descartes thus commenced his search for truth by doubting the possibility of knowing anything, and he ended up by discovering what he took to be certain and eternal truths about man and universe. In contrast, the empiricists commenced on the assumption they could be certain about knowledge gained from experience, and then with Hume, empiricism ended doubting everything. Thus by Hume's time, man was entering a period of crisis in his understanding of himself and his universe. It was a great German philosopher, Immanuel Kant, who sought to heal the crisis and to try to bring about a return of unity and meaningful order to the life of man.

Immanuel Kant

If as a result of the intellectual situation in the eighteenth century things seemed terribly confused, Immanuel Kant (1724–1804) single-handedly took it upon himself to clear them up. He worked so hard at this task that there are those who would say that after he finished, no one could understand anything. Not only did he develop a highly complicated metaphysical system but it seems he took special pains to choose the perfect terms to drive people mad in case his ideas did not do it. On one occasion Kant sent a completed manuscript of his to a friend for appraisal. As the story goes, the friend read half of it then returned it with an appended note informing Kant that if he read all of it, he would surely go crazy. Part of the problem was that Kant went out of his way to express his big ideas in gigantic words. God, he called *prototypon transcendentale*. This could be enough to try a man's faith. Imagine a believer saying, "I believe in the *prototypon transcendentale*." Instead of sensation, he said "transcendental aesthetic." By aesthetic he did not mean what we mean by it today, but what the Greeks meant twenty-five hundred years ago; he also used the word transcendental in a very different way from that in which people use it normally. Kant certainly served up an unpalatable vocabulary. A philosophical dish consisting of such delectables as "transcendental unity of apperception," paralogisms, antinomies, Sinnlichkeit, and noumena could ruin anyone's appetite. The Kantian terminology—the use of words in entirely novel ways —is not easy to swallow, but like much that does not whet our appetite, it has nutritional value. Kant was moving philosophical mountains and could not use molehill terms to do it. He was providing man with a new way of viewing and understanding reality, and for that purpose ordinary terms would not do. Kant was doing something very creative and different in showing us how to understand this world. He needed words appropriate to the task. He needed a *special terminology* to call our attention to the fact that he was doing something very different. Perhaps we should think of his very abstruse vocabulary as a kind of Zen thing whose purpose is in part to shock us out of our usual ways of understanding things.

Kant was not a pompous professor ponderously erecting great castles of metaphysical abstraction. He had his eccentricities, but he was a very human person deeply concerned about questions that matter very much to men. Behind Kant's awesome system of philosophy lay deep concern for the questions that they must cope with to find a meaningful basis for their existence. Behind his complicated technical terminology are simple questions of basic concern to men. Kant understood the work of philosophy to be directed at answering four fundamental questions:

1. What can man know?
2. What ought man to do?
3. What can man hope for?
4. What is man?

Man must have an idea of what knowledge consists in and what its limitations are, or he will not be able to adequately relate himself to the world; he may think he knows more than it is possible to know or he may content himself with less than he can know. To live, man must also discover some basis for deciding what he *ought* to do, for he is constantly confronted with alternatives. How should he choose? Furthermore, man must learn the nature of the world in which he lives, for he needs to know what he can hope for or expect in it. Finally, to know or answer any of these questions, man has to know himself—to know what man is.

The Humean answer to the questions Kant posed pointed up the crisis of modern knowledge. As Hume understood it, there was very little man could know and no rational answer to what he ought to do; and in a world lacking spiritual substance and causal order, there was nothing to hope for. As for the question of what man is, Hume answered that he was a bundle of perceptions—a rather unflattering image.

Hume's philosophical skepticism can be understood as a reflection of man's inability to take science, which was central in his life, and build an adequate philosophy or way of life upon it. Kant saw mankind in the throes of an intellectual power failure. Man could not be certain of his knowledge, neither could he be sure of what was right nor of what to hope for. Science, ethics, and religion were all affected by the Humean thrust. Here was a full-fledged crisis, and the reverberations of it awakened Kant from what he himself described as dogmatic slumbers. Thus his whole being was shocked into mobilization by the skeptical challenge of Hume.

Modern philosophy revealed an important split in man's life—the split between reason and experience. Justice Holmes recognized this split when he remarked that the law is not logic: it is experience, and experience is often not logical. One may reason out beautiful ideas, but they may not be applicable to the world of experience. Both reason and perception belong to the life of man, and there is a serious split in his life whenever he cannot make them compatible. The philosophies of *rationalism* and *empiricism* represented such a division and emphasized the incompatibility between a rational and empirical approach to life. This culminated in David Hume's assertion that reason ought to be and is only the slave of the emotions. Disturbed by this division Kant sought to find a way of synthesis that would return unity and coherence to the intellectual life of man. His means of doing so was brilliant and highly original.

Kant showed how one could make the life of reason compatible with experience. He showed how truths of rationalism and truths of empiricism could be synthesized. The rationalists were certain that all truth was *inside* of men, and all they had to do was reason it out; the empiricists were equally convinced that truth was *outside* in the world, and all men had to do was take it in through their senses. To put it technically, the rationalists maintained that truth and knowledge were innate and *a priori* (before experience), and the empiricists regarded truth and knowledge as external and *a posteriori* (after experience). Kant saw that both schools of philosophy were wrong in one way and right in a different way. The rationalists were wrong in believing they could find truth by unaided reason, and the empiricists were incorrect in believing the discovery of truth to be purely a matter of the senses. The empiricists erred in viewing the mind as an empty bucket that had to be filled with experience to attain knowledge; and yet they were quite right in assuming that knowledge depended in some way upon experience. The rationalists were right in understanding the mind as more than an empty bucket to be filled with experience, but they erred in supposing it could be filled without any experience being poured into it. Where the empiricists put all their emphasis on what went into the bucket and the rationalists concentrated on the bucket itself, the genius of Kant saw that the crucial factor was the way in which the experience that went into the bucket had to conform to the shape of the bucket.

Kant further observed that there was an important sense in which the points made about knowledge by both rationalism and empiricism were irrelevant. On the one hand the rationalists, by concentrating on mind and reason, focused on an unreal *ideal* form of knowledge; the result was that they sought to discover a knowledge superior to any we actually have. On the other hand the empiricists were misguided in overlooking what knowledge really *is*, and instead, concentrated on its *origins* or how it arises. Kant wanted to depart from these fanciful approaches and really get down to business. He sought to analyze knowledge, not in terms of ideals (rationalists) or origins (empiricists), but as it really *is*. Only such an approach could make clear to us what we can really know and show us in what knowledge truly consists.

Up to a point both rationalism and empiricism did have some important insights into this question. Kant once made a remark that may be taken as an illustration of the rationalist-empiricist controversy over the question of knowledge. He said that *concepts without percepts are empty*, but *percepts without concepts are blind*. Rationalist concepts are devoid of experience and therefore *empty*; they tell us nothing. Empiricist sense data in a raw state are chaotic and *blind* and unless they are structured by the mind, they enable us to see nothing. What is called for is a delicate balancing of conception and perception, a blending of rationalism and empiricism. That was the work Kant accomplished, and the resulting product has been called Kantian Criticism.

Kant was illuminated by a rich insight, which had lain hidden in the night for both rationalists and empiricists. It was expressed in his observation that *all knowledge begins with experience, but it does not arise from experience.* What we know *starts* with information (facts and the data of experience), but in that raw state this is not knowledge. Knowledge *arises* when the mind goes to work on unstructured experience and gives it form. A man cannot retire into a stove—as Descartes had done—or sit in meditation on a log to acquire knowledge. To come by knowledge it is essential to come out of the stove, get off the log, and encounter the world. Mere experience, however, does not simply confer knowledge as a God confers blessings. To qualify as knowledge, experience must be ordered and given meaning by the activity of the mind. The empiricists contended the mind was a blank tablet upon which experience wrote. But if the mind was just a blank it would not be capable of reading what experience wrote. The language of experience has to be translated into meaning, and this translating is not something passive, as the empiricist supposed. In empiricist philosophy the mind was too passive and static. It was Kant's contribution to offer us an understanding of the mind in dynamic terms. What Kant saw was that unless there is an active mind to make sense of the complex world of experience, there could not be any understanding.

Kant, who was not very humble about his accomplishments, claimed that what he had done amounted to a *Copernican Revolution* in philosophy. Before Copernicus the sun and other planets were understood to revolve about the earth, but after him the central position of the sun in our solar system was made known. In a similar manner, before Kant the central role of the mind was not understood. As Copernicus revealed the true position of the sun, Kant set out to reveal how the mind shed light on our understanding.

We must be careful not to understate Kant's argument here, for he was claiming something far more revolutionary than that the mind must be considered important because it is the primary source for our understanding the world. Kant said this, but he also went one step further and added that the mind actually *makes* the world, or *constitutes* it. The mind may be said to "make" or to "constitute" the world in the sense it bestows *order* and *form* upon experience, and gives meaningful structure to what would otherwise be a chaotic manifold of raw sense data. It is the very nature of the mind to work in such a way that it has to view reality as intelligible. It is not that man first experiences a world that is unstructured and senseless, and then his mind interprets that experience in an intelligible manner. It is rather that *in the very process* of experiencing the world, order is being imposed upon it by the mind. Bringing order to the world by the mind is not a *separate act* coming *after* perception; it is the mind's way of taking in the world. The rationalists and the empiricists had debated about which was more important—our experiences of the world or the mind's treatment of them. Kant answered by saying that this question did not matter because they were both the same thing; there was no such thing as experience that had not been ordered and organized by man's mind.

Kant revolutionized man's way of understanding reality. Whatever is out there in the real world must be seen by man through the lens of his mind, which is a logical lens, and thus the world must have a *logical* or *intelligible* form. Hume did not live in a disorganized chaotic world, although he analyzed it in such a way. He did so, it might be said, because he understood mind in a passive sense. Hume concentrated on pure experience, or the data of our senses out in the world; he did not realize that, as man receives it, sensed data is already structured.

When Hume asserted there were no causal bonds, no universal laws, and no necessity of any kind *in* nature itself, he did not see the role that the mind might play. If one *concentrates* on sense data, he will not find any *natural links* holding the world together because it requires an understanding of the role of mind, which can see nature only in terms of necessary links, to comprehend the order which exists in the world. A man lights a match. What can we know about this from the *senses?* First there is the *striking* of the match and secondly there is the appearance of the *flame*. On this perceptual level there is no natural link, no *power* or *force* which can be *observed* to produce the ensuing flame. Men *infer* a causal power but they do not *see* it. This was Hume's argument, and as far as it went, it was right. But if man was to see things in proper perspective, he would have to go further. Hume did not see the causal links, the universal laws, and the necessity because he was looking in the wrong place. One cannot understand reality by *just concentrating* on *nature,* for the mind too is a part of reality. The source of intelligibility and certainty is not in nature but in the mind. One must look at the way it works as well as at sense data if one is to comprehend the full story of reality.

The Human mind is definitely not a Humean mind, for the mind is so built as to necessitate our seeing the world as an orderly and logical place. We *must* understand certain events as *causal* and others as occurring in accord with universal laws. This is not an arbitrary intellectual decision, but it is the way things are—that is, it is the way *we* are. The data of our senses are such that they are adaptable to the logical form of the mind, and the machinery of the mind is such that it interacts with experience in such a way as to *inevitably* grind out an intelligible world.

Kant was desperately trying to bring man down from the air of uncertainty in which Hume had left him. In technical terms, doing so meant showing there could be a synthetic *a priori*—that is, there could be necessary truths about the world, the knowledge of which is not dependent on experience. Whether there can be a synthetic *a priori* is of great significance for man. The stakes involved concern whether or not we can know anything with certainty about our world. If we can have no necessary knowledge about the empirical world we can never be sure about any matters of fact.

Kant, in trying to show there could be a synthetic *a priori,* was trying to show how we can demonstrate there is necessary knowledge concerning matters of fact. His efforts here involved philosophic genius and we should examine it closely, even at the risk of being a little repetitious about some fundamentals.

There are two basic kinds of judgment: (1) *synthetic* and (2) *analytic.* Furthermore, there are two basic types of knowledge: (1) *a posteriori* and (2) *a priori.*

A *synthetic* statement is one from which we learn something new about things. Synthetic statements *extend* our knowledge of the world. *Analytic* statements *clarify* rather than extend our information. While no new information is acquired in analytic statements, understanding of the logical implications of what we already do know is often acquired. *Synthetic* statements are of *empirical* significance, and the factual sciences are built of them. Analytic statements are of *formal* significance and are the building blocks for logical and mathematical studies.

In *synthetic* statements the *predicate* in a sentence adds something to the *subject,* but in analytic judgments it does not. In analytic statements the predicate repeats the subject, or we may say *predicate is included in subject.* In synthetic statements they are not equal. A sentence consists of a subject, predicate, and copula (some form of the verb to be); the following is an example of a sentence containing an analytic judgment.

> *A Senator   is   a member of the Senate.*
>   (subject)   (copula)   (predicate)

If we assume every member of the Senate is a Senator, then here the subject and predicate are identical, and thus we have an *analytic* statement. We know such a statement is necessarily true because to assert its opposite is a contradiction and therefore is not even possible. Thus the following sentence is absurd and makes no sense at all: *The Senator is not a member of the Senate.*

A synthetic statement is one in which the predicate tells us something new about the subject. For example:

> *The Senator   is   corrupt.*
>   (subject)   (copula)   (predicate)

In this sentence the predicate "corrupt" is not identical with the subject "Senator," although many might observe that they go together very well. Nonetheless, we cannot discover the corruption of a Senator by just analyzing the definition of the term "Senator," and in that sense we may say the predicate enlarges on the subject, or gives us new information concerning it.

Now it is easy to show that analytic statements can be *a priori,* or can give us knowledge without reference to fact. Because they do not depend upon empirical evidence, they are said to be necessarily true. We don't need to know any facts about a particular Senator to know that he is a member of the Senate. Being a Senator *means* being a member of the Senate. Thus analytic statements are necessarily true because they are *stipulated* to be so. Just as no problem arises in connection with the fact that analytic judgments are *a priori,* so none arises in connection with the idea that synthetic judgments are *a posteriori.* A synthetic *a posteriori* statement is one in which the subject is amplified by the predicate. It is just another way of saying we can get new information from experience. By studying politics we can learn there are corrupt Senators.

Now that we are clear about analytic *a priori* statements and synthetic *a posteriori* statements, that leaves two other possible combinations of these terms (1) analytic *a posteriori* statements and (2) synthetic *a priori* statements. Are such things possible? The first may be, but no one much cares. An analytic proposition is one purely concerned with the meaning of terms and not with facts or that which is *a posteriori,* derived from experience. Anyone who wanted to make an analytic *a posteriori* statement would have to do research to find out if the Senator was a member of the Senate, and even if he were silly enough to bother, his conclusion, "The Senator is a member of the Senate," would be identical to the analytic *a priori* statement.

That leaves the jackpot question as to whether there can be synthetic *a priori* statements. This question is of great importance because it asks if we can get any *necessary* knowledge about the world out there. If we can obtain necessary truths about the empirical world, they will be *a priori* in the sense we will know they must be true even before they are confirmed by facts.

Kant was able to arrive at the synthetic *a priori* from his principle that the very structure of the mind is such that in the process of experiencing the world, it orders and interprets it. This means we never get undiluted or raw experience. Everything we experience is already worked over or structured by the mind. The mind functions so naturally that it imposes upon and therefore discovers in all experiences a certain order, universality, and necessity. All experience has to come to man through the funnel of the mind, and that is a very logical funnel.

Because the mind is responsible for making experience intelligible, it so structures experience that we understand it in the categories of necessity and universality. Thus there can be synthetic *a priori* knowledge. The necessary quality of knowledge is assured not by anything empirical but by the *mind,* and in that sense it is *a priori;* and yet because such knowledge is about the world it is also *synthetic.* The very nature of the mind is such that it forces upon us the conclusion certain things about the world *must* be so. For example, we must experience the world in a context of space and time and things in categories of causality—but the source of our ideas of space and time and causality is the mind, not experience.

Kant said that our experience was *transcendental,* by which he did not mean that it *transcends* or gets beyond the world, but that it is always shaped by the mind. In this sense Kant distinguished *transcendental,* meaning that which is given form by the mind, from transcendent, meaning that which goes beyond experience. The unfolding of Kant's philosophy con-

sisted in an elaboration of the meaning of the *transcendental* basis of knowledge. Kant tried to provide a complete statement of just how the mind
gives form to experience so as to produce knowledge and also to make clear
to us what the limits of this knowledge are. Kant's ambitious program for
doing this was developed in three divisions, which are as follows:

1. *Transcendental Aesthetic:* This has to do with the mind's faculty
for receiving sense impressions, called *Sinnlichkeit* (sensibility). Kant maintained there are two pure forms of sensibility, and these are *space* and *time*.
Without space and time no *objects* would be perceived, and therefore space
and time are a precondition of our experiencing anything. Kant used the
word *aesthetic* in its original Greek sense of having to do with the senses.
All that has to do with the senses is in space and time.

2. *Transcendental Analytic:* This has to do with the faculty of the mind
by which sense data are rendered intelligible, called *Verstand* (conceptuali-
zation or understanding). Through the faculty of understanding the mind
unifies our experience in accord with intellectual categories. Experience must
be understood in terms of these categories.

Both *Sinnlichkeit* (or Sensibility) and *Verstand* (or Understanding)
are required for knowledge. Without *Sinnlichkeit* no objects could be experienced. Without *Verstand* no objects could be thought.

3. *Transcendental Dialectic:* This has to do with the activity of the
mind directed at getting beyond experience and seeking to know ultimate
reality or things in themselves. These are the ideas of Reason, for which
there is no experimental basis.

Kant's philosophy was structured in terms of the transcendental aesthetic,
the transcendental analytic, and the transcendental dialectic. Examination of
these transcendental bases of understanding at once reveals the possibilities
and limitations of human knowledge.

THE TRANSCENDENTAL AESTHETIC

A basic source of the unity of experience is achieved through the mind's
activity in imposing upon all our experience certain forms of intuition. These
forms of intuition are space and time. Space and time derive from the mind,
not from the perceptual world. Kant developed a line of argument to attest
to this, which gave men a very different way of understanding space. Space
cannot be an empirical conception because it is not built out of sensations
or perceptions. Space cannot be a sensation or perception because our sensations are themselves *already* perceived in a context of space. We can think
of space as *empty* of all empirical objects, but we cannot think of empirical
objects as not being in space. Moreover, space is *universal* and as such does
not depend upon the particular data of our sensations. Finally, we hold the
idea of space being infinite, but experience cannot give anything infinite to
the mind. All of this establishes, Kant believed, that space is a mind-derived
entity. It is not possible to see, feel, hear, taste, or smell space, but anything
we can see, feel, hear, taste, or smell is in space. What we see out there is

spread out in three dimensions. The notion of space is *a priori,* or before, experience.

As we have found with space, it is also not possible to derive time from experience. Time does not come in shades, colors, sounds, or tastes. There is no perception of time. Yet no matter what sense objects we think of, they are always in time—they are always *now* or *before, successive* or *simultaneous.* There can be no sensory objects without a time reference. Time is the precondition for everything. It is universal; it is the condition for that which is internal as well as that which is external. Even images of which we think and images in our dreams are in time.

Thus the only way the human mind can arrange phenomena is in space and time. Logically space and time come before experience because, in the absence of space and time, there can be no experience. Thus space and time must be regarded both as *a priori,* or before experience, and in the context that they are essential for the occurrence of all experience. Kant put it this way: space and time are *empirically real* and *transcendentally ideal.* They are empirically real because they are universally present in our experience; they are transcendentally ideal because they do not arise from experience but are a product of the mind.

THE TRANSCENDENTAL ANALYTIC

The transcendental aesthetic concerns the question of how man perceives the world. Kant's investigation led him to the conclusion that everything we experience is in terms of certain fixed forms of intuition—space and time. The nature of the mind is such that we cannot but sense the world in the framework of space and time. The mind determines both the way in which we must perceive the world and the way in which we must think about it or understand it. Just as space and time are invariable categories of perception, there are also invariable categories of thought that set the mold in which we must think. These categories of thought are examined in the *Transcendental Analytic;* they are the concern of what Kant calls *Verstand,* or understanding.

The mind synthesizes and unifies experience and in doing so, makes certain definite judgments about the world of sense data. There are fixed principles or forms of judgment that are absolutely necessary to the activity of thinking about any objects. These judgments, which the mind must make, are responsible for objects appearing intelligible to man. Everything in experience must be thought of or judged as invariant forms or concepts. The basic concepts Kant believed to be Quantity, Quality, Relation, and Modality.

In making judgments men must assert *quantity*—that there is one way, or many, or one aggregate. We make judgments that *all* things are involved, that *some* things are involved, or that one thing is. These three types of judgments can be expressed in universal statements ("*All* Arabian Baboons are Semitic Boojums"), particular statements ("*Some* Semitic Boojums are Baby Bears"), and singular statements ("*This* Baby Bear is a Bore"). All three of these are statements of Quantity.

The mind also thinks in terms of Quality. In doing so, it either *affirms* some things are so or *denies* other things are so. By affirming things we get *reality;* by denying things we get *negation.* The mind also makes limitative judgments, or judgments that give us certain limitations. Thus one might *affirm* that the religious man is *rational;* one might *deny* it and say that the religious man is *irrational;* or one might take a different approach and say the religious man is *nonrational* (limitative). All of these are statements of Quality. Negation is a way of flatly asserting something is not so, whereas a limitative assertion tells us a quality is not applicable at all.

In addition to the categories of quantity and quality, man must also understand in terms of the category of Relation. Statements of Relation may be either *categorical* (that some things must be so without any qualifications), *hypothetical* (if something comes to pass, then another thing will follow), or *disjunctive* (either this will happen or that will). The category of *Relation,* as its name indicates, requires man to understand the world in terms of some fundamental relations. For example a man will judge that one thing is the property of another. Such a relationship must take either of two forms. A relationship may involve the *substance* or essence of a thing, or it may be merely accidental. One might say it is the substance, or essence, of a man that he can think, make judgments, speak, stand upright, and use his hands, but it is only accidental that he is of this or of that color. The mind also has to judge certain things as being the *cause* of other things, and these other things as being the *effects.* People must also make judgments concerning the ways in which things interact. All of these are judgments of Relation.

Finally, men must make judgments regarding what Kant called the Modality of a thing's existence. This means that we must conclude that some things are *possible* and others *impossible,* that some things *exist* and others *do not exist,* and that some things are *necessary* and others are only *contingent.*

Now what Kant concluded was that without all this conceptual machinery of the mind, the world of sense would be unintelligible, senseless, and chaotic. The mind puts the world together and provides us with an orderly understanding of things. The *transcendental* aesthetic provides man with the structure with which to perceive sense objects, and the transcendental analytic provides him with the structure with which to think about the world of experience. The transcendental analytic shows the way in which man *must* understand the world. The matter of our senses is made inherently meaningful by this conceptual machinery of the mind, which provides us with a unified and coherent world. Kant had a very fancy name for all this. He called it *the transcendental unity of apperception.* By this he meant simply that we see the world *put together* in lawful and orderly patterns. This in turn implies that we ourselves must be put together in an orderly way. However complex and differentiated the elements of experience may be, they are all brought together in a meaningful unity. Thus Kant concluded that the mind is *constitutive* of *phenomena,* the world of experience. The mind, in its organizing and unifying capacities, *constitutes* the world or gives it the lawful structure we discover it to possess. This, of course, does not

mean that everything is in the mind. There is a real world out there independently of us, but the orderly universe *in which we live* is a product of the
mind.

The logical categories of the mind fashion a logical pattern out of the
phenomena of the world. And the result is science. The mind, however, may
not be satisfied with the scientific knowledge we get and form from the
mind's interaction with experience. Man may wish to know of that which
exists beyond the world of experience. He may want to know of things that
exist beyond space and time and beyond the experience our minds mold into
unity. Kant brilliantly solved the rationalist-empiricist debate by showing.
that everything that appears in space and time is given pattern by the mind.
But this was not the end of the matter, for it meant that man never gets to
that which exists in a *pure* state. Whatever he gets from perception is already
worked over by the mind—by the categories of our understanding. We
perceive *phenomena,* sense objects as patterned by the mind. But what
about what he called *noumena,* ultimate reality or *things-in-themselves?* The
Transcendental Aesthetic and the Transcendental Analytic do not make it
possible for us to know what *reality* is *independent* of our way of conceiving
it. So far we do not know *das ding an sich,* or the thing-in-itself. But Immanuel Kant was a man of monumental curiosity who could not be satisfied
with stopping here. He wanted to know the thing-in-itself, to explore the
no man's land of *noumena*—that which is beyond the realm of experience.
This brought him—and us—to the *transcendental dialectic.*

THE TRANSCENDENTAL DIALECTIC

Questions of theology, metaphysics, and ethics are not grounded in phenomena and thus are off limits to human reason. When man deals with them,
he gets himself in trouble because there is no reliable way to obtain conclusive answers to such questions. We cannot verify statements concerning
metaphysical, religious, or ethical matters because they deal with a realm
that is beyond the world of experience. Thus it is just as possible (1) to
argue that there is a god as that there is not a god, (2) to contend that there
is a rational soul as that there is not a rational soul, and (3) to maintain that
the world was created as to assert that it is eternal. These questions are
dialectical, which means that there are two sides to them, each one equally
as valid as the other. When one can argue on behalf of something and against
it with equal validity, such arguments cannot really prove anything. When
reason tries to reach beyond the world of experience, it becomes impaled
on what Kant called antinomies or paralogisms, which basically comes down
to the fact that a purely rational resolution of such questions cannot be
attained.

Kant himself had seen that a purely rational approach to all reality was
not entirely adequate. Ever since the days of St. Thomas Aquinas, reason
had been regarded as a most powerful human endowment. Indeed, Aquinas
had such confidence in the power of reason he believed it could be used not
only to solve problems of man and science, but could lead man directly to

God. It is widely assumed that in the Middle Ages respect for reason was at its nadir, but on the contrary, Aquinas was just one among many prominent medieval philosophers who understood reason as a golden key that could unlock all the secrets of the universe. This faith in reason remained largely undisturbed until Kant, living at the peak of the Age of Reason, discovered there were large areas in which the key didn't work. Paradoxically, as the power of science increased the power of reason decreased. In the dialectical hands of Kant, the key of reason could unlock only the door of science, and such matters as metaphysics, ethics, and religion were closed to it.

Insofar as Kant maintained reason could not provide meaningful answers to any questions beyond the realm of experience, he put forth a position that was to be very fully developed by the logical positivists in our own time. The logical positivists concluded that if man could not *reasonably* resolve matters transcending phenomena, then such matters, which include metaphysics, religion, and ethics, must be *meaningless*. Reason is very effective when kept in the confines of science, but beyond these confines it is impotent. "All the worse for the *beyond*," concluded Kant in his *Critique of Pure Reason* and the logical positivists after him.

There is, however, another possibility. If reason and science cannot provide us with knowledge of anything but the empirical world, then it is all the worse for reason and science. Things-in-themselves—what Kant called *noumena*—are not necessarily meaningless or nonexistent. They may be too deep to be probed by reason and logic, but this does not mean that they cannot be grasped by man on another level. This possibility has been taken up by the existentialists in our time. Thus the logical positivists, following Kant's original lead developed in transcendental dialectic, claimed only that which can be empirically verified to be meaningful. The existentialists, on the other hand, took the position that some of the most meaningful things there may be for man may not be susceptible to empirical verification. In this too they were following Kant, for he himself was certain that science was not the last word on the universe. It is certainly a tribute to Kant's philosophical magnitude that out of his transcendental dialectic were generated the seeds for two philosophies—existentialism and logical positivism—which permeate contemporary thinking and are diametrically opposed.

Of the four questions Kant had raised as the fundamental questions of philosophy—What can man *know?* What *ought* man to do? What can man *hope* for? What *is man?*—Kant provided brilliant answers to the first and fourth. But he also opened the way for answering the second and third, as the existentialists showed when they developed their philosophy from Kant. Because we are concerned in this chapter with epistemological questions—questions about what man can know—we cannot do full justice here to Kant's interesting ideas about what man ought to do and what he can hope for. Let us not leave Kant, though, without observing his understanding that man is not just an animal who *knows* but is also one who *feels*. He is not only scientific but also moral and religious. There may be religious and moral experiences that bespeak a truth other than a scientific one about this world. Indeed in the second edition of the *Critique of Pure Reason*

Kant said in effect that he had closed the door of *knowledge* about God, freedom, and immortality only so that he might open the door of *faith* in them.

Kant thus tried to show that science is a meaningful activity, and that meaningful knowledge of a kind that Humean skepticism did not account for is possible. Yet at the same time, he understood that science had its limits. Man's reason could not guide man past those limits, but Kant held out the possibility of other means to get beyond them. In our age of astronomy when so many college students are turning to astrology, we can recognize how fundamentally human is that desire to explore the possibilities of knowledge beyond the sphere of what Kant called *"phenomena."*

Are There Unicorns on Mars?

FROM KNOWLEDGE TO MEANING, AND THEN TO MEANINGLESSNESS

Kant's epistemology was a grand effort to establish that man could have a unified body of scientific knowledge. In forcing the point, however, Kant himself ran headlong into the obstruction of the unknowable thing-in-itself. Contradictions were inherent in the scientific milieu. The world of modern science proved not to be the rational, stable world it was once imagined to be. Promises of a complete rational understanding of the nature of things were shattered, and no one made that clearer than Kant, with his strong case that the very way in which man knows prevents him from gaining access to what is ultimately real. Since the mind gives shape to all material in our process of knowing it, we have no way of knowing the shape of that material in itself, independently of us. Kant, we might say, was the last of the red hot epistemologists—the last to develop so elaborate a theory of knowledge, and with such conviction, that what *man can know* is one of the really big questions of life. When Kant devoted his overwhelming reasoning power and genius to showing that science was possible and that we could have necessary knowledge, and still had to conclude that there can be no knowledge of things-in-themselves, then man had finally come to the end of a long epistemological line.

After Kant it was accepted that science could make it possible for man to achieve crucially important practical things, but that it was powerless to give him knowledge of what the world *really* is like. Science can show man how to come to terms with things and still cannot provide him with knowledge as to what those things ultimately are. Thus the age of science would prove to be one of immense power, but one in which man could easily become lost and get out of contact with reality. Epistemology could never be the same after Kant. And yet, of course, there would have to be some who would try to make it the same. This would particularly be so in the United States, where there was great confidence in man's ability to subdue the real world and make it over so as to satisfy his desires. One might also have expected much the same from Great Britain, an ambitious island fascinated by the power and glory of the industrial revolution that had begun there. In both these nations power was being harnessed for positive and practical achievements, so men tended to be little aware of the resistance of reality and to feel, rather, that reality was in their control and therefore was knowable and without any mystery.

Men engaged in the activity of building, of making a new world, usually have a practical or realistic attitude about things. Their job is to produce results that have testable consequences, not to ponder deeper strata of Being. As the scientific revolution increased man's power, especially in America and Great Britain, a new philosophical style was beginning to manifest itself. Around the turn of this century the main lines of this philosophy were clear: it involved a thorough rejection of idealism.

In Great Britain there developed a bold and vigorous defense of a common sense approach to knowledge. G. E. Moore, one of England's outstanding philosophical minds, dismissed the notion that the thing-in-itself is unknowable. Indeed, he regarded it as sheer nonsense even to suppose that there is any such thing as this mysterious thing-in-itself. Moore took a very straightforward approach. He agreed with Kant that our knowledge of things depends entirely on the way our minds interact with the world out there, but he refused to go along when Kant became puzzled about what those things out there were really like, independently of our knowledge of them. It makes no sense to talk about a thing-in-itself because that is even less real than the thing we perceive. After all, our knowledge of the phenomenal world comes from the combination of our minds with the world outside; we cannot perceive the thing-in-itself. Therefore, all our knowledge of the thing-in-itself would come only from our own minds, and not from the world outside at all. The very question of what things are like independently of our minds is a completely mind-bound question. Besides, Moore did not even think it was an interesting question; it only comes up because Kant maintained that we can never have contact with the world except through our minds and senses. If this is true, then what does it matter what that world, with which we can have nothing to do, is like?

Moore was not just dealing with a troublesome philosophical problem; he was changing a whole style of "doing" philosophy. In a fast-paced age of science philosophers were growing weary with the old philosophical questions. What does it really mean to expend energy questioning whether the world we live in is real? Do such questions make any sense? Surely there must be better things to do. Moore was leading philosophers away from the thankless and fruitless task of trying to discover what we can really *know*, and toward a more profitable task of analyzing what problems can *mean*. He was setting the pace for Analytic Philosophy—the approach to philosophy that does not seek to answer philosophical questions but tries instead to discover what the *correct analysis* of them is.

It is of course generally recognized that Moore was engaged in analytic pioneering. However, he was also doing something else that has been less generally recognized. He was taking an *existential* as well as an analytic approach. Logical Positivism and Analytic Philosophy are often posed as polar opposite philosophical tendencies to existential philosophies. One can understand the contrast between positivistic-analytic philosophies on the one hand and existential philosophies on the other in terms of their very difficult orientations. In the positivistic-analytic orientation, great emphasis is placed upon science and/or logic and analysis, and that which cannot be empirically verified or logically explained is repudiated. On the opposite side, in existentialism there is often a hostility to scientific classification and concern with formal logic; feelings and the concrete *existing* person are stressed. However different these philosophies may seem to be on the surface, it turns out that similarities emerge when pushed to their extremes. One important similarity is that both schools reject traditional philosophical *questions* as well as *answers* in favor of a more direct and uncomplicated way of handling them. Not only did Moore set a precedent for philosophical analysis but, if we think of it, he also pioneered an existential approach. The existentialist believes it is a terrible waste to ask if the very world into which we find ourselves *thrust* actually exists. That world and the things in it provide the context in which our problems arise. To question reality we would have to *abstract* ourselves from it, which is precisely what the existentialists do not want us to do. The existential approach is not to prove to us that things exist by cold argumentation, but to involve us in their reality; and that's just what Moore was doing.. He dismissed Kant's idea of a *noumenal* world of things-in-themselves precisely because it was not a reality with which man could be involved.

Man was moving into a new world dominated by greater power than he had ever possessed. In such a context it was inevitable that philosophers would become less "philosophical" and more oriented toward reality. G. E. Moore was one of the leaders of this philosophical shift from idealism toward *realism.*

In 1903 Moore produced a classic attack against idealism in an article called "The Refutation of Idealism." In it Moore did not set for himself the great philosophical task of refuting the idea that reality is spiritual, the central tenet of idealism. As he saw it, that was too big a question to be handled profitably. Moore aimed at a more limited target, but one central to all idealist thinking. That target was Berkeley's formula that *"to be is to be perceived."* Moore believed that if he could shoot this proposition down, he would be dealing idealism a mortal wound. True, he would not thereby refute the idea that reality is spiritual, but he would annihilate the possibility of *proving* it, and for his purposes, that was quite as good. In other words, reality might be spiritual, but we could never know it; and if we cannot know it, then we have no basis for asserting it is so. Moore's attack was based on the argument that the idealist committed a fallacy in assuming that the statement "to be is to be perceived" asserted an *identity.* That is, the idealist generally operates on the assumption that *being* and *being perceived* are identical, but Moore pointed out that *being perceived* must be different from being, because *being perceived* must follow from the fact there is *something* to be perceived. There is a difference between *being yellow* and a sensation of yellow. To have a sensation of yellow is to have a sensation of something called yellow. The *sensation* and the something are different. The idealists are in error in equating consciousness of objects with the objects themselves.

Moore's "refutation of idealism" certainly breathed new life into the realist movement in philosophy. Soon after the publication of his essay, the *New Realism* was officially given birth in the United States. A group of philosophy professors—Ralph Barton Perry and Edwin B. Holt of Harvard, William Pepperell Montague and Walter B. Pitkin of Columbia, and Walter T. Marvin and Edward Gleason Spaulding of Princeton—came together for the explicit purpose of developing a new kind of realism. They had a few meetings and published "A Program and First Platform of Six Realists" in 1910. This article was followed up a year later by a cooperative book called *The New Realism*. The new realists called for philosophers to cooperate with scientists and to follow the methods of scientists. They insisted that philosophers, like the scientists, must learn to isolate problems and deal with them one by one. Philosophers should not try to know everything at once, as they often had, but should deal with questions specifically.

The new realists claimed that the idealist argument is based on a *tautology*. A tautology is a statement that provides no new information but just gives an identity. Tautologies are always true, but they fail to add to our stock of empirical knowledge. A tautology is of the form A equals A, and the new realists insisted that the idealists' assertion that to *know* an object is to be *conscious* of it is just such a tautology. It goes without saying. But it certainly does not follow from this that no objects exist that we do not know. Following their own advice about using scientific methods, the realists pointed out that if a scientist wanted to refute the astrologer's claim that human affairs depend upon the stars, we would not do it by carrying away the stars and then seeing what happened. Rather, he would show that there are no constant correlations between the behavior of stars and human behavior. In the same way we can refute idealism by showing that the behavior of objects when co-present with mind reveals no constant or causally significant correlations with consciousness. The behavior of objects does not show signs of being affected by consciousness. Just because two things go together, it surely does not follow that one is dependent on the other and cannot possibly exist independently of it. The idealist is just hiding behind a tautology when he takes the obvious fact that knowledge of a thing and perception always go together and deduces from this fact that one of them—the existence of the thing—is dependent on the other— our perception of it.

The new realists also vigorously argued against Lockean, or representative realism. Locke had maintained that what we perceive is just a copy or reproduction of the external world, but the new realists argued that we can directly perceive reality. They pointed out that if Locke were right, the perceptual world would then have to be *inside* the perceiver. For the new realists the decisive fact was that perceived objects *appear* to be external;

by this undeniable fact a presumption is created that the objects are indeed external, and therefore the *burden of proof* rests upon those who deny that presumption.

With various changes, embellishments, and developments, the thorough-going realist refutation of idealism was carried through the first third of this century. But after thirty years of killing idealism, was idealism finally buried? Not quite! On the contrary, more than thirty years after G. E. Moore first wrote his "Refutation of Idealism," there appeared in *Mind,* the same philosophic journal in which Moore's article had originally appeared in 1903, an article by Walter Stace called "The Refutation of Realism" (1934).

The banner of idealism was being hoisted again. W. T. Stace turned the table on the position Moore had taken, a position to which realists were committed. He directed his attack at the realist proposition that an object can exist unperceived. Stace admitted that unexperienced objects *may* exist, but added that we haven't the slightest reason for believing they *do* exist. As Stace saw it, saying that objects exist unperceived is analogous to saying "there is a unicorn on the planet Mars." Not having access to information concerning whether or not there is a unicorn on the planet Mars, Stace confessed he could not prove there is none, but pointed out that there is not the slightest reason for him to believe there is one. That the proposition "There are unicorns on Mars" cannot be denied is beside the point; the point is that the proposition ought not to be believed.

There are, Stace argued, two ways in which we can establish the existence of any sense object. One way is *by sense perception* and the other is by inference from sense perception. We can rule out sense perception as a way of establishing the existence of any object which no one is experiencing for the simple reason that there is no perception going on. As for inference, it is no more helpful. We can infer the existence of something from the fact we experience it, but if we don't experience it, no such inference can be made. Inference from perception works only if there is perception. There can be no valid inference from an experienced to an unexperienced existence. What about induction? Induction cannot help to prove that objects can exist independently of being perceived. The process of induction is a generalization from observed facts. But if there is no perception, there is nothing to generalize from. One might try to prove the realist case by *reasoning,* rather than by experience, by *deduction,* rather than by induction. One might try it, but it doesn't work, for on this level one would have to show that it is contradictory or inconsistent to maintain that objects can exist only when perceived. This certainly does not seem like a contradiction, and to date no one has been able to show that it is.

Having made these extremely persuasive arguments, Stace addressed himself to answering Ralph Barton Perry's criticisms of idealism. Perry had pointed out that because we know objects exist only when we perceive them, it does not follow they *cannot* exist when we do not perceive them. Stace agreed, but he denied that Perry's argument in any way justifies the realist position. Stace very succinctly puts it as follows:

It would be a fallacy to argue that, because we have never observed a unicorn on Mars, therefore there is no unicorn there; but by pointing out this fallacy, one does not prove the existence of a unicorn there. ... As regards the unicorn on Mars, the correct position, as far as logic is concerned, is obviously that if anyone asserts that there is a unicorn there, the onus is on him to prove it, and that until he does prove it, we ought not to believe it to be true. As regards the unexperienced entities, the correct position as far as logic is concerned, is that if realists assert their existence, the onus is on them to prove it; and that until they do prove it, we ought not to believe that they exist. Mr. Perry's argument, therefore, proves nothing whatever in favor of realism.[39]

After thousands of years of debating whether reality is material or not, grown men were still debating about matters it seemed there was no way to prove. As we have followed this debate between realists and idealists, it seems that each side takes its innings and scores some runs, but no one ever seems to win. Indeed, many philosophers were becoming distinctly discouraged with such questions, and began to view epistemology as very suspicious. Trying to devote a life to figuring out what really can be known and what truth is was becoming somewhat of a bore. As we have seen, G. E. Moore had suggested new directions for philosophy in his defense of common sense. Instead of seeking absolute proofs of certain propositions, he put emphasis on the way in which these questions might be *analyzed*.

A new era in philosophy was opening, one in which philosophers would no longer seek substantial *answers* to profound questions about the universe. Rather, what they aimed for was *clarity*. Instead of asking what we can know, it seemed more profitable to ask what we *mean*. We can never really be sure of what we can know, but we can get relatively sure about what we *mean*. In trying to develop some type of ultimate knowledge philosophers have often managed to achieve only an ultimate unintelligibility. Recognizing this, philosophers made the achievement of intelligibility their major preoccupation. If we know what we *mean*, at least we can communicate with one another successfully, and we can also eliminate from discourse those propositions devoid of any meaning.

This task was undertaken by the philosophy of logical positivism or logical empiricism and analytic philosophy, which was characterized by a very orthodox scientific orientation. Logical positivists or logical empiricists insisted that the basic ingredient of philosophical understanding was a *theory of meaning*. They maintained that the only meaningful statements are those which can be *empirically verified*. They were proposing that the only sensible way to deal with problems was to disqualify all propositions which could not be given empirical verification. Visible results can be accomplished by concentrating upon that which can be verified by our senses. Strictly adhering to the empirically verifiable, science can show us how to develop medical cures, build bridges, make and drop bombs, and go to the

[39] W. T. Stace, "The Refutation of Realism," reprinted in *Contemporary Philosophy*, ed. Jas. Jarrett and Sterling McMurrin (New York: Henry Holt and Co., 1945), p. 27.

moon. Theology, metaphysics, and ethics, the statements of which fail to be empirically verifiable, are not productive of any concrete accomplishments. Thus many areas that traditionally drained the energy of philosophers were decided to be meaningless. It is perhaps ironic that the quest for meaning took the form of a demonstration that much of what men value highly is, in fact, meaningless. In looking for meaning, the positivists found meaninglessness.

The Meaningfulness of Intuition: Bergson

Whereas the rational methods of positivist and analytic philosophy were refusing to give man a weapon to unravel ultimate mysteries of life, non-rational methods of discovering truth were gaining new respect in certain areas of philosophy. In the midst of their scientific paradise, men began to turn from the scientific methods to *intuition* to gain true understanding of life. Thus, when scientific philosophers placed ultimate emphasis on intelligibility, clarity, and symbolically communicable information, there also arose counter currents bringing forth *intuitive* and *mystical* philosophies. Renewed interest in Eastern philosophies developed, and in the Western world, a flourishing zeal for *Zen* emerged.

For the Zen Buddhist, humanity is comparable to three billion greyhounds in frantic pursuit of a mechanical hare on a vast race track. Will they ever learn that what they take to be a real hare is just a mechanical hoax? People become subjugated to desires, emotions, and things of the world that should be subjugated to them. In the midst of this dark miasma, Zen offers man enlightenment that can make it possible for him to free himself from the bondages of life. This is achieved through an ego-shattering experience called *satori. Satori* results when man undergoes a fundamental transformation of values that leaves him with a new and meaningful vision of life. An experience so moves a man that he comes to see life in a new light. He learns to find eternal value in the finite things of existence and to rise above the routine traps of life that ensnare so many of us.

To attain *satori,* it is essential to put aside the intellect and to see with a "third eye," the eye of intuitive vision. We, in the West, have spent thousands of years developing our intellect to gain knowledge and control of nature, but we have lost control of ourselves in doing so. Western man has perfected his intellect to gain truth, but has not gained it. The intellect provides external, abstract, uncertain knowledge. This is the type of knowledge required for science—but is the knowledge we need for scientific enlightenment adequate for human illumination? The Zen Buddhist concludes that it is not. Science leads us away from life. Scientific communication is transmitted through language. Yet it may be that the river of life is too elusive to be grasped by the net of language. In what may seem like a paradox, the Zen Buddhist maintains that in order to truly know, one must abandon the intellect.

The centipede was happy, quite,
until a toad in fun

said, "Pray, which leg goes after which?"
This worked his mind to such a pitch,
He lay distracted in a ditch,
considering how to run.[40]

If one thinks too much, he may cut himself off from the art of living. The Zen Buddhist claims that only *Buddhi* knows. Buddhi is the faculty of direct awareness; it is not something that can be demonstrated by logic or understood merely by being told; it is something one must discover for himself in experiencing life.

This perspective is a natural one in the Eastern world, but one much less natural in the scientific world of Western civilization. And yet, a scientifically oriented French philosopher formulated an elaborate defense of *intuition* as a fundamental means of attaining knowledge. Much of the evidence adduced by this philosopher was not solid, but his case was imaginatively and ingeniously constructed.

In rebelling against the mechanistic and overly intellectualistic philosophies that had become prominent in the nineteenth century, Henri Bergson (1859–1941) drew a distinction between two kinds of knowledge. We can know things, he said, either *relatively* or *absolutely*. We gain relative knowledge by *observation* and *description*. If we wish to gain knowledge of some object, we locate it, observe it, measure it, and then write up a description of our observations. This kind of knowledge, according to Bergson, is symbolical or discursive knowledge. It is knowledge that can be communicated to others by objective means. In gaining this knowledge one remains outside of the object, and in so doing one does not gain complete understanding of it. This symbolical knowledge is also *analytical* in the sense that it breaks the object down into its elements. Something precious is lost in this analytic approach, for in so concentrating on parts we miss the *unity*. The drawback of analytic knowledge is that it can't see the forest for the trees; its virtue, on the other hand, is that it can give us a good description of the trees, if that's what we are interested in.

The other way we can know is *absolutely*. Whereas relative knowledge is mediated, or gained through the medium of symbols (language), *absolute knowledge* is *immediate* and direct. It is nonsymbolical. It does not have to be put into words because it is experienced directly. It is intuitive knowledge. Through a feeling of sympathy one merges with the object, and in merging with it one completely knows it. Now relative knowledge is precise and objective, and yet, it invariably lacks certainty. Our scientific tools provide us at best with approximate knowledge however small it may be, some margin of error is always allowable. No matter how high the probabilities are, science can never yield absolute certainty. In contrast, nonscientific intuitive knowledge is absolute—there can be no doubt about it! Thus Bergson felt there is a superiority to intuitive knowledge. The sciences, he maintained, give us only a static picture of reality; therefore, a meta-

---

[40] Alan W. Watts, *The Way of Zen* (New York: New American Library, n.d.), p. 39.

physics of intuition is essential if we are to have absolute knowledge of reality as the dynamic process it is.

The most obvious criticism of Bergson's argument is the claim that intuition may provide us with an insight into reality, but this insight becomes knowledge only when it is tested by scientific means. That is, intuition may be very valuable in giving us a lead, but that lead must be followed up with good scientific confirmation before we can call it knowledge. Intuition does have a romantic aura about it, which is appealing, and it does leave one with a feeling of absolute certainty, but often what one needs is a spice of doubt. Imagine a judge telling a man on trial that even though all the evidence is in his favor, that evidence is only scientific and therefore, inadequate. Then he adds, "I am going to throw out the evidence because I feel very deeply that you are guilty. In fact, I have an intuition amounting to absolute certainty that you are guilty." Now, we would say that it is perfectly all right for intuition to give a detective a lead about a suspect, but that this intuition then will have to be verified by evidence or thrown out. And this is also the case in science. I might *feel* very deeply in my bones that you are a boojum, but that does not necessarily make you one. No one really denies there is intuition, but the question is whether it is a way of knowing or guessing. A person of scientific temper would say intuition is good only for guessing, and we would all agree that there are many areas where we should want to rely on the methods of science and formal procedure in gaining knowledge. But there may also be certain things we can know best by intuition—that is, there may be areas in which intuition seems to give us absolute knowledge, not just a clue we can test later. Thus, if one loves a person very deeply—so profoundly he feels one with that person, he can probably know his beloved better than a psychologist can with all his aptitude tests, observations of overt behavior, and analogies with behavior of lower animals. It might be that a person's entire character can be revealed to another in a flash of intuition. Something happens, and we just know that the person is a phony or is for real. There are times when intuition can show us things that are inaccessible to scientific analysis. If one gets out and immerses himself in the beauties of nature, he may understand them better than he would if he looked at them through a microscope. Indeed, science is full of great discoveries that were made by intuition. To be sure, the scientist then had to collect evidence to prove his intuition to his colleagues, but the point is that *he* knew that what his intuition told him was true even before he did a single experiment.

Thus it seems there are some things we can know best through analysis and others we can know best through intuition. In any case there is certainly one thing, Bergson maintained, we can know better by intuition than by science or analysis. That one thing is our own self. We intuit our self flowing through time. Most people might believe that they should be the ones to know themselves best and could do so by some act of introspection. But behaviorists and positivists all believe that the most reliable knowledge that can be gained is that based upon external observations of the social scientist. Of course, at one point in the *Encyclopedia of Unified Science,* the logical positivist Carnap did become daring and admit that a person might actually know when he gets angry even without looking at his nervous system aided by a psychological instrument or at the play of his facial muscles. Yes, I think one might!

Bergson felt that the malady of modern man was that he dwelled in the world of space rather than of time. In his book *Time and Free Will*, Bergson described space as the sphere of quantity. We conceive of space as homogeneous, even though we really know that it is amorphous. The homogeneity, or uniformity, is not in space; it is put in space by us. It is an abstraction worked out by the intellect to make it possible to deal with space in intellectually manageable terms, for in a purely homogeneous space one can discover similarities and repetitions of events, and on the basis of these, predictions can be made. The trouble with all these efforts to provide us with manageable ideas of space, complained Bergson, is that the spatial world is not the real world. There is no such thing as a *point* in space; a point in space is not reality, but an abstraction from reality. The real world is a dynamic world of action, of never-ending activity. When we think of space, we think of position in space, but even an elementary physics textbook will tell us that a moving object has no position. Now, as Bergson saw it, everything in the world was moving—nothing had position. If there is no position, then there is no point in seeking to understand in spatial categories.

Going a step further, Bergson argued that just as position implies space, so movement implies time. We stand still at a place, but we move through time. In our world where nothing stands still, there is no space, but time is of the essence. Space may be an abstraction from reality, but the world of time and of change is real. But what is time? Time is not the reality discovered through the clock. It is not a long line divided by a series of instants. The scientist thinks he can measure time. He takes a clock and measures time with it by breaking it down into measurable units—into seconds, minutes, and hours. The assumption is that one moment of time is the same as any other moment of time. Although this is true of clocks, it is not true of *men*. To a man, the hour he stands waiting on the cold corner for his girl is not at all interchangeable with the hour he spends parked in the car with her. Bergson is right in believing there are no two identical moments in the life of the self. Time is not a measurable quantity; it is an inner *duration*. It is impossible to break it down into discrete units of measurement because time is an experienced continuity. It is something we can grasp only by intuitions as a felt continuity. Our inner life is a continuous flowing, not a mathematical succession of instants. There is something drastically wrong with chopping time into pieces. It is a distortion of reality to try to measure the *life* of a man by a clock. Bergson well knew that for a man there is no such thing as an *instant* without duration. Man does not live in instants but in durations.

Although the reality of man may be a deeply intuited self flowing in time, Bergson realized that most persons fail to live on this level of reality. Most of the time, people live "outside" themselves, allowing their lives to unfold in space rather than in time. They live for the external world instead of for themselves, reacting to the external environment. In a sense it is easier to live in external space than to live deep within, because doing so provides an outer order. That is, people want to live in a stable environment because uncertainty is a frightening thing and they want to be sure of what will come. But in doing this, they come to live *for* that environment. By living in the world of space, however, one becomes shallow. A man is conditioned by the stimuli about him, mechanically responding to them, instead of living creatively. Such a person is not really *free,* but if he would penetrate to his deepest self, he could gain freedom. Bergson claimed that in moments of great crisis one can oppose his self to the outer course of events, and, in the process, discover freedom. Bergson's insight into the nature of freedom is brilliant, for what can we really mean by freedom except the ability to resist the conditioning influences of our environment? If a man can develop his inner personality so as to resist drifting with the flow of events in the external world, must we not regard him as a free man?

For Bergson, then, reality is *temporal.* In effect, his advice for man is to learn to flow with the stream of time. By being oriented to reality in terms of time rather than of space, men are enabled to experience freedom. Space can be very confining and everything in it can be neatly arranged, including life. The rigidity of being caught in the matrix of spatial understanding is inconsistent with being free. Everything has its place in space, and thus thinking about reality in terms of space limits one to a place. This is too static. Where space is discontinuous and static, however, time is continuous and dynamic. Bergson had a cosmic vision of dynamic becoming, through an understanding of which man can overcome his spatial limitations. Bergson flatly denied that reality could be understood in categories of substance, as it had been by traditional metaphysicians; nor could it be conceived of in terms of Platonic Ideas or eternally unchanging forms. The entire metaphysical structure of *Being*—Ideas, Forms, Substance—was being unearthed by the tremors of the Bergsonian metaphysical whirl of *Becoming.* For Bergson reality was not understood as Being, but as Becoming. That is why time is the essential component of his cosmic vision. The world of dynamic change or flowing time is very real. By perceiving life in terms of time it is possible to grasp reality in its continuity.

Bergson's dynamic intuition of reality had profound influence on the arts and literature. Particularly impressed by Bergson's vision of fluid time was the great writer Marcel Proust who attended Bergson's lectures. In his writing Proust very decisively took us away from thinking of time as we would think of frames in a film strip. His writings forced us to understand that what Bergson called "duration" is the fluid time of real living; time experienced dynamically cannot be cut up into static images.

In a practical sense it is important for us to realize that Bergson's theories of time imply activity, pure movement, doing, and therefore, the emphasis falls on process rather than on form. In the Bergsonian vision the focus centers on how a man is changing—not upon what he is, but upon what he is becoming. To realize this dynamic potential of living and to ignite the spark of existence in oneself meant repudiating thinking in terms of space, and that implied rejecting materialistic and mechanistic assumptions.

For Bergson an especially important proof of the inadequacy of materialistic and mechanistic philosophies was the functioning of human memory. What Bergson calls "duration" refers to the self's experience of its own creative process, of its own apprehension of living time. Every self has its particular temporal continuity, and it is memory that gives this continuity to each man's temporal experience. The successive moments in the life of a human being are preserved in his memory. The meaning of anything we perceive derives from our associating it in our memory with other experiences we have had. Indeed, we could not survive if we had no memory, for memory is what makes it possible for us to make intelligent choices. It binds our experiences together and makes our lives meaningful. People are too prone to break time down into past, present, and future, but by doing so they destroy all sense of continuity and lose the past forever. By understanding time as something objective and essentially outside of us, we see the past as something behind us, with the result that our lives become less full. In reality, the past is never gone. It is conserved by our memory and thus ever remains a part of us. If man truly learns to understand time as duration, his inner being becomes deeply enriched and all of his experiences belong to him forever. Through his memory man can preserve his experiences and retain the past.

Bergson believed that memory cannot be a purely physical function, for it just did not seem possible that a finite, limited mechanism like the brain would have room for the infinite variety of all the images of our lives. Bergson distinguished between the *motor* aspect of memory and *pure* memory. Motor memory is built up through habit formation—for example, walking—and may be simply physiological. But pure memory cannot possibly be mechanical in this way. Bergson maintained that pure memory is independent of the brain and cannot be conceived of in mechanistic terms. Philosophers tried to say that the mind is just an aspect of the body—that the mind, to use their terminology, is nothing but an "epiphenomenon" (or by-product) of the brain. Bergson reasoned that if this were true, then any lesion to the brain should result in corresponding injury to the memory. To check this out, he studied the memory and found evidence that injury to the brain does *not* impair the functioning of the memory. He also found that in certain cases of memory loss, there was no accompanying suffering of injury to the brain. He regarded both of these facts as providing further confirmation that there is no connection between mind or memory, on the one hand, and brain on the other.

Bergson notwithstanding, modern students of brain functioning make a positive connection between memory and the physical brain. One intriguing approach regards RNA (ribonucleic acid) as the carrier of memory through the chemical coding of its molecular arrangement. RNA can occur in such multitudinous patterns and combinations that it may be regarded as possessing the capacity of accounting for any memory load the brain could ever need to hold. Scientists have even found a way of testing if memory is related to these RNA molecules by simply seeing whether or not it is possible to convey it from one individual to another by the transference of these molecules. Experiments have been carried out in which flatworms that were well-trained were cut up and served for dinner to other flatworms that were untrained. The results showed the untrained flatworms that ate the trained ones had a much higher learning capacity than fellow flatworms that had not had the benefits of a diet of well-trained flatworms. Thus, it would seem the memory pattern of the trained flatworms had been transferred to the untrained cannibalistic flatworms.

Numerous other experiments point in the same direction, so it seems we may disregard Bergson's assertion that there is no credible evidence establishing a connection between memory and brain. But this does not mean that we can afford to disregard Bergson. One must be cautious in deciding just what the implications of evidence are. It is a notorious truth that diametrically opposed combatants in the mind-body debate may produce rather similar evidence to support their most different conclusions. Wilhelm Roux, a biologist in the *mechanist* camp of biological interpretation, carried out an experiment in which he cut a frog's egg in half and from it, produced a partial embryo that was responsible for bringing to life the rest of the embryo. Roux's conclusion was that parts *mechanically* reproduce themselves; biologists do not need to speak about the "life" of an organism because the organism is just a bunch of molecules undergoing certain physical and chemical processes. After all, you do not even need a real live frog to make another frog; all you need are enough frog molecules. His experiments, he thought, clinched the mechanist case. The biological theory directly in opposition to the mechanist is the *vitalist,* which denies that life can be explained in physicochemical terms. A distinguished vitalist biologist, Hans Dreisch, carried out an experiment in which he severed a sea urchin's egg into two, and each of the halves redeveloped into a complete embryo. This led Dreisch to conclude that new life could *not* be produced by purely mechanical means. As he saw it, if it was only a question of molecules, then half a sea urchin's egg should produce no more than half a sea urchin. There had to be a vital spark of life that had not been cut by his scalpel. Thus each biologist used virtually identical evidence to support polar opposite conclusions about the nature of life. The lesson to be gleaned from this is that facts do not speak for themselves, but take on meaning in terms of some interpretative scheme. The justification of such schemes often cannot be given merely in terms of factual evidence. Rather, these schemes must be justified in consideration of how well they account for our general understanding of things and our general experience.

Thus the weakness of Bergson's evidence need not finish off Bergson for us. There is a logical point, which Bergson marshaled against mechanists, that is far stronger than his evidence and has much validity. This point is the fact that states of consciousness being closely correlated with neural processes in the brain does not by any means prove that the states of mind are the same thing as brain processes. Consciousness may depend upon the brain to some extent, but this does not imply that it is the same as the brain, any more than the fact that a coat hanging on a hook in some sense depends on the hook implies the coat is the same as the hook. It is a rather gross fallacy to assert that two things are identical just because they are constantly correlated or generally discovered to be associated with or in relation to one another. On this level of argument one may conclude that Bergson was justified in assuming that the materialists had failed to establish their case.

If anything shows that materialism must be consigned to the philosophical rubbish heap it is, according to Bergson, the story of evolution. The essence of reality is the vital impulse, the *élan vital*, a drive toward individuality. *Life* is an upward, creative movement. It is opposed by *matter*, which exerts a *downward* pull. Bergson saw in the story of evolution the struggle of a vital force to overcome matter. He disagreed with Darwin's insistence that variations in species can occur by blind chance. To make this point he had to take on two of the primary theories of the nature of life in the history of ideas—the *mechanist* and *teleological* viewpoints. According to the mechanist position, the living organism is a machine subject to invariable and absolute rules of nature. All events in the universe occur in strict accord with predetermined laws of nature. These laws do not result from any cosmic purpose or from any divine plan. Things happen simply because of the way nature works, not because of any purpose. The teleologist disagrees. He maintains that there is a grand plan in the cosmos, and all that happens does so to fulfill some purpose. Through the history of philosophy, mechanists and teleologists locked in titanic struggle to determine which was right. Bergson denounced both views. He found mechanism wanting in many respects. For example, although molluscs developed in an entirely different evolutionary pattern from that of vertebrates, sight developed in both. It could hardly happen by chance that two such different routes could lead to the same destination. Thus there must be some inner force, some impulsion in life urging evolution in a certain direction. Furthermore, Bergson supposed that the belief, held since the time of Francesco Redi in the seventeenth century, that life cannot be produced by nonliving matter showed materialism is inadequate as an explanation of the origins of life. There is one problem with Bergson's argument here—it is wrong! It is not true that life can be created only from that which is living. In fact, in 1828—thirty-one years before Bergson was born—a German chemist named Friedrich Wöhler had synthesized the "organic" compound urea out of nonliving ingredients in his laboratory, thereby demonstrating that the so-called products of life were no different from other chemicals. More recently, in December 1967, Dr. Arthur Kornberg was reported to assert that genetic material he helped synthesize in a test tube could, with reservations, be considered a primitive form of life. At Stanford University, Kornberg and Dr. Mehran Goulian of the University of Chicago manufactured viral DNA, the nucleic acid essence of life, and it produced active viruses in living cells. The viral DNA molecule synthesized can reproduce itself inside a living cell and generate new viruses.

With these facts in mind, it is obvious why Bergson could not establish that materialist philosophy is untenable. However, his specific arguments against materialism were not as important as his general conviction that any *mechanical* interpretation of life fails to account for the creativity and spontaneity men encounter. On this score Bergson was as hostile to teleological accounts of life as he was to mechanistic ones, for neither leaves any room for the freedom Bergson believed to be a part of life. The mechanist position is based upon the assumption that everything happens in accordance with laws of cause and effect. The teleological position presumes all that occurs does so in accordance with a purposive plan. According to the mechanist doctrine, all events are a consequence of *past* combinations of matter in motion and physical forces; according to the teleologist, all behavior and events are a consequence of a *future* goal or purpose. In either case, man is not creating his own life, but is being created by mechanical or spiritual forces of life. Bergson wanted no part of such an existence, for he believed that a more adequate account of life could be offered by directing attention to man's creative, intuitive life, rather than to his origins or his ends.

In a time of obsessive outward expansion, of manifest destiny, of Faustian madness, Bergson directed us to the unexplored areas within. We have now moved into the domain of outer space and have reached the moon, but we have not yet reached the shores of our inner being. Ours is an age in which the bomb hovers above us and we could physically be blown to bits; it is an age in which products of mechanism, such as our compulsion to compartmentalize all the domains of life and our compulsion to specialize, are blowing us to bits sociologically and psychically. Before we shall achieve any meaningful political integration, we shall have to find *personal* integration. There is a deeper self than the superficial one, which is a product of a *spatial orientation*. It is this deeper self that man must discover in a day when the infinity of space seems ever more real and humanity ever more lost.

The question of *knowing* deeper truths, of knowing a more real and substantial self, of course, all depends upon whether such an entity exists to be known. The question of what is *real*, of what the *object* of knowledge is, is the province of metaphysics.

Summary

1. The discipline of epistemology is the study of knowledge. It involves systematic inquiry into and analysis of such questions as the origins and validity of knowledge, the meaning of knowledge, and its extent and limitations.

2. Epistemological questions are not merely of academic interest, for they emerge from life situations. In many of man's practical activities and in serious matters of reflection, there looms the question of what and how man can know. Can man be certain in important matters? Is he just guessing and formulating an opinion, or is he truly aware of what is? Man is faced

with epistemological issues not just in philosophical speculation but in law, science, economics, psychology, and religion.

3. The basic epistemologies or theories of knowledge in classic philosophy are Rationalism, Empiricism, and Kantian Criticism.

4. *Rationalism* in epistemology is the view that the primary criterion for knowing lies, not in our senses or in perception, but in reason. It is held by many of the leading rationalists that through the process of deductive reasoning, certain necessary truths can be discovered. Inductive analysis and experimental research are accorded inferior status compared to a mathematical approach to understanding. Fundamental truths are regarded as self-evident to reason, and thus, the need for empirical validation of them was obviated. Many rationalists asserted that truth was innate or within man and only had to be reasoned out.

5. Plato, Descartes, Spinoza, and Leibniz are among the great rationalist philosophers. All of these men placed enormous significance upon the role of mathematics in understanding and in life.

6. *Empiricism* is the epistemological thesis that the only source of knowledge is sense experience. Since experience is the source of our knowledge, most empiricists conclude that there can be no certainty and no necessary truths. This is so because experience is contingent. Furthermore, since all is regarded as being derived from experience, the view that there are innate ideas is precluded.

7. Some of the most influential modern empiricist philosophers are John Locke, Bishop Berkeley, and David Hume.

8. Locke maintained that, at birth, the mind is like a blank tablet, and we must write upon it with experience to attain knowledge. Locke believed our senses provided us with knowledge of an objective physical world out there. This view is known as *realism* in epistemology.

9. There are two basic forms of realism. One is *common sense* realism and the other is *representative* realism. Common sense realism is the doctrine that through his senses, man attains *direct* and immediate knowledge of the objective world out there. Representative realism is the view that our senses provide us with a *copy* of the world out there rather than with a direct apprehension of it.

10. Berkeley maintained that since all we can know is what we perceive, we cannot hold anything exists outside of our perceptions. Therefore, we cannot know that a physical world exists. The only things we can maintain that exist are our perceptions and our minds and God, which *have* the perceptions.

11. David Hume developed the modern empiricist theory of knowledge to skeptical conclusions. If all we can know is our perceptions, not only can we not know that an objective world beyond them exists, but we cannot know there is a self, a mind, or a God—for the spiritual or mental cannot be perceived.

12. If things in philosophy seemed to be falling apart with Hume, it was the great German philosopher Kant who tried to put them together again. Rationalists believed we could have knowledge before experience, whereas empiricists insisted we could have it only after experience. With great brilliance Kant showed there was an element of truth in both theories. There must be experience to supply the raw data for knowledge, and yet, this raw data is always being structured by the mind. Thus the mind is not a blank tablet. In the very act of experiencing the world, the mind is giving it shape. This means that man never gets experience as it is in itself, but always as it is colored by his mind. Kant did not deny the importance of the *senses*—the empiricist focus—nor did he minimize the significance of the *mind*—the rationalist focus.

13. One of the consequences of Kant's philosophy was to show that man can never know what reality is independently of the mind's way of shaping it. He expressed this by saying we can never know the thing-in-itself. Contemporary epistemologies tried to show that we can know objective reality, but because there was no decisive or conclusive answer, philosophers began to question whether it was at all profitable to ask what we can know. Instead of expending great energy on a question we may be unable to answer, the idea developed that we should ask what we *mean* rather than what we *know*. Thus in contemporary philosophy, there developed a shift from *theory of knowledge to theory of meaning*. This approach led to the view that many questions and ideals that historically have been taken seriously are actually *meaningless*.

14. The scientific approach to understanding certainly played a considerable role in leading to the conclusion that many of our philosophical concerns are meaningless. It was the scientist Henri Bergson, who became a great philosopher, who sought to show there is a higher kind of knowledge than scientific knowledge. This higher type is *intuition*. He believed there is a fundamental force in life—a vital spirit—that can never be analyzed by science but can be known by intuition.

What Is Real?
Metaphysics

In Pursuit of Being:
Introduction to Metaphysical Problems

We are caught up in an information revolution—never have so many *known* so much, and yet ironically, perhaps never have they *"been"* so little! We are receiving so much information that we are losing the opportunity to experience the world; and we are not making sense of all that information, not being really rational about it. Morris R. Cohen observed the irony in our situation: "Reason lost ground because of the spread of literacy." It is one thing to have information, but it is another thing to assimilate such information into one's life and to live by it. We may express this another way by saying that if we have more *knowledge* than *Being*, we shall not be able to *understand* such knowledge that we have. If our information fails to open us and enlarge us emotionally, it will merely serve to create pathology. Information must have feedback into our human or emotional system, or else our lives, cut off from what we know, will ring false. On a superficial level we hear much talk today about a *generation gap*, but the real gap that is causing havoc in our entire civilization is the gap between *what we know* and *what we are*. Humanly and morally we cannot catch up to our knowledge. Today man has more knowledge—facts and technical information—than he can integrate into his existence.

We have all heard that a little knowledge can be a dangerous thing, but we do not often realize that a lot of knowledge can be just as dangerous. Certainly knowledge, understood in the sense of information, can be profoundly dangerous because it conditions us to be shallow. As Oliver L. Reiser says, "Gloomy predictions have been made about the future of the human race. Of these many prophecies one of the more plausible is that man will eventually bury himself under the mountains of factual data he is piling higher and higher with each passing year."[1] In such a time metaphysics is more ignored than ever, and yet, is probably more needed. It is essential to probe and explore the farthest reaches of reality if man is going to find himself. Metaphysical quest, in itself, should deepen and enrich character.

The ultimate quest of metaphysics is for being and reality. In a world that has been rendered so artificial by the remaking of environment through science and technology, reality has come to seem elusive. Inevitably, man has to try to find a means of getting back in touch with the real. Metaphysics can show the way, for behind all its abstruse technicalities lies this goal of finding reality and putting man in contact with it. Thus it is instructive and ultimately practical to consider some of the great issues of metaphysics, some of the philosophies that have sought to resolve them, and the fundamental stakes at issue in these philosophies.

OF MAKING A LOVER

Suppose you meet the perfect mate, someone ideal in every respect, and who does everything you want. Further, this wonderful mate fulfills the sexual relationship. This mate is physically attractive, and as it is said, very well built. There is one problem, and it is that this mate is really well built because it was constructed rather than born. Your potential spouse is an *android*. Thus you will have a mate who has everything — everything, that is, but a soul. If you are a woman, would you marry your dream man if you discovered he was missing a soul? If you are a man, would you marry your dream woman if you found out she was minus a soul? Are you too prejudiced against computers?

William James has raised this problem, and it is known to philosophers as the problem of the "mechanical sweetheart." The problem gives rise to

[1] Oliver L. Reiser, *The Integration of Human Knowledge* (Boston, Mass.: Porter Sargent Publisher, 1958), p. 39.

the question of whether one could be satisfied with all of the physical requirements of life, if to take advantage of them would mean losing one's soul. A fundamental metaphysical issue is at stake here, for if this android did everything a human did and differed only in one respect, that of not having a soul, how would one *know* the difference? Where is the soul? What is it? What difference does it make? Unless someone tells you this is an android, would you ever miss *soul?* If soul makes no behavioral differences, do we have any basis for assuming it exists? And if it does make behavioral differences, just what are they?

The question is, then, *is* there really such a thing as a soul? What is involved here is a fundamental metaphysical question whether we can better understand reality materialistically or spiritualistically. Can nature be accounted for purely in physicochemical terms? What about man? Must he be understood as a part of nature in physicochemical terms, or is there something distinctive about man? Is he set off from the rest of nature by possessing an immaterial dimension in his being, a soul?

If man is just a physicochemical entity, as the materialists claim, can reality then be understood in terms of unbreakable laws of cause and effect *necessarily* determining all that happens? Yes, if we are to believe the scientific system of Newtonian physics, which seemed to imply that nature could be fully explained in terms of a deterministic scheme. Social scientists, seeking to import the successful accomplishments in the realm of physics to the social sciences, also formulated a deterministic explanation of all human behavior. Behaviorism, associational psychology, and Freudian psychoanalysis all assume human behavior to be induced by necessary laws of cause and effect rather than of free will. The behaviorist views man as a byproduct of his heredity and environment, and thus, what he does is not a result of his choices but of genetic factors and conditioning. The associationist claims that man's mind works by automatically making connections between the bits of information stored there, with no more choice than a computer has when it is programmed to do sorting operations. And Freud took the position that everything a person does or says is based on deepseated subconscious drives over which he has no control.

In each of these descriptions, man is but a complicated machine. He does not *choose* his own life, and because he does not, he cannot be held responsible for it. Thus it would seem that if determinism is true, morality cannot be meaningful; for if morality is to have meaning, we must be able to praise or blame men; but if men are not *responsible* for their actions, then praise or blame are meaningless. Thus, whether or not reality is mechanically determined has exceedingly significant implications for our understanding of our world and of ourselves. Do we live in a universe of unpredictable chance or of necessary laws? Are we responsible for our actions and lives or not? These are fundamental questions with which serious men must come to terms.

To answer these questions, we must know what reality is. It is interesting that every school of psychoanalysis, however it may differ from the other, defines psychosis as a state of being out of contact with reality. The problem is that most analysts are uninterested in the question of what reality is. How are these men to restore their patients to reality when they don't know what it is? Too often they do not look beyond our social structure to discover if it is necessary to put one in contact with something more permanent, meaningful, and real than the social patterns of our society. Thus, too often the analyst takes his task to be one of merely *adjusting* the patient to the social pattern. The analyst usually does not even consider the possibility that it may be society that is sick, out of touch with reality, as Erich Fromm and others have suggested. But if this is the case, then will not the analyst be taking the patient's money to make him sicker? This troubling question provides another demonstration that the nature of reality cannot be ignored by people who wish to live sane and satisfying lives. What is reality?

This advertisement reproduced through the courtesy of The Coca-Cola Company, owner of the registered trademark "Coca-Cola" and "Coke" which identify the same product.

The tradition of Western philosophy has provided three types of answers to this question. *Materialism* answers that the world is constituted of matter in motion (material particles or extended substance), and there are no spiritual components to it. *Idealism* answers that because reality can be *thought* (since it can be grasped by the mind), it must in some sense be of a mental nature; that is, reality itself must be some sort of idea. The third answer is that of *naturalism*. In fact, materialism may be considered as a form of naturalistic philosophy, although not all naturalistic philosophy is materialist in the sense of reducing everything in the universe to physics and chemistry. The primary standpoint of naturalism is that it explains all reality in terms of *nature* and rejects all supernaturalistic accounts of phenomena. The naturalist is also fervently committed to *scientific method* as the only reliable means of understanding nature. Naturalism assumes a much broader conception of nature than materialism, for it does not insist that all is matter in motion or is reducible to that which is physicochemical in nature. The materialist leaves no room for purpose or value in nature.

Such conceptions of reality are not only of interest to the academician or philosopher in an ivory tower but they have significant practical implications. For example, whether one is materialist or idealist seems to have considerable influence on one's political and social attitudes. Historically, materialists have been more radical and reformist in orientation than have idealists. This is natural because their philosophy emphasizes material conditions—economic and political actualities. If there is nothing beyond material conditions, then one will obviously want to make those conditions as beneficial as possible. If there is no hereafter, one had better seek to make life here as heavenly as it can be made. Thus Karl Marx, a materialist, called for revolution to bring about the dawning of a veritable heaven on earth in the form of the classless society.

The Quality of Reality: Materialism vs. Idealism

MATTER MATTERS MOST: MATERIALISM

Those who seek the salvation of paradise, but are impatient about waiting for the kingdom of heaven to come, need wait no longer. They can now go to paradise themselves—by plane. It is not at all an easy trip, but it is possible. For a veritable heaven has been discovered right here on earth. Long have men known legends of Shangri-La, an earthly paradise, but now it is known that such a wonderland of natural wealth and happy health represents a reality. Of course, just as there is no royal road to learning, there is no royal road to paradise; this eternal Garden of Eden is virtually without any road to it at all. And yet, for the stouthearted who persevere, who are fortunate enough to fly *through* mountains (the route by air is through a dangerously narrow gorge), and who are lucky enough to make it along treacherous mountain roads that are constantly being washed out by avalanches, there does lie the magnificent treasure of the good life in a most sublimely beautiful atmosphere. One of the privileged few from our civilization to visit this earthly paradise—the independent kingdom of Hunza in the Himalayas, part of West Pakistan—provides us with a description of this fascinating Garden of Eden:

> In Hunza, people manage to live over one hundred years of age in perfect mental and physical health; and men father children at ninety. But their greatest achievement is the fact that sickness is rare, that cancer, heart disease, heart attacks, high or low blood pressure, and childhood diseases are virtually unknown. There is no juvenile delinquency in Hunza, and divorce

is a rarity. There are no jails, police, or army, and there is no need for them, as there hasn't been a crime reported for the last one hundred and thirty years.[2]

We also are reminded by Renee Taylor, who has been there, that:

While the rest of the civilized world talks of nuclear destruction and fallout shelters, the people of this remote state of Pakistan live in peace, harmony and brotherly love. Fear, hatred and jealousy do not exist. They are friendly, hospitable, and religious people.[3]

Yes, the amazing Hunzakut are religious people, but it does not seem to be religion that makes them amazing. The good life and the long life of the Hunzakut are consequences not of the spiritual but of the material. The astute materialist Feuerbach made no bones about it, and proclaimed that man is what he eats. Modern man has a rather sorrowful diet and a not very happy life; the inhabitants of Hunza, on the other hand, have a beautiful diet and live beautiful lives. A party of visitors, stranded and hungry on a road in Hunza, were brought supplies of wonderful food by a Hunzakut boy. When the boy was offered payment for the food, he backed off, shaking his head, and explained something that is not easy to understand in the civilized world. He said: "Food is given by God to share—not to sell!"[4]

The world of the Hunza is a primitive world, cut off from the nagging tensions and perplexing complexities of our technological world. Man is what he eats, and everything the Hunzakut eats is attuned to the creation of a well-rounded and fulfilling existence. These people eat pure food, drink clear water, and breathe in fresh air. It is said that man cannot live on bread alone, but he would not do badly on *chapatti,* the Hunza bread, which is the mainstay of the Hunza diet. Unlike our "enriched" bread, it is rich in the nourishment of the grain. Made from wheat, barley, buckwheat, or millet, it is naturally enriched with phosphorous, potassium, iron, calcium, and manganese. Renee Taylor comments, "Hunza bread consists of all of the nutrients of the grain. Perhaps, this accounts for their strong nerves and vigor into old age, for they eat plenty of bread with every meal. This may account for the fact that the men over ninety are capable of fathering children and the women able to conceive at fifty years of age.[5]

To sum up, the Hunza paradise is not the result of anything supernatural. On the contrary, the very thing that makes it a paradise is its wonderful naturalness. The religious Hunzakut may seem close to heaven, but that is because they are so high up in the Himalayas. What is really important is how close they are to the earth.

Man may suppose that of all that exists in this universe, he alone stands

[2] Renee Taylor, *Hunza Health Secrets for Long Life and Happiness* (New York: Award Books, 1969) p. ix.
[3] *Ibid.,* p. x.
[4] *Ibid.,* p. 30.
[5] *Ibid.,* p. 99.

apart from things and above them, and that while nature may be objectively studied and comprehended by science, man has an immaterial mind and a free will that utterly elude the grasp of scientific understanding. Man presumes himself to be a creature of fleeting moods, of uncontrollable temperament, of spontaneity and creativity, and capable of taking a courageous stand or of choosing cowardly flight. By his will or his resignation, man can control his body. Against these presumptions, though, he is determined to do what he does by the functioning of his body, and, of course, what man's body is has much to do with what he eats. The more we come to know man, it seems, the more literally might we take the dictum of materialist Feuerbach that man is what he eats. Carlton Fredericks and Herbert Bailey inform us that glands—"pituitary, thyroid, adrenals, and others—control your functions almost entirely. By *functions,* we mean many functions of both body and what we call mind."[6] They continue:

> *Your glandular condition is a determining factor in how and why you will react at any given time to any situation. It will determine what your reaction toward life itself will be: whether one of jubilance, controlled optimism, "neutrality," or deepest pessimism. Although these moods can and do fluctuate within you almost every day, nevertheless the basic pattern of your personality is fairly constant if you are "normal," if you live under fairly regular circumstances and receive a fairly regular nutritional allowance each day.*[7]

So, it is not so much that our will determines what we do, as it is that our glands determine our will. When one does something we truly admire, perhaps we should not say, "That guy really has courage," but "That guy really has great glands." Fredericks and Bailey observe:

> *the endocrinologists have pinpointed many of our actions in our glandular behavior. For example, whether we will fight (be aggressive as the hungry lion) or flee in terror (as the hunted gazelle) depends in part upon the amount of epinephrine (adrenaline) released by our adrenal glands.*[8]

Fredericks and Bailey point out that endocrinologists think this gives "added proof of a mechanistic universe in which one has only to push the correct buttons in order to get the desired results."[9] Man is what the glands manufacture him to be, and they note, "what the glands manufacture and release is dependent upon what the glands receive in the form of nutrition."[10]

Though man may insist that he has a soul and that there is a spiritual dimension to reality, when we get down to hard facts there seems to be little to support notions of a spiritual realm. In explaining the workings of

---

6 Carlton Fredericks and Herbert Bailey, *Food Facts and Fallacies* (New York: Arc Books, Inc., 1969), p. 168.

7 *Ibid.*

8 *Ibid.*

9 *Ibid.,* p. 169.

10 *Ibid.*

the world in general and human functioning in particular, it is not spiritual but material factors to which we must refer. With the rise of modern scientific civilization, the conviction that adequate accounting for all facts of the universe must proceed naturalistically increasingly dawned upon man. This assumption inspired Frederick Engels to triumphantly announce:

> ... we have once again returned to the point of the great founders of Greek philosophy, the view that the whole of nature, from the smallest element to the greatest, from grains of sand to suns, from protista to men, has its existence in eternal coming to being and passing away, in ceaseless flux, in unresting motion and change, only with the essential difference that what for the Greeks was a brilliant intuition, is in our case the result of strictly scientific research in accordance with experience, and hence also it emerges in a much more definite and clear form.[11]

Ernst Haeckel is no less enthusiastic about rendering the universe intelligible in materialistic categories:

> All the particular advances, however, of physics and chemistry yield in theoretical importance to the discovery of the great law which brings them all to one common focus, the "Law of Substance." As this fundamental cosmic law establishes the eternal persistence of matter and force, their unvarying constancy throughout the entire universe, it has become the pole-star that guides our Monistic Philosophy through the mighty labyrinth to a solution of the world problem.[12]

Materialism is defended not only by intellectuals, but in ordinary human understanding as well, it emerges as the most natural explanation of what is out there or what is real. After all, a world of what we perceive as matter is always imposing itself upon our consciousness in so basic a way that we just take it for granted. Our senses are ever at work reporting a hard impenetrable massy world, which we cannot bend to our will. How can one deny the existence of the material world? We are engulfed in it as in a womb—the womb of all life. Matter nourishes and dominates man as a mother does her child. Indeed, "mother" derives from Latin and Greek words meaning "matter." If everything can be explained materialistically, and life arose from purely physicochemical causes, then matter is the mother of life; it is basic. Thus, whatever theories of soul they may develop, men do believe that matter is basic. They say they believe in a nonmaterial Supreme Being and a spiritual heaven, where they will go to reap the benefits of eternal existence after death, and yet, no one is in a hurry to depart from this material world to take advantage of that spiritual heaven. What people want to take advantage of is what they find here on earth.

Our senses communicate to us impressions of a world of matter, and

[11] Frederick Engels, *Dialectics of Nature* (New York: International Publishers, 1940), p. 13.

[12] Ernst Haeckel, *The Riddle of the Universe* (New York and London: Harper and Bros., 1901), p. 4.

since evidence of the existence of the spirit is so scant that sophisticated students of life have been led to assume that all is matter in motion, that all can be explained in categories of the physical or material rather than the psychical or spiritual, and that everything can be accounted for meaningfully in terms of the natural rather than the supernatural. Those who defend any of these views are known as materialists.

Materialism, then, is the doctrine that all facts of the universe may be understood as matter and motion. The building blocks of nature are composed of sheer matter, and so too are those of the human being. Mental or psychical processes can more intelligibly be understood in physical or chemical terms. Because he takes this line, the materialist is considered to be a "reductionist"; that is, he explains things by *reducing* all states of being to purely physical ones or material ones. He admits that there may *appear* to be such an entity as the mind, but there is no evidence of its actual existence. No one has ever seen a mind; indeed, by its very nature it cannot be seen. Of course, he believes in the existence of the subatomic particles postulated as existing by physicists, and these cannot be observed. But, he argues, such physical facts can be empirically verified. On the assumption there are electrons and such, we can predict and infer certain things that can be verified with our senses. But there is nothing we can specifically predict or infer by assuming there is an immaterial entity, "the mind." Those facts that we might consider *mental* can be meaningfully understood, not on the assumption there is a mind but in terms of physical processes, on the assumption that there is a physical organ—the brain. It makes sense to talk of a brain but not of a mind. We know where the brain is, and what it does. But where is the mind, and just what does it do? If one took an X-ray of the head he would not be able to see any mind, and if he opened the skull he could not feel it. No wonder mind has been called the ghost in the machine. Indeed, there seems to be so little evidence of its existence that it does not seem to be even an apparition; it is more a figment. Reliable physical evidence exists of the brain, the nervous system, and the entire physiological makeup of man, but there really is no evidence of an independent substance of a mental nature that we might call mind. Thus the body, including the activity of the brain, may be compared with a machine.

The materialist thus concludes that adequate explanation of our universe must proceed materialistically or naturalistically and not spiritualistically at any level. Research has reached such a point that not only has it become increasingly untenable for the spiritualist or mentalist to show that the material world is essentially spiritual or mental, but the poor fellow can no longer even make a decent case that the mental is mental. What had once been regarded as mental is coming to be understood more and more in terms of physical operations. In this connection it is interesting to note that the dedicated religious person who steadfastly insists that the spiritual exists and that all is not material can himself be changed into a nonreligious person by a simple physical operation. William Sargant reports that "Religious feelings in man may be destroyed if too *extensive* an operation is performed in the frontal lobes."[13] There is the revealing case of a woman Salvation Army worker. We are provided this account of her fate:

> For years she lay in a hospital, constantly complaining that she had committed sins against the Holy Ghost. She complained of it for weeks and months, and her poor husband decided to operate upon her. ... After the dressing had been taken off, I asked her, "How are you now? What about the Holy Ghost?" Smiling, she answered, "Oh, the Holy Ghost; there is no Holy Ghost."[14]

Now the operation, the leucotomy itself, may not directly change the religious belief (it may be changed in the reintegration of the personality after the operation), but in any case the change can be explained in terms of physicalistic principles.

More and more what was once regarded as beyond the pale of physico-chemical explanation is now being brought within the pale. Indeed, even memory, one of the great mysteries of the human mind, is coming to be less of a mystery as it is being explained as the electrochemical storage system of the brain. Memory is now understood as related to the capacity of brain cells for holding billions of pieces of information. Explaining memory as brain cells—in terms of DNA molecules and RNA molecules—has made it possible to understand much concerning this faculty and to carry out many fruitful experiments. Experiments have demonstrated that when a certain site in the brain is stimulated, specific details of information are recalled. Aside from the technical implications of this finding for experimental research, it seems to show that memory is a part of the brain, and cannot be intelligibly regarded as a function of the soul or of that which eludes material description. This conclusion lets the air out of a statement such as the following:

> I am duration, I am consciousness, that is, memory and liberty; therefore I am essentially a spirit, that is, a being outside the bounds of space, having nothing to do with matter; a being freed of materiality and of all that, proceeding from matter. ...[15]

Recent research not only concludes that the existence of memory fails to establish man as a unique spiritual being existing beyond space, but that memory is so much an electrochemical, physical phenomenon, that it may even become possible to take one person's memory and give it to someone else. We know that Dr. Allan L. Jacobson

> trained rats, injected material from their brains into untrained rats, who then speedily learned the same tasks. The only tasks they did learn with such unusual rapidity were precisely those that appeared to have been transmitted.

[13] William Sargant, *Battle for the Mind* (Garden City, N.Y.: Doubleday and Co., 1957), p. 89.

[14] *Ibid.*

[15] Jacques Chevalier, *Henri Bergson* (New York: The Macmillan Company, 1928), p. 161f.

Next, Jacobson and his colleagues reported success in transferring learning in a similar fashion from rats to hamsters and vice versa.[16]

Although the results of such experiments are far from conclusive, they do open the door to some fantastic possibilities. Thus it has been speculated that "if Einstein's understanding of relativity resided in certain RNA molecules of his brain, then the mere transfer of these molecules to another brain . . . should bestow upon the recipient the master's own thorough grasp of the subject."[17] Indeed, there are even more startling possibilities. In the exploration of memory storage, split-brain experiments were carried out on animals. R. W. Sperry carried out research that developed evidence showing either half of the brain cut off from the other can function efficiently on its own. Dr. Dean E. Woodbridge has imagined some tumultuous reverberations that could result from such split-brain experiments. For example, if you take a given brain and call it Tom and sever the two hemispheres,

> *we will then have two Toms instead of one: the two half brains will have exactly the same memories and each will feel itself to be the original individual. . . . A new personality has been created by surgery. . . .*

And that's not all:

> *. . . if you took Tom and Dick, split their brains, and were able to put one of Dick's half brains together with one of Tom's . . . if the combination did work, our theory would predict an interesting new kind of blended individual, possessing in one single consciousness the memories, learned habits, and senses of identity of both Tom and Dick. This would be schizophrenia with a vengeance.*[18]

Considering the direction in which research in cryobiology is pointing, we might see the possibility of taking the brain of an Einstein, freezing it until at some appropriate time in the future when it can be restored to life, and then transferring the contents to whomever we think would make a good Einstein. We could store all types of brains, and whenever there was a shortage of some types, we could produce that type. We would hear no more complaints that Leonardo was the last universal man, for we could blend together the brains of a scientific genius and an artistic genius to produce a modern universal man. And we could do it wholesale, by mass production.

There is no end to the achievements of which we are capable. José Delgado, the brilliant researcher in electrical brain stimulation, maintains that there are basic mechanisms *in the brain* "that are responsible for all mental activities, including emotion."[19] Operating upon such materialist

[16] Albert Rosenfeld, *The Second Genesis* (Englewood Cliffs, N.J.: Prentice-Hall, Inc., 1969), pp. 525–53.

[17] *Ibid.*, pp. 251–52.

[18] Quoted in *Ibid.*, p. 247.

[19] Maggie Scarf, "Brain Researcher José Delgado Asks—'What Kind of Humans Would We Like to Construct?'" *New York Times Magazine*, November 18, 1970, p. 46.

assumptions, man holds in his grasp the possibility of transforming himself as well as his environment. We could make the earth a Mount Olympus and ourselves, Greek gods directing our own destiny.

Of course, the research that reveals the mechanistic functioning of the mind does not in itself prove that *all* reality is matter. It might be that there are spiritual forces in the world, and we just do not have verifiable evidence of them. However, if we lack evidence of mentalistic or spiritualistic entities (and if we continually discover that things once understood to be mentalistic or spiritualistic can in fact be better described as physicochemical phenomena), it seems we have no basis for asserting any reality other than a material one. After all, what has been achieved on the assumption that mind, soul, or psychical reality of any type exists? Not much, really. In contrast, hypotheses based upon materialist assumptions seem to provide much more ground for achievement, and the possibilities are increasing every day.

It seems, then, that we know where man's "*head* is at," but not his *mind.* It looks like the materialist has successfully met the challenge of showing that the world can be intelligibly accounted for in terms of naturalistic forces. Before we consider what he makes of his position, however, let us see how materialist philosophy developed.

We merely open our eyes in the morning, and see all about us a world of material things. At the dawn of history man was particularly attuned to all material forces and environment, but he did not see *matter.* Indeed, it took a considerable period of evolutionary advance before man arrived at the point of seeing matter as such. We observe stars orbiting about in the heavens, encounter the wind and rain, view mountain ranges, flee from wild animals, build houses, and eat and sleep in them. We are fully involved in a material world, observing the physical world and engaging in physical activity in it. Yet the idea that things are constituted of matter is an abstraction from many theoretical or speculative possibilities of what things might be. The great Greek philosophers who, with brilliant perception and insight, began to explain the world in terms of naturalistic properties, were not technically "materialists," but *hylozoists,* for these early Greek philosophers believed that the things of the world were all interfused with *life.* Hylozoism is the view that all matter has life or is inseparable from life. Matter thus was not yet formulated as a distinct concept. Against the background of Greek mythology in which things were understood as happening at the whim of gods, this account of the universe in terms of natural principles constituted a giant step forward.

The first truly noteworthy advance in the development of a genuinely materialist philosophy, however, came with the Greek Atomists, Leucippus and Democritus. Because the materialist philosophy involves the reduction of all in the universe to *matter,* it usually explains material reality *mechanistically* and *atomistically.* The major tenets of the mechanistic view are that matter exists in *space,* and thus has location; it is *not penetrable,* and thus the space a given material object occupies cannot be occupied by any other, object; it has *magnitude,* and thus can be measured; and it has *motion.* The idea of mechanism is that the universe works like a well-oiled machine. All that happens does so because of inviolable laws operating in the universe without plan or design. The machine runs smoothly because of the interaction of material particles, not because of any human or spiritual design or purpose.

The major tenet of atomism is that reality can be analyzed into ultimate constituents that are basic, simple, and indivisible. Democritus explained atoms as innumerable particles—uncreated, incapable of being destroyed, or even of being altered. These ultimate particles, the atoms, can be distinguished from each other only in *quantitative* terms—that is, only by reference to size, shape, and mass. These atoms have the property of motion, and because they move, there must be a context in which they can move. Thus, along with the reality of the atoms there must be the reality of the void, or empty space in which movement of the atoms is possible. As these atoms move about, they collide with each other and rebound like billiard balls. From this interaction and rebounding, the emergence and operation of all things in the universe can be explained.

The philosophy of Democritus was an immense contribution to human understanding, not because of the particular elements of which it consisted, but because it was an effort to explain things in terms of that which can be measured. This was highly important to the formation of the scientific attitude, which contributed to the development of a tradition from which the materialistic, scientific explanation of the universe could be articulated. Before this could take place, however, the idea of matter had to be delimited. Paradoxical as it may seem, the sharpening of this concept was not achieved by materialistic philosophers, but by *dualists*—that is, men who believed that the universe consisted of both material and spiritual entities. This was the case because dualistic theories of reality—maintaining that both spirit and matter are real—absolutely depend upon a very careful circumscribing of their two conflicting principles. Thus dualism paved the way for a conception of the universe in terms of matter and spirit, of mind and body. The great French philosopher René Descartes divided reality into these two categories and clearly distinguished between them. Body or a material object is physical, can be perceived, is located in space, is open to public observation, and can be measured. As opposed to this, mind is not located in space, is not physical, is private, and thus cannot be observed and obviously cannot be measured. In fact, it was not at all clear what one could do with soul or spirit. Because one could investigate material objects scientifically, one could achieve progress in understanding them. Following Descartes, many philosophers completely gave up on the idea of soul or spirit, concentrating their full effort on the idea of matter.

One November night in 1619 René Descartes had a dream—a dream that provided him with a deep insight into most of reality. As he later understood it, the very Spirit of Truth visited him, and gave him vision of all the sciences in which the human mind has no role at all. He explained all nature and the life of all animals—except man—as being based upon purely mechanical forces. The only exception was the human mind. Thus the universe was envisioned as a grand scheme of swirling matter, all inextricably entwined in its precise and relentless mechanical functioning—all, that is, except the human mind, the soul of man. The mind and the soul of man fell outside the orbit of this vast complicated mechanical universe, this great Machine.

It did not take reflective individuals long to conclude that, as bold as Descartes's ideas were, they were not bold enough. He was still dreaming about mind, and an adequate account of things would have to place it, too, in the orbit of the Machine.

In France Descartes's dualist philosophy was quickly attacked by Pierre Gassendi (1592–1655), who developed an atomistic conception of the universe. Gassendi reasoned it was fundamental that nothing can come from nothing, and that nothing can become nothing; thus throughout all change there must be that which remains constant, and that can only be *matter*. Matter must be understood atomistically, as consisting of multitudes of solid and indivisible elements. They are indivisible because physical division, unlike mathematical division, cannot be extended endlessly; in mathematics we can divide a slice of pie into a billion pieces and speak of a billionth of a slice of pie, but we cannot physically cut a real piece of pie into a billion pieces. The motion of these indivisible atoms brings about all changes in nature. There must be empty space because there would otherwise be no place for the atoms to move. Motions can only come into being and go out of it through contact, and that means that every cause is a material cause. Because that which is not material cannot have any effect on that which is not, it must be concluded that even the soul can only move the body insofar as it is matter. With this simple but forceful reasoning, Gassendi claimed that Descartes was incorrect in his dualistic explanation of reality.

The most thorough and systematic statement of materialism at this stage was developed by British philosopher Thomas Hobbes. He developed a system that explained everything by general laws of matter in motion. Thomas Hobbes, who received personal encouragement from the scientific giant Galileo, argued that the entire universe, without exception, could be given account through reference to matter and motion. Number, figure, magnitude, position, and motion were adequate to describe all that is real. In this period of intellectual ferment and scientific discovery, a new vision of the universe, based on physical science, was emerging. Materialism was, less than in the past, an isolated philosophical position and more a general outlook, a world view for modern Western man. Modern physical science, particularly with the contributions of Galileo and Newton, was developing a materialistic image of reality. This outlook has been clearly described by E. A. Burtt:

> ... the great Newton's authority was squarely behind that view of the cosmos which saw in man a puny, irrelevant spectator ... of the vast mathematical system whose regular motions according to mechanical principles constituted the world of nature. The gloriously romantic universe of Dante and Milton, that set no bounds to the imagination of a man as it played over space and time, had now been swept away. Space was identified with the realm of geometry, time with the continuity of number. The world that people

had thought themselves living in—a world rich with color and sound, redolent with fragrance, filled with gladness, love and beauty, speaking everywhere of purposive harmony and creative ideals—was crowded now into minute corners in the brains of scattered organic beings. The really important world outside was a world, hard, cold, colorless, silent and dead; a world of quantity, a world of mathematically computable motions in mechanical regularity. The world of qualities as immediately perceived by man became just a curious and quite minor effect of that infinite machine beyond. . . .[20]

Newton's achievement in physics seemed to present man with an ultimate illumination about all the universe. As the poet Alexander Pope wrote:

Nature and Nature's laws lay hid in night;
God said, "Let Newton be!" and all was Light.[21]

And as the mechanical image of the Newtonian universe advanced by immense strides in the physical sciences, materialist philosophers became greatly emboldened and ever more hostile to any suggestion that there could be more to life than that which meets the physical eye.

A landmark in materialist philosophy came with the publication of Julien Offray de la Mettrie's *L'Homme Machine,* "Man a Machine," 1748. As the Age of Enlightenment blossomed in modern France, thinkers there looked to the world that had once been regarded as one of spiritual light and saw but darkness, the darkness of ignorance and superstition. La Mettrie boldly struck out against all defenders of any nonmaterial principles:

and I hereby challenge every prejudiced man who is neither anatomist, nor acquainted with the only philosophy which can here be considered, that of the human body. Against so strong and solid an oak, what could the weak reeds of theology, of metaphysics, and of the schools, avail—childish arms, like our parlor foils, that may well afford the pleasure of fencing, but can never wound an adversary.[22]

An epochal physiological discovery a few years earlier had really fired La Mettrie's materialistic imagination. It had to do with the fantastic regenerative powers of the polyp, which in 1703, Leeuwenhoeck had classified as a plant. Then one day in 1740 Abraham Trembley was taking a walk in Holland when he came upon a stagnant pool of water and noticed a plant in it. Much taken by it, Trembley examined it meticulously and discovered that what had been regarded as a plant was actually an animal. The polyp could move, contract, expand, eat, and digest. Its main trick, however, was truly remarkable: if you cut up the polyp, each part would regenerate into a whole animal. This discovery of the hydralike quality of the polyp stirred tremendous public interest. In fact, the news was so sensational as to be

[20] E. A. Burtt, *The Metaphysical Foundations of Modern Science* (Garden City, N.Y.: Doubleday & Company, Inc., 1954), pp. 238–39f.

[21] "Epitaph Intended for Sir Isaac Newton, in Westminster Abbey," in Alexander Pope, *Selected Works* (New York: Modern Library, 1951), p. 330.

[22] Julien Offray de la Mettrie, "Man a Machine," in *The Philosophy of Body,* ed. Stuart F. Spicker (Chicago: Quadrangle Books, 1970), p. 84.

remarked that if people were not always talking about war, they would only be talking about insects such as the polyp.

This new information was not only significant for physiology and an exciting conversation topic, but it had profound implications for metaphysics. If each part of the polyp reforms into a new organism after dissection, there seemed to be no other explanation than that the vital center of the animal—the soul itself—must be divisible, and if it is divisible along with the material body, it must not be spiritual but material. This realization not only infused renewed courage into the materialist philosophers but also led to a significant reinterpretation of the mechanist philosophy.

Ever since the time of the early Greek Atomists, Leucippus and Democritus, mechanism was generally understood as implying that it is impossible to construct a system of interrelated causal laws in which we might predict the future and explain why things happened in the past. Reality is held to be purely *deterministic* because all things occur in accord with fundamental and invariable physical laws. What happens does so because of the efficient functioning of the parts of the machine, and not because of any conscious design or deliberate purpose of the whole organism. Thus an event may be asserted to occur, not because of any personal or divine will or intention, not because there is any plan that serves any system of organization, but strictly by the blind interplay of the parts of the machinery of reality. Forces are set in motion according to certain fundamental physicochemical laws, and as these collide, interact, and rebound, purely as a result of mechanical, mathematically predictable combinations, the world as we know it acquires its form.

It should be borne in mind that idealists who deny the reality of matter may also be determinists. They argue all that occurs does so in accordance with an absolutely unbreakable chain of preceding events, but the links in this chain of inevitability are understood as spiritual or mental in nature; for the idealist determinist it is often the will of God, rather than the laws of mechanics, that shapes the chain. Nonmechanistic determinists often assume that there is some purpose to the chain, or that it is leading to some meaningful purpose. Conversely, the atomistic determinists, up to the time of La Mettrie, would deny that there could be any spiritual links in the chain, and just as strongly would deny that the interrelation of the individual links was to serve some ultimate goal of the chain.

Often life does look more like the atomists' deterministic chain than like the idealists' purposive-deterministic chain. So many things seem to happen devoid of reason, sense, or purpose. Someone who had everything in the world to live for is suddenly stricken and taken from the world, while another who may have nothing to live for may live on and on. Wars, famine, earthquakes, disease, and horrible accidents are ever present with man, and they seem to be beyond his control. It truly seems life does go on as an outcome of a mechanist-determinist chain—without any ultimate meaning.

This is where Trembley's polyp comes in. We said before that it revolutionized mechanistic philosophy, and we can now begin to see how: by presenting a new concept of mechanism. Instead of looking to the laws of physics to understand mechanism, men began to look to the laws of biology. Aram Vartanian makes this clear:

> *The vogue of the polyp coincided with a major modification early in the 1740's, of the pattern of teleology with which eighteenth-century France had been nourished. ... The shift of accent was, specifically, from cosmology to biology; or, more explicitly, from the calculable laws of Newtonian mathematical science to the incalculable intricacies of organic nature.*[23]

Vartanian explicitly draws our attention to the crucial importance of this:

> *A new materialism ... was needed, a materialism which would not rest upon the threadbare "atoms-and-chance" hypothesis of Democritus, Lucretius, and their modern successors. The ancient philosophy was contradicted on all sides by the everswelling mass of evidence that the processes of nature, even the minutest, were according to fixed law and undeniable design.*[24]

When the focus shifted from physics to biology and men gave their attention more to the living than the nonliving, they were impressed by the presence here of *design.* Yet, this was not a design imposed by the soul or spirit, but clearly a design that functioned purely in terms of material bodies. Because of La Mettrie's brilliance, a clear articulation of the position that *design is inherent in matter* was developed. He saw that there is inherent in matter the basis for its own functioning and organization. In other words, the need for asserting the existence of God or mind as an independent substance was now eliminated as La Mettrie argued that the capacity to function purposefully is built into the very nature of matter. Thus one could be a materialist without having to give up the idea of design or purpose. La Mettrie's view that the physicochemical can exhibit design or purpose provided a radically new way of presenting the mechanist position. That many scientists in our age of the Computer Revolution talk about the machines working in terms of purpose shows that it was a fruitful insight. Ernest Nagel, a distinguished philosopher of science, has this to say:

> *... it has been possible to construct physical systems that are self-maintaining and self-regulating in respect to certain of their features, and which therefore resemble living organisms in at least this one important characteristic. In an age in which servomechanics (governors on engines, thermostats, automatic airplane pilots, electronic calculators, radar-controlled antiaircraft firing devices, and the like) no longer excite wonder, and in which the language of cybernetics and "negative feedbacks" has become widely fashionable, the imputation of "goal-directed" behavior to physical systems certainly cannot be rejected as an absurdity. ... The possibility of constructing self-regulating physical systems does not, by itself, constitute a proof that the activities of living organisms can be explained in exclusively physicochemical terms. Nevertheless, the fact that such systems have been*

[23] Aram Vartanian, "Trembley's Polyp, La Mettrie, and Eighteenth-Century French Materialism," in *Roots of Scientific Thought*, ed. Philip P. Wiener and Aaron Noland (New York: Basic Books, Inc., 1957), p. 505.

[24] *Ibid.*, p. 507.

constructed does suggest that there is no sharp demarcation setting off the teleological organizations, often assumed to be distinctive of living things, from the goal-directed organizations of many physical systems.[25]

Thus today when machines can do so much, we may even be able to regard them as thinking and displaying purpose in their behavior. The gulf between man and the machine seems to be in the process of being lessened. La Mettrie's point was that there is no gulf. He believed that matter and life were not distinct, and that one can account for movement, thinking, and emotions as matter in motion. He argued that man can be understood as a machine and that not only is there a great similarity between man and animals, but also between man and plants. His vision was of a nature characterized by continuity and uniformity, of a series of gradations from the most simple organisms to highly complex psychical ones at the top of the scale.

If this kind of system was materialistic in character, it did not mean that it was brute and insensible, according to La Mettrie. Rather, he understood matter as having the capacity for feeling; his material world was not a static one of dead matter, but a dynamic, vital universe.

La Mettrie's argument impressed people for he dispensed with the idea that man has a spiritual soul, and, at the same time, accounted for his acting in a meaningful, purposive way. Then, just as La Mettrie made the case that there is no need of a soul to account for man's behavior, Baron *d'Holbach* (1723–1799) went a step further, claiming that there is no need of a God to account for the workings of the world. The universe, he believed, could be explained as a biological-chemical-physical "System of Nature." Continuing along these lines, the French physician and philosopher Pierre Cabanis (1757–1808) developed a "mindless" image of man. He contended that man's thinking is not because of some nonphysical entity called mind, but rather the physiological functioning of the brain. The mind is not a spiritual fount; it is nothing more than the physical brain. The brain takes in outer stimuli as the stomach takes in food and secretes thought like the liver secretes bile.

The materialist outlook grew in strength and confidence, and this bravado reached a high peak in the great nineteenth-century astronomer and mathematician Pierre Laplace (1749–1827), who fervently defended a mechanistic view of the universe. In the Newtonian tradition, he viewed the solar system as one huge mechanism but he eliminated Newton's assumption of a God behind it to correct all irregularities; according to Laplace all irregularities were self-correcting, and the system as a whole was self-regulating. Thus Laplace formulated a perfectly mechanistic and deterministic conception of the universe. In 1812 he postulated the notion of a Mechanical Superman or Divine Calculator; such a Super Intelligence could possess knowledge of *all forces* acting in nature at a given instant, and if he knew the positions of all the physical bodies upon which they act and

---

[25] Ernest Nagel, *The Structure of Science* (New York: Harcourt Brace Jovanovich, Inc., 1961), pp. 410f.

subjected these to mathematical analysis, he could eliminate all uncertainty from our understanding of the universe; then all past as well as the future secrets would be unlocked. We suppose there are mysteries in nature only because we lack sufficient information, but Laplace was saying that the universe is the kind in which everything can be logically and scientifically explained. The universe is a great Machine, and anything we do not know can be explained as a result of our failure to know the workings of its parts. As man extends his scientific knowledge, he approaches the point where he can explain every occurrence in this universe. Theologians may try to tell us that there are matters that cannot be understood naturalistically, and thus we need a God to whom we must pray for certain things, but to Laplace, such theologians were just preying upon man's ignorance. The idea of God was a convenient way of explaining what one did not understand. The story is told that when Napoleon asked Laplace why he left no place for God in his picture of the universe, he answered that God was a hypothesis he did not need.

Materialism had come a long way by the time of Laplace, but it still had a long way to go before it would get to the Laplacean Super Intelligence. Alas, it never got there! The celebration of the universe as a house built exclusively of matter grew to a resounding crescendo in the nineteenth century, but by the end of the century the music of materialism was being played out, and by the twentieth century it could not be heard well at all. Laplace's Super Intelligence was not a reality but a hope, a dream, a faith. As time went on man's capacity to explain the universe mechanistically and deterministically did not increase, but decreased. Man was moving into an era in which, instead of precise prediction, he would have to settle for statistical averages in which he would find that all mystery could not be banished from life, and in which the hard massy supposedly impenetrable particles of the Newtonian world would be transformed into energy in the universe of Einstein.

Thus in the twentieth century when man achieved a zenith in material progress, we discover surprisingly that matter itself has been dematerialized. The late, perspicacious philosopher of science N. R. Hanson bluntly asserts:

Matter has been dematerialized, not just as a concept of the philosophically real, but now as an idea of modern physics. ... The things which for Newton typified matter—e.g., an exactly determinable state, a point shape, absolute solidity—these are now the properties electrons do not, because theoretically they cannot, have.[26]

Hanson can only conclude:

... the twentieth century's dematerialization of matter has made it conceptually impossible to accept a Newtonian picture of the properties of matter and still do consistent physics.[27]

[26] N. R. Hanson, "The Dematerialization of Matter," in *The Concept of Matter*, ed. Ernan McMullin (Notre Dame, Indiana: University of Notre Dame Press, 1963), pp. 556f.

[27] *Ibid.*, p. 557.

As R. G. Collingwood asserts: "in the electronic theory of valency, we see the old theory of matter ... dissolving away and giving place to a new theory in which matter is essentially process or activity or something very much like life."[28]

It is no easy matter to defend materialism against the backdrop of contemporary physics, in the age of dematerialization and antimatter. Both from the standpoint of metaphysics and physics, materialism does not seem to fare so well. Furthermore, in this era of great progress and abundance when the world is filled with material and technical monuments, it appears that men and women are more than ever finding life meaningless and empty. Increasingly it is dawning on people that there may exist a terrible chasm between material well-being and the good life. Perhaps, man cannot live by bread alone—even if it's *chapatti*, the bread of the Hunza "paradise."

Marx's "scientific socialism" reveals a typical aspect of materialistic philosophy in its concern with social conditions. From the time of *Carvaka*, the materialist school of philosophy in ancient India, the motivation for defending materialism has been to better man's social conditions and to liberate him from superstition and fear. The Epicureans specifically used materialistic philosophy to liberate man from fear of death and the gods. Development of modern materialistic philosophy in Germany and France was specifically based upon the effort to formulate a critique of sociopolitical, economic, and religious evils. Materialistic emphasis has ever been placed on wresting control of man from those wielding clubs of supernaturalism and superstition.

It can be refreshingly uplifting to think, as idealists tend to do, that man has a higher calling than to the crass mundane things and experiences of existence. Yet we live in a world in which vast multitudes are downtrodden. Although it is easy enough to say that men do not live on bread alone, when they cannot get their bread they suffer from hunger and perish from disease, and even if they do not die, their bodies are wretched and sickly, and they subsist pathetically in pallor and poverty. Sometimes those who eloquently preach about the higher things themselves overlook the dregs of existence and are indifferent to the plight of the poor who, not having enough bread, can barely live at all. Philosophy then becomes, as Oscar Wilde observed, the study that enables men to bear with great resignation the suffering of others. It is easier to accept the plight of one's fellow men when one is comforted by spiritual assurances or expectancy of salvation in the next life. Thus an important aspect of materialism, which includes no allowance for another life, is to make this life as comfortable as possible.

For this reason a fundamental aspect of materialism has often been its social philosophy. Assuming there is no God nor any life hereafter, and that this life is *it*, materialists have ever exerted their efforts toward making

---

[28] R. G. Collingwood, *The Idea of Nature* (New York: Oxford University Press, 1960), p. 147.

the very best of this life. The fact that man is not going to a heaven up there provides all the more reason for doing something about the hell down here!

Because of this concern with the here and now, materialists have shown a much greater concern with social morality and welfare than idealists. In terms of programs of social enlightenment and efforts to actually *help* human beings, the idealists have not extended their philosophical hand as freely as the materialists have. The idealist has been more in alliance with the political right, and has provided justification for social inequities, while the materialist has tended to fight for social justice. This seems logical enough, because materialistic metaphysics entails a concern with *material* conditions, which idealist metaphysics does not. If men are what they eat, then it is important that they eat well. If men are what they think, as idealists might say, then it is not so important that they eat; they require food for thought more than food for their bellies. Furthermore, the materialist understands death to be final. There is only one shot at living and there will be no replays of life. Idealists argue that materialists, because they deny the existence of God and spiritual values, really have no basis for doing good. The idealist argues that if the materialist is right and this is the only life one will have, then it follows that one should be selfish and care only for himself. Besides, one need have no fear he will be punished later for any evils he gets away with now. The materialist looks at this issue in another way. He argues, just because it is only in this life that human suffering can be alleviated and, being human, one naturally feels concerned about such suffering, it is during *this* life that one may feel a need to do something about improving the human condition. This life is the only one in which to realize human and moral goals and to help one's fellow man, and thus make life on earth more endurable. There will be no paydirt in heaven because there is no heaven.

Of course, some dogmatic materialists who contend that there is "nothing but matter" often stumble upon the facts of life's great complexities, upon the apparent existence of values and what seem to be mental dimensions of life. One might say that such materialism is too uncompromising and fanatic. There are, however, more flexible brands of materialism. Naturalists, for example, who we might regard as materialists in that they deny the existence of the supernatural or spiritual, have a much better grasp of the complexities, the depth, and the richness of life than do the fanatic "nothing-but" materialists. There are also those we might call "liberal materialists" who provide for greater complexity and do so with more flexibility in their account of what is real. For example, there are materialists who recognize that there may be levels of existence that cannot be reduced to the purely physicochemical. Some materialists have developed the idea that new levels of value may *emerge* from a material basis of existence. Of particular relevance here are the ideas of Samuel Alexander (1859–1938), who maintained that life and mind are built up out of that which is physical and chemical, but are not "nothing-but" physicochemical elements. He believed the facts of life showed that novel and distinctive qualities do emerge. The basis of life may be material, but out of this arises life and mind, and these are not simply reducible to that material base. The physicochemical level of existence is purely mechanical, but life is organic. Higher levels of existence could not have been mechanically predicted from lower levels —that is, life with all of its richness and variability could never have been predicted from a mere knowledge of atoms and molecules. Life is physicochemical, but it is not *merely* physicochemical because merely physicochemical processes are not alive. These processes do not give us life until the requisite complexity of integration is attained—the *form* of their combination. That question of form is crucially significant, because not only is it as much a reality as the elements, but it is form that confers their significance upon the elements. It is not patches and color that make a picture, but their selection and arrangement; it is not just the notes by which a melody is conveyed that makes it what it is, but the *choice* and *order* the musician has introduced into them. In the choice and combination of the parts—that is, in the form—the whole attains a meaning that cannot be discovered in the several parts.

As life emerges from the physicochemical, mind emerges from life. What we call mind is, to be sure, a neural process, but again we cannot say that it is nothing but a neural process. There is a selectivity and attentiveness in mind that cannot be accounted for by the anatomy of the central nervous system.

Materialistic philosophy need not by any means be one-dimensional. It can provide a way of accounting for the richness of life and the values we find in it. Perhaps materialism is not adequate to account for all its complexity and variability, but it does not entirely fail to answer some questions. What each person must decide for himself is whether these answers sufficiently satisfy his own need for meaning and purpose.

MIND MATTERS MOST: IDEALISM

If we look about us we can see a hard and fast material world out there. There seems to be little doubt about that. Yet we can only look through the eyes of our mind, for anything we know about that world, we know by having an idea of it; thus we can say that all we really know is our *ideas*. The world of matter lies beyond our ideas, and therefore, *beyond* our reach. So reasoning, very profound minds have arrived at the conclusion that *ideas,* and not matter, are real.

Idealism is derived from the word "idea," which in turn derives from a Greek word meaning *to see* and *to know*. This can be traced back further to a Sanskrit origin, *vid*, which means *to know*. From this source there also evolved the Latin *video,* meaning *I see*. In India a word for philosophy is *darsana,* which is derived from the root "to see." On the basis of this etymology, we may think of fundamental truths as deriving their truth value not from the physical objects but rather from the act of *seeing*. When we want to know if a person *really* understands, we ask him if he *sees*. Thus seeing is important in the significance of the word "idealism": by our *ideas* we *see* and therefore *know*.

Because we see and know through our ideas, it follows that we can know only our own ideas. This is the view of *subjective idealism.* Another approach is that what we can know must be capable of being grasped by our ideas; it must be of a nonphysical nature. Indeed, our studies of nature provide evidence that reality is an intricate, interrelated, and coherent system that can best be expressed in terms of mathematical equations or logical theories. Thus we may conclude that reality is a grand nonphysical system and can best be expressed mathematically and logically. This view is known as *objective idealism.* The *subjective* idealist maintains that one can know only his ideas, and cannot know there is an external world; the *objective* idealist maintains that there is an objective reality, but that it must be explained as nonphysical in nature. The objective idealist can maintain (1) that reality is *all* spiritual; it is one in nature—as stated by Hegel, or (2) that the core of reality must be understood as spiritual, but that there is also a physical dimension to it—as defended by Plato.

Thus when we speak of idealism in philosophy we are not referring to the fact that a person may live by high "ideals," but that life itself is of the nature of ideals. At its core, reality for the idealist is not material but of the nature of value. Vindication of this position should in itself serve to lift us to a higher plane of existence.

In the history of philosophy there have been three basic and varying efforts to vindicate in some form the metaphysical position that ideas are more real than physical things. These are the Platonic, the Berkeleyan or Subjective Idealist, and the Hegelian or Absolute Idealist positions.

If we can find idealism to be a plausible interpretation of reality, it follows that the universe we live in is not inconsistent with our own nature as rational beings, and therefore, we can truly feel at home in it. We may all feel a oneness or common bond in the spiritual value or values that beat at the heart of reality.

PLATO'S STRANGE IDEAS

Some time back there was a popular song that included the words, "it's only a make-believe world." Having enlightened us about the world's not being real, the song also contained the information, "but it wouldn't be make believe if you believed in me." Most persons might have regarded that song as light romantic fare, frivolous and unrealistic. Yet, if the profound philosopher Plato were returned to earth when that song was a hit, he might have said, "Hey, that's my song!" Of course, Plato was quite aristocratic, and he might have experienced discomfort at the thought of his song being warbled by some popular crooner, but nonetheless, upon hearing those words, "its only a make-believe world," he would have acknowledged, "That's my ontology put to music."

That the world of everyday things may only be *make-believe* is an idea with profound possibilities. Like the songwriter, Plato concluded that this empirical world is only a make-believe world; the difference is that he arrived at this conclusion after a thorough logical examination. Plato believed he had discovered, lying behind the variegated, fleeting, and evanescent things of this world, a more stable, enduring, and permanent reality. This enduring reality is not subject to change and decay as particular physical things are, and thus is universal and nonmaterial in nature. Plato called this reality the realm of *Ideas* or *Forms*. The idea or form gives us the *essential* pattern of what actually is, rather than the merely accidental properties of particular physical things.

One goes to the market and locates a nice red juicy tomato. One can gaze at its bright red hue, squeeze it and taste it. If it really tastes good, one can affirm, "Now, that's what I call a real tomato!" But according to Plato that is not a *real* tomato; it is just a particular physical tomato. If it is kept around too long, it will become rotten and undesirable, and its color will become sickly. When one thinks of a tomato, one would no longer think of that sad-looking object. Indeed, even if one eats it before it loses its appeal as a tomato, it will be gone and forgotten. The *real* tomato is an Idea. It is a conception of that which makes the *perfect* tomato. This idea doesn't grow rotten. When we go to the market for a desirable tomato, squeeze one, and make up our mind about it, we are judging if it is a good tomato in terms of our perfect tomato. We only know what to look for in a particular tomato if we have the *idea* of what a perfect one is. No tomato we ever buy is perfect; and yet, unless we have an idea of a perfect tomato, an idea of just what qualities it *should* have, we will not know what to search for in the marketplace or at the vegetable stand. This "real" tomato is the perfect standard by which we can judge all the particular physical tomatoes we come upon. Whereas the "real" tomato is perfect, these particular physical tomatoes are in some sense all characterized by imperfections.

What is true of a tomato is also true of a circle. We can come upon particular round objects, but they never constitute perfect circles. The perfect circle has no given size nor given physical properties; its only quality is its circularity. Yet without the *idea* of the circle, we could never *judge* particular round things to be circular. They are always only approximations and thus, not true circles. The real circle is the perfect idea, which we can never see or sense. Indeed, the very foundation of much work accomplished in plane geometry is the straight line, and yet, the true straight line has length but no width or thickness. No such line, however, exists in the empirical world, for a line drawn even with the hardest, sharpest pencil would have to have some thickness and thus would not be a perfect line according to the geometrician's definition. The real straight line, then, does not physically exist. And yet the perfect line must be real in some fundamental sense, for if it were not, how could we judge whether the lines we draw on paper are or are not approximations of it? It follows, then, that physical things, with their imperfections, are in an important way less real than our *ideas* of perfect forms.

As it is with tomatoes, circles, and lines, so too it is with women. The concrete flesh-and-blood woman one might take in his arms, embrace, squeeze, hold closer, and kiss, is not the *real* woman. To Plato, it is not the particular living and breathing woman who is real; rather, the *idea* or *form* of *womanness* is what is real. The real woman is the eternally feminine, the general idea of woman, and not any particular flesh-and-blood woman. The idea of woman is perfect; it includes all of those qualities that suffer no blemishes. In the physical world no such woman exists. With the concrete woman there is always something wrong. That is why the poet Dante could love Beatrice so completely after that particular flesh-and-blood woman died. When she was gone she became perfection in his mind and could no longer change in any way to destroy her perfection. A man, for whom the *physical shape* of a particular woman who attracts him and makes him hot with passion is what is most meaningful, will invariably grow colder as she grows older and begins to lose that shape. No particular woman is perfect; the perfect woman, like the perfect circle, does not exist in the everyday physical world.

Plato believed that what is real is not a particular *beautiful* girl, who is only a concrete physical thing, but the *idea of Beauty,* which is a universal quality. Just as we only know what a good tomato is by having the idea of Tomato, so we only know what a beautiful woman is by having the idea of Beauty. *Beauty* is unchanging and thus eternal. It is not a concrete physical thing; it is universal. We could never judge any particular things or persons as being beautiful unless we had some standard by which to make such a judgment. Perfect Beauty is not to be found in the physical world; it is that standard by which we can evaluate and decide whether particular things or persons are beautiful. What makes a particular girl beautiful is the fact that she *embodies* the idea of Beauty, but is not herself the real "beauty." Physical beauty is elusive—it cannot be held; the beauty of the Idea is everlasting. Thus one is better off with the Idea than with the woman. Yet it all seems so mad. How many men would prefer to spend a Saturday night with a beautiful idea instead of with a beautiful girl?

The notion that the food we eat, the liquids we drink, and the girls with whom we have sexual relations are only *make-believe* seems so crazy as to be unbelievable. To the seducer, nothing may seem more real than his sexual intercourse. Yet how long does it last? A few minutes. Love, on the other hand, is not physical and remains forever. Love is a value—and anyone who has experienced love can testify that it is a very *real* experience. Plato saw this and developed his philosophy in the direction that reality is more akin to *values* than to physical things. When one is in love, it is often like an awakening to reality—he feels alive and is capable of discerning the greatest values in the smallest endowments of nature. The person in love comes alive to all about him and feels himself the master of circumstances, not their slave. In contrast, someone unable to love does not have much of a sense of reality; he feels submerged by things and does not feel entirely real. Encountering physical things does not put one in contact with reality. It is when one dedicates himself to ideals and values that he feels in command of existence and at one with reality. Plato understood that, and thus knew reality could be described in terms of spiritual values, the Divine

Ideas! In this sense (that they are not *ultimately* real and are not the level of reality that really matters), we may say the physical things are only make-believe.

The Hindus, whose ways of thought are not so far removed from Plato's, speak of the concrete empirical things of the world as being *maya* or illusion. Beyond the particular physical things of this world is the true reality, the world soul called *Brahman.* Physical things are perishable, but the ultimate —the *Brahman*—is spiritual and imperishable. Of course, when a Hindu walks across the street he watches out for oncoming automobiles just like the rest of us. We don't find Hindus standing in the way of trucks because trucks are only *maya.* They act *as if* trucks are realities and get out of the way. But to use this as proof that the Hindus are inconsistent in their idealism is to miss the point. The Hindu would be the first to admit that there is the manifestation of the truck, and that one must react to that which is manifested. But the point is that ultimate reality—the reality that matters most—cannot be understood in terms of such empirical manifestations. Indeed, even in getting out of the truck's way the Hindu is testifying to the reality of ideas. He may never have seen that particular truck before, but he knows, on the basis of the *idea* of what a truck is and of the ideas about momentum, force, and so on, that he should get off the street. If he had only empirical manifestations to go on, every new truck would be a new experience, and he would never know the appropriate response.

Things, of course, do seem real to us because they impinge upon our senses and make forceful impressions upon us. Nonetheless, things are not always what they *seem* to be; there is a difference between the appearance and *reality* of things. Our mouths may water when we behold a delicious-looking apple, and yet when we go to take a bite of it, we may discover it to be a synthetic apple made of plastic. It was not what it seemed to be, as we discovered with one of our senses after another had misled us. But what was it that made our mouths water? It could not have been the apple because there was no apple; it must have been the *idea* of the apple.

A stick, immersed in water, will *appear* bent, but we know it is not because we have formulated laws of refraction that explain this to us. Light rays are bent or refracted when they pass from a rarer to a denser medium —as, for example, from air to water. In the seventeenth century Willibrord Snell articulated the quantitative law that describes refraction. For any two transparent substances of different densities, the ratio of the angle of *refraction* (breaking or changing of direction) is constant, regardless of the angle of *incidence* (incoming ray) of the light. When Snell expressed this in a mathematical formula great progress was accomplished in constructing telescopes and microscopes. Thus although our sight, which is so important to us, reports that a stick is bent, we have a scientific law, mathematically stated, that explains why we see it as bent when it is not. Reasoning and mathematical formulations can give us a more accurate picture of reality than our senses can. This was something Plato understood clearly long ago, and it led him to conclude that what is real must be of a mathematical, logical, or nonempirical nature rather than of an empirical nature.

Science has corroborated Plato's point often by showing that the changing things of the world, when investigated, may turn out not to have the substantiality they appear to have. Particular empirical things grab us, because they hit us where we are most vulnerable—in our senses. Yet when we try to describe the world and put things together by referring to these particular empirical objects, we find that the data of our senses are quite unreliable. To provide an intelligible account of things we must refer to certain patterns—to regularities, abstractions, or generalizations—rather than to particular occurrences. These formal patterns and mathematical formulations turn out to be more substantial than sense data. They tell us more of what reality is like than particular things do. A particular occurrence may have a great deal of impact on us, but it often confers little understanding. If someone punched you in the nose it would have a great deal of impact, but understanding the basic motivation for that punch would be a much more complicated matter. If you had sufficient statistical (mathematical) data, the action might have been predictable, for we understand most fully when we see how things are related to other things, when we discover that things go together which we had not formerly believed to do so, and when we can predict what will happen in the future. Then we may say we know why things happen. Particulars give us no such knowledge. Describing reality involves exhibiting uniformities, patterns, relationships, and abstractions; such descriptions may be bereft of reference to any empirical particulars and often may be stated in terms of mathematical equations. Indeed, contemporary physics very much yields a picture of a mathematical world. Einstein showed us how to understand matter as immaterial structure. Plato, who saw the instability and unreliability of sense data, was led to the conclusion that reality is better *thought* than sensed. This being the case, it is logical to conclude that reality is more akin to the nature of *thought* than to the nature of the empirical phenomena that impinge on our senses.

Thus Plato was led by his logical analysis to what might seem a very strange idea—that Ideas are more real than particular concrete empirical things. To Plato reality is *Eidos,* which may roughly be translated as Idea or Form. The great geometrician Pythagoras had seen *number*—mathematical quality—as the very essence of reality, and Plato learned from him that form is more real than matter or empirical factors. It is form, not matter, that serves to distinguish the things of the world from each other. After all, there is not much difference in the *matter* of a jackass and a person; both are made of just about the same stuff. The difference is in the organization of the matter; they differ because of the *form* the matter takes rather than because of the matter itself. It is always the form of things rather than the matter that makes the difference. Reality must be understood in terms of form and ideas.

When most of us think of ideas, we think of subjective *mental images,* but by idea Plato meant something very different. The *Idea* for Plato is the form of reality—the *essence* of all that which exists. An Idea is not subjective, not something that is on any particular person's mind. The idea of a tree—its essence or *treeness*—would be the same no matter what peculiar notions about trees you or I happened to have. What makes a tree is the same for everybody. This is the sense in which an Idea is an objective reality. Plato's conception of Ideas rests upon the notion that what is objectively real is mental in nature. Particular things are not objectively real in this way; they are real only insofar as they participate in or copy these real ideas. Anything in this world we call beautiful, equal, or good is never perfectly beautiful, equal, or good. When we say two sticks are equal we mean they approximate the idea of equality; when we say different things are beautiful we are noting that, however unlike they may be in all other respects, they do share one quality—Beauty. This quality must be real or they could not share it. We could not call diverse things beautiful without some common quality by which they could be related to one another. It is this common quality—we may call it a universal—which gives meaning to what they are, because without it they would not be beautiful. Plato expressed this by saying that a beautiful thing was so because it *participated* in the Idea of Beauty.

As Plato saw it, this world would not make any sense unless there were such universals to give grounding to things. Our world is intelligible because it is organized as a set of nonsensuous universals culminating in an ultimate unifying principle through which the world is given meaning and purpose. In Idealism, as Plato developed it, ideas are more real than things; things *do* exist, of course, but their existence is shadowy and not capable of the precise articulation that is required of a world conceived of as subject to human knowledge. Our universe is not composed of brute purposeless matter. Rather, it is a universe that has the marks of intelligibility upon it; we can know it through our minds because of this intelligibility, which cannot be accounted for on the assumption that reality is constituted of sense objects. Because the universe can be grasped by thought, it must be of the nature of thought. It is the Ideal patterns that give the scientist, the mathematician, and the philosopher understanding and enlightenment.

HEGEL'S BIG IDEA

We now come to the great German philosopher Georg Wilhelm Friedrich Hegel (1770–1831), to whom another famous German philosopher, Arthur Schopenhauer, paid the following tribute:

> *the greatest effrontery in serving up sheer nonsense, in scrabbling together senseless and maddening webs of words, such as had previously been heard only in madhouses, finally appeared in Hegel. It became the instrument of the most ponderous and general mystification that has ever existed, with a result that will seem incredible to posterity, and be a lasting monument of German stupidity.*[29]

[29] *The World As Will and Representation*, trans. E. F. J. Payne (Indian Hills, Colorado: The Falcon's Wing Press, 1958), I, 249.

It is best to read most philosophers in their original language, but to many, Hegel would not make sense in any language. A man named James H. Stirling was the first to bring Hegel's philosophy to England. Stirling wrote two volumes called *The Secret of Hegel,* and a reader once congratulated him on having *kept the secret.* An Austrian dramatist said, what he liked best about Hegel's philosophy was that it is the only thing he knew to be as incomprehensible as the world itself.

Hegel is certainly not without his enemies in the philosophical community. Indeed, he is so intensely disliked that we may begin to suspect he must have been quite a man to be worthy of so much dislike. People usually do not waste much strength in disliking those who do not make an impression upon them. This suspicion turns out to be right, for throughout the years Hegel's influence has been very great. Certainly Hegel had an obfuscating way of writing, but if we can peel away the husk of style we will find a valuable kernel of meaning. The study of law, history, sociology, and philosophy have all gained much from Hegel's deep insights, and his work certainly deserves study, as difficult as it may be.

Hegel was born in Stuttgart on August 27, 1770. He died of cholera in the 1831 Berlin epidemic. His life was not very eventful. When we say that he was a German professor we have said about all there is to say. His method of lecturing certainly left room for improvement. He sat all crouched up with his head hanging down, coughing and hemming, and only after magnificent effort did he finally produce a disorganized and disjointed sentence. Yet he was greatly respected by his students. There was some spirit in him that people admired. In his student days he used to cut classes like mad. When the French Revolution broke out he planted a liberty tree in Tubingen's Public Square—an acknowledgment of the new French Republic! Soon, however, the Revolution based on reason became a tyranny of unreason. Napoleon smashed the Prussian army in Jena at the very time Hegel was doing research there. At first the German philosophers were excited about Napoleon because the banner of nationalism meant unification of Germany to them. Then the French began to destroy Germany. In particular, Hegel bemoaned the wresting away of the Left Bank of the Rhine. Nonetheless, the ideal of reason, though abused in the hands of unreasonable men, was still believed to be the key to reality. In this historical context, let us try to come to an understanding of Hegel. This is not an easy task. Someone once asked Hegel for a brief outline of his philosophy—and Hegel responded by writing ten volumes. There must be a better way to get to the essence of his philosophy.

It very much appears that there is both mind and matter in our universe. We react to *physical* objects, we react to *thoughts* or *wishes,* and we also get ideas. One might *think* of something unpleasant, worry about it, and get an *ulcer.* The thinking is not material but the ulcer is. Thus it appears that there are material things and mental things, and that they may even be related to each other: I *think* I will raise my hand, and my hand rises. One might ask how material things and mental or spiritual things are related, or if one is more basic than the other. Those who maintain that matter or body is fundamental (or that matter alone is real) are called *materialists*. Many materialists take the position that all so-called mental or spiritual entities or facts are reducible to material ones; they understand thinking as the consequence of electrical processes, as a pure function of the physical brain rather than as "mental" activity. The materialist usually takes the position that matter is real and mental processes can be explained physicalistically.

When subjected to critical examination, a huge flaw can be detected in the philosophical position of materialism. It is that *matter* is itself an *idea*. We know matter only because we have an *idea* of it. But if we know matter through our ideas, then we do not have direct knowledge of it. We have *direct* knowledge only of our *ideas*. What we really know is the idea, not the material. May we not say, therefore, that it is the *idea* and not the material that is real? This is exactly what the idealists do say.

As we saw in the chapter on epistemology, Bishop Berkeley came to the conclusion that nothing except our ideas can exist: *to be is to be perceived*. Only the perceptions or ideas of the individual can be defended as existing. This form of subjectivism was repudiated by Kant, who reasoned that there would have to be something causing the perceptions. If we are perceiving, then does it not follow that there must be *something* to be perceived? Kant knew that had to be the case; unfortunately, he did not know what that something was, so he called it the "thing-in-itself" and admitted that it was unknowable. In developing his view, Kant made a strong case for the thesis that experience is not chaotic, but is given a rational structure by the mind. According to him, everything was logical and meaningful, and yet one did not know what it was that was causing the experience—one could never know just what the thing-in-itself was.

The idea of such an unknowable thing-in-itself bothered Hegel. It left too much unexplained for a rational interpretation of reality. After much thought, Hegel arrived at conclusions that made Kant's unknowable thing-in-itself no longer a problem. It was no longer a problem: he presumed he knew it. Kant had argued that we can have knowledge only of phenomena or appearances, but not of things-in-themselves, not of ultimate reality. Hegel regarded this as a rather strained position. What about these appearances? After all, do they not *really* appear? If they do, which they certainly must, then why say they are not real? Indeed, why call them "appearances" at all. Hegel saw no basis for concluding there is some mysterious thing-in-itself beyond the world of appearances. Instead of understanding the thing-in-itself as some mystical realm beyond the realm of appearances, Hegel interpreted it as the *systematic order* of appearances. We must not think of reality as something lying beyond that which actually appears to us, for then it would be something we could not know and therefore would have no right to discuss. Reality is not beyond appearances; it is the *sum total of all appearances*. It is the *whole*.

From Hegel's argument it follows that if at any given moment we know only a little of all that is, then we do not know reality. In fact, Hegel went much further and claimed if we do not know all reality then we cannot know any little thing. To really know anything, to know it fully, we must know all of its relations—how it affects and is affected by everything else. If one lacks information about how any particular thing fits into the total scheme of things, then there is something he does not know about that thing, and therefore can never contend that he fully knows it. True science in its highest stages of development provides us with the fullest account of all things and illuminates their interrelationships. All of us have probably had the experience at some time of having a good friend do something that would be inexplicable to a stranger. It might be an act that would seem selfish or wrong or stupid to someone who did not know this person. But because we know him so well, we know that what he did is related to something in his personality or his history—perhaps something that happened to him years ago—and that explains it. Because we can see this relationship, we can understand what our friend did, whereas a stranger, who does not know about this relationship, can never really understand that act, even though he was standing right next to us when it happened.

That our understanding of even a simple act may depend upon all sorts of complex relationships is because everything in this universe is related to everything else in some way. The more we study the universe, the more it becomes clear all things are in some way related. Fortunately, this does not mean that we have to know every single thing that ever happened, for the complex interrelationships can be explained by reference to certain fundamental laws. This is to say that reality is a rational system, and all of its elements are interrelated or coordinated in a rational manner.

This was the way in which Hegel saw the universe, and thus his idealism, to a great extent, rested on the assumption that reality is an *intelligible* system. We cannot understand reality in terms of the parts or small elements. Taken out of context, these may seem senseless, but they will always make sense if viewed in the perspective afforded by the whole. The irrational act of an insignificant man may seem utterly senseless, but if one understands his upbringing, his environmental conditioning, the state of the world, and how history has moved it into that state, the act may make sense. Perhaps an act of murder may be so understood. One may say, "How awful and senseless that terrible murder was." Yet on investigation one may discover that the way the killer's father beat him when he was small, the misfortunes he endured owing to his poverty-stricken background, the utter lack of understanding of his fellow men, the climate of violence in society and in the world at large at that time, and the shape of history that brought us to such a period, all went into making one man a potential murderer. Looked at in this light, a seemingly senseless act begins to make sense, and we can begin to understand why it happened. In isolated bits one can understand nothing.

In seeing reality as a logical whole, Hegel was telling us that the parts are meaningful in their relation to the whole just as the individual musical instruments are to the orchestra. In an organism, each organ is what it is in its relation to the whole. A heart out of the body does not mean at all what it does in the body. Everything has some relation to everything else. The whole, as Hegel saw it, is more than the sum of its parts. If we are to grasp reality we must see in terms of wholes, not *bits*.

Today, Gestalt psychology has established that we do not see the world bit by bit, but in terms of general patterns. We know that there is an inherent tendency for any organism, when confronted with an incomplete pattern, to perceive it as complete. Many wholes do seem to have a reality that cannot be reduced to their constituent elements, and this is particularly true of social life where we have *societies, nations, families,* and many *organizational* or group patterns. In this way Hegel's wholistic emphasis contributed a great deal to our understanding of cultural reality.

When the system of reality is understood as a whole, it can be seen to be rational. Hegel maintained that the real is rational and the rational is real. Yet often it may seem that what happens is painfully irrational. The world, full of human misery, is very real and very irrational. In such a world, what sense does Hegel make? Hegel would answer that he was not talking about individual suffering. When he announced that the real is rational and the rational is real, he was not making reference to *particular* misfortunes. Consider the example of our friend's inexplicable action. If we study it in itself, we will not discover reality. Reality in this case must be understood in terms of the laws of psychology, and only then can we make sense of such actions. They are only a small part of reality, and to get to that reality, we must view their causes and see them in relation to fundamental laws of the universe. What is real are those *laws*, and they are not physical or particular things; they are nonmaterial *universals*. What is most real is the *universal*, the total *system* or logical pattern of particular existing things.

Hegel's stress on the importance of the whole and the interrelation of all its parts is a fruitful point of departure for understanding phenomena. An instant, for instance, has no meaning in isolation. We experience in *durations*. A moment can have meaning only in relation to other moments, to a time scale. We must understand the whole to understand the parts. Anything taken in isolation is out of context, and hence distorted. If we apply this principle to the problem raised by individual suffering we can better appreciate Hegel's point. If it can be shown that the system as a whole is good and rational, then one must not view the individual misfortune as an end in itself. In the context of the whole system there may be a reason for it. Perhaps the seemingly meaningless sufferings of an individual are not meaningless in the context of the whole. The truth about the nature of the universe is not to be found in the individual or in fragmentary experiences, but in the whole of reality. For the good of the whole the individual may at times have to suffer.

With such thinking, Hegel may sound like the supreme *organization man* of philosophy, and we may feel concerned that the individual will too readily be lost or sacrificed in the vast complicated system. That is certainly a danger, but there is another way of looking at it. If reality is ultimately not physical but mental, and if all things are interrelated, then there is a natural bond between all individuals. We are all ultimately related to one another, so that no other self is really alien or foreign to my own self. We should all be moved by the suffering of every living being, for we are all bound together. Here is a true basis for political and international harmony, a deep philosophical basis!

Hegel's idealism was a clear rejection of Berkeley's. Berkeley's idealism was subjective, and its point was that we cannot obtain independent evidence of an external world; therefore, it makes no sense to assume the existence of one. According to Berkeley we can only know that of which we can have an idea because all knowledge depends on our *ideas;* we cannot really say anything exists except our ideas and the minds that have ideas. Therefore, it makes no sense to say there is an external world. Hegel found Berkeley's analysis of knowledge convincing, but not his conclusion about what exists. It is true that for us to know anything we must have an idea of it, as Berkeley had reasoned, but to Hegel, that meant that the external world must be of the nature of ideas and not that no such thing objectively existed. As Hegel reasoned, we can know the world only by having *ideas* of it, and if they are adequate ideas they must *resemble* reality; if ideas resemble reality, then reality must be made of ideas. Hegel's point was that if reality can only be known by ideas, we should not conclude, as Berkeley did, that nothing exists except our ideas; rather, we must conclude that the nature of reality is nonphysical or mental. We attain our knowledge through ideas, and the only thing that can be grasped by an idea is something which must itself be of the nature of an idea. We must assume that the ideas that constitute our knowledge of reality are in *agreement* with reality. For one thing to agree with another thing, it must be of the same nature. Thus we must conclude that the reality of which we have knowledge must itself be mental or ideal in nature.

Justice Oliver Wendell Holmes once said that law is not logic but experience. Hegel would not have agreed with this distinction because, for him, experience itself was logic; in a sense, almost everything was logic— except logic. Hegel published three volumes on logic, but they were not really about logic; they were about metaphysics. Logic is the study of the way the rational mind works, and metaphysics, the way in which our universe is put together. In Hegel these were the same thing, so that logic became the same as metaphysics. Both logic and metaphysics teach that real processes must be logical, for the universe is a great *logical* process. The physical, day-to-day world of particular things is certainly real, but *ultimate reality* is the great orderly system of coherent and interrelated experiences. The absolute is the entire system. This is the reality that matters most.

After the time of Hegel this position was given very careful defense by the American idealist Josiah Royce (1855–1916). Most people suppose that the real world is made of physical things, and that it is not only wrong but absurd to say the hard facts of life, the *material* things we perceive, are mental in nature. Royce pointed out that people suppose that hard facts resist us all the time but that ideas can be molded as a person wishes:

socialists can dream of utopias, disappointed lovers can imagine themselves Don Juans, and beggars can attain imaginary riches. In the realm of ideas, anyone can be Walter Mitty. It is different in the world of facts; there, society is organized in accord with hard realities and not with dreams, rejected lovers stand alone defeated, and beggars have only their poverty. At least, that is how it looks. Royce observes, however, that the world of facts is hard, but not nearly so stubborn as people think. Indeed, the dedicated can mold facts. The world can be formed according to ideas; political philosophers do influence the social order, lovers do woo afresh, and beggars can become successful in society. To alter the world, however, work is necessary. We must work in a real world in which house walls do not melt away as in dreams, but stand firm against winter winds. Reality is, indeed, stubborn, but let us not forget that minds, too, can be stubborn. Royce states his case most effectively:

> The lonely wanderer, who watches by the seashore the waves that roll between him and his home, talks of cruel facts, material barriers that, just because they are material and not ideal, shall be the irresistible foes of his longing heart. "In wish," he says, "I am with my dear ones, but alas, wishes cannot cross oceans!" Oceans are material facts, in the cold outer world. . . . But alas! to the rejected lover the world of the heart is all! . . . Were the barrier between him and his beloved only made of those stubborn material facts, only of walls or of oceans, how lightly might his will ere long transcend them all! Matters stubborn! . . . Nay, it is just an idea that now opposes him —just an idea, and that too, in the mind of the maiden he loves. . . . Place me for a moment, then, in an external world that shall consist wholly of ideas— the ideas, namely, of other people about me, a world of maidens who shall scorn me, of old friends who shall have learned to hate me, of angels who shall condemn me, of God who shall judge me. In what piercing north winds, amidst what fields of ice, in the labyrinths of what tangled forests, in the depths of what thick-walled dungeons, on the edges of what tremendous precipices, should I be more genuinely in the presence of stubborn and unyielding facts than in that conceived world of ideas![30]

Royce's claim is that the ideas of people may be the most difficult kinds of facts to influence. Think again of the rejected lover. He would have no cause to suffer if he could get rid of his own idea that he still wants the girl. Thus, not only the ideas of others, but even our own may be unyielding and cruelly stubborn. Someone might say to a rejected lover, "Forget her. Get rid of the idea you need her." If only he could. Royce says the world of ideas has its own horrible dungeons and chasms. We may conclude, then, that ideas can be as hard, as unyielding, and as stubborn as matter— indeed, more so. We can always discover examples of just how malleable and unstubborn matter can be by just looking about us. In fact, all mechanical progress clearly demonstrates the great extent to which man can mold matter. To make this graphic, one need only contrast some technological achievement with some failure in the realm of ideas—for example, how

---

[30] Josiah Royce, "Reality and Idealism," in Daniel J. Bronstein, Yervant H. Krikorian, and Philip P. Wiener, eds., *Basic Problems of Philosophy* (Englewood Cliffs, N.J.: Prentice-Hall, Inc., 1955), pp. 502f.

much more simple it was for man to conquer a physical malady, such as smallpox, than it is for him to conquer intolerance. May we not very legitimately ask, then, which is really more hard and unbending—the physical fact of germs or the mental fact of human attitudes?

The Hegelian spirit was typically the spirit of the nineteenth century in one important respect. The nineteenth century was a period of great historical movement, and the Hegelian spirit was on the move along with everything else. Hegel's ideas were not above change as were the Forms and Ideas of Plato—they worked themselves out in history. In Hegel there was a metaphysics of *change* and *becoming*, not a metaphysics of immutable ideas such as Plato's. The absolute of Hegel was more a subject, life, process, or evolution than a *substance*. In the old metaphysical sense, a substance was something that did not itself change, but for Hegel, absolute reality was dynamic rather than static. This was an extremely important insight. Classical physics had assumed a static theory of the universe, but recent developments have overturned this in favor of a dynamic conception of the universe. Long ago the Greek philosopher Heraclitus had proclaimed that all is change and that War is Father and King of all, by which he meant that strife is built into reality. This model became most important in Hegel and, through him, in Marx and Engels. For Hegel the world was a place of constant change, but the change itself was not arbitrary, for it was seen to proceed according to a well-defined pattern or method. Method was fundamental, for the pattern of the universe was revealed in the unfolding of the dialectical process. The procedure of the dialectical *method* is as follows:

THESIS: assertion of a position—affirmation.

ANTITHESIS: assertion of the opposite position—negation.

SYNTHESIS: the bending of the two opposite positions into a unity on a higher level.

The idea of the dialectic is that reality is full of contradictions, but as it goes on they are overcome, and something new is created. Hegel so much accepted the contradictions of existence that he rejected the principle of identity—the principle that says $A = A$. Although this principle seems obvious and undeniable, that did not stop Hegel from denying it.

According to Aristotelian logic, there are three fundamental laws of thought, and these are required for correct thinking.

1. LAW OF IDENTITY: According to it, if anything is true, then it is true. This is not a difficult idea to grasp. Indeed, it is difficult not to grasp it.

2. LAW OF CONTRADICTION: No statement can be both true and false.

3. LAW OF EXCLUDED MIDDLE: Any statement is *either* true *or* false.

Hegel rejected these Aristotelian laws. He did not reject them entirely, to be sure, nor did he fail to understand them. Rather, he believed that reality is such that it cannot entirely be comprehended by these rational principles. Often when we try to fit reality into our Procrustean bed of logic we distort it. There is a method of *Reason* (*Vernunft* in German) that includes but goes beyond the method of Logic or *Understanding* (which he called *Verstand*). *Vernunft* or Reason does not deny the identities and distinctions of the understanding, but it adds that they may ultimately not be incompatible. The Understanding or *Verstand* is that part of the mind that is always trying to obtain clear distinctions. It has an obsession to make everything precise and cut-and-dried. But reality is not precise and cut-and-dried. Reality is a *process;* it does not stand still; it is a *flow.* At the deepest level of reality, "to be or not to be" is not the question. Life is not static; it is dynamic. Life constantly sees a passing from one stage of being to another, so that to be is not to be, and not to be is to be. It is impossible to make an absolute distinction between night and day, between being and not being. One is always becoming the other. On the level of Verstand—understanding —all the nice, neat, finite distinctions hold, but on the level of Vernunft— reason—they break down, and are absorbed in the totality. As a result our universe appears as a deeply meaningful setting for human life because everything we ever do is connected by unbreakable bonds to everything else in the world—past, present, and future. Life is a complex web of inter-relationships from which things sometimes may seem to disappear, but from which nothing is ever really lost.

Historically, the significance of Hegel's dialectical understanding of life is very great. Mechanistic science reached its high point in the seventeenth, eighteenth, and nineteenth centuries. At the head of this tradition stood Descartes, who had made the most thorough-going separation between mind and matter. The scientific method of observation, description, and analysis was particularly appropriate for doing the work science was called upon to do. But at the same time it provided the metaphysical basis of man's loss of his roots. Man was torn from nature and stood apart from it. Hegel was important because he sought to fuse the disconnected parts. And this, he believed, had to be accomplished on the level of reason. He was not entirely successful, but that is not important. What is important was the brilliance of his prodigious philosophic effort and profound insights. Hegel showed that the method of empirical science may be appropriate on the level of *understanding*, but on the level of reason, the method of dialectic is required. The German word *aufheben* means three things: (1) to pick up; (2) to abolish; (3) to preserve. This word reflects the nature of reality. *Aufheben* is an ideal word to express the dialectical nature of life. Something is picked up and then abolished and then preserved on a higher level.

Surveying the meaning and course of all history and the entire evolution of human thought, Hegel himself formulated a panoramic philosophy of idealism. He saw the history of ideas reaching a high point in the realization of his own absolute idealism. With the articulation of Hegel's idealism the philosophic pendulum had taken an extreme swing forward and was now ready to swing back. In an industrial world being swept forth by tides of material progress, the philosophy of idealism could hardly stand firm amidst the relentless currents. Among these currents was the materialistic and communistic philosophy of Karl Marx. Marx regarded Hegel's philosophy of spirit as a low point—a thesis which had to be negated. Marx appreciated the fact that Hegel was a powerful thinker; indeed, this made it all the more important to crush Hegel's idealistic excesses. Marx believed Hegel was seeing things upside down and he assigned himself the task of turning them right side up.

We have already considered materialism, and logically we might have examined Marx in that context, but doing so would have blurred the focus of historic perspective, inasmuch as Marx's reaction to Hegel is historically of tremendous importance in the development of Marx's thought. Thus we shall depart from our systematic treatment of idealism and materialism here so that we may more fully appreciate the interplay of the positions of Hegel and Marx. There is not time here to give an elaborate account of Marx, but by examining some of the essentials of his philosophy we may be able to appreciate his distinctive interpretation of materialism and better understand his vigorous rejection of Hegelian idealism.

A NOTE ON MARX

Karl Marx (1818–83), the great nineteenth-century thinker and the father of communism, could not accept the theories of other socialists and anarchists of his own time. In contrast to many of his contemporaries, Marx insisted on the need for *force* to bring about the changes men needed. The violent action of the proletariat would speak much louder than flowery words of utopians. Wide awake to the sufferings of the great mass of men, Marx criticized most contemporary socialists and anarchists as dreamers. They committed the cardinal sin of supposing that capitalists were rational men who could be moved by ideas. Men just don't run out and give up their riches upon hearing a socialist sermon. Marx vigorously denounced the idea of basing socialism on rationalistic, moralistic, or theological assumptions. If socialism were to succeed, it must be founded on *science*. Marx attempted to found his socialist theory on a scientific study of history. To him the inevitability of socialism was a natural consequence of basic historical laws. To be sure, in predicting the arrival of socialism on the basis of history, Marx was careful to make sure that these laws would lead where he wanted them to lead. But for our purposes this is neither here nor there, for it cannot be denied that Marx was an intellectual fortuneteller who was to have the most profound effect upon the development of modern history.

The laws of history, the understanding of which provided Marx with a basis for scientific socialism, were understood to operate according to a *dialectical* pattern. According to Marx and his collaborator Friedrich Engels, dialectic is the science of the general laws of motion and of the development of nature, society, and thought. By means of dialectical growth the contradiction of opposites is constantly resolved. Dialectic represents a challenging effort to comprehend reality in terms of its inherent contradictions; in this it is at variance with the generally rationalistic categories of logic and understanding that characterize Western thinking.

Marx developed his system of dialectics on the basis of the philosophical works of Georg Wilhelm Friedrich Hegel (1770–1831), the giant of nineteenth-century German idealism. According to Hegel, the real and everyday world was in fact the external form of the immaterial Idea, a spiritual reality. As Marx saw it, Hegel's idea that the physical and the spiritual were forms of each other was a sound one. The problem was that Hegel had things backward and upside down. Most people assume that ideas are nothing but images, but Hegel claimed they were at the heart of the real world, while the "real" concrete world in which we live was just an image of the Ideas. Marx and Engels felt obligated to turn Hegel right side up. Although reality operates by dialectical laws, Marx and Engels wanted to replace Hegel's interpretation with a *spiritualistic* and *materialistic* one. This is dialectical materialism. Thus in the metaphysics of Marx and Engels, reality was understood to be materialistic and dialectical. Consistent with this metaphysics they defended the epistemological doctrine of *realism*. This is the position that the existence of physical objects is independent of their being perceived. Only one suffering from the insanity of idealism could suppose that if we were not around the world would vanish. Far from the world's being dependent upon our minds, the fact is that mind itself is nothing but an outgrowth of matter. Every idea can be accounted for in terms of a specific social situation, which itself is produced by man's relation to definite material conditions.

Karl Marx supposed all reality to be material, but inasmuch as he also conceived of it as dialectical, his materialism was not of the strict mechanistic variety. Mechanism does not allow the possibility that anything really new can happen, for it sees everything in terms of strictly deterministic laws that reduce all events to simple *quantitative* variations of the same old atoms. Dialectical materialism, however, leaves open a possibility for the emergence of new *qualities*. Biological and psychological sciences rest upon the laws of physics, but they cannot be strictly deduced from these laws as they possess unique qualities of their own. This becomes obvious as one examines Engel's work on the dialectic, which we shall do.

In traditional logic there are three basic laws of thought, which are asserted to be adequate to govern all correct thinking. These are known as:

1. THE PRINCIPLE OF IDENTITY: If any statement is true, then it is true, or "A = A."

2. THE PRINCIPLE OF CONTRADICTION: No statement can be true and at the same time false, or "A cannot be not A."

3. THE PRINCIPLE OF EXCLUDED MIDDLE: Any statement is either true or false.

It may not seem a remarkable piece of information that A cannot not be A. One does not have to be a logician to understand that. But while such information may not be astounding, at least it is sound. We should have no doubts that, if nothing else, at least these are true laws. Yet these basic laws of thought were not good enough for Engels—they were not revolutionary enough for him. And so to Engels, as to Hegel before him, A could be not A. According to Engels there are three basic laws of the dialectic:[31]

1. The law of the transformation of quantity into quality and vice versa.
2. The law of the interpenetration of opposites.
3. The law of the negation of the negation.

These three laws of the dialectic are rather complex and need to be examined rather closely. To understand the first one—the law of the transformation of quantity into quality and vice versa—we should recall that atomistic mechanistic philosophy maintained that the whole universe consisted of identical atoms in various combinations. According to this view, everything that exists or happens is merely the result of various combinations of these essentially identical elements. In this sense, for the atomist, there are only quantitative differences between things, not qualitative differences, for it is all a matter of how many atoms there are and in what positions. Engels disagreed with this; for him, merely quantitative changes could not explain the variety we see in the universe. Although it contradicted traditional logic, he maintained that when we add one atom to another we may get something that is not simply the sum of that quantitative change; new *qualities* may arise in the process of the addition, so that we may say 1A plus 1A produces 2A, but 2A is not the same thing as 1A plus 1A. Two examples are often used to illustrate this argument. One is something we are all familiar with. If we remove one calorie of heat from one cubic centimeter of water, the water will become one degree colder and will contract very slightly. This is a simple mechanical change and is completely quantitative: the changes in the water can be expressed in numerical terms as changes in temperature and volume. But if we get near the freezing point of water, removing another calorie of heat will produce a very different effect: the water will suddenly increase in volume and take on a new quality—hardness. Thus the change in the quantity of heat, when it becomes great enough, produces a change in the quality of the water. The other example is taken from mathematics. Prime numbers are numbers that cannot be divided by any whole number (except themselves or one). One, two, and three are prime numbers because there are no other numbers we can divide them by; four is not a prime number because it can be divided by two. No one has ever figured out a formula for predicting what numbers are prime numbers; the only way to tell is to take a large number and see if you can divide it by anything and not get a remainder. The point is that the quality of being or not being a prime number does not depend upon simple quantitative additions; it is totally unrelated to them. If we add 1 to the prime number 2, we get 3, which is also a prime number

[31] See *Dialectics of Nature* (New York: International Publishers, 1940), p. 26.

and simply the sum of $1 + 2$. But if we add $3 + 1$ we get 4, which is not a prime number; the same quantitative change has produced a change in the quality of the number from a prime number to not a prime number. If we add the same quantity again, we get another change in quality back to a prime number, and so on. If we look at a series of a few of the lowest prime numbers—1, 2, 3, 5, 7, 11, 13, 17, 19, 23—we can see that there is no system by which the quality of primeness can be related to the quantitative changes between one number and the next. Atomism cannot be correct because changes in quantity sometimes produce changes in quality that simple atomism cannot account for.

Engels's second law of dialectics—the law of the interpenetration of opposites—claims that the traditional idea that a thing cannot be both A and not $= $ A at the same time is an oversimplification. On the surface the traditional idea seems irrefutable, but in fact life is more complex than that, and with practically every important true statement we can make there is a sense in which it is not true. Two illustrations, one simple and the other more complex, should help to explain this. We started this section with the simple statement that Karl Marx was the father of modern communism. Now some scholar could come along and point out that actually the communist tradition is a very old one, and he could name numerous forerunners of Marx. We would have to admit that Marx was not the father of modern communism. Then another scholar would point out that, despite the fact that there were forerunners, Marx's contribution was what gave decisive shape to modern communism. To satisfy both of them, we would have to say that Marx was and was not the father of modern communism. The two scholars would probably go on arguing forever, but which of them is right? Well, both are; the case is somewhat like that of the water freezing: Marx's thought is both a continuation of the thought that came before it and something new. Now you may say that these two statements are not really opposites, but they are. Look at it this way: when we say that Marx's ideas are something new, we are not merely saying that they are something new *in addition* to being a continuation of the thought that preceded him. The fact that they are something new makes them different from what went before, and insofar as they are something new they are *not* a continuation of what went before. When a thinker adds an important new element to the system of his thought he changes what came before. Indeed, we have seen this process going on all through this book: Locke adds something new to Descartes and thereby refutes Descartes; Berkeley adds something new to Locke and produces something drastically different from what Locke was saying; and so on. We can say, for example, that Marx was Hegel with a difference (Marx was a Hegelian) or that Marx was different from Hegel (Marx was not a Hegelian). Both are true even though they are contradictory.

Another slightly more complex example of this interpenetration of opposites comes from the world of physics. Ever since the Greek philosopher Heraclitus said so, there have been men who recognized that everything is in motion—or flux, as Heraclitus said. Now motion is a very contradictory idea. You may remember from a physics course that a thing that is in motion cannot be said to have position. Why is this? Because if we were to say that a thing in motion has position X at time Y, then at time Y it could not be in motion. No matter how small a unit of time Y was, if we said that at that particular time our thing was at position X, we would be stopping its motion. If we look at one motion picture frame of a ball in flight, we get the idea that at the moment that frame was taken, the ball was in such-and-such a place. But this is only an illusion, and if we look closely enough and have a good enough camera, we can see that even in that one frame the ball is slightly blurred, indicating that it was moving from one place to another. This would be so no matter how fast we could get our camera to operate; even if it could take hundreds or thousands of pictures a second, no one frame, representing one moment of time, could ever give us a picture of the ball at one place and only one place. Therefore, Engels reasoned, if a thing is in motion, then at any given time Y it must be both at point X and not at point X; in fact, that is what motion is: the being in one place and not being there at the same time. Now, since this is a world in which everything is in motion, it follows that it is a world in which everything is both at a given point at a given time and not at that point at the same time. Whereas, the principle of contradiction from traditional logic said that we cannot describe reality in terms of statements that are true and false at the same time, Engels's law of the interpenetration of opposites proclaimed that only such statements can adequately describe reality, for reality itself is built up of contradictions like the contradiction inherent in the idea of motion.

From the two laws of dialectics we have examined already, Engels derived the third—the law of the negation of the negation. In a sense this is the simplest of the three, and from it we can see how Marx and Engels used dialectics as a method of explaining history. We saw in discussing the interpenetration of opposites that two contradictory statements can both be true. In the technical terminology of dialectic, the first of these statements is called the *thesis,* and the one that contradicts or negates it is called the *antithesis.* When an antithesis negates a thesis, the process does not stop there; we have not heard the last of it when we negate A is at point X at time Y with the antithesis: A is not at point X at time Y. The same logic that applies to the thesis also applies to the antithesis: in short, the negation itself is negated. The negation of the negation, however, is not the original statement. When the antithesis contradicts the thesis, we do not go back to the thesis, for if we did, thought would be a dead-end street and we would just be vacillating between thesis and antithesis. The negation of the antithesis is a new statement that combines what is left of the thesis after it is negated and what is left of the antithesis after it is negated; this new statement, which fuses both thesis and antithesis is called a *synthesis.* Thus we move from a statement (thesis) to its negation (antithesis) to the negation of the negation (synthesis). The process is endless because the synthesis itself becomes a new thesis and is in turn negated by a new antithesis producing a new synthesis, and so on ad infinitum.

It was the belief of Marx and Engels that these laws of dialectics prevail not only in thought and in nature but in all of life. Their main interest was in history, and their efforts were directed toward proving that the dialectical process was driving history inevitably toward socialism. The application of dialectical materialism to society is called historical materialism. As Marx and Engels saw it, history is developing in a dialectical pattern from "I" to "We." The following outline gives some idea of what this means.

THESIS	ANTITHESIS	SYNTHESIS
"I" seeks to express itself.	*The "I's" conflict with one another.*	*Result is a strong Collective Will—a "We" through which the "I's" realize themselves.*

We can apply this mode of reasoning to the actual development of history. For example, we may want to take the Middle Ages as our starting point, our *thesis*. (Actually, we can start anywhere because the process is endless.) In this *thesis*—production was simple, but the means of production were possessed privately by direct producers, the workers. The negation of this thesis produces the *antithesis*—capitalism, in which the peasant and laborer are separated from the means of production and no longer own them. In this phase the industrial system as we know it grows up, and production is no longer simple. By the law of dialectic, this antithesis is itself negation. The process by which the negation of the negation takes place is revolution, and the resulting *synthesis*—communism. The synthesis both contains and negates the two earlier phases. It contains the thesis by reverting to ownership of the means of production by the workers, and it contains the antithesis by continuing with industrial production; it negates the thesis by eliminating simple, primitive methods of production and it negates the antithesis by eliminating ownership by the bosses. The synthesis combines the ownership system of the thesis with the productive organization of the antithesis.

All this historical change can be explained in terms of the economic base of society. Other factors may be important, but in the last analysis only the economic is crucial. The factor of climate, for example, has a great influence on a society, but it cannot account for all social change. Greek climate from the sixth century B.C. to the first century was constant, yet this was a period of immense social change.

Marx and Engels regarded every culture as a structurally interrelated whole. To understand either the art, the literature, or the legal code of any historical epoch, it is essential to see it in a broad cultural context. Marx and Engels more clearly than most understood the *interrelationships* of all aspects of culture and they also saw that culture as a relatively stable social whole is at the same time in a state of constant development. Most philosophies of history can account for either change or stability, but rarely both. If they tell us what factors made the Middle Ages what they were, then we are left to wonder why we are still not in the Middle Ages. If they tell us what forces produce changes, then they generally are not very good at explaining why cultural systems last as long as they do. How can we explain both the persistence of the *pattern* of the social whole and its *development* and change? Marx's answer was that both could be explained in terms of the *mode of production.*

The *mode of production* is the *independent variable* that accounts for both the dominant structural organization of any society and for its development. The economic base of society gives rise to all of its ideas and institutions. The political system, the legal code, art, morality, religion are all, according to Marx and Engels, shaped by the mode of production. What is believed, cared about, or preached reflects the economic structure of the society.

Indeed, although men may proclaim ideas or values are most important to them, they are really at bottom motivated by economic considerations. Men may speak of the almighty God in heaven, but what really drives them is the almighty dollar here on earth. Thus in a capitalist society Christianity becomes just a dressing to make capitalism look good. Religion is, one might say, a front for capitalism, and similarly the state is no more than a means of protecting private property.

Assuming economic factors as the underlying cause of social existence, Marx believed the development of history had to be explained in economic terms. Thus he maintained that the instrumentality of historic development is *class* struggle. Class struggle explains both stability and change because the economic forces that make classes give a structure to society and make it resistant to change; but at the same time these forces produce conflict between classes, and this conflict is the source of movement and change. History produces the pattern it does because, insofar as there are classes there is stability, but insofar as these classes are in struggle there is change. The power conflict that drives classes against one another gets things moving. Ultimately, Marx believed that through class conflicts, all classes would be eliminated, and there would be the establishment of the *classless* society. In it oppression and exploitation would be eliminated.

Although Marx maintained that his socialism was superior to the socialist systems of other thinkers of his time because it alone was scientific, there is much in Marx that smacks of religious prophecy and faith. When he announced what the future course of history would be, and declared it was moving toward a proletarian paradise, he was more engaged in crystal gazing than in scientific prediction.

The fact is that there are many moments of great wisdom in Marx and also many that are rather foolish, but for our purposes—the consideration of materialist philosophy—what is important is that Karl Marx, operating on the assumption that matter is the base of reality, accomplished a brilliant job of showing how we can understand society, culture, and history in economic categories. It was an immense intellectual service for Marx to have focused so clearly on the economic structure of society and to exhibit its relationship to all other aspects of culture. By and large, the significance of the economic province as a fundamental force in civilization was not seen clearly until Marx opened the eyes of mankind to it.

Marx not only formulated a penetrating analysis of civilization and history in terms of economic forces, but also developed a dynamic interpretation of materialism. Marx believed that the mechanistic materialism of the eighteenth century was too static, and thus missed the *process* character of reality. The materialists preceding Marx contended the life of man was a simple function of the material conditions of his existence. There was a tendency for materialists to understand the universe as a great machine grinding out all in existence in accordance with simple and straightforward mechanical principles. This was too static and did not account for the complexity of life and of history. Marx was a materialist, but he did not see anything as simple. Things were complex: a thing contained its own opposite, and there was interplay between the opposites; out of them might emerge a *new* reality. The old materialism did not allow for novelty—for all that occurs is that which is already in the works of the machine. In Marx's vision of things there was always conflict, out of which genuinely new forces might come into being. As Marx and Engels understood it, science could no longer be concerned only with gathering facts and classifying them; they believed science had to be a study of changes, of processes, and it had to be a means of illuminating the great wealth of interconnections between all things.

Marx may have gone too far in making the economic variable the golden key that opened understanding to all aspects of human existence, but he did open new vistas of understanding by analyzing civilization in terms of material conditions, by showing culture to be an interrelated whole, and by developing his dynamic interpretation of materialism.

IDEALISM: SOME CONCLUSIONS

The tomes of Hegel constitute one of the great efforts to construct a metaphysical system providing a complete account of the universe. Of course, there have been idealists since, and highly impressive ones, but none of them is in the big time in the same sense in which Hegel was. The post-Hegelian world was one in which God was moribund and philosophy was becoming morbid. Here was a world dominated by power—by science, politics, and economics—and religious and moral considerations were falling by the wayside. With population beginning to explode and the masses beginning to rise, a new force was erupting into history. The material conditions of the masses were wretched, making them a force to be reckoned with; concern about material conditions was reaching a new peak. The scientific context powerfully reinforced this concern. The scientific epoch of Newtonian physics with the Newtonian image of the universe as a great machine, had ushered in an intellectual atmosphere of materialism. Hegel's whole idealistic concept of reality and historic development was rendered into materialistic terms by Karl Marx. Stress upon science, technology, and political and economic power caused idealistic philosophy to be synonymous with unrealistic philosophy, and, perhaps, to seem less meaningful than it had ever seemed. This may seem ironical as, in the development of relativity physics, contemporary physical theory no longer viewed the universe as a great machine, nor as ultimately reducible to material particles, and it may be that some form of idealistic philosophy would be more defensible than ever before. Einstein eviscerated the universe of all that which might be regarded as absolute; he demonstrated that there can be no absolute space, time, or motion—no absolute standards or reference points of any kind.

And yet, although in an empirical or material sense it may not be possible to formulate an absolute frame of reference, this does not mean that there may not be other grounds upon which the absolute can be validated. The absolute is not a property of the physical universe; it is something other than the physical universe, which men use to give meaning to the material realm. One may still argue that there is an ultimate basis for our relativistic universe. There is much that does make sense in this world, and the fact that we can account for the universe in terms of equations and mathematical principles suggests that it is orderly and intelligible. This has some significance for the idealist case, for the idealist takes the position the universe or reality is orderly and intelligible, and that this cannot be explained physicalistically. Lincoln Barnett reminds us "a curious order runs through our perceptions, as if indeed there might be an underlayer of objective reality which our senses translate."[32] Barnett goes on to explain, "It is the mathematical orthodoxy of the universe that enables theorists like Einstein to predict and discover natural laws simply by the solution of equations." But he immediately adds, "The paradox of physics today is that with every improvement in its mathematical apparatus the gulf between man the observer and the objective world of scientific description becomes more profound."[33]

One can almost feel an affinity with the ancient Hindu idealist who believed the world man perceived through his senses was not real, and that there was a higher order of reality. After all when we think of reality in materialistic categories, we think of it after the analogy of *things*. Talking about electricity, Bertrand Russell pointed out that it is not a thing; it is a way we understand things to behave. In contemporary physics we get away from thinking of reality in terms of things. The basis of reality is not taken to be substance but events. Reality is a reality of process, and that is more consistent with an idealistic than with a materialistic conception.

Of course, objections certainly can be raised against the idealist's contention that a scientific account of the universe entails idealism, but on the other hand it can no longer be maintained, as it was in days of pre-Relativity

---

[32] Lincoln Barnett, *The Universe and Dr. Einstein* (New York: New American Library, Inc., 1952), pp. 23f.

[33] *Ibid.*, p. 24.

physics, that science is inconsistent with an idealistic interpretation of reality

If one can better explain the universe *idealistically* than materialistically, then it may be said that this is the kind of world in which the *ideals* men live and die for have a basis in reality. If matter is not what is ultimately real, then this is a world in which we really may matter.

The Quality of Reality: Dualism vs. Monism

DESCARTES, DUALISM, AND THE "NEW ABYSS"

The time was December 2, 1942, and the place was the University of Chicago. An extraordinary gathering of some of the most outstanding figures in the scientific world was taking place in a very ordinary squash court. On that day scientists, committed to the struggle against the monster of fascism, concluded an experiment with a uranium pile, and in doing so demonstrated the possibility of building the most monstrous weapon ever known to man. Surely that squash court would not have been the scene of atomic drama had it not been for the menace of Hitler; but Hitler is long since gone, and there remains the menace of atomic radiation and nuclear war to pose a greater threat to humanity than Hitler ever did.

On December 2, 1942, the first nuclear reaction was achieved. Always subjected to the power of nature, man was now taking hold of a power brighter than a thousand suns. The nuclear age was upon us and atomic fission—or the splitting of the atom made this possible. Having split the atom, man now could blow up the world. Later, Albert Einstein admitted that if he had known Hitler would not have succeeded in developing an atom bomb, he would not have participated in getting our project for the bomb underway. And Robert Oppenheimer, who played so central a role in producing it, witnessed the first atomic bomb test and was moved to recall those powerful lines from the Bhagavad Gita, the great work of Hindu literature:

> *I am become death, the shatterer of worlds;*
> *Waiting that hour that ripens to their doom.*

The curse of modern existence involves not only the real possibility of a physical shattering of our world but also a philosophical shattering of man. Meaninglessness and despair are in the atmosphere of modern life, making it impossible for people to gain a vision of the future. In an age of plenty, human beings feel empty; in an age of great scientific discovery, they feel lost. Clouds of gloom hang over our cities, and everywhere metropolitan streets are paved with poverty, drug addiction, and violence. There appears to be no wholeness in life. People are alienated from nature, from one another, and even from themselves. One can well explain alienation in economic, sociological, and psychological terms, but to fully comprehend it one should also be aware of the philosophical roots. These roots can be discovered in the philosophy of dualism, which saddles man with an image of himself as an inherently divided being.

An array of great scientists went to that old squash court in Chicago and split the atom, produced a chain reaction, and so launched man into the atomic age. More than three hundred years before this a lonely French philosopher went into his stove, worked on the problem of proving that man exists, and formulated in modern terms the image of man as a dualistic creature. By interpreting all reality as bifurcated into mind and matter, René Descartes in effect split man, thus initiating an intellectual chain reaction that has extended to our own age of alienation.

If it can be shown that there is a relationship between dualism and the development of human insecurity, then we would have to say that Descartes made a contribution to our age of uncertainty and anxiety. Ironically, however, his fundamental purpose was to discover certainty and necessary truths. Descartes was convinced that the attainment of certainty required the most rigorous testing of all assertions. Thus his procedure was to question everything critically. This was the method of doubt. If in the process of doubting all things, one encounters an obstacle in the form of something that absolutely cannot be doubted, then one will have found that of which he can be certain. In seeking such certainty man must go as far as to doubt even his own existence. There is probably nothing a person could be more sure of than that he exists. But could he prove it? Perception cannot provide absolute proof of our existence because we often perceive things that do not exist. There are numerous stories of a man complaining of pain in a leg which, unbeknownst to him, already has been amputated. We may feel sure we see something out there when, in fact, we are seeing only a mirage. We can never even be entirely certain we are not dreaming. We cannot depend upon the orderliness or consistency in what we take to be the waking world, for we can never be fully certain there really is consistency. We cannot even be certain of mathematical truths, because we may be convinced of their truth only because we are being systematically deceived by an evil demon. That is not likely, but it is possible. And as long as anything is possible, even though it may seem absurd, we cannot be *certain* it is incorrect.

It seems that everything is open to doubt, but there is one thing we cannot doubt. We cannot doubt we are doubting because in the very process of attempting to do so, we would be doubting. Doubting is a form of thinking; thus man is a being who thinks. Man's first certainty, therefore, is not that he is a physical being, but that he is a thinking being—or what Descartes called a *Res Cogitans.*

Having proved his own existence, Descartes reached up to do as much for God. To do so he reached back for some medieval arguments, such as the ontological argument that an infinite idea cannot come from that which is only finite—as everything in the physical world is. The idea of the infinite must come from that which is infinite, and that is God.

In this way Descartes got himself and God into existence; after that, all he needed was a world and other people and he would be in philosophical business. He did perceive a world and other selves, and because there is an all good God (Descartes had also proved that God must be all good, but we need not go into that argument here), he reasoned they must exist or God would not allow him to perceive them. After all, what kind of a God would have men perceive a world that was not there? He would be a Fraud, not a God.

Thus reality as understood by Descartes is divided into two substances. There is mental or spiritual substance (God and the *Res Cogitans*) and physical substance (the things we perceive). This view that holds there are two sorts of reality is called *dualism*.

What Descartes called *Res Cogitans*—thinking substance, mind, or soul —is *spiritual* or *mental* in nature; it is *unextended*, which means that it does not extend in space, for it is not a physical thing. Obviously, it cannot be perceived or observed. Thus it is said to be *private*: no one but the individual himself has access to his own mind. No matter how powerful or perfect a technical instrument is, it cannot be used to see what one is thinking. The mind has no spatial existence. This sphere of reality is subjective. Physical substance, which Descartes called *Res Extensa*, is extended, is material, exists in space and time, and thus is amenable to observation. Therefore, it is public. According to Descartes's analysis, reality is dichotomized as follows:

REALITY

MIND (Res Cogitans):	BODY (Res Extensa):
Is spiritual;	*Is material;*
Is free from subjection to mechanical laws;	*Is subject to mechanical laws;*
Exists in time only;	*Exists in space and time;*
Is internal—has consciousness;	*Is external;*
Thus is private.	*Thus is public, and open to inspection.*

To understand reality as composed of mind and body makes sense in terms of our experience. We know people make wishes and have ideas and thoughts, which cannot be perceived. These are of what we would call an intellectual or mental nature. And their reality seems to be qualitatively different from the reality of those things we can feel, see, hear, taste, and smell, such as trees, flowers, rocks, automobiles, vegetables, and houses.

This seems to be a perfect plan for understanding reality, and yet there seems to emerge a technical flaw in what could be a beautiful relationship between mind and body. If mind and body are of such different natures, how do they relate? This is known as the problem of *interaction*. How can that which is of one nature have an influence on that which is of an entirely different nature? One can drive a nail into a board by pounding it with a hammer. Imagine someone trying to drive a thought into a board with a hammer. If a person went about with a hammer trying to nail down a wish, people would soon take him away. There appears to be a real philosophical problem here—and yet, practically speaking, it seems that interaction does occur. A person thinks about an unpleasant idea and comes down with a headache. The unpleasant thought is mental and the headache is physical, and yet it clearly looks as if one has an effect upon the other. One is sitting watching television and *decides* in his mind he will shut the set off and go out—and he does so. The television is shut off and his body goes out. The person thought he would move his body, and it moved.

Somehow, the mental and physical do seem to interact. But *how?* How can that which is spirit be said to interact with that which is matter and is utterly different? Descartes, having interpreted reality dualistically, was intensely concerned with discovering a solution to this problem. The solution he finally worked out was a most interesting one. Descartes had observed that animals have bodies but he saw no evidence that they have souls or minds; indeed, his religion taught that animals do not have souls. Thus they could be understood in terms of purely mechanical principles. Descartes also observed that man has a pineal gland (a small structure at the top of the brain), whereas animals lack one. Because the evidence shows that animals have bodies and no minds and that men have bodies and minds, and further because animals have no pineal gland and men do, Descartes supposed it a reasonable hypothesis to conclude the pineal gland marks the point at which mind and body interact. Descartes regarded this assumption as even more plausible because of the fact no clear function was assigned the pineal gland. This glandular solution of the mind-body problem, however ingenious, is hardly impressive, for inasmuch as the pineal gland is itself physical, it could hardly serve as a principle that would relate the mental and the physical. One would still have to explain *how* the pineal gland could interact with mind. Descartes's solution left much to be desired. What is more, after René Descartes died, Nels Stensen found that the pineal gland exists in animals.

Thus Descartes did not discover a solution to the problems of dualism, but he very clearly articulated the philosophy of dualism in such a manner as to raise some fundamental problems about the nature of existence.

Descartes's philosophy clearly constituted an overthrowing of Aristotelian philosophical principles of physics and psychology. Aristotle interpreted *all* bodies as made of *form* and *matter*. The *form* of a thing is its essential qualities and its specific characteristics. Form reveals *what* a thing is. Matter is that to which form gives shape. Form is inherent in body or matter and animates it and gives it movement. Aristotle believed all bodies to have form and thus, *purpose.* A body always served some end or purpose, which is discernible in its form. *Pure* matter—that is, matter separated from its form—is a brute possibility, an irrationality.

Descartes's viewpoint was entirely different from Aristotle's and had exceedingly significant psychological and cultural implications. In the world view of Descartes, soul (or form) became a principle entirely distinct from matter. It became *alien* to it, whereas in Aristotle the two had been inextricably connected. By freeing matter from interpenetration by Aristotelian soul or form, Descartes made it possible to develop a fully *mechanistic* interpretation of reality. Matter became a *rational* substance, which could be dealt with in its own right. A science of matter could now be perfected independently of a science of man. The following reveals how the Aristotelian view differs from the Cartesian, and how Descartes opens the door to the development of an independent, nonpurposive, nonspiritual physics.

CONCEPTIONS OF REALITY

ARISTOTELIAN:	CARTESIAN (DESCARTES)
All bodies are substances—composed of form and matter.	*Body and soul are distinct and independent substances.*
Form is rational.	*Soul is rational.*
Matter is irrational and dependent for its reality on form.	*Matter is intelligible and exists independently of soul.*

Descartes gave expression to a world in which mind and body were progressively being cut off from one another and in which it was ever becoming more difficult to find a basis for interaction between them. A world was emerging in which that which is most essential to man, his *mind*, was understood as being beyond observation and objective understanding. It was becoming a more and more mechanized world in which there seemed to be no room for the reality of mind. There was no possibility for the *thinking* substance, Descartes's *Res Cogitans*, to be understood scientifically. On the other hand the physical world was entirely open to inspection and to mathematical observation. A science of the physical world could be developed to a state of near perfection. A new and completely objectivized mechanized universe was being built, and in it man as a subjective being was as a displaced person.

The universe in which man must dwell has become *alien* to the essence of his being, and thus man can never feel at one with it or at home in it. Dualistic philosophy plants seeds that grow into *alienation*. Man strives for wholeness, yet he is cut off from the natural world in which he lives and from his own physical nature. To be insane is to be out of contact with reality, but if there is no solution to the problem of "interaction," how can man, whose very essence is his thinking—his mind—ever be in contact with the great physical reality about him?

Man-as-mind becomes a tiny island surrounded by a vast sea of matter. His physical power in the world of matter becomes so immense that he is ultimately able to acquire the use of atomic energy, but humanity develops so slowly that the primary use of the atom is for barbaric purposes. Atomic power, which could have been employed to raise the level of life for humanity, is instead used to threaten it with extinction. The source of man's dignity is his mind, which Descartes saw as the center of his being. But in this mechanistic world of atomic power, what role does the mind have to play? In a recent philosophical classic, British philosopher Gilbert Ryle's *The Concept of Mind*, there is an expressive phrase that describes what has happened to the mind in the modern world: it has become a "ghost in the machine." Only the physical power of the mind is real; the mind becomes virtually nothing. The mind as Descartes explained it is, according to Ryle, a "category mistake." To suppose that the mind exists objectively somewhere in the body in the same way as the body exists is to commit a fallacy. On what basis did Ryle reach this conclusion?

In a famous article written in the early 1930s, "Systematically Misleading Expressions," Gilbert Ryle rejected the principles of logical atomism, which maintained that there is a structural similarity between propositions (statements) and the facts which they represent. The logical atomist position is rather closely related to the mind-body problem of dualism: the dualist says that the immaterial mind is in some way capable of interacting with the material body, and the logical atomist claims that the immaterial products of the mind—our sentences and statements—are in some way structurally similar to the material facts they are supposed to describe. Ryle would have neither of these two philosophical positions; he completely denied that facts or states of affairs in their structure could be anything like or unlike sentences or other types of propositions. Rejecting logical atomism, Ryle devoted himself to the analysis of *ordinary language*. In contrast to A. J. Ayer and the logical positivists, who saw empirical verifiability as the key to philosophy, Ryle came to see the style of the ordinary man's language as that key. A wonderful application of this new method of logical analysis was provided in Ryle's extremely influential work, *The Concept of Mind*. In this work Ryle attempted to show how the misuse of words is a source of bad philosophy. His main point was that *dualism* of mind and body—especially as exemplified in the philosophy of Descartes—is a logical mistake, claiming that the mind is not a *substance;* it is just a *style* of behavior. There is no such *thing* as a mind inside our skull; rather, "mind" is the term for the way in which a person behaves.

This thesis went at least as far back as Aristotle. In *De Anima*, Aristotle's contribution to psychology, the view was put forth that the soul or the psyche is not a thing or substance, but rather is a *function* or an activity of man. Pragmatists in our own times, such as Charles Sanders Pierce, William James, and John Dewey, have viewed mind in somewhat similar terms. But there is a difference between the views of these men and that of Ryle, as there is between Ryle's and a strict psychological behaviorist's, such as John B. Watson. This is so because these other thinkers were interested in the empirical fields of psychology and/or social psychology, whereas Ryle claimed he was not. Ryle's approach to the problem was purely in terms of linguistic analysis.

We have already noted that Ryle accused the dualists of making what he called a *category mistake*. By this he meant that when people say there is a mind *and* a body, what they are doing is mixing up categories.

> *A foreigner visiting Oxford or Cambridge for the first time is shown a number of colleges, libraries, playing fields, museums, scientific departments and administrative offices. He then asks "But where is the University? I have seen where the members of the Colleges live, where the Registrar works, where the scientists experiment and the rest. But I have not yet seen the University. . . .*[34]

But Ryle tells us that the poor man has to be made to understand the "University" is not another collateral institution. The University is not some ulterior counterpart to the colleges, offices, and buildings the visitor has already seen. "The University is just the way in which all he has already seen is organized."[35] According to Ryle the man was making a mistake in thinking that "the University" belongs to the same category as the actually existing laboratories, classrooms, offices, and libraries that compose it. The man got his categories mixed up. René Descartes had done the same thing. He thought the mind belonged to a category it does not belong to. In so thinking, Descartes assigned the mind the status of a *substance*. Ryle, however, found it most insubstantial, and he said of Descartes's theory of the mind: "I shall often speak of it, with deliberate abusiveness, as 'the dogma of the Ghost in the Machine.' "[36] According to Ryle, the mind is not a ghost or some sort of mysterious substance. Rather, it is merely the external intellectual operations one performs. He supposed that the fallacy of dualism is in assuming that observed mental behavior has a hidden cause inside the skull, whereas in fact there is no such thing. For example, we speak of courage, wit, or vanity as though they had a substantial existence of their own. "How could he do that?" we ask. "Because he has courage," someone else answers. However, these words are simply the terms we use to describe a person's way of acting—we say that he has courage when we only mean that he acts courageously.

It was Ryle's contention that Descartes and other dualists all wish to distinguish intelligent behavior from nonintelligent behavior. Ryle maintained that such distinction can be made, but it must be done by describing certain observable behaviors. But instead of distinguishing intelligent from nonintelligent behavior by reference to different types of behavioral manifestations, Descartes had sought for the distinction in terms of some inner cause. According to Ryle, Descartes "had mistaken the logic of his problem. Instead of asking by what criteria intelligent behavior is actually distinguished from nonintelligent behavior, he asked 'Given that the principle of mechanical causation does not tell us the difference, what other causal principle will tell us?' "[37]

[34] The Concept of Mind (New York: Barnes and Noble, Inc., 1949), p. 16.
[35] *Ibid.*
[36] *Ibid.*, p. 156.
[37] *Ibid.*, p. 21.

Ryle built up a beautiful case against Descartes, but the problem is that he was not talking about what Descartes was talking about. Descartes was not a logical analyst like Ryle; Descartes was interested in the *world.* Unlike Ryle, he was not in search of criteria with which to distinguish mental or intellectual from nonmental or nonintellectual behavior. Rather, Descartes was concerned with discovering *why* there is the distinction. Descartes may have been wrong in his dualism—as I believe he was, but that is beside the point here. The point is that if Descartes was wrong, it was not for the reason Ryle advanced: the problem is not that Descartes committed a *logical mistake.* If he was wrong it was because reality is not actually bifurcated into mind and body. And if Descartes is wrong, paradoxical as this may seem, his distinguished critic Ryle must also be wrong, for despite his vitriolic attacks upon Descartes, Ryle is very much a product of the kind of world Descartes's philosophy seems to have given rise to. Looking at the matter historically, we can see that mind was always an important reality for man—was, that is, until Cartesian dualism split the realm of mind off from the material universe. The overwhelming tradition of Western philosophy and religion saw the material and spiritual worlds as inextricably connected; only with the last judgment could they be separated. Of course, Descartes too maintained they were connected, but with him the prime emphasis was upon distinguishing and separating them; with him the connection became a big problem and at best was highly tenuous. In the pre-Cartesian classical world, the kind of attack Ryle carried out upon the notion of mind would have been as out of place as mate-matching by a computer. But after Descartes had so effectively separated mind from matter, and after modern science had had a few centuries to revolutionize the world on the basis of the material side only, the road was thoroughly paved for Ryle to travel on it with the declaration that the "better half" of the Cartesian dual reality was unreal, a figment of the philosophical imagination, and a result of sloppy thinking. In attacking Descartes for believing in the "ghost" of mind, Ryle was actually cutting up the thinking of the philosopher who did most to lay the groundwork for the cutting away of mind altogether and thus making a ghost of what had been so meaningful and real to human beings. The road toward Ryle and our *alienated world* in which mind was so cut off from nature was paved by philosophical developments in materialism and pluralism.

DUALISM VS. MONISM: SOME CONCLUSIONS

Descartes's philosophy gave expression to the reality of man's increasing alienation from himself and from the world in which he lived. To Descartes reality was "clearly and distinctly" a world of mind *and* matter. The problem was that although matter could be treated as something clear and distinct, mind was vague and indistinct. Empirically oriented philosophers and scientists thus devoted their attentions to the material universe. Mind simply did not appear to have any substantiality, and could not be treated in an empirical manner. Thus the reality of mental substance was thoroughly denied by the scientifically trained intellect. In this new age the *res extensa,* or extended substance, existing in space and expressible in mathematical formulae; the material half of Descartes's dualistic world had much more reality than the *res cogitans,* or world of mind. In a period of the scientific, industrial, and commercial revolution, the private sphere of mind was out of reach and fast becoming off limits for men of learning. In this time of great growth in man's physical power and of great historical change, philosophers came to define reality as *matter in motion.* The world was seen as a large machine that operated in accordance with inexorable laws of cause and effect. Man was not exempted from this process; he was no more than a part of it. Descartes had provided arguments showing that animals are automata, merely machines without minds or souls. Men too can be so understood, and they were by La Mettrie, who announced that man is but a machine. Cabanis developed materialism even more carefully than La Mettrie, maintaining that there is nothing whatever spiritual about mind, and that the brain secretes thoughts just as the liver secretes bile.

Of course, neither dualism nor materialism was a new philosophical position; they have both been maintained throughout the history of philosophy. But in the modern world they took on a new meaning and gave expression to the basic dynamics of the reality in which men were living. Never had material conditions been so significant as in the age of Newtonian physics and the Industrial Revolution. With the development of mass production, material values became more a reality than they have ever been in man's past; never before had they so dominated his life.

Here was the start of an age in which man was gaining a material world and losing his soul. So man has come to live in a thoroughly mechanized world with his fate determined by the machine and is unable to be free. Today we are living through one of the great revolutions in material culture—the Cybernetic Revolution. In the Industrial Revolution muscle power was replaced by machines, but in the Cybernetic Revolution brain power—or the mind—can be replaced by computers. We are fast coming to the time when man himself can be replaced. In the past, men anthropomorphized their gods and spoke of them as though they were human. Now philosophers and scientists, having laughed anthropomorphism out of court, are themselves anthropomorphizing computers and speaking of them as if they are human. Worse yet, we are coming to a time when they will no longer speak of humans as if they are human! Material progress has brought us to the point at which a machine can make a decision to start World War III and end man, who made the machine. Dr. Ralph Lapp tells us that men "live in daily dread not only of man-created tensions but also of the frightening technological advance. There is a growing apprehension that the ultimate decision will be taken not by man's own will but by his hardware."[38] He refers us to W. H. Pickering, director of the Jet Propulsion Laboratory at the California Institute of Technology, who has said:

This is the prospect we face: the decision to destroy an enemy nation—and

[38] Ralph Lapp, *Kill and Overkill* (New York: Basic Books, Inc., 1962), p. 8.

by inference our own will—will be made by a radar set, a telephone circuit, an electronic computer. It will be arrived at without the aid of human intelligence. If a human observer cries: "Stop, let me check the calculations," he is already too late—his launching sites are destroyed and the war is lost.

. . . The failure of a handful of vacuum tubes and transistors could determine the fate of our civilization.[39]

IN THE LIGHT OF ETERNITY—SPINOZA

Today social theorists and analysts seem very much united in holding the view that *divided* modern man is falling. The high degree of specialization accruing from our technological civilization and the fragmentation of existence following from it have given rise to alienated, lonely man. Today, when people have moved closer together by virtue of our advanced communication and transportation systems and our unprecedentedly large population, man paradoxically experiences the deepest pain of being cut off and alone. The Industrial and Commercial Revolutions have made possible the building of a paradise on earth, and yet man feels himself to be a stranger in paradise—alienated and estranged. This fundamental problem of *alienation* is often analyzed in terms of economic, political, and social conditions, but it goes deeper. At the bottom of it one will always find a philosophy of dualism. As long as reality is understood as being ultimately *dichotomized,* man must feel himself cut off. If, as is often said, man must be able to feel at *one* with reality to attain satisfaction or happiness in living, then what chance does he have in a universe that is not at one with itself? Thus the dualistic and pluralistic metaphysical conceptions of Descartes and Leibnitz have provided the philosophical basis for our alienated, technological world.

In the modern Western world, a vision of reality as *one*—or what is called a *monistic* conception of reality—was most profoundly provided by Baruch Spinoza (1632–77).

Living in the Age of Reason, when rational methods were proving to be so successful in mathematics and in the development of the new physics, Spinoza was convinced that the tool of Reason could be used to provide a solution to all problems of existence. And yet, although patterned entirely on the model of geometry, his philosophy was not excessively formal, dry, and lifeless. On the contrary, true and existential feeling dwelled in this House of Geometry, and Spinoza never became lost from life within his intricate rational system.

Spinoza understood philosophy to be not an intellectual or an academic game, but a true search for the *best life.* He was convinced that the kind of life man has depends upon what he commits himself to. The objectives to which he devotes himself with his love determine whether he shall be happy or miserable. If he directs his love to objects of his senses or to material things, he will be unhappy, for knowledge of the senses is the most unreliable knowledge attainable; it is always vulnerable to prejudice, error,

[39] *Ibid.*, pp. 8f.

and illusion. Corresponding to this lowest kind of knowledge is the lowest variety of human satisfaction—that based upon pleasure of the senses. Higher than this is knowledge founded upon *reason*. The systematic employment of reason culminates in scientific knowledge, and through science man can understand and control nature. Although this is a very high kind of knowledge, Spinoza recognized an even more exalted type—knowledge that is founded on intuition. Through such knowledge man transcends the narrow confines of the empirical self and attains a vision of the whole— in fact, a vision of reality even as it is seen by God. Man's life thus becomes enlarged, and he is able to rise above the smallness and meanness of the everyday world.

Ironically, as Spinoza interpreted it, love of pleasure, sexual relationships, wealth, fame, and power on earth do not enhance love of self; indeed, they conflict with it. Spinoza observed inside of all men a drive to preserve themselves. He called this impulse to self-preservation *conatus* and used this concept to explain and illuminate behavioral dynamics. The human system will make all kinds of adjustments for self-preservation, Spinoza explained. If a man is ignorant concerning the proper human goals he should strive to retain his dignity as a man, he will automatically adjust and seek to preserve himself by developing such false feelings as jealousy and hatred in order to achieve some measure of self-protection.

The problem is that those who seek preservation by satisfying sensual desires fail to really love themselves and to contribute to that which is most personally fulfilling. Sexual love is often used in this way as a means of preservation. The effort to gain satisfaction and a sense of self-preservation through sensual pleasures is *narrowly* selfish, and hence self-defeating. Actually, the more one can love others, the more he can love himself. A person who truly loves another contributes to his own well-being by filling himself with the goodness of that love, whereas a person who loves another only as a means of satisfying a selfish need gains nothing for either party. Loving others is *constructive* and creates a wholesome feeling within.

Many men who seek to gain pleasure and self-satisfaction go about it the wrong way. Spinoza lived in a period during which the art of sensual and sexual pleasure was being highly cultivated. One could hardly be considered a gentleman unless one had an illegitimate child, or at least syphilis. A real gentleman knocked on the door of his wife's boudoir before entering so as not to catch her with her lover. Spinoza did not believe that such emphasis upon sensual pleasure was truly gratifying. He maintained that the drives for money, sex, and social power were really banalities that were incapable of satisfying the whole man. People falsely pursue such values, Spinoza explained, because they suffer from "inadequate ideas." Spinoza anticipated Freud in his claim that men were motivated by passions they could not understand, and, like Freud, he understood the remedy to consist in bringing deep unconscious strivings to consciousness. Human beings are tormented by fears and anxieties because they have inadequate ideas of what they require as human beings to sustain themselves. Those who choose the narrow trails of life and search for sensual enjoyment miss the true joy of seeing life in total perspective.

For Spinoza the good life consists in understanding what is good for oneself, and that implies not trying to remake the world to fit one's own desires, but remaking one's desires to accord with the ways of the world. He who seeks to control nature is far less free than he who submits to its rule. Because a mere man cannot obstruct the laws of nature, the effort to do so can lead only to anxiety and frustration. There is, therefore, greater freedom in submitting to these inexorable laws than in defying them. Spinoza noted that if a stone thrown through the air had consciousness, it would swear it was sailing through the air because it wanted to. But a stone thrown in the air is not determining its own course, and neither is a man determining his own course as he moves through life. This does not mean that man is not free. He *is* free—free to understand and to accept the ways of nature. What enslaves a man is his desire to interfere with the laws of nature and to make them suit him. The free man is he who knows that he is not free to do whatever he will in the world and has sufficient control over his passions so as not to try to do it. The free man is not he who endeavors to remake the way of the world, but he who detaches himself from the small efforts of men and views all existence *sub specie aeternitatis* —under the aspect of eternity. When a man misses a traffic light, he becomes upset at having to wait twenty seconds; when a person misses a bus, his face becomes flushed and he curses his fate. The world has been going on for over two billion years and will go on another couple billion—political leaders willing—and yet people make so much of a few seconds. If men could only put things in a broader perspective—the perspective of eternity, so many things they regard as important would dissolve into insignificance.

Spinoza invites us to step aside from our petty involvements in the everyday world and to open ourselves to the infinite joy of an eternal perspective. Do not become excited about your big problems; in the eyes of heaven they are but little ones. By seeing things in the light of eternity instead of in the darkness of the moment, one attains the highest kind of knowledge: he has an *intuition* that lifts him above the trivialities of this world and, through a mystic vision, brings true blessedness to his very being. He has not only the highest kind of knowledge but also the highest kind of happiness—the intellectual love of God, which liberates one from the bondage of worldly care.

The possibility of discovering true blessedness and joy in existence provides itself only when one can see that the apparent multiplicity of existence is illusory. In a fragmented world the individual himself becomes divided, and the divided man is always unhappy. Spinoza's discovery of true happiness in this life resulted from his capacity to formulate a *monistic* conception of reality in which there was a oneness of man, God, and nature.

Baruch Spinoza, the philosopher who produced the most thoroughgoing monistic interpretation of reality, was born a Jew. His soul understood the Jewish commandment: "Hear O Israel, the Lord our God, the Lord is one."

Because of his need for intellectual freedom, Spinoza came into conflict with his religion, which seemed to need anything but what he had to offer at that time. The consequence was that he was excommunicated and thus cut off from a unity with the very religion that had ingrained in him the need for unity. Spinoza lost his religion and his taste for it, but he never lost his thirst for unity. He found that fundamental unity in his own metaphysics.

What is *Being*? What is real? If we are to put ourselves into harmonious relationship with our universe, we must establish some contact with or understanding of what is real or what Being is. Historically, most Western philosophers interpreted Being as *divided*. The Greek word for Being is *ousia*. Aristotle insisted *ousia* can be divided into ten categories. The medieval philosophers were greatly influenced by Aristotle, but they understood Being, or *ens* (as the Greek *ousia* was translated in Latin), somewhat differently than Aristotle, for they did not divide Being into ten categories. But they did follow Aristotle in dividing Being into that which *exists in itself* and that which *exists in another*. This division is found in Aristotle, where the terms for these two kinds of Being are "substance" (that which exists in itself) and "accident" (that which exists in another).

Aristotle understood *substance* as that having independent existence in the sense that its being is not dependent upon any qualities outside of it. He contrasted this with accidental qualities that are dependent for their being on the substance in which they exist. Substance is the essence of a thing—the very core of its being—and as such it is that which remains *constant* during all other changes that may occur to it. Thus substance is a permanent dimension of what is real. Aristotle's analysis of change is important as a basis for understanding the idea of substance, for Aristotle believed that change invariably points to something unchangeable. The fact that we experience change in our everyday life implies that there is some underlying, unchanging substance undergoing change.

Aristotle regarded three elements as absolutely necessary for change. They are two contraries and a substratum. There must be that which endures throughout the process of change—the substratum or substance. In addition there is always the terminus at the beginning and the terminus at the end—the two contraries. The terminus at the beginning, the *ad quo,* and the terminus at the end, the *ad quem,* are the boundaries of the change, and underlying the change is the substance. The substratum in Aristotle is any continuing identity. A young man is foolish, but he changes and becomes wise. This presupposes a *privation* (in this case the lack of wisdom), which is the terminus at the beginning, and an *actualization* (gaining wisdom), which is the terminus at the end, and it presupposes substance, which has undergone the change (the young man himself). Aristotle insisted that in order to recognize change it is essential to recognize permanence or substance. Identity can always be recognized in change because there is a substratum or substance. If you see a person for the first time in twenty-five years you may practically not recognize him because he has changed so much, and yet you recognize that he is still the same person you knew twenty-five years ago; he has changed but he is not a new person. Intellectually and physically the person may seem entirely different, yet there is something that makes him the same person and that is his substance, the underlying reality of his being upon which change has operated. The changing qualities, which are not necessary to the being of the man, are the accidental qualities. These accidental qualities depend for their being upon the substance. An example of an accidental quality is the color of the man's hair. It might change from brown to gray to white, but this does not change the identity of the man. Indeed the man could lose his hair altogether and would still be the same man. You might well find a man walking about without a head of hair, but you will not find a head of hair walking around without a man. Substance can exist without some of the accidental qualities with which it is sometimes endowed, but accidentals cannot exist independently of substance.

The word substance derives from Latin and Greek roots that mean "to stand under." The substance is the essence of the thing that stands under it throughout all the changes of its accidental qualities. Indeed, precisely because substance was understood as the underlying substratum in which all qualities inhere and upon which all change takes place, it was virtually impossible to pin down concretely just what substance itself was. This led to the criticism that substance, being a propertyless substratum itself, really was not anything and thus could not exist. This criticism was vigorously put forth by David Hume. However, while some of the British empiricists became very disenchanted with the idea of substance, the Continental rationalists tried to hold on tightly to this elusive idea. The empiricists understood reality to consist only of the various changing empirical qualities that go to make him up. Was there an enduring, underlying self that gives the person his identity? The strict empiricist thought not. The rationalists, however, essentially accepted Aristotle's argument that there had to be some underlying essence of things. Now the first great modern philosopher, the French rationalist René Descartes, defined this substance as that which required nothing but itself for its existence. Substance is that which can exist on its own without external support. But where Aristotle had believed there were a plurality of substances consisting in all of the particular persons and objects of existence, Descartes insisted there were only two substances. These were body and soul. There was spiritual substance and material substance. Beneath the heavens bodies and souls were *finite* substances, but God was *infinite* substance. Spinoza accepted Descartes's concept of substance, but precisely because he did he denied there could be more than one substance. If we must understand substance as that which is complete in itself and is independent in the sense that it does not require any outside assistance for its existence, then it is absolute. This being the case, there cannot be infinite and finite substance. Finite substance, being limited by definition, cannot be absolute. There cannot be anything outside infinite substance because if there were, that would limit such substance and thus it could not be regarded as infinite. Thus Spinoza arrived at the conclusion there can be only one substance, and it must be absolute—God! Roughly, such was the line Spinoza followed on his way to finding the truth. Now let us see in more detail how Benedict Spinoza, the great rationalist, developed his case for monism, or the idea reality consists in one substance.

Spinoza, as we have just seen, defined substance as that which exists in itself and must be conceived through itself. If this were so, it certainly follows that it must be *independent,* completely free of outside influence. And hence it also follows that it is *causa sui* or the cause of itself, for if it were caused by something else, it would be dependent upon that. Furthermore, it is clear there can only be one substance because, since substance is that which exists in itself and is conceived through itself, if there were another substance a contradiction would ensue. This is so because the two substances would *limit* one another, inasmuch as anything that stands outside of another thing places a limitation upon it, just as a wall placed outside would limit me in that I could not walk through it. Whatever is outside of something in some sense diminishes it. Therefore, there can be nothing outside of substance, and it must be understood to be a sole existent. It must be one.

Every person is in some way limited by, or uses, all things outside of him, and therefore is dependent upon them. Thus a person cannot truly be said to exist in himself and to be conceived through himself; nor can he be said to be independent. Things in the world are interrelated by being in contact with one another, by influencing one another, and by being related through universal laws of nature. To explain this interrelatedness and interconnectedness of things, there must be some ultimate unity, and this is substance. There must be some ultimate source for all of the dependent things in the universe, or their dependence is never really illuminated. This ultimate source is substance. In Spinoza the one ultimate substance, of which all things and persons are a part, is understood as God.

Spinoza's God—or substance—is not a personal Being who created the world. Such a conception makes no sense. If God created the world, it would be separate from Him, stand outside of Him, and thus would limit Him. If the universe were separate from God, it would limit and lessen Him, and therefore God cannot be above the world or nature because that would detract from God, and God could not then be said to be absolute. Thus God must be understood as *immanent,* or fully existing in the world. God cannot be transcendent as He was taken to be in traditional theology. The glory of God is not His being above nature, but His being the same as *nature.* So-called "religious" persons who maintain that God is above the world tend to look upward toward Him, and thus they overlook the value of nature and life. Spinoza's philosophy, in contrast, is a celebration of life. God, the ultimate principle, is not beyond nature but is in nature, and therefore nature is sacred, life is sacred, and men who so believe do not defile it while worshipping a God beyond it. Thus Spinoza arrived at the idea of a *Deus sive Natura*—God is Nature. The fact that there is no God beyond the world we live in, actually makes life more meaningful because God is everywhere in it. Nature is truly beautiful because it is God. We thus cannot worship God and pollute the planet, for the planet is God.

To be sure, Spinoza admitted that nature does have a passive, uncreative aspect. This Spinoza called *natura naturata,* or nature as acted upon. This is nature as it is created. But there is also *natura naturans,* or nature as acting, as creative; it is this aspect that provides the fully creative dimension to nature and life. Putting creativity in nature gives it a meaning and value it often lacks when it is merely seen as a consequence and something apart from a supreme personal Being.

Traditional theologians were quite offended by Spinoza's identification of God with nature. Although Spinoza talked so much about the love of God that he was called the "God-intoxicated philosopher," these traditionalists felt that he was not loving God in the traditional sense, but rather nature. Yet, ironically enough, Spinoza had arrived at his view by taking Christian teachings very literally. Christians faithfully maintained that God is omnipotent (all powerful), omniscient (all knowing), and omnipresent (everywhere). As Spinoza saw it, it follows that if God is all powerful, all knowing, and everywhere, he must be everything. However, if God is everything, then He cannot be anything distinct. If God is all powerful and has no limits, there cannot be a world outside of Him, as that would limit Him; thus God must be the same as the world or nature. To equate God with nature is known as pantheism—the belief that God is all, or rather, that everything is God. This was Spinoza's vision of reality, and although it is logically consistent with Christian doctrines, it certainly angered Christian theologians; they apparently were not used to dealing with philosophers who insisted on being logically consistent with their teachings.

In Spinoza's teachings God became an immense interwoven system of nature that excludes the idea of a supreme spiritual power capable of intervening in nature on behalf of individuals. God is not a personal God. God is just the absolute, which is nature. Nature, in turn, is the absolute of which all else is but a part. The beauty of Spinoza's system is that it presents nature as a *unified whole.* There is no God above it, and there are no independent substances within it. All is interwoven in the whole fabric of nature. Thus if one flows with life and relates with reality, there will be no conflict within his life, and he will be one with God. Reality is of one piece, and because it is, anyone who relates to it can be at peace, as there will be no division. There is not even the division of mind and body, for mind and body are but different *modes* of the same substance. They are not different *types* of reality, as Descartes thought; rather, they are just different ways of looking at the same reality. By interpreting mind and body in this manner, Spinoza eliminated the very touchy problem of *interaction* that so plagued Descartes's theory. As we have already seen, the technical deficiencies of Descartes's dualistic theory of the independent existence of mind and body led to some ingenious, and not very successful, efforts to account for the way in which these two completely different entities might interact. On *monistic* accounts, however, such efforts are unnecessary. All aspects of a person's being are of one nature, and similarly, all that is outside of him is akin to that which is within him, and thus he is related to all that is. Therefore, man is not diminished by the magnitude of reality, but enlarged by it. He is related to nature and to all men. There is no alien land. Wherever man may travel, life will always welcome him; he will always be at home in this universe.

Spinoza knew that man can become lost among the multiplicity of things until finally he himself comes to be as another thing to himself. It was in ancient India that the Hindu, looking for the same kind of unity Spinoza sought and feeling the meaning of reality upon the deepest level of Being, discovered an ultimate permanent absolute beyond the shifting things of the material world. The Hindu saw that these many things we become so bound up with make us less than we really are. We prize material things, love them, cheat to get them, lie for them, steal them, kill for them, and we also worship pleasures of the senses. Yet there is a terrible absurdity to this behavior because these things, for which we give so much of ourselves, give us so little. These things are not enduring; they change, decay, and perish. The more we have of them, the richer we think we are but the poorer we become, for these things, by keeping us filled without, keep us from becoming fulfilled within. Thus the Hindu proclaimed the things of the world are not real; they are *maya,* or illusion. When a person is healthy and experiences wholeness, we may say he is in contact with reality. Yet people who devote themselves to the particular material things are divided beings; they feel vague and unreal. Thus it has been the mystics and the deeply committed philosophers who, having renounced the world, have felt the most real and whole. Such men have established contact with that which lies beyond the fleeting, impermanent things of the world. Their lives reveal that there is something immutable, necessary, and eternal—an ultimate absolute by which all is united. The Hindu calls this ultimate something *Brahman,* for to know it is to have one's life touched by the eternal. In the earliest philosophical literature known to man, the Vedas, the ultimate source of all reality is called *tat ekam,* That One. In the later development of this philosophy in the Upanishads, the ultimate One (called *Brahman*) has come to be understood as all the universe. *Brahman* is thus the one ultimate unifying principle of reality. The individual self was called *atman,* and the Hindu maintained that *atman* (or the self) and Brahman (the world principle) are identical. The essence of the self and the fundamental cosmic principle are the same. Man is not a stranger in the universe but is one with its essence. A person who feels and understands the beauty of nature can be deeply moved by it, for there is something in it to which he can relate, something he shares in common with it. Man can know moments of awe-inspiring experiences of the universe in which he may feel a real kinship with it, for ultimately there is something that binds him to reality. Particles of reality composing the essence of man and the universe are not different. Thus man may feel a true oneness with ultimate reality.

When man can somehow feel a oneness with all things, he rises above the misfortunes of life and attains true bliss. Whether in ancient India or in the modern Western world, man can attain that vision that enables him to understand reality, as Spinoza put it, *sub specie aeternitatis,* or in the light of eternity. Viewing reality in this way detaches man from all conflicts within it and frees him from being pulled apart by it. He attains, as Spinoza expressed it, true *blessedness*. His plane of existence is so elevated that his life becomes characterized by *laetitia*, or joy. This *joy* of which Spinoza spoke results when one discovers the true power within his being, the power to discover his oneness with the absolute. Today there is much talk of the need for one world, for a world government and fundamental political unity. There cannot, however, be political unity when the souls of men are divided. Man in our age of conflict and fragmentation must learn how to experience that ultimate philosophical oneness and unity that monistic philosophy teaches is possible. Therefore, let us now see how philosophers in our age respond to such metaphysical challenges.

Contemporary Metaphysics

MADNESS IN THEIR METHOD:
LOGICAL POSITIVISM

There once was a most precocious boy, and his mother was just beaming with pride for him. Her sister Sarah came from far for a visit. Aunt Sarah was really eager to see her little nephew, but her train was late arriving and when she got there he was already in bed. That prevented Aunt Sarah from seeing him that first night, but it did not stop his mother from bragging. She told her sister that he was brilliant and would one day be a great psychiatrist. Not only would little Sigmund be a great psychiatrist, but better yet, he would be a very special kind. "Oh!" exclaimed Aunt Sarah, "what kind?" Mom explained that little Sigmund would cure all of those persons and only those persons who cannot cure themselves. Without as much as batting an eye Aunt Sarah said, "He can't."

"How do you know he can't?" Mom demanded angrily. "You didn't even see him." Very self-assured, Aunt Sarah told her sister that she did not have to see him to know he could not do what his mother claimed.

"But he's a regular genius," Mom persisted. "He could cure all of those persons and only those persons who can't cure themselves."

With a nod of her head and a wave of her hand, Sarah answered, "I don't care if he's a regular Sigmund Freud, he could not do that."

"Why not?" asked Mom, somewhat hurt.

"If he cures all of those persons and only those persons who can't cure themselves," Sarah asked by way of an answer, "what about himself?"

"What do you mean, *himself?*" Mom said suspiciously.

"Well, you know psychiatrists always have problems, but from what you told me about him, he'd really have problems because when he got problems, nobody could cure him," stated Sarah.

"So, how can you know that?" wondered Mom.

Finally came the explanation: "If Sigmund cures all of those persons and only those persons who can't cure themselves, then he can't possibly cure himself because anyone he can cure can't cure himself. Thus, clearly, if he can cure himself, he can't cure himself. Yet according to the formula if he can't cure himself, then he can cure himself because he can cure *who-ever* can't cure himself—and so on. In short, it would be hopeless for him to become a psychiatrist."

Sigmund's mother might have thought that her sister Sarah needed to see a psychoanalyst herself, but in fact it was Mom who really needed to see an analyst—a logical analyst. What is significant in this little story is that Aunt Sarah could determine that there was something wrong with her sister's statement though she did not know little Sigmund or any of the facts. She could tell there was something wrong with the claim just by analyzing the *form* of the statement. And this is exactly the case with analytic statements. The truth or falsity of all analytic statements can be determined exclusively by reference to the form of the statement. With an analytic statement we only need to examine its terms to discover its truth or falsity. Analytic statements are tautological. A tautology is a statement that gives no new information. Thus in a tautological sentence the predicate does not add anything to the subject of the sentence. The simplest form of tautology is the statement $A = A$. A tautology simply presents another way of saying the same thing. The following is an example of an analytic statement: "A bachelor is an unmarried man." The predicate "unmarried man" adds no new information about the subject "bachelor"; it is just another way of telling us the same thing. A fundamental characteristic of analytic statements is their truth is a matter of "certainty" and not mere "probability." We can be certain that a bachelor is an unmarried man because asserting the opposite would result in a contradiction. It would be a contradiction to say that a man is a bachelor but he is married. Thus we know that an analytic statement is necessarily and certainly true because to assert its opposite would be to make a contradiction. An analytic statement *must* be true because it is true by definition: a bachelor is defined as an unmarried man, and therefore a bachelor *must* be unmarried.

The statement, "The bachelor is a swinger," is not an analytic statement. We cannot decide the truth of it just by examining its terms; we have to examine the bachelor and actually watch him operating. This is a *synthetic* statement, and the truth of synthetic statements can only be determined with reference to experience. Because we find the truth of analytic statements *a priori,* or *before experience,* we can be certain of their truth. This is never the case with synthetic statements. We can discover the truth of these statements only by checking them against experience. Furthermore, because experience is uncertain we can only regard synthetic statements as being probably true, never certainly true. Albert Einstein observes, "As far as the laws of mathematics refer to reality, they are not certain; and as far as they are certain, they do not refer to reality."[40]

We can always be *certain* about analytic statements because, as we have observed, they can be corroborated by the test of contradiction. This is not so with synthetic statements. As we have said, to say a bachelor is

[40] Albert Einstein, "Geometry and Experience," in *Readings in the Philosophy of Science* (New York: Appleton-Century-Crofts, 1953), p. 189.

married is a contradiction, and hence it is necessary that a bachelor is an unmarried man. If blue litmus paper is put in acid, it will turn red. That always happens. It is not *necessary*, however, that it will always happen. It would not be a contradiction if litmus paper when put in acid did not change in color. In fact the next time one puts litmus paper into acid, it could turn into a salami. It is highly improbable, but it would not be a contradiction if it did happen.

The problem with analytic statements is that, even though they can give us certainty, they cannot give us any new information. Their value lies in the service they perform in furthering explication and clarification. Perhaps man suffers from no more serious disease than muddled thinking, which can get him into all kinds of trouble in the real world. If this is the case, then the job of *clarification* is one of enormous importance. It is the one the philosopher trained in logic is best able to handle. It is all he is able to handle. The rest he can leave to scientists whose job is to study the world as it actually is.

Using arguments like these, the group of philosophers known as *logical positivists* contend that there can be no necessary or absolute knowledge about the external world. This is the Age of Uncertainty, and there is nothing about the world of which we can be certain; there are no necessary or external truths. Certainty is relegated to life's bin of logic, and uncertainty is the way of the world. This is the way the logical positivist views reality. The logical positivist is a dedicated anti-metaphysician, but often his metaphysics shows. Indeed, one can make a good case that logical positivism is a formalization of the metaphysics of a technological society, for through positivistic eyes nothing more can be seen than a technological world in which only that which can be empirically verified can exist. The positivist concentrates upon techniques and means but regards the idea of purpose as meaningless. How did the anti-metaphysical metaphysics of logical positivism, with its cardinal tenet that empirical verification is the open sesame to reality, develop?

Bertrand Russell (1872–1970) had one very long and exciting life and a great many philosophies, most of them quite unexciting. Before he was eighteen years old Bertrand Russell was a theist, but then he read the freethinker John Stuart Mill and decided there was no God. Then Russell became a Hegelian—until he read Hegel's *Greater Logic,* a work that had a profound influence on him: it influenced him to give up Hegel. From Hegel he went to Plato. Philosophers can be fickle about these things. The love affair with Plato did not last either. As Russell got older, world changes became more tumultuous and precipitous; as technological progress accelerated, specialization became more highly developed and perfected. Bertrand Russell, who became increasingly involved in the swift currents of life, found himself being more and more torn from allegiance to old Platonic and Hegelian metaphysical conceptions. Hegelians defended a position of metaphysical monism, claiming that there is an absolute ultimate reality that is *one* in nature. Russell came to see such a view as a dream that utterly distorted the reality of the diversity with which a man finds himself confronted. Russell came to understand reality as *pluralistic*—that is, constituted of separate and distinct elements making up a multitude of disconnected things. These he called *atomic facts.*

If we are not convinced by Russell, then all we need to do is look to the world. Do we ever find anything that is not individual, particular, capable of being perceived? There are noises, odors, individuals, cars, trucks, and trains, but we have no basis for supposing anything exists beyond such things. For example, someone might say the relationship between New York and Philadelphia is that Philadelphia is ninety miles south of New York. New York exists—some say it is a wonderful town—and Philadelphia exists—some say it is a city of brotherly love. There are many things between the two cities (New Jersey, for instance), but where is the "relationship" that is supposed to exist between them? When we speak of a relationship between New York and Philadelphia, it is just a way of comparing the fact that New York is at 41° North latitude, 74° West longitude and that Philadelphia is at 40° North latitude, 75° West longitude. What we call the "relationship" does not have an existence itself.

Similarly when we say that two persons have a "relationship," we mean that the two individuals do particular things together. When a man and woman have a relationship, there are those who would say there is "something between them." This something may be of inestimable significance but is of no tangibility. (Indeed if the "something *between* them" were tangible, they probably would not have much of a relationship.) Jewish existentialist Martin Buber makes much of this intangible "between." "The fundamental fact of human existence is man with man," he says; "What is peculiarly characteristic of the human world is above all that something takes place between one being and another the like of which can be found nowhere in nature."[41] Buber tells us that language can give only a *sign* of this something between which can be found nowhere. "All achievement of the spirit has been incited by it," he tells us, and goes so far as to claim that man is made by it. But what is it? Buber cannot say. This is what he tells us: "It is rooted in one being turning to another as another, as this particular other being, in order to communicate with it in a sphere which is common to them but reaches out beyond the special sphere of each. I call this sphere, which is established with the existence of man as man but which is conceptually still unapprehended with the sphere of 'Between.' "[42] Buber tells us that the between is the real place and the bearer of what happens to men.

To this, Russell answered by using his logical atomism theory; if two individuals love each other and there is something between them, Russell said in effect, then they had better get it out of the way—particularly when they want to make love. But this was no problem for Russell; as he saw it, this "something" Buber makes so much of is really nothing. In the perspective of this positivistic way of understanding the world, everything mean-

[41] Martin Buber, *Between Man and Man* (Boston: Beacon Press, 1955), p. 203.
[42] *Ibid.*

ingful is capable of being empirically verified. A man may be far away from a woman and yet feel some bond, a relationship, but there is nothing in this situation that is not empirically verifiable. Thus this lover may spend a lot of time thinking about his girl and wishing they were not apart, and he may experience frustration. These *are* specific and particular behavioral functions. This is all there can be to relationship.

Oriented in this way of understanding, Russell repudiated his Platonic philosophy and rigorously denied the existence of Platonic universals. He became convinced that careless use of language gives rise to that kind of philosophizing that ends in asserting the existence of such queer entities as these imaginary "relationships." To counter the metaphysical rush over-populating the realm of reality with all types of fictitious entities, Russell developed his *theory of descriptions.* Russell's mother-in-law, a famous and forceful religious leader, once assured him that philosophy is difficult only because of the long words it uses. Russell did not agree and tried to prove to her that she was wrong. "I confronted her with the following sentence from notes I had made that day: 'What *is* means is and therefore differs from *is,* for *is* is would be nonsense.'" No one would disagree with Russell's conclusion that "It cannot be said that it is long words that make this sentence difficult."[43]

Russell reasoned problems of the above type were caused by the belief that if a word means something, then there must be some existing *thing* to which it refers. Known as the *unum nomen, unum nominatum* doctrine, this idea was defended by the Austrian philosopher Alexius Meinong. This doctrine means that there must be something that has some kind of being to correspond to every noun. Let us consider an example. Most people would agree that the sentence "The golden mountain does not exist" is a meaningful one. Most would also agree that the proposition of that sentence is true. The catch is that the proposition has a subject—namely, "the golden mountain"—which does not exist. Now, if that subject does not designate some object, how can the proposition possibly be regarded as meaningful? Meinong answered by resourcefully concluding that there is a golden mountain. It has three qualities: it is golden, it is a mountain, and it does not exist. Meinong's idea was that there has to be something which does not exist, if we can talk about it meaningfully.

Bertrand Russell believed the world would be better off if such reasoning did not exist, and to further the cause of eliminating such reasoning he developed his *theory of descriptions.* The theory of descriptions is a way of showing that even though a sentence may be meaningful it does not therefore follow that each single word or phrase is itself meaningful. Light was thrown on this problem by Russell's idea of the *propositional function,* one of his more important contributions to logic. A distinction must be drawn between constants and variables, Russell explained. A constant is that which has meaning in itself—such as a proper name like Tom or George. A variable

---

[43] Bertrand Russell, *My Philosophical Development* (London: George Allen and Unwin, Ltd., 1959), p. 63.

has no meaning standing by itself. It may be just a letter, such as "x." The following is a proposition:

Scott was the author of *Waverly*.

This is a meaningful sentence. It means one and only one man wrote *Waverly*, and that man was Scott.

The following is a propositional function:

X wrote *Waverly*.

In this sentence "x" is a variable, and as such has no meaning in itself. Can we say it is true or false that "x" wrote *Waverly*? No; we don't even know what "x" is. Thus a propositional function containing a variable is not meaningful. To be made meaningful we would have to replace the variable "x" with a constant—that is, an entity that can be *described*. If we discover that "x" stands for Scott, then we can know the statement is true. If "x" stands for anything else, the sentence is false. The description "the author of *Waverly*" does have a subject—namely, Scott—and in this significant respect it differs substantially from the sentence about the golden mountain, for the golden mountain is not a legitimate or real subject.

A proper name such as Scott means the person or object to whom it refers. Therefore, plainly and simply, Scott means the person Scott. Taken in itself, however, the golden mountain does not mean anything. Unlike proper names, phrases (such as the golden mountain) are but incomplete symbols and cannot as such be credited with existence until such time as they are filled in with a definite reference—and there is no reference for the golden mountain. Thus Russell's theory of descriptions was an effort to prevent philosophical fraud, and to use the soap of logical analysis to wash out the mouths of philosophers who spoke like Meinong. Russell was determined to show how we can deny any status in reality to such named but nonexistent objects as unicorns, golden mountains, or round squares. Failing to be clear about the meaning of words, men have ever found themselves becoming enslaved to them. Men have lived in fear of mere *words*, such as "god," "demon," "witch," which do not refer to any threatening objects or even to anything that exists. Men have gone to their deaths in defense of myths, such as the *state*, which is nothing in itself. Emotions flare concerning such words as "capitalism," "communism," "democracy," and "freedom." How many people stop to think what these terms mean before they start fighting about them? The demagogue can move men just by employing the right emotionally laden term. Today when the communications media have become so technically perfected, the prospects for demagoguery become truly terrifying. In this day linguistic and logical analysis may assume a new urgency.

If one believes there can be too great a concern with linguistic clarity, he should remember what happened to poor Croesus, the great Lydian king. At one critical moment in history all of his great wealth and power did not serve him, but linguistic analysis would have. Concerned about the dangerously expansive tendencies of the Persians, Croesus decided to initiate a war to prevent Persia from starting one. He consulted the Greek oracle at Delphi to determine if there should be an immediate attack. According to the Greek historian Herodotus, the oracle pontificated that if Croesus would cross the Halys and attack the enemy, he would destroy a great army. Croesus did just that, and the prediction came true; unfortunately, the great army he destroyed was his own, not the Persian. If he had only *analyzed* that statement of the oracle, he could have saved himself a great deal of trouble.

Bertrand Russell carried out the most thoroughgoing program of logical analysis, getting to the bottom of the problem of meaning and seeking to achieve utmost clarity. He developed a *theory of types,* which complements his theory of descriptions, to bring clarity to some seemingly impossible problems concerning paradoxes.

The brilliant mathematician Gottlob Frege devoted his energy to solving problems dealing with the foundations of mathematics. He was committed to demonstrating that mathematics could be solidly based on logic. Frege regarded it scandalous that mathematicians could solve the most complicated mathematical problems but could not answer such a simple question as what the number two is. Mathematics was beset by a lack of clarity concerning the meaning of natural numbers. There were those who claimed that natural numbers were mental constructs. Of course if this were true, it would reduce mathematics to psychology, and Frege believed such a reduction illegitimate. Logic was a labor of love for Frege, who dedicated much of his energy to this problem. He took upon himself the grand task of reducing arithmetic to logic, criticizing mathematicians who had committed foolish errors in spinning their theories about the foundation of mathematics. As Frege proudly consummated his life's effort, a little note arrived from Bertrand Russell pointing out how it is possible to produce a contradiction in Frege's own system. "Now he tells me!" poor Frege must have thought.

Bertrand Russell was referring to the paradox of the class of all classes which are not members of themselves. There is a terribly thorny dilemma of such a nature that if a class is considered a member of itself, then it cannot be considered a member of itself; conversely, if it cannot be considered a member of itself, the nature of the problem is such that it must then be considered a member of itself, and so on *ad absurdum.* Examples of this dilemma, such as the following, were provided during the Middle Ages:

SOCRATES:
   The very next statement Plato makes will be false.

PLATO:
   What Socrates has just said is true.

Now if what Plato said is true, then it must be false because what he said is true (Socrates' statement) means that Plato's statement must be false; but then if Plato's statement is false, it must obviously be true because then the statement of Socrates that Plato's statement is false is not true, and therefore Plato's statement, since not false, must be true. Does such a paradox constitute a basic irrationality before which rational man must stand helpless, or is there some rational means of solution? Certainly Bertrand Russell did not stand by helplessly.

He arrived at the conclusion that a statement is meaningless if one of its terms is or includes the entire statement itself. The assumption behind this reasoning is classes that contain themselves cannot be defined. From this assumption developed a theory of hierarchies of language, for if a class cannot contain itself, then a language cannot talk about itself. Thus there must be a further language in which we can talk about the original language. The original language will be called the *object language,* and the second language in which we talk about the original language will be called the *metalanguage.* In other words the problems produced in the first language cannot be solved within the context of that language itself, and a further language must be developed for solving them.

The problems with which Russell was dealing are not as important as the way in which he dealt with them. Russell was attempting to use logical analysis to handle all the problems of philosophy. Of course, this was by no means a new idea; however, making logical and linguistic analysis central to the philosophical mission was indeed a new departure. This point was really labored by a darling of the logical positivists and British analytic philosophers, the Austrian positivist Ludwig Wittgenstein (1888–1951). Wittgenstein wrote both the Old and New Testaments for this new philosophical movement. His *Tractatus Logico-Philosophicus* was a great revelation and was used as the basis for the development of logical positivism. Subsequently, his *Philosophical Investigations* inspired British Analytic Philosophy. The point of departure for the *Tractatus* was Russell's doctrine of logical atomism. Wittgenstein, like Russell, saw the world as constituted of concrete facts, separate and distinct elements. He understood knowledge as an assimilation or copy of these atomic facts and believed that all universal statements were merely truth functions of singular propositions. This means that a universal statement such as "all men are mortal" can mean no more than that George is mortal, Max is mortal, Hubert is mortal, and so on until all men have been named. He strongly emphasized the idea that the philosopher, confronted with this world of empirical facts, is not responsible for telling us about it. His job must be limited to *analysis.* The real world must be left to scientists, not philosophers.

Wittgenstein believed that philosophy itself is not a theory about reality; rather it is an *activity,* the whole purpose of which is to clarify thought. His stance was that philosophical problems should not be *solved* but *dissolved.* In other words philosophers can contribute no knowledge about the world, but they can untangle confusions *about* the world. Rigorously consistent, Wittgenstein did not even exclude his own work from his conclusion that philosophical problems are logically meaningless and inexpressible. At the end of the *Tractatus,* which one seriously plows through with intellectual blood and sweat, Wittgenstein boldly announces that his own propositions are elucidatory in such a way that he who understands them understands they are *senseless.* Once one has used philosophical propositions (and they have served their purpose), one should hasten to get rid of them. One should throw away used philosophical propositions because, even if he held on to them, he would have nothing. According to Wittgenstein the only propositions that have existential import—that is, the only propositions having any reference to the existing world—are those that are empirical in character. The meaning of a proposition depends upon its being empirically verified.

Wittgenstein's particular development of this view was attacked from within the camp of logical positivism itself by such big positivistic guns as Otto Neurath and Rudolf Carnap. However, despite some rough infighting among logical positivists themselves over some sticky details, there was always unity on the general formula—only that which can be empirically verified can be meaningful.

Simply put, logical positivists were saying: *put up* in terms of what can be verified empirically, or *shut up*. If we expect people to believe us, we have to give them *factual evidence*. When we get down to the nitty-gritty of what we really believe in, we always want something empirically substantial. The logical positivist takes the position that in any area where progress has been made, it was because men were committed to the empirical method and refused to be led astray by metaphysical, religious, or value considerations. When a man tells us that he took a little joy ride up to the moon one afternoon in a flying saucer with some odd little people, we conclude he is crazy. We do not so conclude because of *what* he said he did, but because there is *no evidence* for what he said he did. When an astronaut tells us he went to the moon we believe him even though this is also an absolutely fantastic feat. The difference is that the astronaut has empirical evidence for his claim. In developing the empirical verifiability criterion of meaning, the logical positivists were seeking to move away from traditional philosophical interests such as epistemology and metaphysics. Philosophers should no longer concern themselves with what we can *know,* for that is a problem the solution of which lies beyond the ken of ordinary men, nor with what is *real,* for that is an ultimate question out of the reach of our finite minds. More modestly, the positivists contended that what should be asked is what we *mean,* and to measure meaning, there must be objective standards of an empirical nature.

Some logical positivists took a tough stand on the meaning of the empirical verifiability criterion itself, and we may call them the verifiability hawks; others took a more moderate stand, and these we may call the verifiability doves. Moritz Schlick was an early hawk; he championed what has been called the "strong" sense of verifiability; indeed, his criteria were so strong that they crushed the meaning out of virtually everything. Even statements essential to the development of science were jeopardized when tested by Schlick's standards. Schlick objected that statements of scientific laws fail to be verifiable because they seem to include—built into them— what have been called *counterfactual conditionals;* for example, included within Galileo's law about falling bodies is the assumption that *if* a ball *were* dropped it would behave in a definite way, even though it is never actually dropped. Scientists are quite dependent upon such counterfactual conditionals. Words such as "malleable," "soluble," "magnetic," and "poisonous" are terms that express a *disposition* to react in a particular manner under specified conditions. Such words as these are called *dispositional predicates*, and they serve an important function in science. We believe that *if* a given block of ice *were* heated it would melt and that we can say this is so even though that particular block of ice may never be heated. Counterfactual conditionals are meaningful, and what is more, scientific talk would be hopelessly snagged if this were not the case. The difficulty, of course, is that they cannot be empirically verified since counterfactual conditions are not descriptive of what actually occurs.

To make matters worse, if scientific statements based on counterfactual conditionals cannot pass the strong empirical verifiability test, historical statements fare just as poorly. How could we empirically verify the statement that Washington crossed the Delaware? We would have to get a time machine, go back in history, and actually watch him do it. Existentialists have taken the view that man does not have human nature; he has only history. But hawk positivists will not even let him have history.

Thus the strong sense of verifiability seems too strong to work. For this reason it was modified by Alfred Jules Ayer, renowned British representative of logical positivism. Ayer advocated using the verifiability criterion in a weaker sense. In this "weak" sense a statement would be considered meaningful if it could be shown that any observations, whether actually made or not, would be relevant to determining its truth or falsity. The test for determining whether a statement is capable of verification is seeing whether it is capable of disverification. If a horse can only win and not lose, then we do not have a real race: we have a fix. The same applies to a meaningful proposition. If there is nothing that can count against it or show that it is false, then such a proposition is analogous to a fixed race, and we should refrain from betting on it.

As the positivists see it, that is the case with metaphysical, religious, and ethical propositions. Consider, for example, statements about the existence of God, who is held to be present everywhere but cannot be detected by any of the five human senses or measured by any scientific device. Ayer would contend that such a statement is meaningless not only because it cannot at present be tested empirically but because it can never be tested empirically. When the Russian cosmonaut Yuri Gagarin, an atheist, quipped that while he was circling around in the sky he saw no sign of God; religious people scoffed at him and answered that Gagarin misunderstood the nature of Our Father Who art in Heaven if he imagined that one could find him by going up to the heavens. This is just the point. Ayer would have replied: the fact that not finding him in the heavens does not prove he is not there makes the claim he is there meaningless. Gagarin did not prove the nonexistence of God because it cannot be proved; and if his nonexistence cannot be proved, then the statement that he exists cannot be meaningful.

A statement that there is a sign "Drink Coca-Cola" in the south polar cap region of Mars, now hidden from earthly observational instruments, would be regarded as meaningless according to the strong sense of verifiability criterion. It would be so because at present we have no means of verifying it. In the weak sense of verifiability, however, such a statement would not be deemed meaningless—perhaps ridiculous but not meaningless—because it is not logically impossible for us ever to see that sign. When we land a man on Mars, he could go and look for the sign. We would have a verification if he sees it and a disverification if he finds no such sign. The point is that we know what the relevant observation for testing the assertion would be, even though it cannot be so tested at present. That the statement is *in principle* verifiable is important. A statement that everything happens by the will of God, however, is not even in principle verifiable, for we cannot conceive of any relevant observation by which it might ever be proved or disproved.

Regardless of whether they use the weak or the strong sense of verification, positivists have come to the conclusion that there is no sense at all to metaphysics. In the nineteenth century positivists, such as Auguste Comte (1798–1857), waged a war against metaphysics, claiming metaphysical assertions to be *useless* or *indemonstrable*. In the twentieth century logical positivists went further, maintaining such assertions to be worse than useless—to be utter nonsense in fact. As they see it, metaphysics is just a tissue of statements that cannot be proved or disproved and are thus meaningless. What cannot be proved or disproved can be disregarded, and that is just what the logical positivists tell us we should do with metaphysics.

It has been observed that logical positivists, in doing away with metaphysics, ethics, and religion, also do away with themselves because the empirical verifiability principle itself cannot be empirically verified. Logical positivists meet this objection by contending that the empirical verifiability principle is not itself meant to be an empirical or factual report but is rather a definition or proposal. Despite this answer, one might still object and ask why that particular proposal should be made. Why should we propose as a criterion of meaningfulness for understanding all life a criterion that itself derives mainly from physics? If we are just making a proposal, why propose one with so little meaning to us? As we have already suggested, it even leaves too little of science, for even the *weak* sense of the verification principle fails to account for counterfactual conditionals. This is because counterfactual conditionals, inasmuch as they never occur, are not even *in principle* verifiable.

Curiously enough, logical positivists have been attacked not only for eliminating too much that is meaningful to humans in slashing away metaphysics but also for *not* eliminating metaphysics. After having done his best to destroy metaphysics, Ludwig Wittgenstein ended up declaring in his *Tractatus:* "Whereof one cannot speak, thereof one must be silent." What seems to be implied here is that there exist certain things that we just cannot put into words. Thus the remark could be interpreted as implying the existence of a reality that just cannot be grasped conceptually. It is ironical that so often in life that which is pushed to its extreme does not become "extremely" itself but turns into its opposite. Pushed far enough, dry positivism can move into a sea of negativism, and empiricism—seemingly so clear and illuminating—can move into a night of mysticism. This has always been so with positivists; thus the nineteenth-century positivist Auguste Comte went so far against metaphysics and religion that he concluded by trying to establish a religion of positivism. It takes a powerful man to push a position so far that it reaches its opposite. Wittgenstein could be such a man. He certainly pushed positivism to its boundaries—and perhaps beyond.

Of course logical positivists would vehemently deny that Wittgenstein did any such thing. Commenting on Wittgenstein's remark about being silent whereof one cannot speak, Neurath (a very influential logical positivist) observed that it is true one must be silent about metaphysics, but he added that in this case it is not *about anything* that one is being silent. In plain words one must be silent because there is nothing to talk about, not because there are things that cannot be talked about. F. P. Ramsey put it nicely by pointing out that what we cannot say, we also cannot *whistle*. A rich source of metaphysical nonsense arises from the belief that people can *whistle* what they cannot say or can express what is real without relying on language.

Refusing to be swayed by the whims and whistles of life, logical positivists have contributed greatly to keeping man on the track of logical analysis. The confusions that beset men when they allow themselves to become confused by language or to pay insufficiently close attention to the meaning of their words are gigantic. Therefore, the positivist philosophical medicine is a much-needed antidote to the frequent illogical excesses of irrational man. Futhermore, the technical work of the logical positivists in the area of methodology and logic gives man a sturdy tool with which to understand the problems of linguistic analysis. Of course linguistic analysis should serve as a *means* of helping us understand the world, but for the positivist it tends to become an end in itself. Metaphysics may not make sense, as the positivists claim, but there may also be something nonsensical about positivism. What can be the sense of defining the meaningful in such a way that a large part of the area men find most deeply meaningful is held to be off-limits? Is there a sin of syntax that permits it to alienate one from life? It is easy to become lost from life in logic and language like the schizophrenics who, unable to face the world, sometimes withdraw and create their own language to protect themselves from the outer world. Just as language can serve to open doors to life, it can also close them. As logical analysis becomes more technical, it seems the philosopher becomes more withdrawn from life and human concerns. Scholastic philosophers in the Middle Ages were taken to task for retreating from life into problems of words. Do we have in logical positivism a new scholasticism?

Logical positivists seek to reduce all statements to what Carnap has called the "thing language." This is the language of physics and is based on "protocol reports." A protocol is a direct report of something immediately observable in experience. The positivists maintain that which cannot be expressed in terms of this thing language cannot be. Thus the positivist realm becomes a kingdom of thingdom and an "off-limits" sign is put on areas of life most meaningful to men. As society becomes more complex and calls for greater specialization, man loses his sense of personal unity. He becomes adjusted to the different tasks he must perform. Logical positivism exacerbates this decompartmentalizing of life. Thus when men's souls cry out for an image of unity, the logical positivistic philosophy offers only further fragmentation.

People the world over are groping in the dark and need to find meaning and purpose to give illumination to their existence. The philosopher may have a more important role to play here than the positivist is willing to give him credit for. There is a need for a philosophy that will help man find direction and assist him in learning to live at peace with his fellow men and with his world. If such a philosophy cannot be fully put into words, then it may have to be whistled. If the things that matter most to men are not always capable of empirical verification or quantification, that does not change the fact that they are still the things that matter most. Perhaps the logical positivist should consider the advice of Hamlet:

> *There are more things in heaven and earth ...*
> *Than are dreamt of in your philosophy.*

EXISTENTIALISM

The term existentialism is derived from the Latin *ex sistere*, which means to stand out or emerge. If we think of metaphysics as a branch of philosophy dealing with questions of reality, it is easy to see that in existentialism a most significant departure is taken. In idealism reality is viewed as mind or spirit or as an intricate system of ideas; in *materialism* matter in motion is central, and through the metaphysical lens of *naturalism* a vast and complex system of nature is seen as reality. The emphasis is altered sharply in *existentialism,* as the central focus fixes on existence. What is most real is not some empty mansion of ideas, not an impersonal mechanical universe, but the individual human being—man's own existence. Caught up in an artificial social or political system and submerged by overwhelming forces of nature or technology, it is difficult for man not to be just another thing in a world of things. What does it mean in this universe for man to exist, to be authentic? Man must understand existence in terms of the German word *"Existenz"* as an *"ek-stasis,"* a "standing-out." Man is not just a product of hereditary and environmental forces as nonhuman animals may be; nor is he simply a product of the social organization. Rather, he is one who may break free from bonds of conformity and *stand out.* Such is the perspective of existentialism.

How can a man feel any sense of individuality or personal reality in a world in which depersonalizing forces of life are so dominant? In reaction to the mechanical functioning of a vast, indifferent universe and to oppressive and dehumanizing forces of technology and the ever-increasing concentration of political power, existentialists seek to "stand out," to live what they call an authentic existence—that is, they seek a way of life in which they can fulfill their own unique individual potential and thus be themselves. There is so much in our world that conspires against individuality and contributes to the stultifying power of conformity that existentialists have had to take in hand a sword of revolution. In his *Journals,* the Danish existentialist Sören Kierkegaard (1813–55) demanded that there must be a new Reformation and declared that when it came it would make Luther's Reformation seem a mere trifle in comparison. He said that this reformation will be horrible. He saw people living dishonestly and forgetting their God and humanity, and he saw this had to be changed —thunderously changed. Later in the nineteenth century the German philosopher Friedrich Nietzsche (1844–1900) cried out that a revolution is unavoidable. In his *Ecce Homo,* Nietzsche pronounced that he heralded the coming of a tragic era and predicted Europe would be enveloped in darkness. In his *Will to Power* he announced that, thanks to him, a catastrophe was at hand. He told us it was the coming of nihilism. The nineteenth century was generally a time of grand optimism, but the existentialist saw through the optimism into the sickness of modern man's soul. He not only saw that all was not well, as so many firmly believed, but he saw, in the pages of Nietzsche's *Will to Power,* that soon the earth would writhe in convulsions.

Having great faith in the beneficent possibilities of scientific power, intellectuals of that time—children of the Age of Enlightenment—did not understand the blackness of power that would soon engulf the world with total wars, depressions, concentration camps, nuclear weapons, and arsenals of biological warfare. What most men and women failed to understand, appreciate, or even see—but which was a matter of ultimate concern for the existentialist and was in many ways the starting point for contemporary existential philosophy—is the so-called "death of God." In his *Thus Spake Zarathustra,* Nietzsche describes how the prophet Zarathustra spent years high upon a mountain peak and finally returned to civilization. There he met a pious old saint, and announced to him "God is dead!" This was truly an awful proclamation, for man's belief in God had always provided him with a basis for hope. Take God away and man is left stranded in an infinite, indifferent, and horribly lonely universe. Without God the universe may mean something to man, but man means nothing to the universe, and thus he loses meaning and all the security from that meaning. Thus, according to Heidegger, man becomes "forlorn and abandoned." Man must endure and suffer all the agonies of existence without any recourse to any power beyond.

God as an absolute has always been the ultimate basis for truth and good and evil. Kill God and truth and morality must be buried along with him. This is just the conclusion the existentialist says we must learn to live with. The Russian novelist Fëdor Dostoevski wrote that if there were no God, then all would be possible; this would be a world in which anything goes. Similarly, in *The Gay Science* Nietzsche said that there was no longer any left or right, nor up or down, and this is so because we are just straying through an infinite nothing. Without an absolute standard there is no way of knowing what is right or wrong, good or evil. The result is a cultural atmosphere in which man believes he can say or do whatever he wants. In such a situation it would seem there can be no truth or justice for man, and that we are left in a world in which might is right. This is a situation in which we are bound to despair.

The existentialist, however, refuses to despair. Man need not despair because, although there are no ready made absolute values for man, he does have himself and can *create* his own values. He can build a reality according to his own individual needs, and then his life becomes authentic. In contrast, when absolute values are given to him and he passively accepts what others have created, his life is inauthentic.

The existentialist has pitted himself in a heroic struggle against all those conditions that he believes contribute to inauthentic existence, whether they be the seclusion of the professor in the university, the dull uniformity of life in a highly technological and mechanical environment, the dread conformity of existence in an overpopulated world in which the "organizational" ethic prevails, the dehumanizing effects of a behavioristic approach to the human sciences, the estrangement of man from man in our huge anonymous urban centers, or the alienation of man from God and nature in a scientific and industrial world of "progress" being poisoned with pollution.

The question of alienation, or estrangement, is of special concern to the existentialist, for in a world built upon brute power in which men's fundamental energies have been directed to industrial, technological, economic, political, and military power, God died in the hearts and minds of men. In such a world the individual is dwarfed into powerlessness. With mass production as never before known, man tends to be reduced to the status of just another product, another commodity (or as the existentialists say), "a thing." The existentialist impulse is to lift man up from the degradation of being a thing to the level of authentic human existence.

There have probably been existential strivings in the souls of men throughout all history, and from time to time they have been explicitly articulated in their lives and philosophies, but rarely has an attack on the life's problems been more fully and explicitly existential than the one first launched by Sören Kierkegaard.

Philosophically the point of departure for Kierkegaard was the grand metaphysical system of the German philosopher Hegel. Hegel understood the world in terms of the development of what he called Spirit. He believed that reality was ultimately nonphysical in nature and subject to an evolutionary process that followed certain fundamental laws outside man's control. Supreme value was seen in the development of the "Spirit," and man as *fuel* for that development. Thus men were viewed merely as means for achieving the ends foreordained by an impersonal force evolving in the world. All human suffering was justified in terms of this Spirit, for Hegel maintained that any evil or suffering in the world would be negated by the final triumph of the Spirit. Such logic failed to comfort Sören Kierkegaard, who was then suffering over a love affair with Regine Olson, and he could discover no solace in this impersonal Hegelian Spirit. However small a man may seem, his own suffering can feel as large as the universe, and it means little to be told his suffering is not important in the ultimate scheme of things. Hegel claimed that there is a big plan of the universe, which is more basic than any plans of us mortals; men must serve this ultimate plan of the universe rather than their own life projects. But as Kierkegaard saw it, this meant there were no real *possibilities* in life. The only possibility is that this ultimate spirit shall fulfill itself. But even this does not offer much help, for it meant that men could never "stand out" in the existential sense because they would always be subordinate to the Hegelian "Spirit."

For Kierkegaard there are real *possibilities* for man, and he must choose from among them. Kierkegaard expressed this by saying that "Both/And" is the road to Hell, but "Either/Or" is the key to heaven and, more importantly, the key to life. The point is that if man is to lead an authentic life, he must constantly make choices, for in deciding *"either* this *or* that," man is making his own life instead of leaving it to be made for him. He must accept the pain of responsibility, for only by doing so can he gain the joy of freedom. No one else can choose for a man; he must choose for himself. Nor can a man put off making choices and try to have it both ways. To avoid the necessity of choice is to let oneself be morally cast adrift and therefore, to be inauthentic. Thus Kierkegaard was particularly disturbed that so few persons who called themselves Christians chose to be Christian. To be a Christian involves the deepest dedication and commitment, and one cannot be both a Christian and a man of the world. To imagine that one can is to live by the "both/and" principle—the principle of inauthenticity. One cannot choose both God and practicality, both Christianity and making money, both Jesus and fame or power. Christians who do not understand this mock Jesus and live false, inauthentic lives; thus society becomes filled with so-called "Christians" who have no feeling for the anguish of the Christian life. When one *chooses* to be a Christian and opens himself to God and to a life of love, he then becomes the *truth.*

To Kierkegaard truth was not understood as something one *has,* but as something one *is.* Thus one cannot *have* the truth of Christianity by intellectually subscribing to a set of dogmas, but one can *become* the truth by having a real personal mission and by living as Jesus lived. One must make Christian doctrines not a part of his abstract understanding but a part of his concrete life. Thus in opposition to all Western schools of philosophy, Kierkegaard was telling us that truth is *subjective* rather than *objective.* For him truth was not a matter of logic but a matter of life.

As with so much else in his philosophy, Kierkegaard's view of truth collided head on with Hegel's. Hegel understood truth in terms of the principle of *coherence.* For anything to be true it must cohere with the whole system of reality; whatever is inconsistent with an accepted and established body of principles cannot itself be accepted. In either words, something could be considered true only insofar as it could fit in with the whole. Kierkegaard lashed out against this idea; he insisted that man is not just a fragment of some totality but is himself a whole and can himself be the truth. Indeed man was the whole truth. Attacking the Hegelian metaphysical edifice head on, Kierkegaard boldly proclaimed his refusal to be but a *paragraph in a system.*

Throughout history great philosophers had made reason, ideas, definitions, and abstractions more important than concrete flesh-and-blood human beings. This is summed up by saying that for these philosophers *essence precedes existence.* Kierkegaard and the existential philosophers who came after him thought that Hegel and, indeed, most of the philosophers of the Western world had it backward, and so they insisted that *existence precedes essence.* These are two famous phrases that are often used to sum up the differences between existentialism and other philosophical approaches. It is therefore important to understand what they mean. At first glance, this talk about essence preceding existence and existence preceding essence may seem a bit confusing, but behind it is a straightforward and very important idea—an idea that is crucial to philosophical thought in the twentieth century. Nowhere has the meaning of this idea been more fully illuminated than in the philosophy of the great French existentialist Jean Paul Sartre, to whom we now turn.

NOTHING DOES MATTER: SARTRE

In the midst of a technical civilization deeply committed to objectivity, Jean Paul Sartre (1905–   ) proudly claims subjectivity as the starting point of his existential philosophy, and in doing so he goes against the entire history of Western philosophy. We can see how by going back to classical Greece to that giant among philosophers, Plato. According to Sartre, Plato lost sight of the real world of imperfection here on earth by gazing up to the perfection of the heavens in his search for truth and justice. As we saw in our discussion of Plato in Chapter 2, Plato believed that eternal forms, or what he called "Ideas," were prior in existence to and more real than all of the particular things of life that surround us. To Plato it is not the scent we smell, the sounds we hear, the succulent food we taste, or the lips of the woman we kiss that are ultimately real. Rather, it is the *essences* or eternal forms, the universals lying behind these that are real. Plato would tell us that the beautiful girl a man holds in his arms is not as real as the pure disembodied *Idea* of beauty. In the phrase "essence precedes existence," the essence is the Idea of Beauty and the existence is, of course, the actual girl who exists. When we say that according to Plato's theory essence precedes existence we mean: *chronologically,* there must have been an Idea of Beauty before this particular girl was even born; logically, we could not speak of this girl as beautiful unless we already had an Idea of Beauty in our minds; and *ethically,* the Idea of Beauty is more important than any particular beautiful thing.

To Plato the girl (the existence) was just an accident and thus not as important as the Idea of Beauty. Particular girls come and go, grow old and gray, and lose their loveliness, but the Idea lasts forever and is beautiful always. The Platonic point is that if we are really to know anything, we must grasp its essence or the Idea of it. A definition conveys the essence or idea of the thing. Thus if one has a definition of a building he can know just what a building is even though he may never have seen a particular building. On the other hand, should one see a building without having the idea of what one is, he would not as much as know what it was he was seeing. One must have general understanding before one can know or appreciate the particular. One would have to understand the general idea of humanity before one could come to see that a particular person shared the properties of the class of humanity. Thus the essence "humanity" precedes the existence of any particular human being.

Most philosophers have agreed with Plato on this point, but Jean Paul Sartre felt that they were all being too farsighted and thus missing what was near and dear. Sartre argued that when essence is made to precede existence in the case of man, then man is degraded and treated not as a human being but as an object. Consider the case of the manufacture of a paper cutter. A paper cutter is an "object" made by an artisan using a model based on a concept. It is produced by referring to the concept of what a paper cutter is and by following an established method of production, which is also part of the concept. In this case it is true that essence precedes existence: there would be no paper cutter unless someone first had the idea of one. But to say that this is also true of man is to accord him no more dignity than a paper cutter. No better job has been done than that done by Christianity in making man a paper cutter, for by conceiving God as a superior artisan, it follows that "God produces man, just as the artisan, following a definition and a technique, makes a paper cutter. Thus the individual man is the realization of a general concept in the divine intelligence."[44]

In fact this view has become so deeply embedded in our thinking that even those who do not believe in God do not really believe in man either, for they also put essence prior to existence. Thus Sartre observes that many atheistic philosophers and psychologists believe man has a *human nature*. This belief makes each man no more than a particular example of the universal concept of man. All such efforts to define man in terms of human nature do injustice to what it means to exist.

What is it for a man really to exist? Sartre carefully explains by drawing a very fundamental distinction in his tome *Being and Nothingness*. His definition is essentially dualistic, for he maintains that there are two types of being, which he calls "being-in-itself" (*en-soi*) and "being-for-itself" (*pour soi*).

Being-in-itself is the type of being characteristic of objects. An object can be fully understood with reference to its mathematical and physical dimensions and its function or use. We can know an object when we know its measurements or size, the material of which it is made, and what it is used for. In contrast, if we know all of the physical characteristics of a man,

[44] Jean Paul Sartre, *Existentialism*, trans. B. Frechtman (New York: Philosophical Library, 1947), p. 17.

and know what his use is in his community, we still know practically nothing about him. This is because there is another dimension to man—what Sartre calls his consciousness—which cannot be measured with a ruler and cannot be physically observed. By his consciousness man can transcend his physical being—that is, he can transcend the level of being as an object (being-in-itself) and reach a level of subjective being in which he can choose for himself the kind of life he wishes. This is being-for-itself.

Of course, a price has to be paid for this. In gaining the freedom to be *for* ourselves, we have to give up some of our sense of security. A rock has great security. No wonder; it has no problems because it is just a rock and that is all there is to it. If, however, a rock had within its being the capacity to choose not to be a rock, then even Gibraltar would be rocked by insecurity. Similarly, a table has no problems because it is made by a carpenter according to a plan. But man makes himself; of course he does not originally create himself, but once tossed into the world he becomes responsible for all he does—for his life. That man can choose in this way means he has not only consciousness but also has freedom, and because the price of this freedom is insecurity, Sartre concludes that man is *condemned to be free.* For a man to realize he is responsible for every choice he makes and for the effects each choice may have on his own life or on the life of others can be a cause of a terrible anxiety. One bad choice, and a whole life can be spoiled.

Man is condemned to freedom. As Sartre sees it, man is not a homosexual, a waiter, or an anti-Semite in the same way he is a certain blood type, has blue eyes and naturally curly hair. If a girl does not like her brown eyes, there is not a great deal she can do about that. (Of course, if she doesn't like her brown hair she can do something about that.) While one may not like the color of his eyes or skin, he cannot really change them. However, he can change the color of his character. The color of eyes and skin is fixed genetically; it is being-in-itself. Character is not fixed; it is being-for-itself. Thus what man becomes, in the most important sense of the term, is fixed by man himself. This is why the existentialists generally maintain that there is no such thing as human nature. The Spanish philosopher José Ortega y Gasset (1883–1955) announces that man has not a nature but only history. Being-for-itself makes it extremely difficult for a man to feel secure, but it does provide him the opportunity to be free and to really be himself.

Many reject the opportunity. The painful agony of freedom inherent in being-for-itself becomes too much to bear. In the throes of a terrible world war when men claimed they were fighting and dying for freedom, a book appeared that (elaborating on this existential insight) argued men were really dying to get away from freedom. Called *Escape from Freedom,* it was written by Erich Fromm, a German-American psychoanalyst. Fromm's point is echoed by Sartre: both agree that people are always seeking to trade in their freedom, their being-for-itself, for the security that comes from living like an object, from being-in-itself. Throughout all history men have been in quest of freedom and for just as long have been afraid of finding it. Perhaps this idea has never been expressed more eloquently than by the Russian novelist Fyodor Dostoevski in a passage from *The Brothers Karamazov,* which describes how an autocratic dictator recognizes that the common people will always choose the path of security over the path of freedom.

"In the end they will lay their freedom at our feet," Dostoevski's Grand Inquisitor proclaims, "and say to us, 'Make us your slaves, but feed us.' "[45]

Sartre expresses the same idea by saying that the durability of the stone has a great attraction for man. It is most appealing to man to be as impenetrable as a stone and not to have to change. Sartre wrote a book called *Anti-Semite and Jew* in which he analyzed how this works in a particular instance. The anti-Semite is a man who simplifies his life by not going through the trouble of deciding whether or not he likes each Jew he meets. It is easier to hate them all in advance. Besides in this way one always has an explanation when things go wrong in his relationships. Anti-Semitism, like any other form of prejudice, is a means of avoiding the uncertainty present in human encounters. If things go badly and one does not have a scapegoat to blame, then he may end up having to blame himself. It is much more comfortable to have a Jew to hate! The creation of a scapegoat is an excellent means for people to avoid having to face what is wrong in themselves.

The anti-Semite is not the only one who tries to avoid the responsibility of freedom by simplifying his thinking in this dishonest way. Many others who would seem to have much better motives are in the same boat. Thus the communist deceives himself that his brutality is justified because eventually it will lead to the perfect society. Similarly the Freudian analyst, who is supposed to have such deep insight into human motivation, deceives himself with such oversimplifications. His deception is that everything is the fault of the family or of libidinal energy. The Freudian cannot accept the fact that he must answer for his own life. Sartre calls all such thinking "bad faith" or "self-deception." The tragedy is that so many live in bad faith, deceiving themselves in this way. The social patterns into which human relations fall render it virtually impossible for men and women to live in good faith. The fact is that most relations with other people threaten one's freedom and tend to reduce one to the level of being an object, or just a thing. This is why Sartre tells us that Hell is "other people." In human relations men constantly treat one another as if they were not human and thus come to understand their existence on this dehumanized level.

In the Age of Reason the French philosopher René Descartes presumed he could prove he existed through reasoning. It was his view that man most clearly knows himself in the act of thinking. He knew himself as a thinking being, and thus concluded, *"Cogito, ergo sum"* (I think, therefore I am). In an age growing ever more remote from the Age of Reason, Karl Marx, caught up in the political storms of his time, built up a philosophy based on an assumption the very opposite of Descartes's. As Marx understood things, man exists first and thinks second; Marx would have said "Man *is*, therefore he thinks." Although existentialists reject Marx's economic determinism and historical materialism, they fully accept his idea that man is caught up in existence and only out of that does his thinking emerge. As the existentialist

[45] Fyodor Dostoevski, *The Grand Inquisitor On the Nature of Man,* The Liberal Arts Press, 1948, p. 30.

sees it, man does not have to *prove* he exists, for he is so involved in the misery and absurdity of life that he knows it only too well.

In traditional metaphysical and epistemological undertakings, a philosopher had to forget he existed so that he could establish his profundity by proving it, but for the existentialist there is too much suffering in the world to let a man forget he exists. He finds himself thrown into a world full of grief and unhappiness, and that bears down upon a person too heavily for him to be able to seriously deny or doubt that he exists. As early as 1938, before he formally developed his philosophy, Sartre worked out his ideas of being and existence in a novel called *Nausea* (*La Nausée*). In this novel Antoine Roquentin is made to tell us that existence is not something that can be thought from a distance but is something that weighs heavily on your heart like a fat loathsome beast. How unreal Descartes's philosophy appears to the existentialist: first he proved he existed, and then he proved the world existed. The existentialist, entangled in the absurdity of existence and the pain of life, knows not only that he exists but that the world around him exists as well. How can one doubt it?

The problem is: it would not make sense to doubt our own existence, but we often lose sight of the fact that we exist as being-for-itself. In interaction with other human beings, who often treat us as objects and can do us considerable harm, a person can tend to lose confidence in himself as a being of freedom and worth, as a being-for-itself. Just a glance, a little glance, and one person can throw another completely off balance. Confronting the world of dead objects, a person might feel he has the world by a string, but in encountering other living beings one may suddenly feel as if the string is around his own neck. It is all too easy to become locked in the frame of reference of the other, to be reduced to the status of an object. We have all felt this way at times when confronting people more powerful than ourselves—as if these people in authority have the power to do with us as they wish. This is why the existentialists put a lot of emphasis on acts of rebellion as a way of breaking the shackles of those in power who tend to make one feel like an object. In rebelling, a person asserts his being-for-itself. We all know that while doing something he should not, a person may well feel that the whole world belongs to him, but if he discovers he is being observed he will come to feel he belongs to the world and is just an object and no longer a free agent. Instead of feeling a sense of freedom, he may feel shame. When one becomes ashamed, he loses the understanding of himself as being-for-itself.

So prevalent is this tendency for people to reduce one another to the status of objects that they manage to do so even when in love. When people love someone they say they want what is best for their beloved. Now the highest fulfillment of a man's existence is to be free, so if a person loves another he should want that person to be free. Yet one of the first things a person tries to do when he is in love is to take his beloved's freedom away. One wants the person he loves to *belong* to him. As Sartre sees it, behind all love is the impulse for possession. One wants the person he loves to become like a piece of property. Throughout history poets and philosophers have found great words to describe love. Sartre also found an interesting word to describe love; it is *sadism*. In loving another, one is ever seeking to possess and enslave him and thus to reduce the other to the condition of being-in-itself—to the status of an object. There are times, of course, when love is not sadism; but Sartre believes then that it is masochism. When one is not seeking to conquer and dominate the beloved, then one is seeking to be conquered and dominated. One not only tries to take the freedom of the other but one also gladly yields up his own freedom to the other.

Protesters in our time often shout "Make love, not war," but when one finishes reading Sartre on love he may feel love is worse than war. Sartre's theory of love may seem rather grim, but then love can be rather grim. After all Sartre is a perspicacious observer of human behavior, and when he spoke of love he was not basing his words on something he had dreamed up in his imagination but on what he observed in the reality of human interaction. Men do talk of "conquering" women, and women do have devious ways of controlling men; it is widely recognized there is a battle of the sexes. Love certainly can be and often is what Sartre says it is, but the question is: *Must* it be? Can it be something more? Although people often do objectify themselves by living selfishly, is it not possible that individuals may free themselves from the narrow confines of egoism and become more human through love?

There is no denying that much of human behavior bears out Sartre's seamy image of human existence. Sartre saw with painful clarity how dim life can be, but he did not therefore succumb and expect man to dwell in the darkness of pessimism. Rather than give in to the darkness, men must learn to live in it. What is more, they must find a light within themselves—a light of creative individual action. Although a man is "condemned to be free," he practices self-deception; he resorts to all kinds of devices to gain mastery over others, reduces himself and others to objects, and turns love into a sado-masochistic enterprise in order to commute this sentence of freedom. Yet man cannot avoid his basic freedom. To be free is to choose, and even if man does not choose he must make the choice not to choose. In the final analysis he cannot escape his freedom. This being the case, he should give up his futile efforts and try to cope with the burden of freedom; he creates his own life with this freedom, and there is great reward in that. Sartre believes man must bear his unhappy fate and find redemption in a life of freedom—a freedom that emerges out of facing the suffering and anguish of the human situation and resolving not to be conquered by it. The existentialist sets himself the task of portraying that dreadful situation against which man must affirm himself.

If one is to live realistically he cannot deceive himself about the nature of this world; he must admit what a horror it is. Atheistic existentialists such as Sartre are concerned that for the man who believes in God, the world can never be horrible enough. Theists who regard themselves as existentialists refuse to stand idly by and accept such an insult. They insist life with God can be just as much of a horror as life without Him. After all, imagine the horror, the terrible anguish that must result when man—who is impure, a sinner—must stand before the almighty, pure, and all-good God. It is the most humiliating encounter there could possibly be. Sartre is not convinced and observes that, humiliating or not, existence would not be meaningless if it were grounded in a supreme being.

Without God man has no standards to guide him and nothing outside of himself upon which he can depend, Sartre contends. Because of that man must turn within, and find strength in himself; because man *has* nothing he must *do* something: he must act. For Sartre the answer to the meaninglessness of life is action. In the metaphysics of nineteenth-century German philosopher Arthur Schopenhauer (1788–1860) the emphasis was on the *will to live;* in that of Nietzsche it was on the *will to power;* in that of Sartre we find the *will to action.* In the metaphysics of existentialism substantial reality has broken down, and thus man is left with only his own functioning, his own actions, and his own deeds. In the nineteenth century Newtonian physics provided man with an image of a solid impenetrable world of matter; ultimately reality was held to be made up of indivisible material substance. But with the Theory of Relativity, matter was transformed into energy. According to this Einsteinian idea, the whole world is a system of ceaseless energy. All man has is his action, his energy! In physics matter was changed into energy, and in existential metaphysics the idea of a substantial self is changed into the energy of pure action. For Sartre man cannot be said to have a self; all he can be said to have is action. Thus the being-for-itself, which Sartre has made so much of, is not considered anything substantial. Man is not an object; he is as we observed earlier, a consciousness, and consciousness is not something that can be defined in terms of positive properties. It has no solidity; it is not extended in space nor is it quantifiable. The self cannot be touched; it is not something positive. And what is the destiny of every self? Utter negation. At the center of a man's existence there always looms the possibility of his nonexistence. Men work so hard to attain things, but in the end can keep nothing, not even themselves. Every life, seemingly so full and so real, leads to ultimate absurdity, the negation of all. The consummation of a man's destiny is a naught, nothingness. In his *Republic of Silence,* Sartre lets us know that for men in the French Resistance death became the habitual object of concern. He says that death has to be considered not as some constant threat or danger but as man's lot, his destiny, the profound source of our *reality* as men.

Thus, thinking about death (the universal negation which is the condition of all our lives), Sartre discovers negative realities (*des nègatités*). Today physicists talk about nonmatter, and literature is filled with nonheroes. This is appropriate, for we are living in an age of anxiety when people are disturbed by the discovery in their midst of a void, a feeling of meaninglessness and barrenness. No one can read modern literature and poetry, wherein we may find such deep insights about life, without appreciating the prevalence of this spirit of negation. If we think about it we can see that negative reality—things that are not there—can exercise a much greater force upon us than things that are there. Think of a man or woman deeply in love awaiting a phone call from the beloved, but the phone never rings! No actual ring is more real than that nonring. Think of a great friend with whom you experience wonderful joys and pleasures, a constant companion and source of inspiration. He dies; he is no longer there. You then experience his absence as fully as you had experienced his presence.

Sartre's philosophy is profoundly expressive of the nihilism inherent in our age, an age of terrible frustration and disillusionment. However in another sense, we may think more of the existentialist discovery of nothingness as a forward movement in the direction of uniting the Western with the Eastern soul. One thinks of Sankaracarya's commentary on the Brahma *sutras* (Hindu philosophy) in which he maintains that the self is silence— that is, that the self cannot be known through any positive description. As the Hindu Yajnavalkya explained it, of anything one can predicate of the self in seeking to articulate what the self is, it can always be said, "*Neti, neti,* not this, not this." How can we define the self? We cannot say it is just our body; it must be more. Similarly, any other definition we offer can be recognized to be inadequate. Thus when man is so positively conquering nature, when he has attained very positive technical and scientific progress, when he reaches the moon and actually takes hold of it in a very positive sense, it is ironic that we find our hands empty and we seem to be drifting through an infinite sea of nothingness. When we have left the Eastern world behind us materially, we are finding we may have to broaden our perspective to include as a part of our existence that which was known eons ago as the utmost reality by wise men of India. Alexander the Great, with all the Western aggressiveness within him, conquered India, but in turn was conquered by it. We may just be learning something about that now in our own existence.

In the twentieth century, when mankind might have expected so much of a good civilized existence and instead has found unlimited savagery and barbarism, we should not be surprised to find negativistic philosophies emerging. Sartre's philosophy is very negativistic, but it is negativistic in a most positive way. The Oriental, who is more aware of the possibility of synthesizing life's contradictions, can appreciate this better than Western man. Thus while Sartre thinks of freedom in negative terms, the possibilities of it are magnificently positive for man. Although man may not be free to tear away all shackles that bind him and may not possess the power to fend off those who would coerce him, he still can say "no." A man can say, "You can imprison me, torture me, and kill me, but you can't convert me to your way of inhumanity." It is along these lines that Sartre understands freedom. And this is not a viewpoint he formulated in an ivory tower; it is one he found fighting in the French Resistance during the Second World War.

Existentialists may be criticized for being morbid, sensationalistic, too irrational, insufficiently analytical, and for many other sins against philosophy, and yet morbidity, crass sensationalism, irrationality, and violence are all part of living, and the existentialists were trying to develop a philosophy of life. Sartre may be condemned for not being as methodological or technical as one might expect a philosopher to be, particularly in an age of science, but he may also be commended for not losing sight of human concerns in a time when technology casts so large a cloud above humanity. Logical positivists and linguistic analysts may be much more precise, careful, and logical than Jean Paul Sartre, but often their philosophy, which devotes itself to telling us what is meaningful, is so technical that it seems itself to be but part of the meaninglessness of a technological wasteland. Besides, the existentialists, although contributing to the success of the image of irrational man, are anything but irrational in the defense of their theses about existence.

As a matter of fact, existentialists are by no means as unanalytical as many analytic philosophers maintain. They are not nearly as different from positivistic and analytic philosophers as is often suggested. There are important differences, of course, but what is interesting is that there are also some revealing similarities. It is not difficult to make a case for the affinity of logical positivistic philosophy with a technically oriented industrial civilization, but what is less obvious is that existentialism is also very much in the orbit of such a civilization. The difference may be said to lie in the fact that while logical positivism appears very much to be an expression of the forces of a technical world, existentialism is a reaction to them; and if this is true, then both are shaped by the same set of circumstances. It should be remembered that when we react too strongly to something we tend to become dominated by it.

Thus we find much in common in these two philosophical tendencies. It is widely held that existentialism is an anti-intellectualistic philosophy; it is a rebellion against rationalistic philosophy. But for all its emphasis of the rational disciplines of logic, mathematics, and science, logical positivism is no less anti-intellectualistic. Its interest in these disciplines is *technical*, not intellectual. Logical positivism does not see reason, science, or logic as an answer to any human problems; it sees them rather as *tools*, as devices, for solving problems. Thus for the logical positivists, reason is no more a way of understanding life or reality than it is for the existentialists. If the existentialists let reason be dominated by the emotions, the logical positivists let it become the slave of technique.

Neither the existentialists nor the positivists are very positive. Neither has time for contemplation of positive eternal truths or values; both schools, if they can even be called schools, disdain traditional epistemological questions. Whereas so-called "ordinary language" philosophers, who really grow out of the logical positivist tradition, concentrate on the way men talk, existentialists pay attention to the way men feel. The style of existentialism and logical positivism is very different, and they are quite at odds on what types of question a philosopher might legitimately try to answer, and yet after all these philosophies are just different sides of the same coin (but a coin very different from the one of classical philosophy).

Sartre himself, although rebelling against the dehumanization of Western values and world civilization, cannot give us much to help us move in a positive direction. He praises freedom, but he does not tell us much what it is. Although there is emphasis on man's freedom, there is not much of a philosophy of freedom. It may be in these difficult times man needs a theory of freedom to find it in his existence. It may be true that he can find freedom when he says "No," but behind this "No," shouldn't there be some standard, some value to which one is willing to say "Yes"?

One is also bothered in reading Sartre by his view of love. He is unable to forge an image of human beings rising above possessiveness, sadism, and masochism in their relationships of intimacy. Certainly such relations can be that (under dehumanizing conditions of life love can degenerate into what Sartre says it is), but one would hope it could also be more than that. Sartre, in sum, has a purely negative view of freedom, value, man, and love. One would expect this from one caught up in the mechanism of this over-organized, overmechanized, and overpopulated civilization. But should not the existentialist, who rejects these aspects of modern civilization, find that which is affirmative in existence?

Sartre fought in the resistance against the Nazis, and this experience had a profound effect on him. But perhaps he should now stop resisting, which is negative, and start existing, which might be positive. In extreme situations, extreme responses are called forth. What the extreme situation may demand from man is resistance and the courage to say "No." Most of us, however, do not live in a trench nor are we fighting in the underground. What most men must face are not bullets from the enemy out there but the dullness of everyday life. Their lives are threatened not by oppressors and secret police but by the unseen anxieties of a life with little meaning in alienated societies. What dehumanizes man is the boredom of routine, the anonymity of the bureaucracy, and the lack of a community sense to enrich living. All of these say "No" to man, and we need a philosophy that will lift man to the heights that can be obtained only by saying "Yes" to life.

Existentialism is not that philosophy. Although existentialists fervently protest against the alienating forces of a technological civilization, they do not really rise above the level of protest and provide man with a philosophy that can lift him to new human heights. They gallantly say "No" to the possible entrapments of overorganized and overmechanized existence, but they have not found a way to say "Yes" to something beyond this existence. They fail to provide a philosophical synthesis to direct man toward a new space-age philosophy. There is resistance, but no real new vision. In an age characterized by fragmentation, existentialism no more than logical positivism offers a new perspective, a new unifying framework for mankind.

Thus existentialism is sometimes regarded as an ignoble philosophy. But we should recognize that in its emphasis on the need for heroic resolve in the face of the overwhelming odds life stacks against man there is much nobility. Throughout the history of ideas, the model of man adopted by philosophers, theologians, psychologists, and social scientists has been that of a being made by forces beyond his control. Sartre, however, accords man the dignity of being responsible for making his own life. Such a philosophy, even if it cannot lift him to new heights, can provide him with the motive for struggling to lift himself; and this is no insignificant achievement.

Sometimes it almost seems as if we are no longer awake but are struggling through a deeply disturbing nightmare, and the central image in this nightmare is the mushroom cloud of atomic destruction, at once the symbol of man's power over nature and of his powerlessness to create a human world and to live at peace with nature and his fellow man. The creation of atomic energy comes as the culmination of man's great efforts to attain power over nature, the unpredictable and harsh workings that once so threatened human security. Man developed science and through it gained power over nature—so much power that he lost balance, and finally, holding deadly atomic power in his hands, he fell in danger of blowing up nature and himself with it. An important aspect of modern science was its insistence on looking objectively upon nature, and man—his own existence deeply subjective—became isolated from nature and incapable of feeling at home with it. As man's power over nature increased, his world became more objective and less human, and he began to find himself in a vast kingdom of objective artificiality in which the synthetic was fast replacing the natural. Thus man became alienated from nature.

Every day in our civilization we stand witness to the barbaric packing together of vast herds of human beings, who remain unrelated to each other despite being packed together. Sociologist David Riesman has christened them the "lonely crowd." Jammed in subways, trolleys, and buses, elbowing their way through forests of people on overcrowded streets, in shopping malls, and at entertainment and sporting events, frantically dancing without relation to their partners, people whirl through life like atoms in a void. Today one rarely feels anywhere a sense of human harmony or community. This atomic-age man, space-age man, scientific man is alienated not only from nature but also from his fellow man.

In this maddest of all possible worlds everyone is speeding through life, awakened by the ringing bell of the alarm clock. Think of the very name of it! *Alarm* clock. We must not awake naturally to face the beauty of life; we have to be alarmed, forced up so we can face the artificiality of dehumanized work. And so multitudes of men and women mechanically migrate back and forth to work to devote themselves to jobs that lack meaning to them. Everywhere the individual is being lost amidst perilously large mobs. Overpopulation, overmechanization, and overorganization proceed apace and threaten the autonomy and independence of man. A man comes home from work at night and makes a dash for his television, which he has to turn on almost as an addict makes his dash for dope to get turned on. People seem to have to get something from the outside to keep them going as their own life energy appears to be in a state of power crisis. The older generation has to go to movies, sporting events, and vacation resorts and the younger generation has to go to drugs, electronic sounds, and communes. No one seems to go to himself anymore. People joylessly drift through life. In this mechanical world there is so much being done and so much to do externally that man has no time for himself, no time to get to know and be with himself. And so man is alienated not only from nature and from other selves but even from himself.

If one had to find one word to describe the plight of modern man, he could not go wrong with the word *alienation*. Today man finds nature alien to him, he finds other selves alien to him, and he finds his own self alien. There is hardly a social analyst of any importance who has not diagnosed the modern situation in such terms. Because of this alienation, he finds himself torn up from the roots. How deep do these roots go? How great is the alienation, or estrangement, of man? The social analyst rarely plunges to the depths of these roots. Thus there is something superficial about most of the explanations and remedies for man's condition offered by social scientists. Rarely do they get to the core of the problem, for they do not see the *philosophical* grounding of these conditions. Martin Heidegger (1889–   ) sees that the problem goes far deeper than the vision of the social scientist extends. Most social scientists analyze the problem in terms of certain observable conditions in the family unit or in terms of the dynamics of society or of the development of history. But, Heidegger maintains, these conditions themselves cannot be understood except in the context of the philosophical problem of *Being*. Therefore Heidegger undertook a most profound and original analysis of Being.

The fundamental roots of man's problems are not economic as Marxists tell us, nor sexual as Freudians tell us, nor environmental as sociologists tell us. They are, Heidegger tells us, ontological. The basic alienation of man is alienation from Being itself, and his sickness is based upon the very way in which we in the Western world look upon Being. It is for this reason that the primary aim of Heidegger's philosophy is the construction of a new ontology, a new way of conceiving of reality. Heidegger came to destroy the old tradition of metaphysics, which he saw as already rotten at the roots, and in developing a philosophy of Being he was planting new seeds that can be the basis for a new life.

Heidegger was thoroughly convinced that the whole history of Western metaphysics had been erected upon an improper base, and thus it had to be taken down. It was falling down in any event. The improper base involves a misconception about the nature of Being. Western man has gone through his whole history serving the wrong idea of Being. When we try to understand Being, it is crucial for us to realize that Being may be understood, or apprehended, in two ways: (1) in a narrow technical sense and (2) in a broad philosophical sense.

When we seek to understand the meaning of Being in the narrow, technical, and objective sense we view it as a noun, as designating a particular being—a thing or an object. Being in this sense refers to that which is specific and definite to somebody or to something. This we may call the "thing" notion of being. There is another way in which "being" can be comprehended, and that is not as a noun but as a verb, not objectively but subjectively. Just as we may think of being *as a* creature, we may also think of the being *of* that thing. Thus being can be taken as designating some particular thing, but it may also be taken as the act of existing of the thing.

Being can tell us about *what something is* or it can tell us *that something is.* When we regard it in this latter sense as a verb, we are talking about what Heidegger calls *being itself,* the sheer act of existing. It is not easy to put this idea of being into words because as such nothing specific or definite is involved. We may describe all the physical properties of a man and thus define him in an objective sense, *as a* being, but there are no words to express the being *of* him; nouns and adjectives can express the fact that he is *something,* but words cannot really convey the simple but all-important fact that he *is.*

To get to the act of existence of the person, his "isness," we must sheer away all objective properties until what is left is so abstract that it seems to be almost nothing. Yet this "isness" constitutes the very core of one. We can understand this in love. When we love a person it is not for what the person *has* but for what the person *is.* Someone else may *have* the same things or even more and yet just leave us cold. The true lover cannot say he loves the beloved because of this or that or the other thing, but just because the beloved *is* who she is. One really loves the other not *as a* thing but rather the being of the other, the other's unique act of existing. It is not something specific that leads us to love another but the very "isness" of the other. This "isness" is the most basic fact about beings. It cannot be put into words but must be experienced. This is what we refer to when we understand being as a verb. Most languages provide words that designate each sense of being—being as a thing on one hand and the being of things on the other. Unfortunately, English does not provide us with two words for the two senses of being. That makes it difficult for us to understand the profound meaning of being, but Heidegger's native language of German very aptly conveys the distinction between the two concepts in its words *das Seiende* and *das Sein:*

BEING

(1) DAS SEIENDE	(2) DAS SEIN
Being understood on the analogy of concrete things, in the sense of being a noun, as a specific, as an object.	*Being understood in the sense of the being of things. This is being as a verb, as an activity rather than a thing. It points to reality in its subjective dimensions.*

Das Seiende, or being *as things,* has to do with the objective world out there, but there is more to existence than that; there is also the deeper reality *of* things. This latter sense of being, *das Sein,* is what Heidegger believed must serve as the basis for a new ontology, a new fundamental philosophy. It is because he concentrated on understanding Being on so fundamental a level that we may regard his philosophy as far more profound than Sartre's or that of most existentialists. Sartre argued that existence precedes essence, but existence for him whirls about in the mad world of *becoming*, in the physical world of constant change. Heidegger went deeper and showed the necessity for understanding existence itself as rooted in Being. We might contrast the positions of Sartre and Heidegger by noting that where Sartre proclaims that existence precedes essence, Heidegger agrees but goes one step further, insisting that being precedes existence.

Heidegger maintained that Western man set foot upon the wrong philosophical road far back in his past. At the very dawn of philosophy in ancient Greece, the first philosophers isolated *being* and understood it as a noun on the analogy of things. Instead of the Being of things, they concentrated on things themselves. Being itself is so fundamental it cannot be put into words, and yet it is something we live and breathe. Its very fundamentality renders it conceptually difficult to articulate. Thus we are liable to overlook it. It is not likely we should so easily overlook *things* because they present themselves more overtly to us. Indeed it is very easy to become lost in a sea of things, and that is precisely what happened in Greek philosophy. The result was the erection of metaphysical constructions upon the foundation of *das Seiende* instead of *das Sein*. In Western philosophy each metaphysician has described Being in terms of some specific kind of being. Philosophers have not thought of Being in terms of "isness" but in terms of "thingness." Of course, it is very difficult for us to even understand what Being is apart from things, but that is because of a history of conditioning to this perspective. We should not think that Being as "isness" does not exist just because it is difficult to conceptualize. There may be more to life than meets our conceptual eyes. Our philosophies in the West have attained vision too much through that conceptual eye. Aristotle theorized that metaphysics is the science of being as being, but he thought of this being as if it were *substance*—something definite. He understood "being" on the analogy of a "thing." Even Plato's Idea of ultimate reality was something conceptually definite. Similarly, the medieval philosophers' idea of God was not really the idea of Being; it was the idea of the highest *thing*. God was conceived of not as Being but as one who is some*thing*.

BEING "AS" THINGS: THE OBJECTIVE WORLD AND THE WILL TO POWER

Thinking of being in terms of *a* being, or some definite thing, makes it possible to be very objective about reality. It is quite different with the being *of* things, for that is not amenable to objective description. The being *of* things cannot be observed, measured, and described with precision, but being *as* things can be. Things can be classified and organized; indeed this is precisely the job science performs. Thus when the Greek philosophers abstracted being *as* things from the being *of* things, they set the stage for the development of science. This is at least in part why there was a glorious flowering of science in the Western world, whereas in the Orient, where being is not conceived of on the analogy of things, there was no such development of science. The Western world has a long tradition of emphasis on *objectivity* and *organization*. This orientation has vigorously seeped into our lives today, so that everything has to be planned and organized. When one goes to a foreign country, one has to have a planned tour. The basic premise of such a tour is that one will thereby get to see every important *thing*. And so one goes through a whirlwind routine and sees everything, but never gets a real feel of the country—never acquires insight into the being of the country. This is symptomatic. Increasingly people want their lives organized. They have to set plans for things to do for long periods in advance. This is interpreted as the full life. Notice the resort lodges that advertise they have every moment of the day arranged for their guests. From the moment one arises in the morning until one falls into bed at night worn out, a detailed schedule of things to do is provided. In short they wear people out right around the clock working them more arduously than any boss could—and this is known as enjoyment. This fetish for organizing one's life, planning it around things, and searching for things to do, reaches its point of diminishing returns. People get tired of things and of doing things. Thus a general boredom sets in. People can handle things, but when they become tired of them they are unable to open themselves to being. Not having roots in Being, people become lonely, even in a crowd. In this sense, our crisis is at its root philosophical, and merely political, psychological, sociological, or economic solutions will never get to the heart of it.

The quest to objectify and organize life, which is made possible by the reduction of being to things, involves a desire for control over things. Indeed the impetus to organize is based on the need to get things under control. This produces a vicious circle because the more one is devoted to things, the more one usually loses control over one's inner life, and hence the more one needs control over things in the outer world. People need power over things to compensate for the lack of power over themselves. Thus, underlying the drive to organize is a strong *will to power*. It is significant that, as Heidegger calls to our attention, the culmination of the entire tradition of metaphysics in the West was reached in Nietzsche's theory of the *will to power*. Nietzsche was thus the natural conclusion to the history of metaphysics in the West, both in the sense that he took it as far as it could go and in that he in no small way aided in the destruction of that history. Nietzsche loudly announced the death of God and with Him of the entire realm of transcendental values to which He gave support; yet Nietzsche retained the concept of power, which had always been seen as emanating from God. Like Francis Bacon a few centuries earlier, Nietzsche saw the effort of science and knowledge generally as a will to power—an expression of the need to get power over nature and over man. Today this compulsion for power might well lead to our own destruction.

In contrast to this Nietzschean vision of man activated by a will to power, Heidegger and the philosophers in the East do not believe that it is necessary to take power over the world in order to have it. If one opens himself to the world he will understand it, and this is possession enough; if one opens himself to life it will flow into his veins, so that nature and life become part of him, and he becomes infused with them. We can know life only by flowing with it, not by striving for power or mastery over it. This is not an easy principle to explain, and there is no simple formula for understanding it. One thing is certain: one cannot learn to open himself to being by giving it "fifteen minutes a day" for a few weeks. There is no instant salvation, no royal road to Being. It involves a more basic change of values, and changing one's values is not an easy matter. One must give up the desire to control things and learn to find worth in life itself. This involves virtually a total reconditioning, for most of us in the West are conditioned to be *dualists*. Like Descartes, we tend to think of reality as divided into the mental or spiritual on one hand and the physical or material on the other. Duality has the effect of rendering us strangers unto nature. Heidegger was convinced that it is impossible to heal the estrangement from being unless this "subject-object" distinction is overcome. Hence he set as a basic aim of his fundamental ontology the destruction of dualistic philosophy. He did not see the world as bifurcated into two irreducible kinds of being: man and nature, subject and object, or mind and matter. Heidegger, who gave man so much understanding of himself, did not even use the word "man" to describe man. He christened man *"Dasein"—being there*—because he felt that this concept is not conducive to thinking of man as *cut off* from reality. Heidegger provided us with great insight into man, but his own basic interest was not in man as such—not in psychology or philosophical anthropology. His primary interest lay in ontology, but a type of ontology that had to be built on an understanding of man rather than of the world. The general procedure is to synthesize our knowledge of the universe in order to formulate an ontology, but Heidegger supposed an understanding of man and what is in him can give us greater insight into reality than knowledge of the universe can. Heidegger strongly believed that if we are going to understand reality, or Being, we must not do it on the basis of *things*—objective properties that stand outside of us. Because the human being has Being and insight into his subjectivity, he may provide the clue to what Being is. Thus ontology should be based on an understanding of the Being of man rather than of any things in the world. Heidegger, who maintained that man is not an object or thing in the world, sought to understand him as Being in the world. Heidegger regarded it indispensable to distinguish between man and things. Things, he pointed out, are simply *present;* they have no more being than that which is openly observable. Secondly, things can be understood in terms of *general categories*. Thirdly, things have *functional value*—that is, they can be *used*. In contrast, man is not merely *present*, is not just a part of a general category, and is not a functional creature to be *used*. It is therefore crucial that man not interpret himself as a thing, for when he does, as Heidegger observed, his existence becomes *inauthentic*. This inauthentic mode of existence is one that is completely externalized; in it one lives for things and for others and as such does not really live at all. Instead of looking to one's own potentialities, one finds oneself merely drifting through life, living only on the surface, and never reaching those levels of one's being below what is openly observable; one finds oneself compulsively conforming and thereby becoming part of some general category; and one begins to define oneself in terms of what one does, especially in terms of one's occupation, thereby being reduced to the status of a thing to be used. Thus man *falls away* from his true self. He becomes estranged from his human potentials and lives not with himself but with the crowd. He becomes an anonymous or faceless man who is free but who, tragically, has chosen to run away from the possible realization of himself. His being lacks the factors that are part of an authentic existence, the kind of existence that separates the "men" from the "things." These factors are:

1. *Befindlichkeit*—awareness of one's true condition
2. *Verstehen*—understanding
3. *Rede*—discourse

The anonymous man, instead of being aware of his condition, is aware only of overt occurrences. He never sees what is going on beneath the surface. The surface level is his reality. He does not have *Befindlichkeit.* Furthermore, his life is characterized by *ambiguity* rather than *understanding.* He is confused about his own meaning and about the causes of things that happen. And finally, he is not capable of *discourse* but only of *prattle*— not *Rede* but *Gerede!* Through true discourse one can establish an inner tie with another *Dasein,* or person, but for the anonymous, externalized existence there is just meaningless chatter; over and over again there resounds the hollow ring of empty phrases and shibboleths.

It might seem pedantic to poke fun at the "conventional" utterances of everyday speech. Perhaps, there is really no harm in the conventional greetings and clichés of ordinary "small talk," but they can be a measure of one's depth. People reach the point at which they stop taking the small talk for what it is, and instead take it for reality. Small talk is meaningless, and when it becomes the basic ingredient of one's dealings with others, it reflects the meaningless existence of the small talker. Often people try to hold on to one another with words. They feel that to relate, they must keep talking. But when people do this they are communicating only with their lips, not with their selves. Often silence can speak more eloquently than words. Words can never really take hold of another being. If somehow amid a deep silence two persons feel they are together and feel this deeply within themselves, it may be something more than that which can be put into language. Such persons utter no words but yet may speak to one another. Understanding cannot be a mere matter of intellectual comprehension. To understand something is not just to possess information about it, but to appropriate it into one's being, and know it upon a nonverbal level. When one understands himself as "subject" and views what he wishes to know as "*object*," then he is precluded from opening himself to it and cannot bring it into existence. Understanding has to be with the entire self. When one understands with his whole being, he brings truth into his life.

Heidegger vigorously protested against the objective theory of truth that makes truth a purely intellectual affair. He located the unfortunate origin of this objective theory, which was an intellectual conception of truth, in Plato. But to find the real meaning of truth Heidegger went further back in Greek philosophy, back to its basic origins. The original Greek word for truth was *alethia,* which means revelation. And this is what truth really is; it is a revelation to the whole person. By living according to his true potential man lives in truth. Like Kierkegaard, Heidegger saw truth as something we *are,* not something we *have.* One must know truth with his full being, and there is no need to have it put into words. All one has to do is open himself to it, and it will *reveal* itself to him. Somehow, though, people have become too closed through their externalized lives to be able to open themselves. How many persons can stroll through a countryside without bringing along thoughts of their day-to-day existence—the job, money worries, or thoughts of what tomorrow will bring? Such concerns close one to the wonderful simplicity of the nature about him. One cannot really take it into himself because it is blocked off by his preoccupation with daily occurrences. People are so caught up in their daily activities that they cannot free themselves to participate in life. If one could only pause a moment in his race to keep up with the demands of daily life, he might find some release from the bondage of an inauthentic existence.

A man who chooses to run away from his possibilities finds that anxiety invariably catches up to him. He cannot sever himself from his own potentialities without producing disquietude. Then he tries to run away from anxiety, and estrangement follows. Man tries to avoid the anxieties and tensions of life by absorbing himself in practical activities. But the practical activities demand that he respond with only a *part* of himself, and he soon gets to the point at which he is only *in part* alive. He does not engage in life fully. But man *is* a full being, although this fact is usually concealed except during certain intense emotional experiences. Intense emotions can overtake one's entire self. When a man becomes depressed, he is not just depressed with part of himself; his total being is gripped by a feeling of meaninglessness. Things that ordinarily make him feel good suddenly seem without point or meaning. Everything seems useless and hopeless. Conversely, positive emotions like love can make the entire world seem wonderful. The possibilities inherent in such intense emotion reveal that man does have the potential to live fully, although he only does so on rare occasions. Man can only go so far in running from himself and can only refuse to face life for so long; sooner or later he will reach the point at which he finds life staring him in the face. In an externalized existence man can avoid many of the deep emotions of life, but when crisis strikes, his entire emotional system is affected, and he lacks a basis for responding to the crisis. Not being accustomed to responding to life fully, he cannot cope with a situation that deeply touches his emotional life.

The externalized life modern man lives is such that everyone is much like everyone else, and thus any particular person is invariably expendable. One man's job can be performed by another. A person can always get someone else to do his work for him, but there is one thing that one has to do alone—he has to die all alone. No one can help another die. People who are not used to facing reality try desperately to avoid having to face the inescapable reality of death. Thus they place death outside of themselves and can only think of it abstractly. They do not think of it in terms of their own lives but in terms of the lives of others. Death is not real to them; it is just another external event that happens to men generally. People generally do not consider death as *their own* possibility. Thus they can speak glibly about a nuclear war, for they have no existential conception of death. To have such a conception, to be realistic about death would be very torment-ing, and people always try to avoid such anxieties.

In general, Heidegger contended that people would be stronger if they would accept anxiety. Like Kierkegaard and Freud, Heidegger distinguished between fear and anxiety. Fear is of something definite, but anxiety—though all-pervading—refers to nothing definite, which makes it all the worse. Yet, in a sense, anxiety is a condition of life—especially in the atomic age—and so man must learn to live with it. To try to avoid it is to flee to inauthen-ticity.

Now it might seem that Heidegger is a very melancholy philosopher. His concern with death must strike many as a morbid interest. Yet this does not alter the fact that he is talking about a real problem that affects every one of us. I am not sure that the interest in linguistic analysis of many of our philosophers is not somewhat more morbid for it is a type of living death. There is no escaping the fact that the end of man is death. This is not a problem of quantitative analysis; it is not something that can be explained away. Anyone who is alive must know that *annihilation* awaits him. Thus Heidegger's discussion of "nothing" and of "death" does not result from the fact that he is an expert in creating pseudoproblems, as the positivists would have us believe. They tell us that Heidegger's metaphysics, with its talk of annihilation and nothingness, is nonsensical because the idea of nothingness is unreal; it does not correspond to any empirical reality. But people who fall into a state of *despair* come face to face with nothing-ness—they know it is real. Anyone who reaches the point at which he must face his own death knows that there is nothing more real.

Some people have objected to Heidegger's philosophy by saying, in effect, "It is true that death is a reality we must all face. But what good does thinking about it do? I admit that death is each man's fate—the fate no one escapes. But why dwell upon it?" Heidegger would answer that only by coming to grips with the problem of death can we gain strength to face it when it comes. We can also gain, in facing death, a more profound understanding of what is really valuable to us. As people go along in their everyday lives, they get in the habit of assigning the most monumental importance to the most trivial occurrences. But when one faces death, things that he has made overly important come to seem insignificant to him. He cannot help but see his values in proper perspective. When one's own life is at stake, his money, his possessions, and his small desires simply do not make much difference anymore. In meeting with death, one learns what really is and is not important. The imminence of death can teach more about values than any treatise on morality.

Man must also learn that just as no one can die for him, so no one can live for him. In the face of anxiety and death man must resolve to fulfill his human potentials. To do this he must have an adequate conception of time. Most people think of time as a series of instants along a straight line. On this conception of time, the past is something that is *no more* and the future is something that is *not yet;* both past and future are defined in negative terms, and only the present is seen as positive. The consequence is that man must live for the moment. Such a way of living inevitably is superficial because it fails to do justice to all the dimensions of man's life. These dimensions can be understood only when time is not divided into instants but is seen as a structural whole. In an authentic existence man must tie together the past, present, and future. Instead of regarding the past as something done with and gone, man must accept the burden of it as a present reality; instead of regarding the future as something that is *not yet,* one should regard it as something that *will be* and is in fact coming into being at every moment. The future is that into which man constantly projects himself, but he cannot realistically project himself into the future without fully accepting his past. At any given moment the crucial question is whether man will take the responsibility for his past into his being and resolve to move into the future in truth, or whether he will deny his past and thus "fall away" from a future of truth and authenticity. One must bind the three tenses of time together, taking his past into his present by making a resolution for the future. In this way man can free himself from the necessity of drifting with the stream of time. When one thinks of time as divided into discrete instants, the instants that were in the past are forever gone and there is not much one can do about them. Time flows on like a river, and one is caught in the flow. But when time is seen as a structural whole, then man does not lose the parts that make up the past. In talking about time Heidegger used the term *ekstasis*, which means "standing out," and the point is that man stands out and is not caught in time. The consequence is that the past has not been lost, thus leaving man free to bring it into his present and do something about it in his future.

One might object that, by Heidegger's own account, the future man has is not much, for it is his own death. To this Heidegger would answer that, although there is an emphasis on death in his philosophy, there is also an emphasis on life. That we must be aware of death does not make life meaningless. On the contrary, only by being aware of it can we know what really matters in life. We cannot ignore the reality of death, but we can be fully honest with ourselves about it, and if we resolve to live authentically in spite of being aware of it, then in the meantime we can live with meaning.

Summary

1. Metaphysics is the study of what Being is, or of what is real.

2. In classical philosophy two basic answers to the nature of reality are to be found in the metaphysical philosophies of materialism and idealism.

3. The assumption of materialism is that material particles, or some form

of matter, constitute the fundamental elements of reality and that all emerges from, can be explained in terms of, or can be reduced to, physico-chemical matter. Mechanistic and deterministic materialism presupposes that the universe and all in it runs like a well-oiled machine according to physical laws that are ironclad and purposeless.

4. Historically great representatives of materialism are the Greek Atomists Leucippus and Democritus, and in modern philosophy, Thomas Hobbes, the French Encyclopedists, and Karl Marx and Friedrich Engels.

5. Idealism in metaphysics is the position that the nature of reality is mental, or spiritual, rather than physical. Essential reality is held to be more akin to values than to things. It has been argued that we can only know reality through ideas of it, and if the nature of reality is such that it can be grasped by an idea, then reality must be consonant with the idea. The case can be developed that all we know is what we perceive, or what ideas we have, and thus we do not know a material world—that is, we do not know the reality of matter, but only the reality of ideas.

6. Great idealists in the history of philosophy were men such as Plato, Bishop Berkeley, and G. W. F. Hegel.

7. Plato held that the particular physical things we encounter are only fleeting. Particular physical things generate and decay; it is not possible to hold onto them. Investigation of them points, however, to a more permanent reality beyond, one that is nonphysical, universal, and eternal. This reality Plato called the Idea or Form. When we try to understand the structure of reality, we do better with mathematics than with our senses. This is because reality is not a physical thing. Particular physical things are not real in themselves but are only *copies* of the real Ideas. The line one draws is never completely straight but only an approximation of the perfect real line, which is the ideal. A particular man only fulfills some of the qualities of the ideal of manhood. Particular men come and go, are born and die, but the idea of man lasts forever.

8. Bishop Berkeley was a *subjective* idealist. He maintained that all one can ever know is what he perceives. Since one's own perceptions are the source of all knowledge, there is no way for one to know that an objective world exists outside them.

9. Hegel argued that there is an objective reality, a reality outside of our particular perceptions and ideas, but since we can only grasp it by having an idea of it, then it must be of the nature of the idea. Hegel saw the world as spiritual or ideal in nature and also as evolving according to a definite plan. Hegel believed that through a process of struggle, spiritual reality was evolving to ever greater perfection.

10. Whereas the ancient Greek philosopher Democritus maintained all of reality is constituted of matter, the nineteenth-century German philosopher Hegel explained it as composed of spirit. Democritus and Hegel were at polar ends in their views, but both philosophers believed the world was made of but *one* substance. Thus although Democritus was a materialist

and Hegel an idealist, both were *monists*—they believed reality was completely composed of only one kind of substance. A very different way of understanding reality is provided by the modern French philosopher René Descartes who believed reality was composed of *two* substances—spirit and matter, or body and soul. Descartes was thus a dualist.

11. Dualism assumes that reality is divided, and the implications of such a view may be that man has a difficult time understanding himself as a whole person. Thus there may be an important relation between the philosophy of dualism and the problem of alienation. A monistic philosophy provides a world view in which there is no essential fragmentation of things. The philosopher Spinoza developed an uncompromising philosophy of monism. He vigorously insisted that reality could be explained in terms of one substance, the absolute, which he called God. By this, however, he referred not to the personal God of the Judaeo-Christian tradition but an all-embracing system of nature.

12. In the twentieth century, an age of science and power, philosophers have increasingly turned away from traditional metaphysical interests. Logical positivists maintained that only that which can be empirically verified is meaningful. They denied that metaphysical propositions were capable of empirical verification and thus found the field of metaphysics to be nonsense. At about the same time existentialism arose—not in support of our scientific and technological world but in revolt against it. Like the logical positivists, the existentialists turned from traditional metaphysics, but unlike them did not reject metaphysics altogether. Instead they developed a radical metaphysics based on the idea that man's existence—his living creative activity—rather than any substance such as matter or spirit, is the central reality. This idea was expressed in the existentialist formula that existence precedes essence.

4

What Should We Do?
Ethics

Introduction to Ethical Problems

If someone tells you that if he throws a copy of the *Congressional Record* in a fire it will burn, and you tell him you do not believe him, there is a way he can prove it. He can throw one in a fire, and if it burns, you will know he is right. Statements that purport to tell us what does happen in the world we may call *descriptive*, or *factual*, and we can resolve argument concerning them in a definite way—by testing them. Now suppose an advocate of the New Left school of politics tells you that you *ought* to throw a congressman in the fire. You can throw one in the fire, but even if he burns that would not prove he *ought* to have been thrown in the fire. How can one prove who is right with questions concerning what ought to be? This type of question is a central concern of the branch of philosophy called *ethics* and is also a central concern of men. Yet men have never been able to find any easy answer to questions of what ought to be. All the factual and descriptive information in the world still leaves us with the terrible burden of deciding what we ought to do about it. This is a problem to which all human beings are heir. How do we decide?

Suppose you had the power to make yourself invisible. What would you do once you were invisible? Would you visit a group of friends to hear what they were saying about you when they thought you were not around? Listening in on what others are saying isn't supposed to be a nice thing to do, but would this bother you if no one could ever find out that you were doing it? While invisible you probably could get away with stealing or killing. Would you do it if there were something you wanted to steal or someone you wanted to kill? If there were someone you disliked very much, would you do things to torment him? You could get away with a lot while invisible.

Remember, no one would ever know you were doing any of the things you do while you are invisible, nor could there be any punishment for your doing them. Perhaps you still might not do these things because your conscience would know and God would know. But suppose the magic that made you invisible were so powerful that it would even make you invisible to God, or suppose that you do not believe in God. In either of these cases, do you still think your conscience would bother you? Perhaps it would at first, but after a while you probably would get used to it and not care. After all if you are beyond the reach of God and men, what would be the basis for conscience? None of these questions should be easy to answer, and if you think you can answer them easily, you undoubtedly are fooling yourself by being overconfident about your own ethics.

Thus far we have considered selfish pursuits an invisible man might undertake. Maybe you would do things primarily of benefit to humanity rather than to yourself. You could break crime rings, expose corruption in high places, and punish the guilty. If you knew of a very evil man, would you kill him? If you would not because killing is wrong, would you change your mind if you knew that doing so would prevent him from slaughtering multitudes in a war he was planning to instigate? Are there any circumstances under which you would take the life of another human being?

In Robert Sheckley's novel *The Tenth Victim* society arranged for The Big Hunt in which people were licensed to kill each other. In it Polletti was the victim and Caroline the hunter. How do men and women behave in such a world?

> *"Do you know what she told me tonight?"* Polletti said. *"She told me she loved me. And all the time she was planning to kill me."*
>
> *"The treachery of women is proverbial,"* Gino said. *"What did you tell her?"*
>
> *"I told her of course that I loved her,"* Polletti said. . . .
>
> *"She's killed nine men,"* Gino reminded him.
>
> *"You can't really hold that against her,"* Marcello said. *"That's simply a manifestation of the times."*

"Perhaps you's right," Gino said. "But what will you do, Marcello?"
"I shall perform the counter-kill exactly as I had planned," Polletti said.[1]

Caroline and Polletti had more than the ordinary problems of lovers, for they were contracted to a duel of death against one another. When Caroline mentioned love in connection with her victim, she was told her contract expressly forbade her to fall in love during her hunt and particularly with her victim. Caroline pointed out that love existed a long time before contracts. It was then called to her attention that contracts are more enforceable than love. Which should be more binding on one, a contractual obligation or love? If a contract is more binding, then one should carry out its stipulations even though it may cause great harm to those whom one loves. If love is more binding, then how can people trust each other to keep their promises? Maybe neither is absolutely more binding than the other, and it all depends upon the particular circumstances. But in that case, how is it possible to determine whether one *ought* to give priority to one rather than the other? What are the criteria?

Should one do good because of a contract (or legal obligation) or because of love? Do you do good because you love to do it or because you fear the social ostracism that may result from not doing it? Do you refrain from doing bad things because of principle or because of the legal consequences if you were to be caught? In 1920 the Boston police went on strike, and apparently there were an awful lot of decent citizens there whose honesty did not derive from love of honesty; people went on unprecedented shopping sprees—after the stores were closed! Not only did people who were ordinarily honest help themselves to all types of merchandise, but it is reported they tried to sell it at such exorbitant prices that they would make even professional criminals blush. If people would so behave just because the gendarmes are on strike, imagine what they would do if they could become invisible. Are people inherently immoral and only held in line by laws?

Is it wrong to cheat on examinations? Most schools take a very dim view of this practice, and the punishment for cheating may be automatic failure or even expulsion. A student may cheat by deviously gazing at another student's paper or at carefully secreted cue cards, and then writing what he learns there on his paper, passing it off as his own work. Many administrators and teachers regard this as immoral, and some have sought to trap cheaters as if they were criminals on the Most Wanted List. Honest students are those who stay up all night diligently memorizing what someone else wrote in a textbook. The next day these students come in and carefully write down what they remember from their reading last night. What they write down is something copied from someone else's work, too, but the difference is that the diligent students remember what they copy for a few hours longer than the cheaters. Thus, in the sense that cheating consists in copying from an-

[1] Robert Sheckley, *The Tenth Victim* (New York: Ballantine Books, Inc., 1965), pp. 138f.

222

THE WORK
OF THE
PHILOSOPHER

other's work, we may say everyone who takes the test cheats. The difference seems to be that a given system honors one variety of cheats—those who are willing to work themselves weary memorizing—and dishonors another variety. From this fact arises the problem of *contextualism* in ethics, for questions of value must be understood in terms of some type of framework or context. When a species of behavior is morally evaluated in terms of a given legal system, people often forget the contextual dimension of ethics and tend to take the given legal system as an unquestioned framework on the basis of which moral problems are to be resolved.

With respect to the example of cheating, it would seem that in a society such as ours, which is devoted to success at getting ahead by any means, cheating might be positively valued as a means of survival. Suppose a student who received an "A" subsequently revealed that he had cheated to get it. Should he not be rewarded for being so industrious? One would think he might at least be honored as one most likely to succeed. In fact, however, he would be severely criticized. Why? Because we do not condemn cheating with reference to our actual social practices but with reference to our ideals. Understanding the matter in the context of our assumed ideals rather than in the context of our actual practice makes it clear that it is not the actual cheating that gets people so upset but the flaunting of our ideals by people whose cheating comes to our attention. For a person to acknowledge that he cheats (either by getting caught or by confessing) reflects poorly upon our ideals, whereas the cheat (who covers up his actual practice) shows thereby that he accepts our ideals. We more or less expect people to cheat and keep their big mouths shut about it as a sign that they respect our values even though they do not practice them.

Yet this does not mean that practice is irrelevant to moral evaluation. Most people recognize the necessity of invoking practice as a basis for judging behavior. For example, people generally accept the idea that in times of great crisis or of extreme situations certain ideals simply may not be applicable. Thus in time of war people will justify violent behavior they would ordinarily condemn and say, "Well, war is war!" *The Wall Street Journal* conducted a survey on an alleged American massacre at Songmy in Vietnam, and got responses such as follows:

> "Oh fiddle! Every war has that. War is war," matter of factly says Mrs. Mary Halsem, a retired nurse in Los Angeles. The alleged massacre wasn't a tragedy at all, agrees Patrick Kupper, a 55-year-old elevator starter in Boston. "It was good. What do they give soldiers bullets for—to put in their pockets? That's the way war is." Defending the reported killing of children, a Cleveland woman says, "It sounds terrible to say we ought to kill kids, but many of our boys being killed over there are just kids, too."[2]

At Songmy American soldiers were reported to have ruthlessly killed defenseless women and children without provocation, and not in self-defense. If these men had done anything remotely similar in time of peace, they would be universally regarded as the most wanton fiends, and it would

[2] *The Wall Street Journal,* December 1, 1969, p. 1.

be said the civilized world could never be safe while such men were permitted to be on the loose. Yet in time of war they may not be condemned, and it is even thought that it is good to have such men on the loose.

The point is that what at first may appear to be a relatively simple moral question, such as the one concerning cheating, may turn out to involve very difficult complexities. Anyone can condemn something as immoral, but understanding and justifying such statements is no easy matter. To understand moral questions one must concern oneself with the meaning of terms, whether he is judging in terms of actual practice or in terms of ideals, whether such judgments are prejudiced and subjective or are objective, and whether or not the framework in terms of which he makes his judgments can be validated. There are big headaches in coming to terms with what might seem to be little questions of morality. Indeed it may even be the case that there is no justification at all for moral judgments.

Why should we be moral at all? Perhaps, there is no reason to be. Is it immoral to steal? Most people think so. People hold property in reverence, and society has taken meticulous care to make crimes against property a major concern of criminal law. Some maintain that property is a civil right, whereas there are others who go further and insist that it is a natural right. If people so cherish property, it is easy to understand why it should be thought that crimes against it are so important and so immoral. However, some have asked where property came from in the first place. Pierre Joseph Proudhon, the French anarchist, responded to the question "What is property?" with the answer "It is robbery." As Proudhon saw it, property originated when someone put a fence around land that had been the common property of everyone and announced that it was his. By being strong enough or clever enough to make people accept his claim, he had invented property, but what he had done really amounted to theft. Obviously, anyone who accepts this definition is not going to take crimes against property as seriously as do most people in our society. On the contrary, those who accept this definition would be concerned that people are used for the sake of property. In this sense one might regard property as a crime against humanity. This is the position socialists and communists may take. Is property a right? It is a wrong? Are there any means by which we can know?

Is vandalism immoral? People generally deplore it. If a person should see a vandal tearing up his car, he would probably feel like tearing up the vandal. A vandal is a terrible person who does damage to our property and lowers its value. But automobile manufacturers who sit around and plan how to make our cars obsolescent and valueless are highly respected. Styles are changed so frequently that the value of a car diminishes at a far more rapid rate than it does when vandals work on it. Should automobile manufacturers be ranked, morally, as no better than vandals? Are their practices morally wrong? Or do they have a right to do what they will with their products? How can anyone say that someone does not have the right to do what he likes with that which is his own? If he does not have this right, who does? Who decides what can be done with what? What criteria are used? Where do the principles by which we decide come from?

A good way to test one's own operating morality and the ideals to which one subscribes is by projecting oneself into certain extreme situations and attempting to decide how in fact one would behave and how one ought to behave therein. Here are two such cases.

King David was deeply in love with Bathsheba, and she loved David madly. Everything would have been fine but for one thing—her husband, Uriah. David took advantage of the fact that Bathsheba's husband was a greater soldier than a lover and decided to honor him by shipping him out to fight—and die—for the glory of his country. David was certain Uriah would die, and that Bathsheba could then be his. The prophet Nathan was just as certain that King David was a very immoral man and told him so in rather strong terms. God would raise evil up against David in his own house, Nathan said, and would take his wives before his own eyes and give them to his neighbor to lie with them, and this not in secret but before the sun. Yet if David was wrong to steal another man's wife, why would it be right to do the same thing to him? Should one consider extenuating circumstances? After all, David truly loved Bathsheba; he was not simply fooling around with another man's wife. Indeed David cared for Bathsheba far more than her own husband Uriah did, for Uriah was terribly ambitous, very inflexible, and not at all sensitive or understanding of Bathsheba. What is more, David's decision to send Uriah to his death was only a last resort; he had sought many other means by which to resolve the triangle, but they did not work because of Uriah's own obstinacy. In addition to this, the situation was complicated by the fact Bathsheba was pregnant, and when this became public knowledge she would have been stoned as a harlot, thereby killing both her and the baby in her womb. Could a man permit that? Can we condemn David for not wanting to permit it? Was Uriah's life worth that? How can one come to an objective moral conclusion in such a complex existential predicament?

In George Bernard Shaw's *The Doctor's Dilemma,* a distinguished doctor is prevailed upon by a lovely and fascinating young lady to treat her artist husband. The doctor, Sir Colenso Ridgeon, agrees to help her husband. However, he soon learns the artist husband Dubedat is a worthless scoundrel. The problem is that Ridgeon is the only person who can save Dubedat, but he can only take one more patient; if he helps Dubedat, he must neglect a true and dear old friend who is very sick. Who should be saved, a dishonest and insincere young man who can make an artistic contribution to the world, or a good man and an old friend? Are there any moral rules to guide one? Sir Colenso Ridgeon decides to save his old friend, and there certainly seems to be a moral basis for his doing so. Yet in a fifth act of the play we learn that the reason Ridgeon chose to cure his friend and not the worthless Dubedat was not in consideration of his feeling for his friend but in consideration of his love for Dubedat's charming wife. Ridgeon's own assessment was that he committed a "purely disinterested" murder, but was this the case? Is his decision any less moral because it served his own selfish purposes?

Moral situations are often richly complex like this. Who deserves greater condemnation, King David or Ridgeon the doctor? Is there any justification for what either did? Are we humans completely lost in a moral jungle, or is there any way we can logically decide about moral problems?

In our changing world of scientific discovery it becomes increasingly more difficult to deal with classical moral problems. Just think of the possibilities in an age of cryobiology when it is possible to store people at death and later to restore them to life. Under these circumstances a political leader who sends young men off to protect our freedom by waging a war in some far-off jungles, where it will not be possible to freeze them when they get killed, will be robbing young men not only of their present life, but of their future life as well. In pre-cryobio times one could always rationalize about death by remembering that everyone has to die sooner or later. But when people are frozen at time of death in liquid nitrogen at $-197°C$ and then maintained in that condition until medical science discovers a cure for what killed them, this rationalization will no longer be true. However, it would still be true for those blown up in a war. Under the circumstances could anyone justify war? Could even the most committed warnik say it was morally just?

Such developments as cryobiology mean that we will have to redefine death. Is a person who refuses to be frozen at time of death guilty of committing suicide? What about that part of the marriage ceremony that commits two persons to each other until death do them part? Does it mean that two persons are stuck with each other even after they are unfrozen and brought back to life in an entirely different world? If only one of them were revived, would he be a widower or a married man? If he remarried and his first wife were then revived, would he be a bigamist? How should we look at such questions morally?

All of the questions raised in this chapter are *ethical* questions. Some of them are, admittedly, rather far-fetched, and others are more practical questions that you may well have to answer for yourselves at some point in your lives. The process of living gives rise in men to the need of determining what is *right* and *wrong* and of establishing ideas with which they can praise or blame others and even themselves. More than this, men want to understand their own *obligations,* or what they *ought* to do. Even though we know something is right, it does not follow that we are obligated to do it. Thus it may be *right* for us to risk our necks to save someone's life, but does that mean we have an obligation to do so? How can we know when we *ought* to do something, when we have a moral duty to do that which is right—whatever that may be? For clarity concerning such issues we look to the field of ethics.

The effort to discover if there are, or if we can formulate, any moral rules in accord with which we can play the game of life is a concern dealt with in an area we might call *normative ethics.* Philosophers seek to develop and work out ethical theories, principles, or laws in terms of which we can understand what is right or wrong, good or bad, and what we ought to do. The ethical philosopher will make an effort to demonstrate that his set of ethical principles or values constitutes the most adequate means of dealing with ethical and moral issues. He will use logic and empirical evidence in defense of his ethical views or system. Normative ethics, then, has to do with building an ethical house in which man can live, with giving us workable moral principles to guide us, and with showing us the way to decide what is right and what we ought to do.

Another very important concern of the ethical philosopher is a methodological one: it concerns the question of the status of ethical statements, principles, and systems. How can ethical principles themselves be justified? Are ethical principles objective and universally valid, or are they merely subjective, depending upon need or personal social bias? If ethical statements and principles are only subjective, then the only way we can ultimately deal with someone who does not believe as we do is either to have nothing to do with him or to kill him. If there are no valid principles by which we can convince people who disagree with us on ethical matters, then all that avails is sheer force—a very frightening proposition. Because this problem is so crucial, the ethical philosopher is concerned not only with what is right and what we ought to do but also with the question of whether there is any way of establishing the validity of *any* ethical principles. This second type of ethical question brings us into the field called *metaethics*.

Not only must the ethical philosopher attempt to find ethical principles by which men can live (normative ethics) and not only must he attempt to discover the meaning and function of such principles and labor at justification of them (metaethics) but he must also come to grips with some *factual* questions. The first factual question the ethical philosopher has to deal with concerns human nature, for an ethical theory inconsistent with the nature of man would be worthless. Is the nature of man such that he is more directed in his behavior by *biological* or by *cultural* factors? Sigmund Freud assumed that biological determinants were more fundamental than cultural ones, whereas Erich Fromm maintained that cultural factors were more basic. If Freud was right, there is not much we can do about such perennial human activities as war because the aggressive instinct is built into the very nature of man. However if Fromm was correct, we can condition man's need for aggression out of him by changing the social structure in which he lives. Indeed the whole question of changing society greatly depends upon the question of whether behavior is primarily a consequence of cultural or of biological forces. Similar questions concern the nature of women. With extremists on one side saying that for women anatomy is destiny, and extremists on the other side saying that there are no important differences between men and women other than the sexual apparatus, how can we determine what is right unless we have the facts? In these and other questions we cannot decide what a man can or ought to do until we have a clear view of the facts of human nature.

One of the most crucial questions about human nature for the ethical theorist concerns whether man has *free will* or whether his actions are simply an outcome of heredity and environment. If the actions of man are not based upon free choice but on circumstances beyond his control, then he can be neither commended nor condemned for them, for it would be meaningless to praise or blame those who are not responsible for their behavior. If someone through no fault of his own gets hit on the back of the head, it would be very odd indeed to blame him for hurting his head in that way. If men are not free, they are not responsible, and if they are not responsible, then telling them what they ought to do is like talking to the wall.

In addition, the ethical philosopher is also concerned with the question of whether man is essentially an egoist or an altruist. If it is truly a man's nature to be selfish, can we with any sense tell him he ought not be selfish? The kind of society men might seek to organize takes on meaning in terms of this question. If man is altruistic by nature, then he can seek to develop a cooperative society. Of course, there may never be an either/or answer to any of these *factual* questions, but whatever turns out to be the case will have some bearing on the way we vote for what *should* be.

Finally, the ethical philosopher must deal with the factual question of whether we can know a man's intention independently of his behavior. If the behavioristic interpretation of man is valid, then we must understand his functioning on the analogue of a machine. Intentions do not matter; we can evaluate man only in terms of consequences of his actions. Others maintain that consequences may be out of a person's control. If the results of a man's action are something he did not intend, then it makes no more sense to praise or blame him than it would if he did not have free will. Before we can decide between these two arguments, we have to determine factually whether man can have intentions apart from actual behavior.

We may sum up by observing the varieties of problems the student of ethics must struggle with as follows:

Normative Ethics.   The task of developing and formulating principles and systems of value and obligation. Some of the basic criteria by which we might decide what is right and/or what we ought to do are as follows:

Pleasure
    Duty
        Power
            Love
                Man
                    Nature
                        God

Metaethics.   The question of how to validate or justify principles or systems of value. Study of the meaning and function of ethical predicates and principles. Analysis of ethical questions with a view to establishing the prospects for the creation of a science of value.

Factual Questions. Determining the nature of man in order to assure that our ethical principles will be realistic and appropriate. Some of the questions that must be answered are as follows:

Is man a biological or cultural animal?
Does he have freedom or are his actions determined?
Is he essentially egoistic or altruistic?
Are there such things as intentions or are there only consequences?

To live and breathe as human beings, men cannot ignore questions of value. The answers of the great philosophers to these questions can help us formulate our own answers and can provide us with an opportunity to see if their answers can be applied to our practical existence. If we can arrive at some working conclusions about what is good and right and about what we ought to do, perhaps it will help us to live better, to improve the quality of existence, and to make a contribution toward constructing a more human world.

The House of Pleasure: Hedonism

I built my soul a lordly pleasure-house,
Wherein at ease for aye to dwell.
I said, "O Soul, make merry and carouse,
Dear Soul, for all is well."[3]

One of the earliest discoveries a person makes is how much he would like to take residence in a lordly pleasure-house and how eager he is to flee from any abode of pain. However, there are those for whom pleasure turns out to be so difficult an experience to find and get along with that they learn to make friends with pain; we call such people masochists and do not regard them as normal. This is because it is almost universally assumed that pleasure is desirable and pain undesirable. The philosophy that teaches that pleasure is man's most precious treasure is known as *hedonism.*

A hedonist may maintain either that all of us *are* in fact pleasure-seekers or that we *ought* to be pleasure-seekers whether in fact we are or are not. In other words, hedonism may be a normative thesis or it may be a descriptive factual account of the way in which man actually behaves. When it is asserted the very nature of man is such that he always seeks his own pleasure as a good in itself, we have an example of the descriptive thesis. This is known as *psychological hedonism.*

The other branch of hedonism maintains that in fact everyone does not seek pleasure at all times. One need not be a masochist to repudiate the quest for pure pleasure; one might be a martyr. Perhaps martyrs are masochists, but perhaps not. In any event, those who adopt the prescrip-

[3] Alfred, Lord Tennyson, *The Palace of Art.*

tive, normative branch of hedonism admit that it is not a descriptive account of how men do behave, since some men obviously do not seek pleasure; instead, they maintain that the principles of hedonism tell men how they *ought* to behave. This doctrine is known as *ethical hedonism.*

One might deny the truth of psychological hedonism and still affirm the truth of ethical hedonism. Thus one might say men *do not* always devote themselves to the attainment of pleasure, but they certainly *ought to.* Of course, it is perfectly possible for one to defend both psychological and ethical hedonism. After all if man is so built that he naturally *seeks* pleasure, then it is reasonable to maintain that he ought to seek pleasure. If some puritan tells us not to try to live by pleasure, the ethical and psychological hedonist would answer that this advice is wrong because it exhorts us to do what is unnatural. This psychological hedonism can be taken as a basis for ethical hedonism, and any contradictory theory can be regarded as an attempt to move us against nature.

If one does or ought to seek pleasure as a good in itself, an important question is "How?" Should one seek instant pleasure, or is it wiser to wait for a pleasure payoff later? Should one make an effort to acquire pleasure primarily for himself, or should one pass the pleasure on to others? The latter question gets us into the philosophy of *egoism,* for hedonism is the position that pleasure comes first and egoism is the position that *I* come first—that is, *my* pleasure comes first.

As with the case of hedonism, so too with egoism: we may distinguish between a psychological and an ethical version. Psychological egoism argues that individuals do in fact consider themselves before anyone else, and ethical egoism argues that regardless of whether they do or not, they ought to. The English philosopher Thomas Hobbes (1588–1679) was a psychological and ethical egoist, taking the view that the individual both does and ought to regard himself and his welfare before that of others. The contemporary American novelist Ayn Rand is an ethical egoist but not necessarily a psychological egoist; she complains that people are not selfish enough and exhorts them to egoism.

Of course, underlying all these questions is: what is pleasure. Is pleasure basically physical or is it mental, intellectual, or spiritual? Jeremy Bentham (1748–1832) believed all pleasure was physical, and thus pleasures could only be distinguished quantitatively. John Stuart Mill (1806–73), a follower of Bentham's who thought Bentham wrong on this point, claimed that there were higher and lower types of pleasure, thus making it possible to distinguish pleasures *qualitatively.* In the pages that follow, these and other positions will be examined more closely.

ASK WHAT YOU WILL DO FOR YOURSELF: EGOISTIC HEDONISM

Thomas Hobbes may be regarded as one of the first significant contributors to the development of modern ethics; he formulated a comprehensive theory of ethics independent of theology. Whereas previous ethical theorists looked to the heavens to get their ideas of what was right, Hobbes looked to man. In fact he held a very low view of man, and there are those who have criticized him on this score. His defenders, on the other hand, argue that he was simply being honest and realistic.

Influenced by the spirit of modern science, which was flourishing when he was a young man at the end of the sixteenth century, Thomas Hobbes endeavored to build a system of philosophy by relying exclusively on the tools of reason and experience. Starting from the premises of science, Hobbes argued that material objects are the only things that men encounter in this world; to believe anything else is superstition. In fact, Hobbes regarded religious views not only as fanciful and superstitious but as downright dangerous to the security of the state. He called for meticulous regulation of religion by the government to keep religion out of the government's hair, and he was undoubtedly right because when he was fifty-two years old, the government was overthrown by an army of religious zealots.

Greatly influenced by mechanistic science, Hobbes left nothing for spiritualistic reality. Ultimate reality is composed of bodies in the form of particles of matter, which are in a constant state of motion. So thoroughgoing a materialist was Hobbes that, even though he conceded there was a soul, he insisted that it too was material—when a man's body went, the soul went with it. Indeed all was reduced to matter in the system of Hobbes. In this sense the body of his philosophy was the human body, for he reasoned that the body alone was real. It is the only thing of which man can have knowledge. To formulate a perfect system of philosophy Hobbes sought to deduce everything from the laws of matter (or of the body). Starting with matter in motion Hobbes sought to deduce the fundamental truths of nature, man, and society.

The scheme Hobbes adopted divided philosophy into two branches —the Natural and the Civil. The subject of Natural Philosophy is material bodies made by nature, whereas Civil Philosophy has to do with those made by men. Civil Philosophy is concerned with the commonwealth, which is, in Hobbes's terminology, a "body corporate." The primary division of Civil Philosophy is in ethics and politics, with politics founded on ethics, and including materialistic psychology.

If all that exists are material bodies, then all man is must be understood as a material body. From this it follows that man's main concern is with the preservation of his body. It is all he has, and thus there is a natural urge for him to take good care of it lest it be destroyed by violent death. Man thus is dominated by two fundamental impulses—the impulse for self-preservation and the fear of death. This is not a pretty or dignified picture of man, who seems to have no higher purpose than keeping himself alive, but Hobbes insisted that it was a fully accurate one.

From Hobbes's argument it follows that man will always act with his own interests uppermost. This is true not only in big life-or-death issues but also in the small details of normal living because anything that threatens a person's interests makes him that much weaker or poorer or less able to take care of himself. Now it is certainly true that life in the modern world can be pretty much a cutthroat business with every man for himself, but, one might object, this is not the whole picture. For example, when we say that life in the modern city is pretty much a jungle, that is just a figure of speech; there is a lot about it that is like a jungle but also a lot that is not at all like a jungle. There is cooperation, people are somewhat restrained in their selfish actions—there is, in short, social organization. Has Hobbes overlooked this? If it were just a question of every man being out for himself, why would there be social organization? Why would life not be completely a jungle?

Hobbes would answer that in fact he had not overlooked the evidence of social organization. On the contrary, it was precisely because every man was out for himself that led to the development of society. Before society was formed, Hobbes said, life had in fact been a jungle; human life was one continuous war of "each against all." If one man wanted something he took it from whoever was weaker than he was, and if the weaker man were smart he would take any opportunity to kill the stronger one before being robbed and killed himself. The problem with such a mode of living, as in all jungles, is that life is solitary, poor, nasty, brutish, and short. Recognizing this problem, prehistoric men figured out that if they could make life less of a jungle, they could live longer. If we could get together and organize things so that if someone robbed me, the rest of the people would gang up on him and punish him; then he would not rob me, and I would not try to kill him before he could get the chance. I would have to give up the chance of taking whatever I wanted whenever I could get it, but in exchange I would know that other people were not always trying to rob or kill me. In that way we could all live longer. Reasoning such as this, Hobbes argued, led to the formation of the first society. Man did not organize himself into societies because he had higher aims than a selfish one; on the contrary, he organized into society because he recognized that in the long run his selfish aims could be better served by doing so.

There had been great philosophers in the past who would not have agreed with Hobbes on this. In ancient Greece Aristotle had written:

> When several villages are united in a single complete community, large enough to be nearly or quite self-sufficing, the state comes into existence, originating in the bare needs of life, and continuing in existence for the sake of the good life. And therefore, if the earlier forms of society are natural, so is the state, for it is the end of them, and the nature of a thing is its end. . . .
>
> Here it is evident that the state is a creation of nature, and that man is by nature a political animal. . . .
>
> . . . The state is a creation of nature and prior to the individual. . . . He who is unable to live in society, or has no need because he is sufficient for himself, must be either a beast or a god: he is no part of a state. A social instinct is implanted in all men by nature. . . .[4]

[4] Aristotle, *Politics*, trans. Benjamin Jowett in *The Basic Works of Aristotle* (New York: Random House, Inc., 1941), Book I, Chap. II, pp. 1129f.

Aristotle did not see the state as artificial creation; rather, it is deeply rooted in human nature, of which it is a natural expression. In other words, there is a social part of man beyond his merely selfish needs. In the modern world, just twenty-six years before the appearance of Hobbes's *Leviathan,* the Dutch philosopher Hugo Grotius offered mankind a novel presentation of the Aristotelian view of man as a political animal. Grotius developed a doctrine of sociability (*socialitas*), the point of which is simply that there resides in man an impelling desire for society. Even before man developed law and a state to assure him of security, Grotius contended, men could get along with one another because of this natural sociability, which is an inherent part of the human makeup.

Hobbes's philosophy was an answer to such thinking. Aristotle and Grotius, he felt, could not have looked closely enough at the actual behavior of men if they believed them to be naturally social animals. If there were not laws and sanctions to uphold them, men would be at each other's throats. In a state of nature there would be no sociability; every man would be for himself in a state of all-out war. As Hobbes saw it, there is no natural sociability; there is just natural selfishness. Hobbes was certain that an examination of the plain facts of life would bear him out on this.

Hobbes would admit that there are many actions that seem altruistic. People give to charity, donate their time to worthy causes, help their friends when they are in trouble, and even sacrifice their lives for others. But are these actions really as altruistic as they seem? Leaving aside for the moment the case in which a man sacrifices his life, all the actions just mentioned can be done either publicly or anonymously. If they are done publicly, then the person who does good benefits by being thought well of; if they are done anonymously, the person still benefits in terms of the pleasant self-image he gains by his action. Indeed people we think of as good, charitable people say all the time that they like to do good things because they get a lot of satisfaction out of it. That is just the point, Hobbes would say: they are not doing good because of the good it does for the recipient; they are doing so because of the satisfaction they get from it. Imagine two people, one who gets his kicks from beating people up and the other who gets his satisfaction from giving people money. There is no question that the world would be better off without the former and is a better place to live because of the latter. But as far as the egoism-altruism question goes, that is neither here nor there. Both are working for the same thing —their own satisfaction—and we consider one of them good because his satisfaction comes from things we approve of and the other bad because his satisfaction comes from things we disapprove of. We should certainly not forget that there is quite a difference between these two men, but this difference has nothing to do with egoism and altruism. We may think that the world would be a better place if people were more altruistic, but if we think about it what we mean is that the world would be a better place if people could get more of their egoistic kicks out of things that help others.

But what about the man who sacrifices his life for someone else? Surely he cannot be gaining anything out of it? It is hard to imagine how he could be doing it for satisfaction, inasmuch as he won't be able to enjoy the satisfaction when he is dead. Indeed the case of a man who lays down his life for a friend is the toughest nut egoistic philosophy has to crack. There are, however, a number of answers the egoist can make. We must bear in mind, he would point out, that any decision as to whether a man who lays down his life is acting out of egoism or altruism will have to depend upon the psychology of the one in question, and this is an area about which, by the nature of the case, we do not know very much. It would help to know what such people are thinking as they decide that they will give up their lives for the sake of others, but of course we cannot. We can only guess. We do know, however, that one very common fantasy many people have involves being dead and seeing others' reactions to their deaths. Adolescents are especially prone to imagining that they have killed themselves and are hovering over their homes watching how guilty their parents feel for having driven them to suicide. Most of them, of course, just think these thoughts; a few more deeply troubled ones actually attempt such suicides, and we have testimony from those whose suicide attempts failed that the imagined reactions of others after their deaths played a part in their motivation. Perhaps much the same sort of thing is at work with the person who sacrifices his life for another. He does not think of his death as real in a sense, for he imagines himself knowing of the gratitude of those for whom he made the supreme sacrifice. We do not really know, but that is one explanation. In other cases, persons who give up their lives for others may actually be committing suicide. And in still other cases, the person may simply be deranged. In the final analysis, the egoistic philosopher cannot fully explain away all cases of self-sacrifice, but he can say that they do not offer insurmountable proof that his theory is wrong. Just to play it safe, he would probably say: Give me a concrete case of someone who gave up his life for someone else; let me find out all the facts about him that I can; the chances are very good that I will come up with a plausible explanation that will be consistent with my theory—that people always act out of some egoistic motive or other; and even if I cannot convince you in one particular case, that would only prove that perhaps we did not know enough about this particular man's psychological makeup.

Behind all this reasoning is the basic assumption that if we dig deep enough, we will find all acts that seem to be from altruistic motives can really be traced to egoistic motives. This argument is well illustrated by a story told about Abraham Lincoln. Lincoln was riding in a coach and arguing with a fellow passenger, a man named Ed, over this question of egoism. Despite the fact that he is regarded by many as an altruist, Lincoln took the position that even when men do something good, the motive of their action is *selfishness*. He and Ed debated the issue as they rode on. They came to a bridge, and as the coach passed over it Lincoln noticed through the window a poor pig stuck in the mud. He beckoned the coach driver to stop, got out and assisted the pig out of its distress. When he returned to the coach, Ed laughed—confident that he had won the argument. He told Lincoln that after all his protestations against altruism he himself had just acted as an altruist. Lincoln smiled and answered:

> *Why, bless your soul, Ed, that was the very essence of selfishness. I should have had no peace of mind all day had I gone on and left that suffering old sow. . . . I did it to get peace of mind, don't you see?*[5]

Hobbes did a thorough job in seeking to establish that human behavior can be explained egoistically. The problem with this explanation though is that Hobbes and the confirmed egoist always cheat in making their point. The dice always roll egoism because they are loaded. When they claim that human behavior is always egoistic, they are purporting to tell us something about the world. The statement that all behavior is egoistic is what is known in philosophy as a *synthetic* statement—that is, a statement that gives us new information about the world. The opposite of a synthetic statement is an analytic one. An analytic statement does not give us new knowledge but makes clear the knowledge we already have. We have to look to the world to find out whether or not a synthetic statement is true. If someone says "The cat is on the mat," we have to look at the mat to learn if it is true. The truth of analytic statements is not a matter of fact but of definition. If someone says that her sister is a boy we do not have to look, for we know that this cannot be the case because a sister is *defined* as a female.

The statement that all behavior is based on self-interest on the face of it is synthetic, and thus the truth of it should be established by empirical corroboration. In actuality the egoistic position is usually defended as if it were an analytic statement and is thus true by definition. The defender of egoism *defines* the term so broadly that it includes all behavior. Egoism then is made true by definition and is not empirically found to be true. The function of a definition is to limit a term so that it may be distinguished from other terms. The way the egoist proceeds to defend egoism, however, there are no limits to it: indeed by Hobbes's definition of egoism *nothing* could possibly be counted as an instance of altruistic behavior. There can be no altruism, not because we could never *find* people who show primary concern for others but because we would say that such concern must have an egoistic basis, even though we cannot empirically pinpoint it. Egoism is so defined as to embrace all instances of behavior. This reduces the altruism-egoism question to an absurdity. Of what possible value is a term that is incapable of distinguishing between extremely different varieties of behavior? On a freezing day St. Martin of Tours cut his cape in half and gave it to a beggar. Of what value is a thesis that concludes his behavior is no different from that of the crook who steals the coat off your back? Does it advance our understanding to hear that two such different persons are equally selfish?

[5] Frank C. Sharp, "Egoism and Altruism," in Dewey, Gordon and Loftsgordon, *Problems of Ethics* (New York: The Macmillan Co., 1961), p. 14.

An egoist is one who considers the good of himself before that of others. An altruist is one who considers the good of others before that of himself. To discover if there are altruists is not a matter of playing with definitions but of finding if there are individuals out there who fulfill the requirements of the definition. What we have to do is discover if there are instances of behavior in which individuals actually consider the well-being of others before their own and do not have any *ulterior motives* that we can empirically establish. What Hobbes and others claim is that there is always an ulterior motive. But if we cannot *specifically* find it, do we have the right simply to assume it is there, as Hobbes does? The motive springs of human behavior are extremely complex, and there are so many variables that we can never be certain of exactly why a man does something. To say he always acts for his own individual self-interest is to say that we are certain of exactly why he acted. Even if it can be established that a person derives self-satisfaction from helping someone, this is irrelevant. The requirement of altruism is that one consider another before himself and does not imply he has to feel miserable for so doing. What is really significant is that there are individuals who find satisfaction from considering the well-being of others even before themselves. The trouble with the world is that not enough people get satisfaction from helping others. It is preposterous to brand those who do as egoists just because they experience satisfaction from devoting themselves to their fellow men.

It simply is not meaningful to assert that because people always act out of self-interest they are selfish. Since man is by *definition* a self, no doubt there will always be self-interest—unless he degenerates to the consciousness of an oyster. The question that is crucial is whether his self-interest is identified with his family, his friends, humanity, or just with his own skin. If a man defines his self in very narrow terms, we may regard him as egoistic; if he defines his self in very broad terms, he may be considered altruistic. The question is not simply whether or not man is concerned with his self but rather with how big his self is. He will be a selfish person if his understanding of the self is limited to his own physical needs. (Ironically, it is doubtful that he will be serving his self-interest by pursuing this selfish course, for he will be imprisoning himself inside his skin and cutting himself off from the fulfillment one finds from flowing into the world.) Thus we may say it is axiomatic that man acts out of self-interest but that it is an open question as to whether or not he acts *selfishly.* In other words, egoism is acceptable as an analytic statement but doubtful as a synthetic statement.

One of the most interesting rebuttals of Hobbes's doctrine was developed by Bishop Joseph Butler (1692–1752). Butler made a most damaging observation against the egoist position that man seeks above all else his own pleasure. Butler very perceptively called to our attention that a person really never does directly desire pleasure; rather, he desires some *specific object.* For example, if a person becomes hungry, it is not pleasure he aims at but food. Pleasure may be the by-product of that eating, but it is not the direct goal of a hungry man. Thus it cannot be correct to describe man as an egoistic hedonist for the very simple reason that man is not always seeking *hedone,* or pleasure. Psychologically, man is highly complex and cannot be described in terms of any simple motivation. Thus Butler thought it more accurate to say that, although men do have impulses of self-love, these are modified by impulses of regard for the happiness of others. Butler took a rather different view of the nature of man than Hobbes did. Where Hobbes thought of man after the analogy of the machine, and in that context saw man mechanically functioning so as to maximize his pleasure, Butler took a more organic view, understanding man as a whole functioning system. His different drives were regulated to the functioning of the entire system rather than to one predominant motivation, such as pleasure.

Despite Butler's argument, however, the verdict against egoism was anything but final. As modern history progressed, there accumulated increasing reaction against absolutism, and revolution was in the air. This period was characterized more by selfishness than by sympathy. Ludwig Feuerbach proclaimed that Man is to Man the Supreme Being, Bruno Bauer announced that Man has just been discovered, and Max Stirner said that it was time to take a look at this supreme being and new discovery. It seemed in this historic period that man was truly coming into his own; this idea was expressed most clearly in Stirner's *The Ego and His Own,* an aggressive statement of egoistic philosophy. Hobbes, who developed his doctrine of egoism in a time of political absolutism, was fearful that egoism could get out of hand, and for the individual's own security he wanted to put man in the hands of the all-protecting and all-powerful state, the "Leviathan." Stirner, coming later when liberty and revolutionary ideas were filling the air, demanded that everybody, particularly the state, keep their hands off the individual. Whereas egoism was defended by Hobbes in conjunction with political authoritarianism, Stirner completely junked authoritarianism and gave egoism an anarchistic form.

In *The Ego and His Own* Max Stirner—the name was the pseudonym of Kaspar Schmidt, a respectable Prussian citizen, who taught at a very sophisticated and very proper girls' school—argued that idealistic concepts, such as of God or of one's Nation, were nothing but vacant abstractions. The nation was nothing but a large assemblage of individuals just like himself, and so when one is told he must live his life for his nation or die for it, only a fool would take this seriously, for there are only selfish individuals.

Although such ideas sound rather revolutionary, Stirner was so uncompromising an egoist that he wanted to have nothing to do with revolution. He was concerned with the individual rebel, and the individual rebel can be just as well destroyed by the revolutionary as by the statist. The individual must go on his own and cannot devote himself to any such abstractions as humanity. For, in the end, what is humanity but a bunch of individuals? If this is so, then the best way for the individual to serve humanity is by serving the individual, starting with himself.

Ultimately, Stirner's defense of egoism amounted to an all-out war against idealism, or spiritualism. Stirner expressed his hostility to idealism in no uncertain terms:

> *Man, your head is haunted; you have wheels in your head! You imagine great things, and depict to yourself a whole world of gods that has an existence for*

you, a spirit-realm to which you suppose yourself to be called, an ideal that beckons to you. You have a fixed idea!

Do you think that I am jesting or speaking figuratively when I regard those persons who cling to the higher, and (because the vast majority belongs under this head) almost the whole world of men, as veritable fools, fools in a madhouse. What is it, then, that is called a "fixed idea"? An idea that has subjected the man to itself. . . . Is not the stupid chatter of most of our newspapers the babble of fools who suffer from the fixed idea of morality, legality, Christianity, and so forth, and only seem to go about free because the madhouse in which they walk takes in so broad a space? Touch the fixed idea of such a fool, and you will at once have to guard your back against the lunatic's stealthy malice. For these great lunatics are like the little so called lunatics . . . they assail by stealth him who touches their fixed idea. They first steal his weapon, steal free speech from him, and then they fall upon him with their nails. Every day now lays bare the cowardice and vindictiveness of these maniacs, and the stupid populace hurrahs for their crazy measures. . . .[6]

There is no greater enemy to an individual than a fixed idea, Stirner says; instead of living for themselves, men live for fixed ideas and become enslaved to them. These fixed ideas have no place in a changing world, yet men become possessed by them as they once were *possessed* by the devil. It is a form of insanity.

Ludwig Feuerbach had rejected religion and replaced it with the idea of man-in-society as the source of all values, but Stirner rejected even society. In a sense his philosophy was an expression of the new man of the nineteenth century. Stirner wanted to sweep away all restraints in order to fulfill the nature of this new man, who was essentially egoistic and hedonistic. Stirner's philosophy represents that stage in which man, having lost the protection of the gods and of traditional values, was making a kind of god of himself. Such a line of development could not be pushed very far without inevitable disillusionment setting in, and when it did men turned for protection to theories of collectivism. Thus the world was being prepared for the rise of communism and national socialism.

In the twentieth-century world, the magnitude of power has grown so great that the dimension of the individual has necessarily been dwarfed by comparison. In a characterological study of modern society, David Riesman has pointed out that in our history we have witnessed a transition from the tradition of the inner-directed man to that of the other-directed man. In other words, we have moved from individualism to conformism, from the Protestant Ethic to the organizational ethic. Mass movements and tidal waves of collectivism are drowning the individual in this world of galloping totalitarianism. In this context there has arisen a voice that cries out for individualism and for *egoism*. With socialistic and communistic ways of thinking and dealing with problems becoming increasingly accepted by intellectuals and liberal politicians, this voice, which belongs to novelist Ayn Rand, has sounded out loud and clear for egoism and individualism and has done so in conjunction with a defense of capitalism. Thus, whereas Hobbes de-

[6] Max Stirner, *The Ego and His Own*, trans. S. T. Byington (New York: Libertarian Book Club, Inc., 1963), p. 43.

fended egoism in connection with political absolutism, and whereas Max Stirner defended it in connection with anarchism, Ayn Rand defends egoism along with capitalism.

According to Ayn Rand the trouble with the world is that men are not sufficiently free, selfish, and capitalistic. Her defense of egoism differs from those of her forerunners in that earlier schools of egoistic philosophy based their argument on feeling, whereas Ayn Rand bases hers on reason. The usual tactic had been to maintain that man *feels* he must serve his own interest first, that his emotional makeup is such that he seeks to attain his own pleasure before that of any other. But as Ayn Rand sees it, if man does not serve his own interests before others, he is a slave. A slave does not live in accord with reason but with the demands and orders of his master, which may be irrational. Egoism with Ayn Rand is not simply a matter of following one's drives; rather, it is a matter of rationally leading one's own life. Understood in this way, her contention that there are not enough egoists in the world makes sense; if we look at what she says superficially, it seems she is wrong, for surely there is no shortage of selfish people in the world, as moralists have been saying for some time. But Rand's point is more profound: it is that most of those who pass for egoists are not really egoists in her sense—that is, they are not rational egoists and are not leading their own lives.

Another important point about Rand's egoism is that, in contrast to many egoists who develop their position that man ought to be an egoist on the assumption that psychologically he is one, Rand argues that men often are not egoists but ought to be. In other words, most egoists affirm the truth of *psychological egoism* (the factual thesis that men *are* egoists), and then conclude that because men are egoists, it follows they *ought* to be. Thus psychological egoism serves as the basis for ethical egoism. Rand, however, points out that many persons fail to live for themselves first, and yet maintains they ought to.

Rand developed her doctrine of egoism in her novels. In an age when the leading character in fiction is the so-called "nonhero" or "antihero," Rand's novels stand for an unembarrassed kind of romantic hero worship. Two heroes particularly give embodiment to her egoist ideal. In *The Fountainhead* it is the brilliant architect Howard Roark, and in *Atlas Shrugged* it is John Galt.

In *The Fountainhead* the uncompromising Howard Roark designs the government housing project Cortlandt House. All he asks is that the work be done his way. Roark is a creative giant, a great artist; he works not to please the whims of himself or others but to express his prodigious talents. He designs for no one who would place restrictions upon his creative imagination. He creates neither for profit nor for humanity but only for himself. This, Rand contends, is the only sincere way for an artist to work. If an artistic product is not to have a hollow ring, it must come straight from the heart and mind of the artist—which it cannot do if the artist thinks of others first. In the novel Roark's design for Cortlandt House was accepted, but somewhere along the line some officials made changes in his plans, which he felt prostituted his art. He argued that they had no right to do this to his design, but there was nothing he could do about it. Finally, as an expression of his self-respect and in order to keep his work true to himself, he got some dynamite and blew the building up. Then he waited to be arrested. At the trial he would state his case. On trial is not Roark but his philosophy of egoism. The theme of the novel is individualism versus collectivism, egoism versus altruism. Cortlandt House was a government housing project—a home for the poor, the destitute. At the trial Roark reminds the court of this, for his point is that the fact the people are poor does not give them the right to his work. No one has a right to one minute of his life; no matter how vast the multitude of people concerned may be, he will not be a man who exists for others. This is a man of great integrity, and he is acquitted.

This story is obviously far from realistic. The way in which the man of integrity and principles triumphs in the free enterprise society makes the novel an expression of what we might call "Utopian Capitalism." The experience of history teaches us that the Howard Roarks do not survive. This is an unrealistic dream. Its hero worship is laughable. In this age when impersonal forces of existence threaten to bring about the extinction of individuality of personality, one might hope for a defense of individualism—indeed one would welcome it with open arms. But in Rand what one finds is sheer autistic thinking. It is a nice fantasy, but a fantasy nonetheless. The individual—armed with his reason, ability, and integrity—can affect power only in Hollywood and in Miss Rand's novels.

The case for egoism here suffers because its sense of history is unrealistic. For example, in his chapter on "The Moral Revolution" in his book *Who Is Ayn Rand?* Nathaniel Branden, one of Rand's disciples, asserts that to the extent countries adopted capitalism, the rule of brute force vanished from men's lives. Capitalists, we are informed, substituted the principle of trade for one of violence as the ruling principle of human relationships. We are also told that Individualism was the creative power revolutionizing the world and that capitalism closed the doors to force and "offered men a market instead of a gun."[7] In the light of history, anyone who starts with the premise that capitalism closed the door on force is opening the door to farce. Capitalism may have "offered man a *market*" but not "instead of a gun." On the contrary, it gave man a gun to take the market, and equipped him with a gun to keep it. It was egoistic capitalists who carried out the practices of colonialism, imperialism, racism, and militarism, which Rand and Branden seem to think of as an example of *rational self-interest.*

Rand and Branden do not develop a very convincing defense of egoism, but their work is important because it reveals the inherent difficulties of defending egoism on the ground of reason rather than feeling. To regard egoism as a matter of rational choice rather than of emotional drives is to

[7] Nathaniel Branden, *Who Is Ayn Rand?* (New York: Random House, Inc., 1962), p. 12.

disregard human behavior. One finds Hobbes's defense of egoism compelling precisely because it is so well rooted in the way men's drives lead them to actions aimed at fulfilling their own self-interest. In contrast, the rational approach of Ayn Rand takes on the air of a romantic dream.

Pass the Pleasure: Utilitarianism

There is a great deal of evidence to support the contention men act selfishly, and yet there is also evidence that some men consider others before themselves. From our analysis of egoism one cannot conclude that it has been established with certainty that man is essentially egoistical. Even more tenuous is the effort to establish that he ought to be. It is not so easy as it might seem to defend egoism. Indeed one might wonder why the truly selfish person should want to defend egoism. If the egoist is a person truly out for his own interest, why should he alert everyone else to be out for their own interests. Is that not self-defeating? If I am truly out for my own self-interest, I should seek to recruit other men to serve *my* interests. Thus is not the egoist being an altruist when he tells others to be egoists?

Historically, most hedonistic theories—that is, theories that put pleasure at the source of their system of values—have been built on an egoistic foundation. Because this is not a very sound foundation a number of hedonistic philosophers have attempted to broaden the foundation of support. They have tried to found hedonism not on the basis of individual interest alone but on that of group interest or the interests of many. The philosophy that pleasure should be reserved for the greatest number and not just for oneself was given classic expression in the writings of Jeremy Bentham and John Stuart Mill. Their philosophical position of hedonism is known as *Utilitarianism*.

JEREMY BENTHAM

Jeremy Bentham (1748–1832), the first important philosopher of Utilitarianism, developed the principle that good is the greatest happiness for the greatest number. The starting point of his ethical philosophy was the brutal fact of man's slavery. All men are slaves, Bentham said; they are slaves to their drives for pleasure and from pain. Nature has placed man under the governance of these two sovereign masters; pleasure and pain alone determine both what we ought to do as well what we shall do. Some men may pretend to abjure the empire of pleasure and pain, but in reality they will remain subject to it all the while. One cannot escape their authority. Upon this *natural* foundation Bentham erected the principle of utility and set out to demonstrate how moral science can be improved.

Moral science can be perfected by recognizing that it is based on the principle of utility. Utility is that property in any object whereby it tends to produce benefit, advantage, pleasure, good, or happiness on the one hand, or prevents mischief, pain, evil, or unhappiness on the other to the party whose interest is involved.

Pleasure and pain tell us what we ought to do and see to it that we

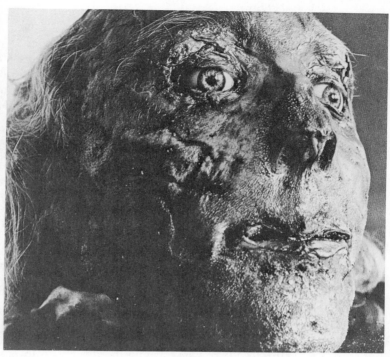

Jeremy Bentham's dressed skeleton and mummified head at University College, London. Used courtesy of John McKenzie.

actually do it. Good is that which gives the individual pleasure, and bad is that which gives him pain. Sympathy, moral sense, duty, the Will of God, and the love of esteem are all impotent as ultimate motives; it is true that they may operate as sanctions, but they all are themselves based on pleasure and pain, which are the inescapable points from which any realistic ethical science must start.

In formulating the principles of utility Bentham insisted that pleasure and pain must always be measured in terms of *individuals*. He stressed individuals in this way because he was a *nominalist*—that is, he believed that only individuals or particular things exist, and that group or corporate entities are only unreal abstractions. The corporate entity has no real existence above and beyond the individuals who compose it. For example, the "state," for which men are often asked to lay down their lives, is just a shorthand expression for referring to the particular individuals who exercise power. Similarly, all corporate entities, according to Bentham, are purely fictions: they give the illusion of being something, but are not the reality; they have no objective existence. Bentham proposed that men judge things in terms of the way they actually function instead of what their essence is supposed to be. This eliminates abstractions and corporate entities. The community or state must then be viewed as a fictitious body, consisting entirely in the individuals who are its members. When we speak of the interest of the community, all that we mean is the sum of interests of the several members who compose it. It follows then that one cannot talk about the interest of the community or of the state without talking about the interest of individuals.

Although Bentham stressed pleasure as man's greatest treasure and theorized that reality is only to be equated with individual existents, his view did not culminate in a narrowly egoistic or selfish approach to life. Insofar as Bentham understood good and evil in terms of the individual's natural drive to secure pleasure and to abjure pain, he may be classified as an egoist. However, because Bentham believed that the pleasure of each individual was good, he reasoned that the more individuals there were to receive pleasure, the more good there would be. Good is to be understood in terms of the pleasure of the individual, and because each individual counts as one, there will be more good in the world as more pleasure is passed about. Thus Bentham cannot be regarded as an orthodox egoist in the usual sense, for he is very much concerned about the general or common good. If each individual's pleasure is to count as one unit, the highest good will consist in the greatest amount of pleasure to the largest number of individuals. Thus Bentham formulated a definition of good as being *the greatest happiness of the greatest number.*

Bentham thought that with this definition of good, Utilitarianism provided a much sounder foundation for democracy than any abstract theory of natural rights. By happiness Bentham meant physical pleasure. which can be calculated and dealt with empirically; in contrast, natural rights are abstract ideas, which cannot be dealt with in practical terms. Bentham was very suspicious of the natural rights that democratic theorists said men enjoyed by birth. Men are born with ears and eyes and hands and feet. We say a man has ears (not "natural ears" just because it is natural for him to have ears) and we do not have to call attention that the ears are natural. When we say that a man has natural rights, on the other hand, we do so precisely because they are so *unnatural.* Ears or hands or legs are empirical and observable; when we speak about them, there is no doubt about what we are speaking. But the case is altogether different with natural rights. Because we cannot see them, there is nothing but doubt about what they are. No one says the ear is located in the belly button and we smell things through it. Everyone who speaks of ears says they are located in the same place and that through them we hear. Yet one person says there is a natural right that we are all equal and free, and another person says there are natural masters and natural slaves. One person says property is a natural right and another insists it is a natural wrong. Natural rights turn out to be subjective prejudices, not objective moral principles.

Bentham saw if there was to be a science of value it was essential to deal with an empirical quality, something susceptible of observation and measurement. This is why he emphasized *physical pleasure,* which is very concrete and can be dealt with scientifically. He believed we can measure units of pleasure and pain. Very impressed with the development of calculus, he imaginatively proposed a calculus for measuring value—a *hedonic* or *felicific calculus.* This was to be a means by which all laws, policies, or actions could be evaluated. The hedonic calculus was to be a way of determining the units of pleasure or pain produced as a consequence of human behavior. It could tell us what we *ought* to do by establishing what in *fact* would give the greatest pleasure or the least pain. To accomplish this the hedonic calculus employed the following criteria by which we can measure pleasure and pain:

1. INTENSITY—how intense

2. DURATION—how long

3. CERTAINTY—how sure

4. PROPINQUITY—how soon

5. FECUNDITY—how many more

6. PURITY—how free from pain in the case of pleasure and from pleasure in the case of pain

7. EXTENT—how many.

All questions can be dealt with in terms of the calculus. The value of legislation, or social policies, may be considered with respect to the elements of the hedonic calculus, and then it will be possible to decide moral questions in an objective way. For example, consider the case of a city that wanted to levy a small tax on all income in order to make improvements in its yacht harbor. The inconvenience (pain) caused by the tax would not be very *intense* because the tax would only amount to a few pennies. But it would be tremendous in *extent* in that everyone had to pay it. The pleasure it brought to the few people with yachts on the other hand would be rather more intense, although not very much so because a few improvements cannot amount to all that much. The clincher, though, is that the pleasure would be of very small extent, so that the low-intensity but extensive pain caused by such a tax would outweigh the moderate-intensity but unextensive pleasure produced by the improvements. Thus the tax would be unjust. Now if the city wanted to levy the same tax, this time to improve the libraries in the schools in the wealthy part of town, it would have a slightly better case. The same calculations of extent and intensity came into play, but there is the added dimension of *fecundity*. The pleasures that come from knowledge and reading are such as can produce additional pleasure for the same initial investment, raising the sum on the pleasure side. Finally, if the city decided to use the tax to acquire books for all the libraries of the community, it would have the best case yet because the extent of the pleasure would be multiplied tremendously, and for some among the rich who might have felt bad consciences from benefitting at the expense of others, the pleasure would be of higher *purity* since it is unmixed with the pain of guilt. Using calculations such as this, Bentham analyzed a number of the laws of his day and arrived at the conclusion that they often satisfied the selfish desires of the few and were unjust because they did not take into account the extent of pain and inconvenience they caused for the many. In his hands, the principle of utility became a tool for a radically democratic critique of government in which the happiness of every man was to count for one and no man for more than one.

Bentham, as we have seen, thought it quite legitimate for an individual to pursue his own pleasure, and to that extent his philosophy was tinted with the color of egoism. But at the same time an altruistic shade was blended in the ethical picture, for one had to consider others and to take into account whether or not the pleasure I derive from what I want outweighs the pain my action might cause in them. One must balance his own search for pleasure with considerations of the pleasure of the majority.

If we follow the hedonic calculus and balance our pleasures against the pains of others, we produce the greatest good possible. But what is an individual man's *motive* for doing so? What if he only cares about the greatest good for himself, not the greatest good of the greatest number? Bentham answered that there are *sanctions* that see to it one will not overindulge in one's own pleasure or exclude consideration of the general good. A sanction motivates one to follow a moral course and assures one not to overplay the hand of pleasure. There are four sanctions—*physical, political, moral,* and *religious*. These sanctions make binding moral principles or laws. For example, if one eats too much he will become ill and if he drinks too much he will have a hangover. This is the *physical sanction*. One might rob or kill to satisfy his pleasure, but there are courts and prisons to throw a damper on that line of fun. Here one would be bound by the *political* sanction. Aside from laws and courts and the pokey, there is the fear of being censured or ostracized by public opinion, which will make one watch his step. We can gauge its importance just by considering the oft-pronounced question, "What will people think?" There are those who fear offending public opinion and those who fear God. They are kept in line not with a view to laws or public opinion as much as a desire to keep on the right side of God. This is the *religious* sanction.

Assuming that the sanctions work and that men make an effort to keep on the right side of their appetites, of the law, of public opinion, and of God, there is in Bentham's utilitarian philosophy the rudiments of a philosophical foundation for a just and democratic society. Throughout history elites have indulged their own appetites for greed at the expense of vast multitudes; minorities of men in power have sent majorities off to their deaths in wars having no meaning for them; and the few have lived in great luxury but the many have dwelled in the darkness of hunger and poverty. And now here was a man to plead for the good of the people, to make a case for the happiness of the majority. Bentham was proclaiming that no man has more right to pleasure than any other. Each individual's pleasure counts for only one. In the philosophy of utilitarianism some men are not *more equal* than others. The more pleasure there is, the better it is. This is a democratic theory of value.

By focusing on the majority, however, the utilitarian may disregard minority rights. If a policy of burning witches (a minority) makes the majority happy, then that policy would seem to be justified by Bentham's theory. What if by vivisecting a man we could very likely find a cure for cancer and thereby save millions of lives, would it not be justified to experiment on that man? If the pleasure of each counts for one, surely the life of that man could not be worth the lives of millions. Surely it would be a contribution to the greatest happiness of the greatest number to experiment on the one man for the benefit of the majority. Bentham would answer that when we sacrifice one life for many, we are sacrificing the many as well, for the many is composed of individuals and no one can be safe or secure if any one at any time can be sacrificed. Thus to refuse to sacrifice one man is not just to be romantically idealistic but to stand firm on the principle of utility. The idea that the greatest good of the greatest number justifies sacrificing one man for many is not true, Bentham would say, if we really understand the hedonic calculus; for the calculus tells us that the guilt and anxiety the many would suffer if they lived in a society so indifferent to the life of an individual in it would far outweigh the possible benefits.

The case might be made that Bentham's emphasis on the *greatest happiness for the greatest number principle* contributes to the debasement of cultural standards. If all opinions are equally valid, that which is excellent will be debased and the mediocre will be exalted. Personal worth will be determined by popularity, political leaders will be sold as products, fundamental policies will be viewed through the eyes of public opinion surveys, and the value of entertainment will be decided by ratings and box office lines and not by quality. One just cannot determine such important questions—as war and peace, truth or morality, the excellence of leadership, great art or literature—by counting heads, particularly when there may not be much in the heads of "silent majorities" or any kind of majorities. If it fills the silent majority with loud laughter to throw Christians to lions, that does not make it right. Bentham was biased in favor of democracy, but it seems he has not realized that for a democracy to be viable it must protect minority rights.

Despite shortcomings in Bentham's views, he did make a significant contribution. The mere effort to deal more realistically, practically, and empirically with questions of value constituted an important historic step forward. And although there are serious problems in using *utility* as a final criterion of value, it should not be neglected as a factor in the valuable, and Bentham's emphasis on it reminds us of its importance.

JOHN STUART MILL

John Stuart Mill, one of Bentham's most ardent supporters, was brought up to believe in the general good of all men and women and he was full of genuine feeling for his fellow man in whose happiness he was truly interested. However, though Mill agreed with Bentham that good could be understood on utilitarian grounds (in fact it was Mill, not Bentham, who used the word "utilitarian"), nonetheless he disagreed with Bentham's idea that happiness could be understood simply in terms of physical pleasure. Therefore he set about to develop his brand of hedonism, which he explained in a tract called *Utilitarianism.*

Mill believed that man should strive for the general happiness of mankind and not just for his own particular happiness. Where Bentham tended to emphasize the individual's private pleasure, Mill broadened the base of hedonism considerably and located the source of moral obligation in one's fellow feeling for all human beings. All human beings harbor within them a feeling that they are an integral part of society. This is a natural feeling in all men, but it only blossoms forth in proportion to the development of one's sensitivity and thoughtfulness. The feeling of unity with one's fellow creatures is, Mill concluded, a natural desire of one who has a properly cultivated moral nature.

In general, John Stuart Mill had a much better appreciation of *character* in man than did Jeremy Bentham. This made it possible for him to deny Bentham's assertion that the only way to distinguish among pleasures is on a quantitative basis. Bentham held that one could never say one type of pleasure was *higher* than another; the only way to show pleasures differed was on physical grounds. Mill argued that intellectual or spiritual pleasures are higher pleasures—that is, better in kind—than physical pleasures. He felt Bentham was wrong when he said that all pleasures are equal in quality and differ only in quantity. If one man enjoys poetry or art and another enjoys bowling, these pleasures are not equal, even if one man enjoys his pleasure "just as much" as the other enjoys his. Poetry and art are higher types of pleasure, and society should give preference to such things in establishing its priorities.

Mill arrived at this ideal in a most dramatic way, one worthy of Hollywood. He was wondering whether it would be more desirable to be a happy pig or a miserable man. He decided in favor of the pig, and as he went to write the word *pig*, his hand proved incapable of doing so; and so Mill knew he was not for the pig. From that moment forth Mill knew utilitarianism should be a *big* morality, not a *pig* morality. Mill concluded it would be better to be a human dissatisfied than a pig satisfied, better to be an unhappy Socrates than a happy fool. Of course the fool or pig might well disagree, preferring to be ignorant and blissful. If a pig could talk, he would probably tell Mill that he would rather be a happy pig wallowing in the mud than an unhappy philosopher carrying the world's problems on his shoulders. If people derived more pleasure from reading Mickey Spillane's novels than Shakespeare's sonnets, can anyone say they are wrong? In essence Mill's answer was that a man of culture can be a better judge because he knows both the novel—which appeals to base emotions—and that which appeals to the intellect. All the pig knows is wallowing in the mud. A pig cannot read a poem of Milton's or appreciate the moving beauty of a great symphony. Thus he obviously is not in a position to judge whether wallowing in mud is better than viewing a great painting. In order to judge one thing is better than another, one must know both. The person who judges all things by whether or not they are productive of physical pleasure for the most part has not given himself to the experience of intellectual, artistic, and cultural products. His experience of life is narrow and limited. He is not really competent to say rock and roll is better than the music of Mozart because he does not know Mozart. Had there been rock and roll in Mill's time, he would have said that one who came to understand both would always prefer Mozart. The man of culture can understand Mickey Spillane, rock and roll, or tap dancing, but he can also understand Dante, Beethoven, and the ballet. His judgment is more valid because he can compare. Perhaps this is why the artistic achievements he places value upon withstand the withering of time but the so-called popular products quickly fade into oblivion.

If one defends hedonism on a purely physical basis, as Bentham did, there is a tendency to reduce human life to what Mill regarded as a lower grade of existence. If one accepts this view, then it matters not what one does so long as it gives him *pleasure*. Mill, as we have seen, argued that there are *higher* and *lower* types of pleasures. Although his argument is very appealing, the problem with it is that it tends to lift Mill's philosophy altogether beyond the level of hedonism. For how can we say pleasure "A" is better than pleasure"B"? There has to be some *standard* or *criterion* by which we say this pleasure is better than that one. But the moment we say there is such a standard, that (standard or criterion) rather than pleasure, becomes the basis of value.

Mill's attempt to defend the values of the cultural elite led him to a nonutilitarian position, for in saying there were *higher* pleasures, he introduced a quality which would have to be evaluated in nonutilitarian terms.

Thus, of the two utilitarian philosophies—Bentham's and Mill's—Bentham's was flawed by its crassness in not recognizing that there are higher values in life than physical pleasure and in not offering adequate protection for the rights of minorities, whereas Mill's was flawed by the logical inconsistency of being a pleasure philosophy that acknowledged some unnamed principle "higher" than pleasure as its criterion of value. Nevertheless, both Bentham and Mill undeniably had a strong point in maintaining that utilitarianism cannot be disputed; it is so basic that it underlies whatever ethical position one might take. People naturally do seek pleasure and try to keep away from pain. That is just the way we are. We cannot deny that we like pleasure, for it is by definition what we get from something we like. Indeed Sigmund Freud, the man who made the greatest modern contribution to the scientific understanding of human motivation, made the pleasure principle basic to his system. Freud saw the pursuit of pleasure and the flight from pain as the ultimate purpose in human behavioral dynamics; the human organism, he maintained, was *automatically* regulated by the pleasure principle. Whenever there is tension (which is painful), the organism finds some means of relaxing the tension (which is pleasurable). Freud's hedonism was not based on philosophical reasoning but on what he took to be basic facts of biology. In Freud we get a clear reversal of the classical image of man as *homo sapiens*, or rational man. The idea that man is essentially rational was very clearly developed in the ancient world by Plato and in the modern world by Descartes; they defined man as a *thinking* thing, a being whose very essence is to think. Freud turned this around by announcing that man is a *desiring* animal, an animal seeking reduction of tension and the pleasure that ensues from tension reduction. During the First World War Freud saw men driving themselves to destruction which led him to be driven beyond the pleasure principle. Thus in 1920 there came a far-reaching change in Freud's understand of man. In his *Beyond the Pleasure Principle,* Freud came to see that there is more than a light of pleasure in man's life; there is also a dark side, for in addition to the basic pleasure instinct there is also a basic *death instinct.* Freud detected a desire inherent in the very makeup of man impelling him to return to his original inorganic state. Thus alongside *Eros,* or man's sexual instinct, is a terrible aggressive instinct of which the very aim is death. This strong destructive tendency is directed not only against others but even against oneself. Thus one travels the route of pleasure as far as it can go and finds it leads not to a city of happiness but to a very dead end. If one goes back to the beginnings of Western philosophy, one will find the great Greek materialist philosopher Democritus who was immortalized in the poetry of Lucretius. Democritus, called the "laughing philosopher," was probably the first Western philosopher to explicitly develop the idea that *good cheer* or pleasure was the ultimate good. Twenty-four hundred years later pleasure was no longer a laughing matter, and with Freud arose the idea man has a need not only for pleasure but also for destruction—not a very comforting thought in the nuclear age! Life had become too absurdly tragic to be understood on the assumption that the pleasure principle was basic.

Thus, with Bentham, Mill, and finally Freud, we have a very strong case for the importance of pleasure in determining human values. This does not, however, close the book on what philosophy can teach us about what man should do in the world. These three said, in one way or another, that man should satisfy his desire for pleasure. But there have been many philosophers who raised very serious doubts about whether pleasure, which unquestionably is important to people, really has much to do with goodness or not. Men desire pleasure but also desire to eat and sleep and breathe. We would never think of calling someone a good man because he managed to supply himself with food, rest, and oxygen. Perhaps pleasure is the same sort of thing. It is nice to have, maybe even essential, but it has nothing to do with whether we are good, moral, ethical people. In this sense pleasure may not be a factor in the Good at all. To pursue this possibility further we will next examine some nonhedonistic theories of value. These theories locate the center of value in reason, will, duty, love, or power rather than in pleasure.

Deontological Ethics: Kant

Immanuel Kant's attitude toward morality was somewhat paradoxical. In his monumental *Critique of Pure Reason* Kant implicitly scorned and flouted morality by showing that whenever we race beyond the empirical we run our heads directly into stone walls of contradiction. Then, almost as if he had recanted, in his *Critique of Practical Reason* he defended the view we cannot live without it. However, the paradox was more apparent than real, for if we properly understand what Kant was saying about morality, we can see that in fact he was quite consistent. But before we can understand what Kant had to say about morality, we must understand Kant's theory of knowledge.

Kant claimed he had achieved a Copernican Revolution in philosophy, and he was not exaggerating. He brought about a transformation in man's way of understanding the universe by showing that in receiving knowledge man's role was creative, not merely passive. The world is not just out there, ready-made, waiting for man to find it. The world man lives in and understands is a very different world from that of all other species. It is different because his way of understanding it makes it different. What man knows as reality is not just a world of brute fact but his intelligible way of viewing it. The reality we know is a product not only of the raw material out there but also of the sensory apparatus that perceives it and of the rational mind that gives it form. Thus what man knows as reality is never simply a world out there but a world to which he has given rational shape in his very process of understanding it, and in the act of knowing the world man plays a very creative role.

Science, Kant showed, does not really tell us that there is a perfectly ordered and solid world out there, for neither science nor man can ever come face to face with a world of brute facts. Interposed between man and the world is always his own mind structuring it. The mind furnishes the intelligibility we discover in the world and thus satisfies the basic need man has for an orderly and meaningful world. Kant's philosophy was thus an answer to David Hume's challenge to the idea that we live in a rational universe. Hume, you may recall, had argued that all one can show with respect to the relationship between two events is that one thing happened and was followed by another. No one ever sees the *cause* that allegedly links or binds the two things. The statement that the first event is the *cause* of the second, Hume argued, is only an inference. Thus he tried to show that there is no rational basis for assuming a law of causality. Kant, however, pointed out that what Hume had failed to understand was that man's mind so functions that he can only see the world in terms of certain rational principles such as causality. Man is so structured himself that he has to make *sense* out of chaotic sense data. Hume was wrong to say there is no rationality in nature, for there is—it is in *human* nature.

Thus Kant brought good news for the building of a rational science of nature. But could his arguments be extended to the field of morality? Morality, after all, has to do not with what *is* but with what *ought* to be. Could one find principles that would make ethics rational?

In his *Critique of Pure Reason* Kant did not seem to think one could. However, in the *Groundwork of the Metaphysic of Morals* and the *Critique of Practical Reason* he seems to have reversed this position. So inconsistent does the spirit of these works seem to be in relation to *Critique of Pure Reason,* which provides no basis for morality, that some scholars suggest

Kant just tacked morality on as an afterthought. Indeed Bertrand Russell expressed his objections in quite strong terms. Considering how tough Kant was on God and morality in his *Critique of Pure Reason,* his softening up on them in the *Practical Reason* seemed to Russell like a sellout:

> *The first German to take notice of Hume was Immanuel Kant. . . . As he says himself, "Hume awakened him from his dogmatic slumbers." After meditating for twelve years, he produced his great work,* The Critique of Pure Reason; *seven years later, at the age of sixty-four, he produced the* Critique of Practical Reason, *in which he resumed his dogmatic slumbers after nearly twenty years of uncomfortable wakefulness.*[8]

It is possible, however, to view the *Practical Reason*—in opposition to Russell—as an ethical awakening complementing Kant's awakening to Hume's doubts concerning the possibility of scientific knowledge. One might interpret Kant in such a way as to show that the *Critique of Pure Reason* and the *Critique of Practical Reason* are far more harmonious than usually thought. It is true that scientific phenomena and ethical phenomena must be understood on different frequencies, but it is not contradictory to assume the nature of man is such that he may operate on *both* frequencies. Interpreting Kant in this way, we may say *Pure Reason* shows how man may operate on the scientific frequency and demonstrates that ethics cannot be tuned in on this frequency. Man, however, need not drop out morally. He can operate on another frequency, and it is this ethical frequency with which the *Practical Reason* deals. In one work Kant seeks to establish that the nature of man is such that he must see the world he lives in as intelligible, and in the other work he develops the thesis that man is such a being that he must understand life in moral terms. Man is both a rational and a moral being, and therefore reality must have both a rational and a moral character. Just as man cannot watch someone strike a match and then observe a flame without automatically assuming a causal relation (that the striking necessarily produced the flame), so man cannot live without making moral judgments and being guided by moral ideals. In this sense although Kant was a great rationalist, the ground of his morality is existential, for he finds morality not in the objective universe but in the imperatives of human existence that demand its creation. Kant does not put it in these terms, but I think we can so understand what he was actually doing. What Kant did maintain was that man is a moral being; although it is true he cannot strictly prove the truth of such ethical postulates as the existence of God, freedom, and immortality, it is nonetheless true that the requirements of human fulfillment call for these assumptions.

Thus we need not accept the charge that in his later works Kant artificially added morality; rather, he showed that as there is an answer to man's need for intelligibility in the universe there is also an answer for his most basic hopes. The human image would not be complete if it did not embrace man's need for morality as well as his need for intelligibility.

Assuming that man is moral, the problem then is to analyze and show

[8] Bertrand Russell, *Unpopular Essays* (New York: Simon and Schuster, 1950), p. 51.

just what morality consists in. Morality is not anything empirical. The empirical concerns what *is*, whereas morality has to do with what *ought* to be. This being the case, Kant argued, the field of ethics does not have anything to do with the consequences of our acts. These consequences involve questions of what happens in the empirical world, which is a factual matter. What one ought to do, therefore, cannot be a question of consequence, as the utilitarian philosophers insisted. It must be a question of *duty*. Kant's ethical theory is *deontological*. The word comes from the Greek "deon" which means duty or obligation. When a person does something following an inclination, he is doing it for a psychological rather than a moral reason. When a man acts for moral reason, however, he is really involved in a creative endeavor. He may have to resist the world—including his own inclinations—to follow duty. This is moral effort. In a period of social ferment when the scientific, industrial, and commercial revolutions were awakening men to practical and utilitarian interests, Kant took his stand on a deontological or duty ethic in direct opposition to the utilitarian theory of morality.

In deciding whether an act is moral or not, it is necessary according to Kant to determine if it arises from a *motive* of inclination or duty. If the act, even though its consequences may be beneficial, results from a sense of inclination, it is not moral. To be considered moral an act must be undertaken purely from a sense of duty. A utilitarian like Jeremy Bentham would say that it does not matter whether an act is from the motive of inclination or from duty because motive is irrelevant; morality depends entirely upon consequences. That which bears good fruit is good, and that which bears rotten fruit, no matter how pure the motivation, is rotten. What good is it for someone to be a prince of a fellow in his intentions if he is always bungling matters and causing injury? A person may have the best intentions in the world, but if he is incable of translating them into action, the world will be no better for them.

Of course, Kant would admit that consequences are important—to whoever is involved in them. But he would answer Bentham that they are not important morally. Where Bentham would say that a man is good if his acts have good consequences, Kant would insist that a man is not good unless he has a good will. Now if we go along with Kant and rule out consequences as an ethical standard we may want to consider the thorny question of inner motivation. There is no instrument by which we can look into a man and see his motives. How can we ever know what a man really *intends?* It will do no good to attempt to infer his motives from his overt behavior, for that would mean we could know motive only in terms of consequences. The jurist is faced with problems similar to those that confront the moralist. In fixing legal responsibility he cannot avoid dealing with motives as against consequences. It is a problem human beings have to come to grips with, and it is interesting to see how the juridical mind has done so.

Included in the very structure of our legal system is recognition of the necessity of taking into account both intentions and consequences in determining legal responsibility. A man cannot be convicted of a crime (except in certain specified instances of negligence) unless *mens rea,* a guilty mind, can be established as well as *actus reus,* the committing of an actual overt act. The crucial question philosophically, of course, concerns how it is possible to test what one's intention is. In fact it may be necessary to construct *mens rea* on the basis of *actus reus*—that is, it may be necessary to infer intention from the overt act. This may be acceptable for a court, which has to make a practical decision one way or another, but is not really satisfactory for a philosopher, who should have and can afford to have more rigorous standards. Thus it has been held that if one bites another's ear so hard that he tears it off the other's head, it is legitimate to assume he intended to do something wrong.[9] Interesting decisions have been made concerning whether we should judge one on the basis of his intentions or on the basis of the consequences. These decisions have been developed in "attempt" cases. Attempt cases must always be predicated upon some specific overt act. In order for a person to be charged with *attempting* something, there must be some actual consequences of his attempt. The crucial and really interesting question emerges at just this point, for once we have a given act, how can we know it constitutes an effort to achieve a given end or result? In answering this question some jurists have relied upon assumptions similar to Kant's while others have adopted the kind of criterion Bentham employed. In other words, in "attempt" cases it must be decided whether a given act is a specific and definite effort to achieve a particular end or result, and some jurists have concluded that if the act implies the *intention* to achieve that particular result the person must be held guilty of "attempt" even if it would have been impossible for him to commit the crime he was "attempting." Others have held the only really relevant consideration is whether the initial act could *actually* have been carried out and if it would have produced the specific end or *consequence.* Those judges who place guilt even where consummation is impossible seem to be relying on very Kantian assumptions, whereas jurists who maintain the crucial criterion is in the possibility of the consequences actually occurring seem to be making presuppositions quite similar to Bentham's.

There are then no clear and set standards in this area of law. One set of jurists decides that if, in the nature of the case, there cannot be a realization of the specific consequences, then there cannot be a verdict of guilty on the charge of attempt. Other jurists say, in effect, that if the intention is there, then the possibility of consequences is irrelevant. What is needed is greater clarity and precision regarding the problem of whether we should think in terms of the actual possibilities—in the spirit of Bentham's moral philosophy —or whether we should adopt "intention" as a basis for our understanding— a sort of Kantian procedure. Perhaps, a careful job of synthesizing both into a consistent policy is required. It may be that if we entirely neglect either intention or consequences what we get will be foolish. This has often been the result in actual cases. Such cases illustrate that we have here a practical, legal problem that needs to be ironed out by clarifying our philosophical assumptions.

[9] *State v. Skidmore,* 87 N.C. 509 (1882).

In a number of cases it has been held that if an impotent man, not know-ing of his disability, attacks a girl with intent to rape her, he can be found guilty of attempted *rape*. In such cases one would have to say the standard for determining whether there was an attempt falls back upon intention. A sixty-seven-year-old man enticed two little girls to his home; one of them was ten and the other eight. He took one to a bedroom and undressed her, but he took off none of his own clothing. Then the little girl's grandmother arrived on the scene and put an end to that business. The jury was informed that the man was impotent and could not have raped the girl. Nonetheless, it found him guilty of attempted rape. He appealed, and the verdict of the trial court was upheld. Impotency is not a defense against *attempted* rape. It must be frustrating for someone to have to go to jail for *attempting* some-thing he could never succeed in doing. In the case of the sixty-seven-year-old man it was held that as long as an *apparent* possibility existed that he could have raped her, his impotency could not be allowed as a defense.[10] The man has to suffer the double pain of discovering his inadequacy on the one hand and of being accorded criminal credit for his effort on the other.

There are other cases in which it would seem consequences rather than motive or intent dictate the judicial verdict. An American soldier fully in-tended to desert his army unit and join the enemy. The soldier went over the hill, as it is said, and he specifically sought out the enemy in order to join them. To avoid detection by the American army he followed a circuitous route around to the enemy camp. After a desperate journey he finally arrived at the enemy encampment. Just at that apparently triumphant moment when he believed he had achieved success he made an embarrassing discovery. The enemy had retreated during the night, and his own unit had taken over their camp. He had deserted into his own company. He was arrested, charged with attempted desertion, and put on trial. To the surprise of many, he was found innocent. The court held that he could not be found guilty of attempted desertion because it is not possible to attempt that which is im-possible, and it was reasoned that it is impossible to desert into one's own army. Unquestionably this man's *motive* was not to do his duty—it was specifically to desert; and yet because desertion could never have been the *consequence* of his action in that particular situation, he was found not guilty.[11]

Other cases confirm this approach. Thus when a man took a shot at what he believed to be a person whom he hated with a passion (and it turned out to be in actuality a tree stump), it was held he could not be found guilty of attempted murder, for it is impossible to *attempt* to kill a man by shooting at a tree stump. The man's malice aforethought had no bearing on the decision in this case. Yet if a man shoots at another and completely misses him, or if he shoots and does hit him but does not wound him because he is wearing armor, it has been held he can be found guilty of attempted murder. One of the most interesting of these cases involved a very passionate guy, burning with sexual desire, who cast his hungry eyes upon a truly volup-

[10] *Preddy v. Commonwealth*, 184 Va. 765, 36 S.E. d 549 (1946).
[11] *Respublica v. Malin*, 1 Dall. 33, 1 L. Ed. 25.

tuous girl and decided to rape her. Can you imagine his embarrassment when the object of his sexual desire turned out to be a clothing dummy! What a dummy he must have felt like! He was brought before the bar for this and found not guilty of *attempted rape*. The court held that regardless of what kind of problems one has, one just cannot have sexual relations with a clothing dummy.

Now let us pose a hypothetical question, bearing on this discussion. Suppose a rather distinguished-looking gentleman is standing on the end of a pier observing the rolling waves rushing forth. Suddenly his tranquil contemplation is broken as he sees a man in a rowboat topple over and fall into the whirling waters. The fallen man, gasping for breath and in a state of desperation, calls for help and seems to be going down. He shouts, "Help me! Help me! I–I– can't swim." The gentleman on the pier knows that as far as Kant is concerned one should do his duty though the heavens may fall, and he believes he has a duty to help his fellow man. However, he has also read Jeremy Bentham, and believes he should consider the consequences of his acts. But at this moment he forget's Bentham's formula that the good is the greatest happiness for the greatest number, and remembers instead the egoistic hedonistic position that good is the greatest happiness for himself. "Sorry old chap," he tells the drowning man, "I'd really be delighted to help you, but after all this is a brand new suit I have on, and I would hate to get it wrinkled—have a date tonight you know." About to go down for the last time, the drowning man makes one further effort and yells, "Don't wrinkle your suit, but do toss me that life preserver up there." The gentleman assures him he would be glad to, but makes the point that the damn thing is frightfully dirty and that he would not even think of getting his hands all grimy from it. The poor soul then drowns. "Pity," the gentleman comments as he resumes watching the majestic ocean.

If a policeman were informed of the gentleman's behavior, could he arrest him or charge him with any crime? But what crime? The gentleman could defend himself by averring, "I did nothing." Precisely. For it is *generally* the case in our legal tradition that there is no law against doing nothing. One may have very bad intentions and may even stand by to let another die, but as long as one does nothing the usual rule is that nothing can be done to him. Of course, there are significant exceptions to this rule, as in certain negligence cases and in certain instances involving police assistance on which special legislation is required.

Now what if another man on the end of the same pier sees another man drowning. This man, having read Kant, feels he has a *duty* to come to the aid of his fellow man. He does not know how to swim, but he tosses in a life preserver. Unfortunately the preserver conks the drowning man on the head, and as a result he drowns. This good samaritan has the very best intentions, yet he may be in the worst trouble with the law. Once one becomes involved in a precarious situation, in the eyes of our legal system he starts to incur liabilities. On the basis of such legal decisions, intention or a sense of moral duty is not given recognition. This principle is very well illustrated in *People* v. *Beardsley* (150 Mich. 206, 113 N.W. 1128, 1907). It was decided that if a woman *voluntarily* goes to the quarters of a married man, there to dwell in adultery—while his wife is away, of course—and attempts suicide, the man has no obligation to stop her. If the man has good intentions and tries to stop her he will probably be opening the door to legal difficulties, but if he has bad intentions and lets her kill herself he will have nothing to worry about from the law. The general law is that one cannot be held guilty of a crime for an omission to act unless a specific obligation is spelled out or unless one is the cause of another's being put in a precarious position.

Lawrence H. Boyd, a taxi driver, came upon the scene in time to find three guys ganging up on two victims and really giving it to them on a seamy South Side street in Chicago. Boyd pulled his cab to a halt and came to the rescue. The result was that he got shot twice in the chest and once in the hand. He was treated as a hero, "hailed by police, his boss, the press. The Illinois Medical Society even announced it would 'take care' of all his medical bills."[12] Some years later we are let in on a glimpse of how Boyd was taken care of. He was living "in one of the city's all Negro ghettos—penniless, broken and bitter." The fruits of good intentions! Four years after the incident his $1,269 hospital bill was still unpaid as was his $1,000 doctor's bill. The Illinois Medical Society had not taken care of it. His employers at Checker Cab Company bluntly told him they were paying him for driving a cab, not for stopping robbers. Boyd said they had advised him that he should have minded his own business.

From these conflicting cases it seems clear that we cannot turn to the law for answers to ethical problems; it is nevertheless true that concerning such matters as whether we should judge a man in terms of the ideal of *duty* or his overt acts do seem deeply embedded in the fabric of social existence and therefore do cry out for some workable solution.

Take the case of the bystander and the drowning man. A utilitarian such as Bentham could say that the bystander who failed to act at all was immoral if it could be shown that the consequences of such inaction were harmful. Intention would be irrelevant. On the other hand, intention was so important to Kant that he would say that acting might not be moral, even though the actor might save another from drowning, if the action was done from selfish motives—such as a desire to get his picture in the paper and impress his girl. This, of course, would not matter to Bentham or to the drowning man, but it mattered to Kant, who felt that acts in themselves do not count concerning moral questions. Saving another man for selfish reasons rather than for reasons of duty may be socially useful, but it is not a moral act. Of course it is not immoral either; it simply has nothing to do with morality.

Perhaps duty is not as absolute as Kant maintained, but it certainly is of more importance than our practical society usually admits. Perhaps the conflicting judicial decisions in our legal history on the problem of whether to weigh intention or consequence more heavily reflect the difficulty of coming to absolutistic conclusions in actual life situations. It may be necessary to

[12] Lois Wille, "Good Samaritans, Law and the Golden Rule," *The Nation,* April 26, 1965, p. 447.

take a flexible position on the question of duty, which is just what some contemporary ethical philosophers are doing. Nonetheless, in discovering just what is involved in holding an ethics of duty and in determining the degree of importance we should wish to attribute to it, it is most instructive to examine a position like Kant's in which duty is an absolute obligation.

The law does not always encourage man to do his duty and sometimes even punishes him for trying. Kant would never excuse man from his duty, even if that meant he would be punished for trying. Kant went directly to it in the first line of the first section of his *Fundamental Principles of the Metaphysics of Morals:* "Nothing can possibly be conceived in the world, or even out of it, which can be called good without qualification, except a Good Will." Kant had no doubt that intelligence, wit, judgment, courage, resolution, or perseverance are all good qualities under certain conditions, but all can easily be perverted if the will is mischievous. It is the same with power, honor, wealth, health, and even happiness. All of these can be good, but they can also lead to presumption and pride. These qualities can be truly good only if the will is good. The will is the key to morality, and thus if we wish to determine the moral worth of a man we have to discover whether or not he acts out of a good will. If the will is not good, anything he does will be tainted and soiled. If a man makes an anonymous donation to a charity and, even though he cannot boast about it, feels pleasure with himself for so doing, he may become very self-righteous. Thus he acts not from a moral but from a selfish motive. The good man should act out of a sense of pure duty.

To many people it has seemed that Kant was expecting too much of man. It was absurd to suppose man could act out of a pure sense of duty devoid of pleasure. The German philosopher Friedrich Schiller, himself influenced by Kant, objected to Kant's ethics on the grounds that if doing one's duty implies that one can feel no natural desire to do the act in question, a mother who loved her child and did what was best for him for this reason could not be considered good; nor, by the same reasoning, could we regard any wholehearted friendship as moral. This seemed an unnatural conclusion to Schiller. Actually Kant did not maintain that one could do his duty without love, nor that one had to feel something was distasteful before one got moral credit for doing it. The mother who acts out of both love and duty is acting morally; the mother who acts only out of love is not a worse person, but her acts have nothing to do with morality.

Kant was not just against fun and games and doing what we want, but the point is they are not relevant to morality. They have to do with what people enjoy, not what they *should* do. This is why duty is so important to him, for it alone is relevant in determining if one has acted morally. The basis of moral worth must be a good motive, and the only invariably good motive is the desire to do one's duty.

In getting on in living, in doing things, in making decisions, a person will invariably have some rules to guide him. Kant describes this by saying that a person decides upon a maxim—that is, a general rule which he plans to follow in his actions and which tells him what his duty is. This maxim is subjective in that the individual chooses it for himself. It is policy for him, and having a policy gives him a consistent way of acting. If a person is led into dilemmas or inconsistencies by seeking to follow the maxim he has adopted, then there is something wrong with his maxim, and he really has no policy and no duty. The test of whether one's maxim is valid, therefore, concerns whether the rule one adopts as the basis of his actions can be consistently followed. If it cannot, then the rule will break down, will prove not to be a real rule, and one's duty will be dissolved. Suppose someone decided he would always drive his car on the left side of the road. This maxim or rule would not last very long, and neither would the person. The maxim decision would come to a crashing halt when another car coming down the same side of the road crashed into him. In the same way a maxim that does not give a clear road ahead will lead to a moral crash. If a maxim cannot be consistently applied to life's situations it will break down. This being the case, Kant wanted to know if there was a maxim that would not break down, one that can be applied with perfect consistency, which we could always be able to follow.

A truly consistent rule is one that can be universalized—that is, it can be applied *without any exceptions*. It will always apply in all situations. Such a rule would have no conditions attached; it would be unconditional. One's duty to follow this rule would also be unconditional. Therefore Kant called this rule, which was the basis for his system of morality and duty, the *categorical imperative*.

An imperative is a command. There are two types of commands—hypothetical and categorical. A hypothetical imperative is always conditional; it is of the form: *if* this is so, *then* that must be so or must follow. A hypothetical imperative is always an "iffy" thing; it can tell us what we must do *only* if we desire to achieve certain consequences, but if we do not care about those consequences then it tells us nothing. A categorical imperative tells us what we must do, and there are no *ifs, ands*, or *buts* about it. At first it might seem that laws are *categorical*, telling us what we must do and, much more frequently, what we must not do, but a moment's consideration will reveal they do no such thing at all. Our laws are indeed *hypothetical* imperatives: they tell us we should not do such things as break windows if we do not want to go to jail. The structure of law is such that we are told what we should expect to follow *if* we engage in certain patterns of behavior. If a poor, cold, and hungry man wants a place to sleep, he may throw a brick through a window so he can get a warm night's rest in the pokey. We are not told we *must* not exceed the speed limit, but that if we do we may get arrested.

Moral law is quite different from legal codes in this respect. It has nothing to do with consequences and it is unconditional. If a man says, "I will save your child and carry it out of that burning house if you will give me a thousand-dollar reward," he may be doing a valuable service, but he is certainly not acting out of a moral motive. Morality is not conditional. A mother does not say she will love her baby *if* it doesn't cry, nor does a moral man say he will do good *if* he is given recognition. The call of moral duty is a categorical imperative and unconditionally obligates us. It is only rational beings who are capable of conceiving universal laws, and therefore only rational beings are absolutely bound by moral laws. The moral law must allow no exceptions and must permit no extenuating circumstances. Therefore it must be based on a maxim that can be universally applied. For this reason Kant says we should act only on that maxim through which you can at the same time will that it should become a universal law.

Suppose someone should quickly need some money and in order to get it makes a promise he has no intention of keeping—that he will repay the money. Kant would analyze this situation by pointing out that if the man in question adopts a policy of breaking promises, before long no one will believe him and he will not get any more money. Thus his maxim cannot be universalized, for if everyone broke the promises he made when doing so served his needs, then the teeth would be taken out of the notion of promise and its meaning would be lost.

Kant gives three main formulations of the categorical imperative, all of which mean the same thing, although there are different ways of emphasizing that meaning.

1. Act as if the maxim of your actions is to become by your will a universal law of nature.
2. Treat every human being as an end in himself, and never as a mere means.
3. Act as if you are a member of an Ideal Kingdom in which every man is both subject and sovereign, and thus a principle of conduct is only binding if it can be regarded as a law one imposes on himself.

These three forms of categorical imperative express Unity, Plurality, and Totality:

UNITY: There is one universal law which all men are bound to obey.

PLURALITY: There is a plurality of rational subjects, and each and every one is to be treated with dignity and as one having absolute worth in himself.

TOTALITY: Totality results from the fact that unity can be discovered in the plurality. In subjecting oneself to the universal moral law, not only does one not thereby renounce any individual rights but on the contrary confirms his own absolute worth.

The categorical imperative imposes an absolute obligation upon a man and in so doing confers upon him absolute worth as a rational being. There is only one problem: it absolutely fails to tell him specifically what he should or should not do. The categorical imperative is a purely *formal* principle. Justice Oliver Wendell Holmes once remarked that law is not logic but experience. Does that judgment about law not apply to morality with even more force? Does not such an insistence upon abstract duty render man, who must bend with the winds of life, too inflexible to deal meaningfully with the complex problems of existence? Considering the endless variety of situations and predicaments in which man can become involved, is it not quixotic to demand of man in every situation the absolute duty of truth? Yet that is exactly what the categorical imperative does. Suppose a man should decide in a given situation it would be profitable to lie. Can the maxim that embodies that decision be universalized? Hardly, for if everyone lied, then no one would believe anyone and it would be impossible to lie. Lying would become meaningless. Thus one should never lie.

Is it always wrong or amoral to lie? Or is Kant's unyielding insistence on truth as a moral duty a *reductio ad absurdum?* Suppose one tells a little lie to avoid hurting someone's feelings. Surely there is not anything wrong with that, is there? If a very sensitive person asks how she looks, is it really moral for one to tell the truth and say, "awful"? Isn't it really preferable to lie and tell her she looks nice? Remember, however, that to do so is to compromise the truth, and once that starts, who knows where it will ever stop? Deceit is most contagious and spreads like a plague when it begins to infect men.

Thus, although Kant himself was disinterested in consequences from a moral standpoint, it may be that even in terms of consequences Kant's absolute demand for truth makes sense. Would not people be better off if they bore a truer image of themselves? A personal incident comes to mind. One day I was riding in a bus, and across from me were three girls. I couldn't help but overhear two of them go out of their way to compliment the third on her new hairdo. They said it was *just* stunning. It didn't look very stunning to me, but I figured I really don't know anything about these matters. I did think it strange however. It was all piled up on the top of her head and to me looked like a black elevator rope. Then the bus came to one of its stops and the girl with the stunning hairdo got off. At that point the other two stunned me. No sooner was the third girl off than one of the two said to the other, "Was her hair ever a mess?" The other responded, "Awful, just awful!" I decided to participate and thus inquired of them why they had not told their friend what they really thought of her hair style, and they justified their lying ways by telling me they did not want to hurt her feelings. "So," I answered, "you let her walk around looking ridiculous all the time the poor fool is encouraged to think she has a 'stunning' hair style. You don't want to make her feel bad, but apparently you have no reservations about letting her look bad." They seemed to think I was crazy, and so we didn't pursue the question of truth any further. I think it is widely accepted, however, that it is moral to keep the truth from someone if that will spare him suffering or misery. If a person is dying from an incurable disease, does it do any good to tell him he is practically a dead man? Why not let him live out what little remaining time he has in peace? Indeed, telling him may even hasten his death by causing heart failure. Truth is dynamite and can explode; one might even want to argue that it should be used only with great care. On the other hand, perhaps, not telling the dying man will hasten his death by encouraging him to live with less care. More significant is the consideration that perhaps he might want to know and as a rational being he has that right. If a person knew he only had a limited time, perhaps he would do things he always wanted to do before his time ran out. If the man is so sick he is bed-ridden and cannot do anything, then he would probably get the idea himself that his condition was pretty serious. Under such circumstances, how much harm would result from telling the truth? In any event, Kant still has a most valid point in addition to consideration of these consequences. Should we seek to universalize our policy that it is right to lie to spare one unpleasant news, it would follow that anyone who inquired about his condition, health, or fortune could not believe what he was told. Everyone would know it is policy to lie concerning such matters, and therefore the purpose of the policy would be destroyed.

Truth is not a tool that can be used to fix up particular problems we may have; it is an abstract principle. We cannot use it to suit our own purposes, for then we would not be serving truth but seeking to use it. Our interest would not be in truth but in employing it to realize certain consequences. Truth is very powerful. Men who have the courage to accept it and build their lives upon it find that they thereby become free from the lies and mea-sures of deceit that shackle so many. If all men were committed to truth, this would probably be a better world to live in despite the fact that the truth might hurt in specific instances. Our attitude toward truth should be like that of the pacifist who takes an absolute stand against killing. To justify killing on certain occasions is to open the door to it on virtually any occasion that suits the purpose of some men and thereby to diminish the general reverence for life. Similarly, to justify lying in certain instances diminishes respect for truth.

That this danger of diminishing respect for truth is a very real one can be seen in the tremendous problem of the "credibility gap" in our govern-ment, which opened up during the Johnson Administration and has not closed yet. Arthur Sylvester, who was in charge of dispensing information for the Department of Defense from 1961 to 1967, asserted that a government has an inherent right to lie in situations that it considers grave enough. A state-ment such as this does irreparable harm to that government's credibility. If a government makes a policy of lying, no one will believe it. Commenting on Arthur Sylvester's statement before the House Subcommittee on Govern-ment Information, Charles S. Rowe, chairman of the Freedom of Informa-tion Committee of the Associated Press Managing Editors Association, testi-fied:

> In its efforts to deceive actual or potential foreign adversaries, the government has also deceived the American people. The credibility of their government has suffered in the eyes of many citizens. This erosion of faith in the veracity of government, if long continued can result in serious harm to a democratic society. ... If we should accept a premise that the government has a right to lie to the American people under one set of circumstances, there is a serious danger that this repugnant philosophy will be extended to more and more circumstances and we will find ourselves being lied to with increasing frequency. ...[13]

[13] Quoted in Bruce Ladd, *Crisis in Credibility* (New York: The New American Library, Inc., 1968), pp. 144f.

In a sense Charles Rowe, who is a very practical man, seems to be sending out a Kantian message, saying that if we adopt the maxim that we can lie in certain situations we will be adopting a policy we cannot universalize, for it erodes the meaning and value of truth. The Kantian position must really be taken seriously, for there is an important truth in the idea that morality must be based on a categorical imperative and that true duty must be that done for its own sake rather than for any ulterior motive. And yet, although we admit we must take Kant's position seriously we may still ask if it is a philosophy we can morally live by. It certainly is not an absurd position, but is it sufficiently flexible? Consider the following predicament:

The setting is World War II in Nazi Germany. Fritz hates the Nazis but feels helpless and thus tries to stay aloof from all that goes on. His mother, whom he loves very much, is quite different. She works for the underground; in the basement of her home she has a secret press on which she prints leaflets and a clandestine transmitter on which she sends out radio messages against Hitler and the Nazis. At the same time as she does this in the secret basement, her son sits upstairs reading Kant. A heavy knock is heard; Fritz opens the door and is confronted by a Gestapo agent accompanied by two storm troopers. The Nazis inform Fritz that they know his mother is a traitor against the Third Reich and ask him if he knows where they can find her. Since Fritz hates the Nazis and loves his mother, he lies to the Nazis, telling them he does not know where his mother is. The Nazis believe him and are about to depart. Fritz sits down at the table to continue reading Kant when he suddenly has a pang of conscience. He calls to the Nazis to come back. He remembers the categorical imperative and informs them his mother is downstairs in a secret basement printing propaganda against them. The Nazis apprehend Fritz's mother, drag her out, torment and torture her awhile, then line her up against the fence in front of Fritz's house, and shoot her. If Kant was right about the absolute duty to tell the truth, then Fritz has done his moral duty.

If that was moral duty, one can only conclude that humanity is in more trouble than even the most radical critics of our society maintain. Perhaps Kant was right insofar as he said that the maxim we adopt as our rule for living must be one we would be willing to see universalized, but he was wrong to imagine that "I shall always tell the truth" was such a maxim. It may just be that in real life universalizing truth telling would lead to completely unacceptable and untenable human predicaments. Indeed, in terms of the logic of life it might just be that there is not *anything* we can universalize or make absolute. An abstract duty to be done for its own sake, unrelated to the dynamics of actual life situations, does not qualify as a guide for us in such situations as in the story of Fritz. If a lie will protect anyone from the atrocities of inhuman oppressors, there must be a *human* imperative that we ought to lie in such a situation.

In this respect we should notice the attempt by the twentieth-century philosopher W. D. Ross to introduce more flexibility into Kantian ethics. Ross believed it most important to clearly distinguish *right* from *good*. *Good* is that which has beneficial consequences, and good things are worthy objects of satisfaction. Right is what we ought to do whether or not it leads to that which is good. Thus, in the case we have just seen, it may have been right to tell the truth but the good thing to do would be to lie to the Nazis.

Similarly, where Kant would say that the mother who cared for her child out of love rather than out of duty was not doing anything morally *right*, Ross would agree, but he would add that what she was doing was unquestionably *good*.

Ross's system was an improvement on Kant's because it was more flexible. More wisely than Kant, Ross did not hold that a duty was absolute. Instead he spoke of *prima facie* duties. Thus on the face of it there is a duty to keep a promise or to tell the truth, and all things being equal, one should do his duty. However, Ross recognized the significance of extenuating circumstances and thus took the position that if it would alleviate great suffering, then one should break his promise. Doing good sometimes can be more important than doing right. A *prima facie* duty is a conditional rather than an unconditional duty, and performance of it should not be blind but should be dependent on whether it is fitting to the situation.

Of course, Ross's approach still leaves us with problems. He insisted duties were conditional and also insisted their validity was intuitive. We intuitively know we have a *prima facie* duty to act in a given situation and that good may sometimes outweigh duty. But how do we know when? What is more, Ross believed there are many different *prima facie* duties. If in a given situation more than one duty calls, how shall we know which to answer? Ross told us that duties are not absolute and that in different situations one duty may be more binding than in another, but he provided us with no rule by which we might determine which one is more binding. Falling back on intuition may just be morally falling on our face. Different men will have different intuitions, and the intuitions that may seem valid in one class or in one group may not seem so in another.

Despite these problems, however, it is important to add something like Ross's flexibility to Kant's rigid system, for if allowance is not made for filling in the form of duty with human content, how can we preclude the possibility that certain individuals or interests will make use of duty to serve inhuman or immoral ends? It has been written:

> There is no atrocity and no crime which has not been enjoined at some time and some place by conscience and duty or which is still not enjoined today. Murder, scorching and laying to waste, the slaughter of the defenseless, of women and children without regard to guilt or innocence, robbery and betrayal, debauchery and orgies count as in accord with duty or at least as not against conscience; and so too actions that appear to us as morally quite indifferent are enjoined by this strict command.[14]

John Dewey went even further in his *German Philosophy and Politics*, claiming that a tyrant could give any content to the form of duty and thus demand unquestioning obedience to his ruthless policies. He saw that Kant's moral philosophy could be used for the most intolerable abuses. As Dewey understood Kant on this, nothing could better serve a dictator than a

---

[14] E. Becher, quoted in Julius Ebbinghaus, "Interpretation and Misinterpretation of the Categorical Imperative," in *Kant*, ed. Robert Paul Wolff (Garden City, N.Y.: Doubleday & Company, Inc., 1967), p. 217.

categorical imperative. In this connection it is rather interesting that Adolf Eichmann, during his interrogation by Israeli police, claimed that he sought to follow the philosophy of Kant throughout his military life. When Judge Raveh asked Eichmann what he believed the main principles of Kantian philosophy to be, Eichmann answered that what he found most attractive was the *categorical imperative.* The charge against Eichmann by the Israeli court was that he and others caused the death of millions of Jews by gassing and by other means in the extermination camps of Auschwitz, Chelmno, Belzec, Sobibor, Treblinka, and Maidanek. He was further charged with taking the necessary steps to put millions of Jews to work in forced labor camps, organizing mass persecution, and having some responsibility for the sterilization of Jews and gypsies as well as for other atrocities.

If someone like Eichmann found the categorical imperative attractive, what does that say about the attractiveness of the categorical imperative? In fact, it does not say anything against its attractiveness for the categorical imperative as formulated by Kant was consistent with none of the practices undertaken by the Nazis. The categorical imperative does say that one should always do one's duty but it does *not* say that that duty is always whatever the state says it is. In defending his deontological ethics Kant was certainly not saying that man must do his duty and not reason why. On the contrary, doing one's duty in the Kantian sense is quite the opposite of blindly following a command. Indeed, one must do his duty not only with his eyes wide open but also with his mind wide open. In this sense neither Dewey nor Eichmann really understood it.

The fact is that the categorical imperative as formulated by Kant cannot be filled with any content a tyrant wishes. Kant understood the categorical imperative as a uniquely human moral duty. The kind of duty that alone can arise from the categorical imperative is one consonant with rational human existence. The policies with which Eichmann was associated could not only not be universalized but were directly contradictory to those forms of the categorical imperative that demand each individual be treated as an end in himself and that the individual himself be the source of any principle of conduct binding on him. The categorical imperative is based on the rational nature of man, and no one can invoke it as a defense for carrying out any unreasonable or irrational acts. There is built into it those two fundamental principles of any truly democratic society—that man is an end in himself and that any man, just by virtue of being a man, is a member of the kingdom of ends.

There is no higher testimony in behalf of the worth of man than that contained in the principle that every man must be treated as an end in himself and not as a mere means. This principle recognized the uniqueness of man and asserts—in that uniqueness—that a very special worth inheres in man. Man is to be respected just because he *is*, not because of what he *has*. Thus man is not to be used, for he is not a tool. In totalitarian states men are regarded as tools, as a means. The end is not the man but the state. Of course, a tyrant is not the only one who can use a man as a mere means to an end. A man may use himself as a mere means. It is for this reason that

Kant opposed suicide, for he reasoned that anyone who commits suicide is using his own life as a means. Indeed, it is often the case that a man may degrade himself far more than a dictator ever will.

If man could ever learn to take the categorical imperative seriously, there would be an end to the degradation of man. There is no principle that contains a greater tribute to the nobility of man or a higher defense of individual rights than the categorical imperative. Even the golden rule is far less golden, as we can see in the case of professional prizefighters and professional soldiers whose ethics permit them to hurt or kill others because they are willing to take the risk of letting others do the same unto them. To be sure, such behavior is not consonant with the spirit of the golden rule, but logically considered such behavior may be deduced from it—or at least it is not precluded by it. No such subjectivistic interpretation is logically possible in connection with the categorical imperative. It flatly declares that all individuals must be treated as ends in themselves and never as mere means. Thus no matter what a person would be willing to let another do unto him, he must always treat the other as an end in himself.

The only problem with the categorical imperative is whether or not it is realistic. Are the cards life deals us such that we shall always be able to play out the hand of existence and still treat everyone as an end in himself? This is the kind of objection an existentialist such as Sartre raises. A girl loves her fiancé dearly and at the same time feels a deep dedication to her lonely, invalid mother. When her father was dying he had asked only that she promise always to be good to her mother and never to desert her. The mother had suffered greatly throughout her life, and now all she has in the world is her beloved daughter. Then the daughter's fiancé gets a transfer to Tokyo. If he refuses he not only will miss out on a great opportunity but will lose his job, and it will be difficult to get another. He suggests to his fiancée they be married and go to Japan together. She wants this more than anything in the world, but if she goes there will be no one to stay and care for her mother, and the mother's condition is such the doctor will not permit her to travel overseas. What is more, the doctor advises that if the mother is left home alone she may worry herself into a heart attack.

How can this girl treat everyone as an end in himself? If she goes, she treats her mother as a means to the happiness of her fiancé and herself. If she stays, she treats herself and her fiancé as a means to her mother's well-being. If she takes the categorical imperative seriously, what can she do? She can't even give up in despair and kill herself, for that too is prohibited by the categorical imperative. It sometimes happens that whatever one does he will have to end up treating someone as a means. Life is often that way, and therefore however meritorious the categorical imperative is, it may just not work.

All one can say is that although there may be occasions on which there will be enormous difficulty in applying the categorical imperative (if it can be applied at all), still there will be many occasions on which we shall be able to live by it. There is no higher ideal toward which we as rational beings may strive, and although ideals cannot always be realized, they still serve to give us valuable direction. We can at least endeavor to treat all men as ends in themselves. This in itself should move us ever closer to that truly human kingdom, described in the third form of the categorical imperative as the kingdom of ends. A truly human community must be a kingdom of ends in which man regards every other man as an end in himself and in which he accepts no law as morally binding that does not have its source in his own reason.

Kant designed this third form of the categorical imperative to express the idea that the morality of man must be based on man's own rationality because he noticed that all other moral philosophies were heteronomous— that is, they were based upon that which lies outside of man. A heteronomous morality is one in which the good, right behavior or duty—is legislated from the outside. According to such theories the motive for being good may be God, the law, society, the promise of attaining pleasure, or some such external consideration. If morality is imposed from the outside, then men are being used as means by whatever outside force imposes its rules on them. If it is God's law they must follow, then they are serving God's ends, not their own; if it is the law that establishes the rules, then the state is using them as a means; if the laws are those of society, then it is their fellow men; and if it is pleasure that is calling the tune, then they are treating themselves as a means. The first gives rise to religious superstition, the second to totalitarianism, the third to the tyranny of the majority, and the fourth to alienation.

For Kant morality had to be *autonomous;* it must be *self-legislating.* Only if man finds the moral law for himself can he be fully at one with himself as a free, rational being. Man best fulfills his humanity through such a rational existence. What better hope can there be for a democracy? Despite constitutional guarantees and laws, if men do not really understand themselves as ends in themselves and as free, rational men capable of deciding for themselves, democracy will not work, for it will turn out that many individuals will be *used*, treated as tools, for the interests of others. There will not be true democracy, in which men choose their own destiny; rather, there will be what has been called *manipulative* democracy. Not only is the categorical imperative *not* a preparation for totalitarianism as Dewey charged but, quite to the contrary, it is the finest preparation for democracy.

No ethical philosophy treats man with more dignity than Kant's. Kant forged an image of man consistent with the ideal of a truly virtuous life. For man to live virtuously and act out of the motive of duty is for him to achieve the *summum bonum,* or the highest good. But to speak of the summum bonum—of man's virtue, of his undeviating performance of moral duty—is not to tell the whole story of morality. Before we can understand man as a moral being, we must still deal with the question of whether or not he lives in the kind of universe that complements his existence, for if man is to be eternally frustrated in seeking to do his duty, then man as a moral being would be undercut by the very universe in which he lives. Is this the kind of universe in which the cry for morality can be heard anywhere outside the heart of man? If it is not, then the entire climate of existence is hostile to the nature of man. Or is this the kind of a universe in which man's moral nature is meaningful because it has an appropriate setting in which to act? If it is, then what kind of universe would that be? It would be one, Kant answered, in which there is Freedom, God, and Immortality. Here is his reasoning.

We only commend or condemn people when we believe they are responsible for their actions. They can only be considered responsible, however, if they are free to choose their actions. Thus if morality is to have any meaning, if we are ever to regard anyone as virtuous, we must assume there is *freedom*. Those men who are commendable, we believe, should be rewarded for their virtue. Of course they do not behave virtuously in order to be rewarded, but justice seems to require that they should be rewarded for having behaved virtuously. Frequently, however, the good that men do in this life is not rewarded, and perhaps even more frequently the evil they do is not punished. This leaves a rather messy picture from a moral standpoint. It cannot be redressed by man; this is work for a *God*. There must be an ultimate standard-bearer for morality, and that can only be a personal God who cares. Now God does not catch up with all of the bad guys in this life, nor does he do right by the good guys. Since He is a good God one must assume there is another day for the good guys and the bad guys when justice will be meted out in proportion to deserts. In short, there must be an assumption of *immortality*.

Complementing the summum bonum—that is, the intrinsically good, or action willed for the sake of duty—there must be the *Bonum Consummatum*, or the distribution of happiness in precise proportion to virtue. Together these two forms of the good make up the complete good. At this juncture many get the idea Kant was selling out, for in the first place he told us the only absolutely good thing was a good will, and that consequences did not count; but in the second place he informed us that morality will find ultimate fulfillment only when there are appropriate rewards and punishments. Perhaps Kant, after all, turns out to be nothing but a hedonist. Kant's philosophical enemy Bertrand Russell had something to say on this score:

> *Kant was never tired of pouring scorn on the view that the good consists of pleasure. ... If you are kind to your brother because you are fond of him, you have no merit; but if you can hardly stand him and are nevertheless kind to him because the moral law says you should be, then you are the sort of person that Kant thinks you ought to be. But in spite of the total worthlessness of pleasure Kant thinks it unjust that the good should suffer, and on this ground alone holds that there should be a future life in which they enjoy eternal bliss. If he really believed what he thinks he believes, he would not regard heaven as a place where the good are happy, but as a place where they have never-ending opportunities of doing kindness to people whom they dislike.[15]*

[15] *Bertrand Russell's Best* (New York: A Mentor Book, 1958), p. 121.

Here is a case in which Bertrand Russell's wit is sharper than his wisdom. Kant did not make pleasure and happiness equivalent. It is not entirely clear what he meant by happiness, but he did not seem to understand it in purely hedonistic terms. In any case, Kant did not declare either pleasure or happiness to be bad; he claimed only that they were not proper motives for duty. Kant never relented in his insistence that the moral agent must always act out of a sense of duty, regardless of the consequences. This in no way is inconsistent with such a pure person's being rewarded for his virtue as an *unintended* consequence. A good person does not do good *in order to* receive a reward, but would it not be better if such a person were rewarded? If during battle a soldier under fire risks his life to save some of his buddies because he is a glory seeker or because he wants a medal, Kant would not call him moral, although he would admit that what the soldier did was a good thing. On the other hand, if a soldier risks his life purely out of a sense of moral duty and for no other reason, then he is truly moral. After having behaved virtuously in the Kantian sense, is it not better that he should be given a medal than that he should not be recognized at all?

Kant's argument that God, freedom, and immortality are necessary if morality is to be meaningful is a relatively strong one, but it must be admitted that there is something sneaky about it. Even if we admit that the existence of God, freedom, and immortality certainly would render ethics more meaningful, that does not mean they do exist. In fact, Kant himself, in his *Critique of Pure Reason,* had a case on the basis of which one might say they do not exist, and nothing in the argument we have just seen refutes it.

What is significant is that Kant showed that reality cannot be deduced from facts external to man; rather, the very nature of man's mind is such that it enters into and molds these facts. The way man is built necessitates his understanding the universe as an intelligible system. Although the intelligibility of the physical universe does not entail the existence of any extrasensory reality, Kant recognized that the physical universe—what he called the world of phenomena—is not the whole of reality. The reality of man demands not only a physically intelligible universe but a morally intelligible one as well. Just as man must see the physical world in terms of such principles as causality, so he must see life in terms of some kind of moral interpretation. What is more, Kant also claimed that the only thing that will really make any moral interpretation ultimately meaningful is the assumption of God, freedom, and immortality.

Although many have argued that Kant's demonstration of the existence of God, freedom, and immortality is not philosophically sound, there is a sense in which we can see that what Kant was doing here was not all that different from what scientists do in their work and therefore has more validity than Kant's critics usually recognize. Scientists, it has been pointed out, do not merely collect facts and then build generalizations and laws from them; rather, they build and formulate *models* of explanation that will provide the best account for man's problems. Such models are not empirical generalizations; they are theoretical constructions. They derive not from facts but from the mind of man and are acceptable because they make most sense of the facts we possess. (This view will be more fully explained and elaborated in the section on scientific methodology.) By the same token, although one cannot legitimately demonstrate the existence of God, freedom, and immortality on the basis that all men seem to have some sense of moral obligation—some recognition that some things ought to be done and others not—one can claim that this assumption is *justified* as a model that makes most sense of moral experience. That is to say, whether or not the existence of God, freedom, and immortality can be proved, it remains true that we can best *understand* the world human beings live in on the assumption that they exist, for without such an assumption something as central to the human fabric as the sense of morality is left without any real grounding. Thus although one cannot prove the existence of God, freedom, and immortality on empirical grounds, there may be other grounds on the basis of which they may be postulated.

Kant sought to show that man has a dual nature. On the one hand, he is part of the empirical world and thus is subject to its ironclad mechanical laws, and his behavior can be accounted for on the principle of causality. But man is also more than just an empirical being; he is also a self, an ego. The self cannot be defined in purely empirical terms; it cannot be identified with the body, although this is not to deny that the body is a part of the self. Kant tried to show that it is only on the assumption of the nonempirical reality of a unified ego or self that we can understand the intelligibility we find in the universe. There has to be some unified entity that can apprehend the chaos of sense experience as a unified whole. Thus an important base of the self is not empirical and thus is not a citizen of the world of space and time. In the sense in which the self can be seen as more than one's body, it can be understood as free.

For this reason we must never equate the whole of reality with the empirical. If it cannot be strictly proven on empirical grounds that ultimate reality is built upon the foundation of God, freedom, and immortality, it cannot be disproved either. What is more, it does not really matter that it cannot be answered on empirical grounds, for it is not an empirical question. Rather, it is a conceptual question. The problem concerns what concepts, what model of explanation, will make most sense of the meaning of ultimate reality for the human being. A major part of Kant's contribution to ethical philosophy was his argument that the only possible model of such a universe was one in which man's moral nature was reflected in the moral nature of the world outside him. Because the physical world in which man lives so obviously contains injustice and immorality, then it must be the case, if man's moral nature is to make any sense at all, that behind this physical world there is moral order, which guarantees man's freedom, provides a context of immortality in which justice can work, and is presided over by God. Kant may not have proved that such a moral universe exists, but he argued convincingly that man's life cannot be meaningful unless it does.

Man has been honored by the title *homo sapiens,* rational animal. He has the capacity to analyze matters logically and to make decisions on the basis of evidence. However, man is not simply a logical calculating machine. Frequently his emotional wires short-circuit his reason, and the dangers of passion have been pointed out often. But on the other hand if the sinews of man were nothing but logic and reason, he would be something like Laputans in Jonathan Swift's *Gulliver's Travels.* These people devoted their whole lives to rational speculation and as a result were not otherwise well-fitted for living. Swift describes the inhabitants of Laputa as follows:

> *Their heads were all reclined either to the right or the left; one of their eyes turned inward, and the other directly up to the zenith. . . . I observed here and there many in the habits of servants, with a brown bladder fastened like a flail to the end of a short stick, which they carried in their hands. In each bladder was a small quantity of . . . little pebbles. . . . With these bladders they now and then flapped the mouths and ears of those who stood near them. . . . It seems the minds of these people are so taken up with intense speculations, that they neither can speak, nor attend to the discourses of others, without being roused by some external taction upon the organs of speech and hearing. . . .*[16]

The Laputans were so up in the air in thought that they had to have a "flapper" strike them to keep their attention from wandering during a conversation. And Swift adds:

> *This flapper is likewise employed diligently to attend his master in his walks, and upon occasion to give him a soft flap on his eyes, because he is always so wrapped up in cogitation, that he is in manifest danger of falling down every precipice, and bouncing his head against every post, and in the streets of jostling others or being jostled himself into the kennel.*[17]

The good life hardly emerges from such a world of abstract reasoning. Gulliver complained that he never saw a more "clumsy, awkward, and unhandy people" than these highly intellectual Laputans. Though they were great in mathematics, they were perplexed in everything else. Perhaps, nothing more effectively testified against their failings in *human* matters than the deep contempt their own wives had for them. The Laputans were great in cogitation but not very good in bed, and their wives were exceedingly fond of strangers. And they didn't even have to worry about getting caught, "for the husband is always so rapt in speculation that the mistress and lover may proceed to the greatest familiarities before his face. . . ."[18]

In short, these men of abstract reason leave much to be desired as men. Although the element of reason has often been regarded as the crowning

---

[16] Jonathan Swift, *Gulliver's Travels* (New York: Rinehart and Company, Inc., 1948), pp. 148f.

[17] *Ibid.,* p. 149. The word "kennel" refers to the open sewers, which ran down city streets in Swift's time.

[18] *Ibid.,* p. 155.

glory of man, many men have denounced it. The very word, Laputa, which Swift employed to name the homeland of these creatures of abstract reason, comes from the Spanish *la puta*, "the whore."

Jonathan Swift lived before the rise of Romanticism as a major intellectual influence, but in his thorough job of discrediting abstract reason and rationalism's overemphasis upon cogitation and pure thought, he anticipated many of the points to be raised later by the Romantic movements. As time went on in modern history, it increasingly came to be realized that man has a heart as well as a mind and that, as Pascal said, the heart may have reasons of its own that the mind cannot understand. Intellectuals throughout history exalted reason. However, in the nineteenth century a realization that there was an emotional tempest in the fragile teapot of reason seemed to be very clearly emerging. The idea that this is a rational universe or that man is a rational being was being very forcefully questioned, and there arose in philosophy an extremely vigorous defense of *will* as superior to reason. This philosophy of the will, which is called *voluntarism*, was not a new philosophy, for it had been well developed in the Middle Ages. But it was being taken up with a new vigor and excitement and was being given a deeper meaning in the new spirit of the turbulent modern industrial world.

Increasingly in the modern world there appeared voices to assert that the life of passion is higher than the life of reason, that the savage is more noble than the civilized man, and that will is more fundamental and more important than thought.

Although there were many who praised the will, not all of those who believed will to be a greater force than reason or thought were elated by this discovery. Indeed many found this thought frightening, for if will is supreme, man will find himself helpless and at the mercy of the blind striving force. Thus there are philosophers who recognize the importance of the will and set themselves in opposition to it.

Indeed, the recognition that the will is so fundamental and basic that it can be explosive and therefore should be renounced, occurred far back in Oriental religion. Buddha carefully and deeply reflected upon life and found will everywhere, driving life to misery and suffering. Buddha understood that it was not disease, poverty, old age, discomfort, or even death that causes human misery but what he called *tanha*, or desire. Desire emerges from a basic will to live and brings in its wake terrible frustration. For example, what pains someone who has lost in love is not that he no longer has his beloved but that he continues to *desire* to want her. Because people cannot fashion the universe to fit their desires, it will be true that as long as there will be desire, which is a product of the will, there will be frustration and unhappiness. Only through the elimination of desire, the renunciation of the will itself, can man be free from this frustration. This was the underlying assumption of the *Four Noble Truths*, which Buddha taught. The First Noble Truth is that life itself is *dukkha*, suffering: all life is tainted with suffering. The Second Noble Truth teaches that the cause of this suffering is *tanha*, or *desire*. The Third Noble Truth is that one must overcome and renounce all desire. And the Fourth Noble Truth is the prescription for effecting the cure. This is the Eightfold Noble Path that shows the roads to the renunciation of will and desire.

The Western world has always been more expansive, explicit, and active than the Eastern. Thus it was the womb out of which was born modern science, the Industrial Revolution, and capitalism. Thus the philosophy of Buddha might be seen as an expression of the more negative way of the East as compared to the more positive and confident way of the West. Thousands of years after Buddha, however, and in the midst of the most vigorous assertion of Western will, in a time when nationalism, imperialism, and militarism were flourishing and in an age when men confidently praised and affirmed the ideals of progress, a German philosopher named Arthur Schopenhauer (1788–1860) returned to the inspiration of Buddha and negated the expression of Western will.

Schopenhauer saw that all of Western man's science, industrialism, and material progress could do nothing to make life meaningful or give man happiness. He believed the only thing that could help living would be to renounce living. At the very moment of the triumph of the Western will, Schopenhauer announced that it was doomed. In his metaphysical theory Schopenhauer admitted the primacy of the *will to live* as the very basis of reality, but in his ethical theory he insisted that man ought to deny the will to live if he is to find salvation.

Schopenhauer saw that all life is eternal strife in an irrational and evil universe. He insisted that life is a "bad bargain." What is one's future? Decay and death! Schopenhauer supposed that if the dead were given a chance to come back to life, they would turn it down. The story of life is one of decay, grief, and disappointment. Why should man want to live? Because he is irrational, Schopenhauer answers. Man *is* himself the very will to live. He cannot extinguish the fire of the will. "Will" lights his fire and burns eternally. Men cannot help but desire and hope, even though there can never be fulfillment. Even love, which we should most expect to redeem us, is of no use, for is not the very essence of love pain? It seems that life is a punishment inflicted on us for being born. Considering that he felt this way, why did Schopenhauer not suggest that everyone commit suicide? Would that not add an optimistic note to his philosophy, for then man could be spared the dull and painful drudgery of existence? Actually Schopenhauer gave this idea serious consideration, as he was much disturbed that suicide was accounted a crime. There are many stupid laws on suicide. For example, where attempted suicide is a crime it has been ruled that if two people get together and decide to commit joint suicide, and one makes it and one does not, then the survivor is guilty of murder. Thus the state says it is a horrible crime for one to take his own life, and if someone tries to do so and does not succeed—as in the above case— then the state will convict him for murder and do it for him. Schopenhauer would regard such laws as utterly unethical, pointing out that there is nothing in the world to which a man has a more unassailable right than to his own life and person. What possible right could the state have to tell one he cannot do what he wants with his own life? If your own life is not your own, then what can be? If you do not want to live, who is the state to say that you must?

Despite these arguments that suicide should not be regarded as criminal or even as an act of insanity, Schopenhauer recognized that it is no solution to man's plight. A man may kill himself, but he cannot kill the general human will to live. By taking one's own life he merely thwarts one manifestation of the will to live, but mankind—and the evil world—continue to go on. Schopenhauer simply could have killed himself, but he did not want to be selfish about it. If he could have marched all mankind to death, then that would have been a valuable contribution, but why should he have killed himself and have allowed the rest of the world to suffer on? One person here or there might commit suicide, but for every suicide there will be millions of killjoys who will refuse to give up their lives.

Humanity has no chance, for nature conspires against it. With the maternal instinct, combined with the sexual urge, there is no way of getting away from the propagation of mankind. Before Sigmund Freud, Schopenhauer had brilliant insight into the importance of the sexual impulse, which, he said, "constitutes even the very nature of man."[19] The fact that the sexual impulse is basic to man is manifested in many ways. An interesting "expression of this natural sentiment is the well-known inscription on the door of the *fornix* at Pompeii, adorned with the phallus: *Heic habitat felicitas* [Here dwells happiness]."[20] Schopenhauer claimed that the sexual impulse is the kernel of man's basic will to live: ". . . therefore I have called the genitals the focus of the will."[21]

Schopenhauer even understood the ambivalence of love, pointing out that sexual love is compatible with the most extreme hatred toward its object: "I love and hate her," as Shakespeare has Cloten say in *Cymbeline* (Act III, Scene 5). In any event, the maternal instinct and the sexual impulse make the prospects for the end of mankind rather poor. Nature sees to it that the will to live is unending. Indeed that is what love is about. Schopenhauer himself denied that love is primarily romantic; no matter how sublime love may seem, it can ultimately be reduced to the instincts toward "generation." This is the irrationality that is responsible for the perpetuation of the human race. In acting on nature's behalf, man strives after woman "in defiance of all reason, sacrifices his own happiness in life by a foolish marriage, by love, by affairs that cost him his fortune, his honour, and his life, even by crimes. . . ."[22] Thus man is duped: he has been had —by nature!

Schopenhauer believed that if reason were really a basic force in human life, then man would never be attracted to such a creature as woman. Therefore life must be will, which is not rational. How can the will be tempered? Suicide cannot silence the will, because there are males with

[19] Arthur Schopenhauer, *The World As Will and Representation* (Indian Hills, Colorado: The Falcon's Wing Press, 1958), II, 513.

[20] *Ibid.*, p. 513.

[21] *Ibid.*, p. 514.

[22] *Ibid.*, pp. 539f.

their sexual impulses and a villanous force: woman, who attracts men to have children. Is there any deliverance from the will?

Schopenhauer envisioned two avenues of escape. One is to be found in *art,* and the other is to be found in *ethical renunciation.* It is particularly through *ethical renunciation* that man must come to terms with the force of will. We are literally caught in the trap of life, and it is a painful trap, but to a certain extent *art* can liberate us. In devoting oneself to art, one can forget about the cruel struggle of life. Art can lift one above this lowly world of pain and suffering. In art one can contemplate the eternal forms that transcend the restless world of becoming. One can open himself to the world of music or absorb himself in the forms of painting. But even with art the effects cannot last forever. When the music is over, the beautiful dream is finished and life, in all its painful and gory details, stares one in the eye again. There must be a more permanent means of escape. There has to be. The answer is suggested in the art of tragedy. The paradox is that in tragedy we are forced to directly encounter the dreadful realities of life: wickedness, the pain of uncertainty, the destruction of the innocent. If life is so terrible, why would one want to be so glaringly reminded of it in the art of tragedy? Schopenhauer's answer is that we learn a lesson of great wisdom from the tragic heroes. The tragic heroes wage the losing battle of life with all their heart and soul. Invariably they fall, but in the process they learn to renounce their vain ambitions. Through the agony of existence comes the wisdom that they must renounce the will to live. Similarly Schopenhauer turned from the relentless West to the restful East and pointed out that instead of wishing to change the world, man has to change his *wishes.* In art one learns of the worthlessness and absurdity of life by being shown that the tragedy of life consists in trying to change the world.

Thus for Schopenhauer the ethical way out of the dilemma of life is through *renunciation.* Every man must recognize that his own plight is just one tiny element in what is a universal condition. All humans—and, indeed, all life—are not alone in having to face a dreadful existence. We are all related through suffering and must therefore develop compassion for all living beings. We must renounce our selfish ways. Schopenhauer said that suffering expresses itself to all existence as its true destiny. Life is very deeply steeped in suffering, and there is no way out. We enter it amid tears, find its course always tragic, and die absurdly.

When Schopenhauer examined existence he did not find any Christian God to redeem man, but he could see the need for certain Christian virtues. Saintliness is the only way to flow with life and to protect ourselves from being badly wounded by outrageous fortune. Schopenhauer saw, that to be driven by our petty desires, jealousies, and angers is to bind ourselves in slavery. Man does not need his envy, his disturbing passions, or his hatred. Let him give them up then and give up looking upon the world as a place designed only to make him happy. Let him *deny* his will. Man needs to inscribe in his heart the commandment "Thou shalt not want." In our modern world it took an atheist to be one of the first to deeply and truly understand this Christian value.

If anyone had told Schopenhauer that his misanthropy resulted from his sickness, he would have answered that the sickness was not his but mankind's. If he were wrong in his pessimism about life, then it would be an easy matter simply to disregard him and get on with our living. If he were right, however, then we would have to dislike him for making us face an unpleasant reality. We usually dislike him, which may indicate that we find what he says disturbing.

If life was bitter to him, it is because he had tasted of it, as optimists often have not. And who can say that his way of deliverance—the way of saintly renunciation—is not the way for man in our world of turmoil and hydrogen bombs?

God and the Good

In their search for value, men have found answers in the way of pleasure, reason, virtue, duty, or in following the will. Arthur Schopenhauer thought that none of these answered the primary problem of human existence—suffering. Pleasure is never lasting, for it invariably gives way to pain. Men were once confident that the very universe itself was rational, but Schopenhauer found no basis for such confidence. Man, who has flattered himself as being *homo sapiens*, rational man, is a prisoner of blind irrational urges that govern his life. In this world of misery and pain, of irrational striving, of power and violence, how frail and weak virtue becomes. In such a world what meaning can duty have? How can it help alleviate the inherent pain of existence? It cannot, and in the face of such odds against a good life, one might as well give up. Thus Schopenhauer concluded that man should live by renouncing life. There seemed to be no other answer.

The theist—that is, the person who believes in a supreme being, a personal God—might well say that Schopenhauer's attitude provides an excellent illustration of the consequences that arise from the assumption of a godless universe. If Schopenhauer had believed in a supreme being, then he would not have seen the universe as simply the result of blind swirling atoms or as merely brute matter in motion; rather, he would have seen that it is the result of design and therefore has purpose. It is in terms of such purpose that human beings find meaning, find a reason for being and a reason for morality.

After all, why should one be moral? Why does it make sense to be moral? There must be some *basis* for morality but what can it be? Certainly if this standard or basis for morality is not eternal or absolute, it can work only within narrowly circumscribed limits, and whenever one gets beyond those limits one would become free of moral responsibility. This is not true morality, for when one is behaving according to certain norms only because of certain empirical sanctions—whether these be of the police, of public opinion, of learning experience, or of one's own guilt—then one is acting out of a sense of expediency, not out of a moral sense of right. If, however, there is a Supreme Being, who is all-powerful and eternal, then there is no end to His authority and therefore no end to moral responsibility. If God is *everywhere* and *always* is, then so is morality! One can get beyond the norms of his society or even beyond the norms one has internalized as a result of his own conditioning, but no one can ever get beyond the authority of an all-powerful God.

God's existence thus becomes an absolute basis for morality, for only if there is a God are moral norms always binding. It provides an answer to one of the most difficult problems of morality—the methodological problem of justifying *ought* statements. When one says something *ought* to be done, what is the source of that *ought*? If one says this ought to be done because of pleasure, of power, of the law, of society, or of one's own psychological needs, one is basing what we *ought* to do on something that *is* the case. Yet it is a fallacy to derive what *ought* to be from what *is*, for *ought* and *is* refer to different logical orders. There is thus no basis for ought statements in the physical world. The only case, the theist argues, in which we can derive what ought to be from what is, is the case of God. Because God is above the universe, not merely in it, we can derive moral statements from the fact of his existence. God does not exist merely in the way the things of the world exist. His existence is ultimately normative in character and can therefore serve as an ultimate standard for what ought to be done.

As far back as in ancient Greek philosophy Plato had recognized the problem of founding a workable ethics and appreciated the need for an absolute standard. In search of this he developed and formulated his theory of the Good, which was, in essence, the absolute that served as the normative basis for all life. The *Good* in Plato was not a personal God and thus lacked a certain existential force, which was to be supplied in the philosophy of St. Augustine. In Augustine, all morality was totally dependent on the Divine Absolute. A very perspicacious observer of man, Augustine saw that man is psychologically weak and cannot be left moral on his own. He expressed this idea by asserting that man was tainted by original sin and could be moral only by the grace of God. Unfortunately, St. Augustine's penetrating insights into the nature of man were couched in theological language and therefore lack appeal to the modern secular mind.

There seems to be a block or two on which the philosophy of Augustine, like many theistic ethical theories, invariably stumbles. Thus, it may indeed be the case that the assumption of God's existence can help with the problem of how man can know what he *ought* to do, but the question remains of how man can know there is such a God. We must also admit that philosophers and theologians have been trying to figure out arguments for His existence for the last twenty-five hundred years and still have not found a proof that conclusively establishes it. We may admire their tenacity but we must also doubt their credibility.

Furthermore, if one could believe in God, which God would one believe in? Theologians, philosophers, and religions have provided man with a variety of Gods. How is one to choose which to follow? The God of one religion may ordain a very different moral system than the God of a different religion, and the only way to settle it seems to be for the members of the various religions to go to war with each other—and thus we are back to power.

Even if one could prove that one specific God does exist, there would be the virtually insurmountable difficulty of knowing what He really believes is right, or is the Good, or is what we should do. Gods are not in the habit of discussing these matters of morals with us ordinary mortals. For the most part men have to interpret what they think God wants, and there is a striking tendency for people to imagine that He wants what they want. In this sense God is a supreme Charlie McCarthy, and man is the ventriloquist who puts moral words in his mouth.

Thus if we want to use God to solve certain problems of ethics, we still have to solve the problem of God. This predicament has led many thoughtful persons to agnosticism, or the position that one cannot know whether or not God exists. Others have answered that *the question of* the existence of God is not simply a rational question. It is not merely a question for the mind but also for the heart—for the whole man—and one has to find God in his guts as well as in his brains. When one does, one will be completely committed to God and will know in his whole being what he ought to do. This is, we can see, an essentially existential approach to religion and ethics. The great Danish philosopher Sören Kierkegaard took such an existentialist approach to ethics. Kierkegaard saw that neither the question of the existence of God nor the most important ethical decisions are matters of reasoning things out or of following certain religious or ethical rules. They are matters of deep religious faith and commitment by the individual. A man cannot safely follow rules and thereby do what is right; he must take a *religious* leap, for only if he does so will he know what he *should* do.

Kierkegaard's philosophy, we can notice from the little we have said of it already, straddles an important dividing line in the history of Western thought. From his vantage point in the nineteenth century he looked back into the past and forward into the future. On the one hand, his intensely Christian beliefs would seem to put him back in a period before traditional religion had been attacked by modern skepticism; on the other hand, his existential sense of God and man puts him much in the twentieth century. Kierkegaard's philosophy bridges two worlds, and we will now turn to it to see how this significant feat was accomplished.

The Existential Way to God: Kierkegaard

"Christ's judgment after all is surely decisive, inopportune as it must seem to the clerical gang of swindlers who have taken forcible possession of the firm 'Jesus Christ' and done a flourishing business under the name of Christianity."[23] Such a bitter denunciation of Christendom probably could

[23] *Attack upon Christendom*, trans. W. Lowrie (Boston, Mass.: The Beacon Press, 1956), p. 117.

not have been made with such deep feeling by an atheist, a materialist, and a communist such as Karl Marx, for the problem of Christianity was not felt in Marx's soul as it was in the soul of Sören Aabye Kierkegaard, the Christian. Marx attacked Christianity because he did not believe in it, but Kierkegaard found it unbearable because he did. Christians go to church, he said, to seek comfort, not God. Jesus, however, died in agony on the cross for he had asked everything for the truth in which He believed. Thus Jesus' life provided the first great example of the fact that it is dangerous to be a Christian. Of this Kierkegaard was completely convinced, for he recognized that the *explosiveness* of the truth of Christianity was so great it could destroy men living false lives. Thus he put aside the easy protection of the Church and the traditional philosophy of reason. To exist one has to put aside the easy ways of modern life and harken back to primitive *Christianity*. This was Kierkegaard's message, and nobody received it when he first sent it.

For Kierkegaard the central fact of modern life is the loss of Christianity. It had been lost because men wanted to *use* it to shelter and protect them. They used Christianity to close them to existence rather than to open them to it. Instead of giving man greater existence, the Church, by guarding him from the suffering and anxiety of life, gives him *nonexistence*. Man can exist on different levels, according to Kierkegaard, who saw three basic levels or stages of existence: the *aesthetic,* the *ethical,* and the *religious.* Of these, the richest, fullest, and most meaningful level is the religious. Only he who reaches the religious stage can truly be said to *exist.*

The first stage on life's way is the *aesthetic.* By aesthetic Kierkegaard did not mean that which refers to the beautiful as we usually understand the term today. Rather, he went back to the original Greek meaning of the word which is to sense, perceive, or feel. The man who remains at this stage of existence wishes primarily to gratify his sensual needs; he devotes his entire life to the pleasure of the moment. When that moment passes nothing is left but boredom, so that the man who searches only for pleasures of the senses loses meaning in his total life.

The aesthetic mode of life is riddled with contradictions, for when one seeks pleasure he finds only the pain of despair. Life does not work properly on this level. In an important sense man on the aesthetic stage of life is like a child: he searches for pleasure but tries to avoid responsibility, for it would necessitate taking a broader view of life, which would mean that he often has to forego many momentary satisfactions. The *esthete* attempts to avoid choosing; he wants everything—like the child who thinks he can play with all the toys in his closet at once. But the very attempt to avoid choosing is itself a choice. One chooses not to choose, to live without responsibility, and one cannot avoid the consequences of that choice—the uncertainty, the despair! One finds himself at the mercy of external circumstances, for his well-being is dependent not upon himself but upon events in the world.

If one grows up at all one learns that this is an unrewarding mode of behavior. Thus in order to overcome one's despair one chooses to live on a deeper level—the *ethical* level—where man becomes aware that there is more to life than the pleasure of the moment. He turns from the outer world and the aesthetic stage to his *own* inner world. The true ethical level as Kierkegaard understood it is not what philosophers, with their theories of ethics, imagine it to be. The job of ethics is not analyzing ethical concepts; it is living ethically. Ethical theory must be *subjective,* and ethical propositions should be *lived,* not merely *stated.* One can become ethical only by choosing with his life, and in so doing one moves beyond the aesthetic stage. To Kierkegaard, the logical positivist would be an example of an intellectual who thought he had reached the ethical level but was really still functioning on the aesthetic level, for he never explicitly commits himself.

Although the individual becomes responsible for himself on the ethical level, he still does not fully realize himself as an individual. He does not do so because choosing on the ethical level involves making a choice in accordance with a universal principle or a rule. An ethical rule is useful because it helps us make our decisions. One knows that one should not steal because there is a rule that says "Thou shalt not steal." One knows one should not kill because there is a rule that says "Thou shalt not kill." But there are existential situations of life to which no rule applies. Life is too rich and involved to be covered by rules. In fact, often our ethical choices are not between a good and an evil but between opposing goods or opposing evils. No rule is applicable in such cases. One has to decide for oneself, fully as an individual, and one cannot do this on the ethical level. In his *Fear and Trembling* Kierkegaard drew the line between the ethical and religious stage of life, showing how it becomes necessary to "leap" beyond our universal moral rules.

Kierkegaard began his argument by telling us that the ethical is universal, applying to everyone at every instant. Yet there are times when this universal might have to be suspended and when the individual may have to stand opposed to that universal. For example, there is an ethical rule that a father ought to love his son even more dearly than himself. Yet God came to Abraham and told him to sacrifice his son. Murdering one's son is hardly ethical, yet Abraham prepared to sacrifice his son. Was Kierkegaard here presenting philosophical justification for murderers? Leopold and Loeb, the famous "thrill killers" of Chicago in the 1920s, believed they could put aside the ethical and thus reasoned they were free to kill. As exceptional individuals, they took the position that moral rules were not applicable to them. This too was the assumption of Napoleon, who regarded himself as above morality. The same idea was dramatically presented in Dostoevski's *Crime and Punishment,* where the hero Raskolnikov did not see why a superior person like himself should feel restrained by moral rules against murder. And of course Nietzsche called for man to go beyond good and evil. Like Raskolnikov, Nietzsche felt that moral rules had no validity for superior individuals such as himself. Was Kierkegaard traveling in such company when he cited Abraham as an example that one may go beyond the ethical level, even to the point of killing one's own son? In fact he was not, for after announcing that the ethical should be suspended, he immediately parted company with his immoralist friends. Kierkegaard never said that the ethical should not be taken with utmost seriousness, nor that one should arrogantly put himself above it. Leopold and Loeb sacrificed their victim to their own vanity, but Abraham sacrified his son to God. This makes quite a difference. Abraham did not cooly decide that moral rules had no application to him; on the contrary, it was only with terrible anguish that he decided he had to put aside a moral rule to answer a higher calling. Indeed, Abraham was never easy in making his decision. He could never really be sure it was not a devil, pretending to be God, who came to him and demanded that he sacrifice his son Isaac. And even if it were God who demanded this sacrifice, it was still something that could be done only in *fear* and *trembling*. Isaac and Abraham went to the place where the sacrifice was to be made and Isaac got some wood for the altar. He was puzzled because there was no lamb for the burnt offering, for Abraham had not yet let Isaac in on the fact that he was going to be the lamb. It is not easy to tell one's son one is going to make a sacrificial lamb of him, but God had asked this of Abraham, and Abraham believed in Him so strongly that he could not turn away from Him. Abraham began to tie Isaac to the altar, but it was excruciatingly painful for him to do so. His hand trembled in great fear, and he felt a need to cry out against God who would demand a man's own son. Yet Abraham had faith and made ready to plunge the knife into Isaac's heart. At that very moment, an angel of Jehovah appeared and saved Isaac. Although many may feel turned off by this Hollywood ending, the main point of the story is important. It is that one must hold one's faith against all odds. To do anything else is to lose one's contact with God, the ultimate reality of existence. By religious faith a person can leap into existence, for he truly becomes himself by relating himself to God in faith.

Kierkegaard's point was that existence is not something that comes to a man without tormenting inner struggle and there are no easy smooth solutions. One cannot use a rational or logical system to figure out life; one cannot reason his way into existence. One can come to exist only through an "existential leap" into faith. Logical systems cannot answer the questions raised by life, for life does not work in a nice, neat, and logical way. For this reason Kierkegaard wanted to oppose all attempts of philosophy to rationalize or systematize life. In so doing, this lonely man in nineteenth-century Denmark developed ideas that not only have become foundation stones for existentialists of our day and have greatly influenced thinking about depth psychology but have great relevance for troubled men in the twentieth-century world. Against the impersonal forces working to destroy the individual and against the thought currents that discount the individual by overrationalizing and objectifying him, Sören Kierkegaard stood opposed with his very life.

In our own day, much more than in Kierkegaard's, one of the threats to the individual is the crowd, the modern phenomenon called the mass man. The crowd is the monster that eats individuality alive. Today social analysts clearly perceive the threat of a mass society in which man becomes lost in the organization and generally lives a life that is not his own but the public's. Kierkegaard felt this threat in the very marrow of his bones long before our present analysis of the *mass cult* and, what is most remarkable, he foresaw all the dangers, which have only recently emerged. Kierkegaard realized that the mass is shallow and crude and will not allow the individual any pure air to breathe. In giving himself over to the mass, man alienates himself from himself, for he loses what is uniquely himself to share in abstract group characteristics. His opinions belong not to him but to "them," and anything that is excellent is depreciated. The face of the crowd is empty and cold. The crowd is not truth, Kierkegaard said, thereby radically altering the conception of truth. We tend to regard truth as a property of propositions rather than as a property of things or persons or people; we think of it as highly objective, involving no personal considerations. But Kierkegaard denied that truth is always objective. In fact, in the most important matters he regarded it as *subjective*. We might say that something a man says is or is not true, but we would not ordinarily say a *man is true*. But Kierkegaard would. If a man lives a lie, if he pretends he is what he is not—as men who live in the mass do—then the man himself is untrue. Conversely, if one plunges into existence and does not pretend he is something he is not, then one is true. Kierkegaard wished to point out that the most important kind of truth is the truth that must be internalized. Knowledge that certain mathematical principles and factual statements are true is entirely an external matter. This is not the case with truths of religion. They must be a part of a person. The most educated clergyman who knows all truths of religion may himself be untruth incarnate; and the most ignorant peasant, if he lives with kindness, love, and humanity, may be a true man. In religion truth is not something you know; it is something you are.

This means, of course, that man must find truth for himself and must then appropriate it into his life. Truth cannot be given as a present. This is why many institutions of modern society are so inimical to man. They are designed to protect him from the pain and insecurities of life, and in doing so they actually protect him from the truth. If an individual is to find value and truth in his life, he must live as a free man. Because being free involves making real choices and because real choices involve conflict, they cannot be made without anxiety. Thus freedom is born in painful anxiety. Most men would rather live without freedom than with anxiety, and so they cut themselves off from the truth of their own being. The result is, ironically, that anxiety overtakes them anyway. Like contemporary psychoanalysts, Kierkegaard distinguishes between anxiety and fear. Fear is bearable because it refers to a *definite object*; we know what we are afraid of and can combat it. But anxiety is a sort of objectless fear; it is brought about by an unseen enemy, and that makes it all the more frightening. In two books, the *Concept of Dread* and *The Sickness unto Death*, Kierkegaard analyzed this terrible anxiety and the way it turns into *despair*. He had the perspicacious insight that despair, like anxiety, is not caused by anything *external* but by something internal. For example, if a man is in despair after having lost his fortune, we would conclude that the loss of his money caused him to despair. This is a false analysis for it is really the loss of his self that has caused the despair; the loss of his fortune only made the despair apparent, for without the distraction of his wealth he has become aware of the void in his existence. This becomes clear when we realize that the loss of fortune does not matter so much to a person who has a strong self. The same is true of all that is outside of us; the loss of any external thing disturbs us deeply only if we have no *inner* meaning.

The tragedy of this situation is that religion actually contributes to this spiritual sickness instead of healing it. With modern religion one is guaranteed all the·answers by the church and is thus really deprived of the authentic faith that comes only when one works through the problems of religion for himself. This is why Kierkegaard feared the institutionalization of religion, for with institutionalized religions one becomes religious as a way of escaping from himself. If one simply goes to the church he is supposed to go to, then one has not *decided* for himself to become religious. What could be a more basic part of man than his religion, and if he does not choose that for himself, how can he be himself? The church gives man all of the objective guarantees that cut him off from personal communication with God. If Christians really believe Christianity is the greatest thing in the world, they should become aware that it cannot be had for the asking. A man cannot go to the corner church to pick up religion as he would go to the corner store to buy bread. To be truly Christian one has to understand all of the paradoxes of Christianity; one has to doubt it, accept the terrible anxiety of that doubt, and still choose it. Only then can one really appropriate in his own being the very truth of Christianity. One then finds meaning within, for one has found God within. But when one tries to escape the doubts and the pains of life, one cuts oneself off from God and from one's own self: one is left, without strength, to face the despair of life.

Kierkegaard's philosophy was existentialist in the deepest sense, for he understood completely that man must get beyond the artificialities of life. This means that he must not take the easy way out by following forms and rituals. He must live spontaneously and respond, not to preconceived prejudices or abstractions but to what is essential to life.

> *It is said to have chanced in England that a man was attacked on the highway by a robber who had made himself unrecognizable by wearing a big wig. He falls upon the traveler, seizes him by the throat and shouts, "Your purse!" He gets the purse and keeps it, but the wig he throws away. A poor man comes along the same road, puts it on and arrives at the next town where the traveler had already denounced the crime, he is arrested, is recognized by the traveler, who takes his oath in the courtroom, sees the misunderstanding, turns to the judge and says, "It seems to me that the traveler has regard rather to the wig than to the man," and he asks permission to make a trial. He puts on the wig, seizes the traveler by the throat, crying, "Your purse!"—And the traveler recognizes the robber and offers to swear to it—the only trouble is that already he has taken an oath. So it is, in one way or another, with every man who has a "what" and is not attentive to the "how": he swears, he takes*

his oath, he runs errands, he ventures life and blood, he is executed—all on account of the wig.[24]

People go through life deciding, making judgments, condemning, and existing on the basis of the wig rather than of the man. This was Kierkegaard's way of telling us that men subsist too often on the hollow nourishment of *formalities*. They eat the husk and throw away the corn and never get to the essence of things. For him the essence of life was to be found in *God*. This was not the God the Sunday Christians bowed down before in church but a living God to be eternally encountered in life. Kierkegaard bore witness to this truth by giving up his own comforts, by sacrificing his physical well-being and financial security in order to go out into the streets to bring men the message of God. He deeply loved a girl named Regine but gave her up, not because he did not want a comfortable and happy life with her but because such a life would deflect him from his mission to serve God. People who involve themselves in mundane pleasures tend to become distracted from God, and Kierkegaard loved God with all his might.

There are many philosophers who have based *all* on God and have understood value and ethics only through Him, but none provides a better illustration of devotion to God. Not ethical rules or moral precepts but only a valid existential leap into faith can enable man to make an adequate ethical decision. Ultimately one must decide what he should do on the basis of faith, not on the basis of rules, and this involves a radical existential commitment. Such was the ethical ground on which Kierkegaard stood.

Is Might Right? The Ethics of Power

Traditionally the idea of Good and Evil in this universe guided the behavior of men, but as man gained more and more power on this earth, the world has become ugly with violence. Men thirsting for even more power are renouncing morality in order to get it. By the time of Friedrich Nietzsche (1844–1900) the traditional world of value was being blown to bits. With the rise of the industrial age the fuse of power was lighted, and the philosophy of Nietzsche was the dynamite that exploded in the world of ethical theory, driving men beyond good and evil. Power has always been important to men, but men have never had such an awesome amount of it, and that does make a difference. We live in a world in which power corrupts and crushes traditional values. Even our heroes, such as James Bond, are hired killers, creatures who put themselves above law and morality because they are licensed to kill. Ours is an *ugly* world of undreamt nuclear power, of nightmarish violence, of totalitarianism, of pollution and contamination, of lavish wealth alongside dreadful poverty. In such a world, has the doctrine that Might Is Right at last become a valid description of what the world has come to?

[24] "Concluding Unscientific Postscript: Postscript to the 'Philosophical Fragments'" in *A Kierkegaard Anthology*, ed. Robert Bretall (New York: Modern Library, n.d.), p. 258.

Perhaps there stands no more monumental symbol of the ugliness that the human being is capable of than Dachau. A suburb of Munich, Dachau is the site of the death camp Adolf Hitler had erected. Over 200,000 human beings were gassed to death there. When the war was over the United States took over Dachau, closed the camp and then reopened it as a United States army prison. At the end of January 1969 a news release from Munich informed us about the results of a court-martial at Dachau. Seven soldiers imprisoned at Dachau signed statements or testified under oath that certain beatings had taken place at the army's Dachau prison. Guards were alleged to have employed plastic hoses, wrapped in tape and doubled over, to beat the prisoners. One of the soldiers tried was Sergeant Wesley Williams, who was quoted as stating, "When they [the army prisoners] were brought into the maximum security block from the mess hall, one by one, my men and I were waiting behind the door. I told the prisoners to put their duffel bags on the table. Then one by one, the guards grabbed them and I hit them on the shoulder two to four times each."[25] Complaints were made that for no apparent reason prisoners were punched in the stomach, hit in the shoulder blades, knocked on the floor, and kicked. The commander of the prison, Major Moore, was quoted as saying, "Sometimes preventive force is necessary to deter prisoners. I have seven children at home and I hit them when necessary with a big wooden spoon, but I don't think I maltreat them."[26]

The guards who served under Major Moore were charged with maltreating prisoners at their court-martial. How did these guards plead? They pleaded innocent. On what ground? Did they deny beating prisoners? No! Their defense was, rather, that they were obeying orders. When Nazi guards from the Dachau concentration camp were tried as war criminals for their brutal and inhuman treatment of prisoners they too invoked the defense that they were only obeying orders. That defense was disallowed. There was, however, precedent for such a defense. In fact, in 1940 the American government published *The Rules of Land Warfare* in which soldiers were explicitly given the defense of *respondent superior*, in accordance with which a soldier could not be found guilty for doing what he was ordered to do by a superior officer. Paragraph 347 of *The Rules of Land Warfare* states "Individuals of the armed forces will not be punished for these offenses in case they are committed under the orders or sanction of their government or commander. . . ."[27] Such a defense, however, was overruled when the Nazis were tried at Nuremberg. New American guards at Dachau were using the same defense Nazi guards at Dachau had used. What was the decision? An Associated Press item, which appeared in the Philadelphia *Evening Bulletin* on January 31, 1969, announced that "A court-martial last night acquitted two U.S. Army stockade guards charged with maltreating prisoners."

[25] *The National Enquirer*, February 5, 1969, p. 12.

[26] *Ibid.*

[27] Quoted in Rene A. Wormser, *The Law* (New York: Simon and Schuster, 1949), p. 565.

Not only were these two acquitted but all the guards tried were found not guilty. Their defense of complying with a legal order from a superior was accepted. Were they acquitted, we must wonder, and was their defense of obeying an order accepted because the magnitude of their unlawful orders was so much less than that of the unlawful orders obeyed by the Nazis? Or were they acquitted because they represented those who were in power rather than those who had been vanquished?

During World War II, Dresden, the capital of Saxony, was so widely regarded as a great cultural center and was of such little significance militarily that it was never considered as a bombing target. What is more, thousands of Allied prisoners were quartered there and Dresden had in fact become a hospital city. Yet, in February 1945 on the eve of the war's end, Dresden was devastated by a "fire storm" bombing raid. In such a raid thousands of individual fires are combined into a gigantic single blaze, which brings in its wake terrible destruction. Hospitals and schools were destroyed and women and children were slaughtered by dive bombing attacks. R. H. S. Crossman states that a fire storm "was deliberately created in order to kill as many people as possible, and that the survivors were machine-gunned as they lay helpless in the open—all this has been established without a shadow of a doubt."[28] This massacre did not even have military significance. In fact, it so shocked the Germans that they resisted with greater effort than ever; if anything, the attack prolonged the war. Sir Winston Churchill was behind the raid, and the evidence is that it was carried out not to teach our Nazi enemies a lesson but to impress our Communist friends or allies. Churchill reasoned that after the war Stalin, whose soldiers were moving deep into Germany, would have to be dealt with in terms of realistic power, which has nothing to do with principles. Something dramatic was called for, and thus Sir Winston Churchill ordered the destruction of Dresden.

Shortly afterward, atomic bombs were dropped on Hiroshima and Nagasaki. The mushroom clouds of death signaled the truly horrible devastation that resulted from the bomb. General Eisenhower was deeply disturbed by the use of such power, but President Truman showed no signs of moral perplexity. Indeed Truman explicitly stated he never had any doubts about using the bomb.[29] Truman's justification for dropping these weapons of destruction was that doing so stopped the war and saved millions of lives. The available evidence, however, seems to indicate that this was only a rationalization and not the actual reason for dropping the atom bomb. As a matter of fact, the Joint Chiefs of Staff, who are not exactly what one would call a ban-the-bomb group, were all against using the bomb. General George C. Marshall maintained that there was no need to use the bomb because Russia's entry into the war with Japan would in itself be sufficient to bring the war to an end. Admiral William D. Leahy asserted:

[28] R. H. S. Crossman, "Apocalypse at Dresden," *Esquire*, November 1968, p. 154.

[29] See the quotations from Truman in Gar Alperowitz, *Atomic Diplomacy: Hiroshima and Potsdam* (New York: Simon and Schuster, 1965), p. 113.

It is my opinion that the use of this barbarous weapon at Hiroshima and Naga-saki was of no material assistance in our war against Japan. The Japanese were already defeated and ready to surrender. . . .[30]

The official American position was that we dropped the bomb to get Japan to surrender. The problem with this explanation is that all the evidence shows Japan was beaten so badly she was ready to surrender, although not *unconditionally*. The Allies had just about smashed the Japanese Imperial Navy, and Japan was being bombed to bits. The culmination came on March 10, 1945, when a bombing raid on Tokyo exacted 124,000 casualties. Japan was already sending out peace feelers. Chiang Kai-shek had been approached concerning the possibility of the surrender of Japan in December 1944, as was revealed in the diary of Secretary of War Henry L. Stimson. Furthermore, in April a new Japanese government had come into office, headed by a moderate man, Admiral Suzuki. His new foreign minister, Shigenori Togo took his post on the explicit understanding that he would be able to initiate efforts to end the war. To this end exploratory talks were undertaken with Russia. All of this suggests that there was no military necessity to use the atomic bomb on human beings. Why then was it used? Gar Alperowitz, who undertook the most careful analysis of this question, arrived at the conclusion that there is no conclusive answer to the question, but that the evidence suggests the bomb was used to end the war with Japan before Russia could get into it and thereby gain a foothold in Asia. This view is not based merely on circumstantial evidence, for Secretary of State James F. Byrnes had been quite explicit: "We wanted to get through with the Japanese phase of the war before the Russians came in," he said.[31]

If it is true that the terrible devastation of Dresden, Hiroshima, and Nagasaki was carried out not to save lives and shorten the war, not against our enemies but against our friends so as to provide the Western Allies with political advantage, would it not seem that such acts were crimes against humanity, and should not the perpetrators have been tried at Nuremberg? Why is it that only the defeated are ever found guilty of war crimes at War Crimes Tribunals? Is it that those who win never do anything wrong? Or is it that might makes right and that therefore whatever the mighty do cannot be regarded as wrong? R. H. S. Crossman says, "only Germans were brought to trial at Nuremberg" although "the Russians displayed their fair share of insensate inhumanity" and "the Western democracies were responsible for the most senseless single act of mass murder committed in the whole course of World War II."[32] Surely if the Axis powers had won the war, instead of us thinking of Eichmann as a fiendish war criminal, we would have had forced upon us the idea that Churchill and Truman were the fiendish war criminals. If the Nazis had emerged victorious, they would have told

[30] Quoted in Gar Alperowitz, "Why We Dropped the Bomb," *The Progressive*, August 1965, pp. 12f.

[31] Quoted in Alperowitz, *Atomic Diplomacy*, p. 112.

[32] Crossman, *op. cit.*, p. 149. The reference is to the bombing of Dresden, of course.

the world that what Eichmann did was necessary to shorten the war and save lives in the long run. And with the Nazis in power, the world would have believed them, just as the world believes the allied justifications for their destruction in Dresden, Hiroshima, and Nagasaki. Is it not the case then that what is taken as right and good is that which rests upon power? The idea that might is right and that morality is based upon power is one that has been very ably defended by some of mankind's most perceptive philosophers. In the Western world one of the first explicit statements of this power morality goes back to the Sophists in ancient Greece.

THRASYMACHUS

It was the view of the ancient Greek sophist philosopher Callicles that the people gang up on the few exceptional individuals among them. The inferior use their power to make the superior cower, and because of its power the majority is considered right by conventional opinion. There is one difficulty with this position: if there are individuals who are so superior by nature, how is it they always turn out to be losers? And if the inferior can band together and obtain power over the superior, then there is no point in calling them inferior. After all they have managed to overcome their handicap of inferiority and dominate society, whereas the superior, who are unable to take advantage of their natural abilities, end up dominated. The fact that these superior individuals are always in an inferior position does not say much for their superiority. Callicles insisted there are individuals who are naturally superior by nature, but if they are at the top of nature, why is it they are always at the bottom of the heap in society? How can we know there is natural superiority unless it *manifests* itself? We cannot know what nature intends except by actual *effects*. Thus if men are not in power, what basis is there for asserting that they belong in power?

Just this point was raised by Thrasymachus of Chalcedon, an otherwise obscure figure who is remembered today for his debate with Socrates in the first book of Plato's *Republic*. Thrasymachus' point was one for which all history provides testimony, and that is that *justice is in the interest of the stronger*. There is no natural right. Right is whatever those who have Might say it is. Callicles had claimed that inferior people of the world, who undoubtedly were not in the right, united to overpower superior people, who undoubtedly knew what was right but were not as strong as the masses. But Thrasymachus, who was an empiricist going only on empirical evidence, believed that those who actually had power had to be right, for right is whatever those in power say it is. Those in power make the rules—and make them for their own interests. If they can attain power, then it is not meaningful to call them inferior or to say that what they do is wrong. Those who cannot survive are actually the inferior ones. Thus what the strong do can never be wrong, and justice is always in their interest.

Thrasymachus' defense of an ethics of power is a classic in philosophic literature. No similar defense of power was explicitly formulated until modern times, when some great prophets appeared in the rank of the philosophers. Of these, Hobbes and Nietzsche are the most important, and both learned a great deal from the Italian historian, political scientist, and philosopher Machiavelli, whose name has come to be synonymous with the unprincipled exercise of power.

SUPPORT YOUR LOCAL SHERIFF: HOBBES

In the ancient and medieval world, men thought about politics by and large in terms of theoretical, moral, and religious principles. When philosophers talked about politics they concerned themselves with what *ought* to be. Men have always understood the importance of power, but they had never before held as much power in their hands as in the modern period of history. In a world consisting mostly of forces beyond his control man had always felt somewhat impotent, but as science developed man began to reverse the process and to subject nature to his own power. Now holding power in his own hands, man could get a better look at it and could attain a better understanding of its significance. No one understood more clearly the importance of power nor looked at it more squarely in the face than Niccolò Machiavelli (1469–1527). In discussing politics, he did not talk about what ought to be; he talked about what *is*. He understood politics in terms of the realities of power rather than in terms of moral or religious ideals. Machiavelli did not discuss such questions as the ideal political being, but he unashamedly discussed the best way to eliminate a political rival. That may not be nice, but that is what politics is about. James Burnham, himself a careful student of the realities of power, very clearly states the significance of Machiavelli:

> *Machiavelli delineates with sufficient clarity the field of politics. What are we talking about when we talk politics? Many, to judge by what they write, seem to think we are talking about man's search for the ideally good society, or his natural aspiration for peace and harmony, or something equally removed from the world as it is and has been. Machiavelli understood politics as primarily the study of the struggles for power among men. By so marking its field, we are assured that there is being discussed something that exists, not something spun out of an idealist's dreams or nightmares. . . . If our interest is in man as he is on this earth, so far as we can learn from the facts of history and experience, we must conclude that he has no natural aspiration for peace or harmony, he does not form states in order to achieve an ideally good society, nor does he accept mutual organization to secure maximum social welfare. But men, and groups of men, do, by various means, struggle among themselves for various increases in power and privilege. In the course of these struggles and as part of them, governments are established and overthrown, laws passed and violated, wars fought and won and lost. . . . Machiavelli's implied definition of the field of politics as the struggle for power is at least insurance against nonsense.*[33]

Machiavelli understood that there could be a political *science* only if men would look at facts rather than ideals and if they would understand the

---

[33] James Burnham, *The Machiavellians* (New York: The John Day Co., Inc., 1943), pp. 41f.

realm of politics in terms of moral hopes. Thomas Hobbes accepted these Machiavellian postulates and extended them in an effort to understand ethics itself in terms of the realities of power.

Hobbes started out by accepting what he took to be the plain fact that each man is not out for some general, universal, or abstract good but for his own particular, individual, and concrete power. In the state of nature, which existed before the political state developed, every man, out for his own power, was at every other man's throat. The natural condition of man, Hobbes said, is one of *"bellum omnium contra omnes"*—a war of all against all. According to him, the state of nature is characterized by "continuall feare, and danger of violent death," and the life of man in such a state can be described as "solitary, poore, nasty, brutish, and short."[34] Because man cares about his own skin, he has to do something about this state of affairs. In the state of nature, man is helpless. He cannot even appeal to a distinction between right and wrong because there is none. There is no right or wrong, no just or unjust, for everyone has a right to anything he can get away with, even another's life: "It followeth, that, in such a condition, every man has a right to everything; even to one another's body."[35]

This situation simply would not do for a creature who was concerned about his own well-being. In order to gain peace and security, men had to enter into a contract, by which Hobbes meant a mutual renunciation or transference of rights. Thus, men wanting to protect themselves from one another mutually agreed to transfer all right and power to one man, or a council, on the condition that everyone else would do the same. Man could escape the dreadful insecurity that comes from living in a state of nature by transferring all of his rights to a sovereign. As Hobbes saw it, a state in which every man had a "right" to anything he could get was a state in which no man had a right to anything. Therefore, the selfish individual has to place limits on his egoism, for if society were nothing but selfish individuals all fighting for narrow interests, then no one would be safe. If people all carried guns and lived by the law of the gun, everyone would get shot or would be in constant danger of getting shot. Even being the "fastest gun in the West" offers little security, for as we know from countless movies, the most powerful are often the most vulnerable because they make such inviting targets. The stronger you are and the more you can get from other people, the more ambitious men will try to figure out ways to beat you. Thus arises the need for one strong gun to keep order. Those who wish to live in peace and security would do well to support their local sheriff.

Hobbes recognized only one type of pact, the *pactum subiectionis*—that is, a pact that invests the ruler with virtually unconditional power, the only exception being that he must govern and keep order. If the sheriff or sovereign is going to keep order and protect us, he must have power. Men must accept his rule and are obligated to obey it in return for order. Right and wrong must be determined by the laws of the sovereign, and they cannot be questioned. Thus men cannot contend there are laws higher than the sov-

[34] Thomas Hobbes, *Leviathan* (New York: E. P. Dutton, Co., 1950), p. 104.
[35] *Ibid.*, p. 107.

ereign's and cannot appeal to some sort of "natural law" or "moral law" by which to judge the positive law of the sovereign. "This town isn't big enough for two kinds of laws," they would say in the movies, and thus positive law must become the basis for moral law. This makes it possible to assure order. If right and wrong are to have meaning, they must be backed up by power, and the sovereign has the power to do it. Hobbes thought that covenants without the sword are only empty words. To be meaningful, morality must be based on power: "The bends of words are too weak to bridle men's ambition, avarice, anger and other Passions, without the feare of some coercive Power. . . ."[36]

Hobbes formulated his views in a most systematic and circumspect manner and did so with an understanding of the complicated social conditions of his time. Yet in essence his message was much the same as that of Thrasymachus—*Might Is Right!*

In the classical world Aristotle explained the motivation for knowledge in terms of curiosity. In the modern world, with science making it possible for man to attain more power than ever before, Francis Bacon explained knowledge in terms of power. Knowledge gives man power, and that is why man should seek knowledge. Man needs knowledge not to satisfy his idle curiosity to understand what the world is like but to control the world. This impulse for domination increased as modern scientific civilization progressed. No man understood this better, or expressed it more explosively, than Friedrich Nietzsche.

THE POWER AND THE GORY: FRIEDRICH NIETZSCHE

According to Arthur Schopenhauer, the basic driving force in all nature is will. This will is not only a will to life but also a will to peace and contentment. Naturally, Schopenhauer was gloomy about this will and its prospects for satisfaction, because there is no peace or contentment to be found in this crazy world. Nietzsche, however, declared that there is no reason to be pessimistic; the will of man, he said, is not just a will to life or to peace: it is a will to power. "Only where there is life, is there also will: not, however, will to life, but so teach I thee—Will to Power."[37]

If peace were the most important goal for man, we would have to agree with Sophocles that we could "Call no man fortunate that is not dead." But if life is the will to power, then one does not have to be dead to be fortunate, for one can accept the struggle and turmoil of life as part of the never-ending contest for power. Today, there is perhaps too much emphasis on peace of mind and peace of soul, much of which seems to involve an attempt to escape from what is involved in life. Even psychiatry tries to find peace for its patients, calling such peace "adjustment." But, we might ask, "adjustment to what"? In a world seething with violence and suffering, there may be something absurd in making a fetish of "adjustment" and ultimate

[36] *Ibid.*, p. 113.

[37] *Thus Spake Zarathustra*, in *The Philosophy of Nietzsche* (New York: Random House, Inc., 1927), p. 25.

satisfaction. What is more, this emphasis on adjustment contributes to the factors that tend to make man a thing, for we approach the task of "adjusting" him as though it were not very different from adjusting a machine. In such a context, the philosophy of Nietzsche, who refused to be "adjusted," may be just what we need.

Nietzsche was, of course, a great psychologist. He saw the inside of man—how he rationalizes, feels guilt, compensates, and sublimates—long before Freud. And he saw, as Freud never did, that man ever strives for power.

Nietzsche's metaphysic of the will to power explains much that alternative theories of value fail to explain, accounting for much that is involved in the process of valuation. The most influential theories of valuation, the Kantian and the utilitarian, fail to account for much that can be explained on the theory of the will to power. According to utilitarian theory, the good is that which gives pleasure. The problem with this theory, as we have seen already, is that most people insist on making a distinction between pleasure and good. A life of crime might bring a successful criminal much pleasure, but even the criminal probably would not describe his activities as good. On the other hand, Kant maintains that *only* duty and a good will can be good. The trouble with this theory is that if the utilitarians go too far in saying that pleasure is always good, then Kant also goes too far in saying that pleasure is never good.

Nietzsche's theory avoids both of these errors. By saying that the good is a will to power he meant that men *create* their own values; they do not find them ready made. According to the utilitarians we much value the things we possess, but according to Nietzsche things possess value only insofar as we *interact* with them. In a sense, things do not just have value for us; we have to *make* things valuable. For this reason Nietzsche saw no reason to be pessimistic, for the fact that life does not provide value for man is no problem in his eyes. Man must create his own values.

The most fundamental observation that can be made about Nietzsche's philosophy of the will to power is that it was the ultimate consummation of metaphysical theories in the Western world. For Plato reality consisted in eternal Forms, which he called Ideas; for Aristotle, Spinoza, and most of classical philosophy reality was understood in terms of the category of *substance*. When Kant showed that reality cannot be found *independently* of the perceiving self, the objective order of things was beginning to break down. Kant was one of the first to *effectively* make reality ultimately unknowable, and without a knowable objective reality, man would be left with nothing—that is, nothing but his will. Accordingly, Schopenhauer focused on will, seeing the main form of will as the will to live. Nietzsche went one step farther, transforming this will to live into a *will to power*. This transformation had been inherent in Western philosophy ever since Sir Francis Bacon announced in the seventeenth century that the aim of knowledge was to get power over things. Thereafter men no longer wanted to know about the universe because it was God's, and by knowing it they could know him. On the contrary, they wanted to know about the universe because it was *theirs,* and by knowing it they could control it. Indeed, God became unnecessary in a world that belonged to men and that men could control.

Nietzsche did not flinch from the fact that God had no place in the modern world. Although he is famous for announcing, in his *Thus Spake Zarathustra,* that "God is dead!" we must recognize that Nietzsche did not kill Him. Rather, he was recording a cultural fact—the cultural fact that God no longer occupies the place in the life of men He once did. God is dead not in the sense that He once objectively existed and then ceased existing; He is dead in the sense that He has died in the hearts and minds of Christians, for they no longer believe in Him. Instead, they believe in science, utility, economics, the nation, and they manage to reserve a few minutes for God on Sunday. Like Kierkegaard, Nietzsche recognized that the various churches in modern society were not temples of God; on the contrary, they were nothing but *tombs* of God.

The question of God's existence cannot be reduced to the level of an academic game in which one side produces arguments to show that there is a God and the other side, to show there isn't. If one is going to argue that God does not exist, then the important thing is to face the consequences of His nonexistence. Many atheists are so involved in the trivialities and details of their arguments about God's nonexistence that they fail to realize if God does not exist, then man's own life loses its meaningfulness. The Russian novelist Dostoyevski declared that if God does not exist, then there is no moral order to the universe and everything is permitted. Only when one realizes the truth of Dostoyevski's statement and still can affirm that there is no God can one really be an atheist. But few ever dare face that consequence, for it means facing the fact that *all* the values that have ever given man any comfort or hope lose their anchor, which had been firmly rooted in God and disappear into the sea of nothingness. Man is left alienated in a lonely and hostile universe.

Nietzsche faced this consequence, fully understood it, and refused to back away. God is absent in our lives today because he has slipped out of our hearts and souls, and thus man has lost his internal sense of meaningfulness. Yet, Nietzsche argued, man can find distractions to make him forget God or substitute gods embodied in totalitarian collectivities. In this way Nietzsche, who suffered deeply and thoroughly in his soul all the tormenting consequences of the loss of God, was able to say yes to life with the truest heroism. As Nietzsche saw it, if there is no God, then the only thing left for men is power. Men can forget there is no God by devoting themselves to the attainment of power; and if they get enough, they can in a very real sense make gods of themselves. Thus Nietzsche celebrated power, rejecting the peace of God for the fury of Dionysius. He exalted power and would not shirk cruelty. He placed himself in opposition to all sentimentality.

But let us not forget that Nietzsche did not kill God; he was merely the coroner who looked at the facts of modern life and found Him dead. It is as though Nietzsche, who went mad in the later part of his life, was personally suffering the death of God for all mankind; like Christ, this anti-Christ suffered for our sins. In fact, he signed one of his letters "The Crucified One."

Nietzsche once said that he was "dynamite," and this is true. Tragically for him, the Dionysian forces he took within himself exploded and he blew himself up. Still more tragically, what happened to Nietzsche psychologically could happen to all of us in a much more literal way, for today when man has turned from God to the search for power, he has gained the power to blow everything up. Like Nietzsche we must, as he beseeched us to do, somehow learn to say yes to life even in a godless world. But we must also learn to very carefully control our will to power, and this is something that Nietzsche, who did not clearly enough delimit the power concept, failed to do. We cannot afford, inwardly or outwardly, to unleash all the fury of Dionysius, as he did. We must make sure our will to power is for power over our own selves and not over the rest of the world, or else we shall lose the rest of the world and ourselves with it. The power man learns to gain over himself can result in human glory. The power man attempts to win over the world can only have a gory ending. Nietzsche, in his career, dramatized the struggle we must all fight, and his fate is a sad reminder of the high cost of living that struggle.

Man, Nature, and Metaethics

Traditionally ethical philosophers sought to formulate moral systems. They developed theories of right and wrong and good and evil, in terms of which they derived guidelines for human conduct. They gave us moral principles and rules to live by. These ethical systems or doctrines were based upon such assumptions as pleasure, duty, reason, will, God, power, and with the development of evolutionary theory, nature. Yet, despite the thousands of years spent in developing these systems, no one has ever succeeded in *proving* what is right or good. Physical theories can be proven because they can be dealt with experimentally. But because what ought to be has nothing to do with the factual, there seems no way to experiment with it. Thus philosophers have finally become fed up with trying to tell us what is right and good. They have become disenchanted with ethics. For this reason they have shifted from ethics to *metaethics*—that is, instead of developing theories of ethics directly, they began to talk *about* ethics. They concerned themselves not with what is right or good but with the meaning of such terms as right and good. On the metaethical level, philosophers studied the meaning and function of ethical terms and gave consideration to such issues as how ethical predicates or theories might be justified. Work on the level of metaethics is more concerned with analyzing principles of value than with formulating them.

On the metaethical level of analysis, some philosophers came to the conclusion ethical terms have no meaning; since they cannot be verified in an empirical sense, they are just nonsense. In his examination of what ethical terms can mean, however, John Dewey developed an intriguing approach by which he showed that ethical terms could be empirically verified. Thus Dewey laid the foundations upon which it might be possible to construct a science of value. He took human nature as a norm for measuring value and showed that it is far less changing than relativists assume. Since ethics has to do with the conduct of men, taking Man as the measure of value seems a most meaningful way to deal with traditional ethical problems. The procedure is to find the universal needs of man and to employ them as normative ideals. One need of man, which is increasingly coming to be regarded as basic, is *love*. There are rich possibilities in building an ethical theory on the idea of man and love. Thus, out of metaethical analysis emerge interesting suggestions for the direction future analysis might take.

Contemporary Ethics

In the last century one of the main attempts to create a science of value on the model of *empirical science* was undertaken in the framework of utilitarianism. Bentham had insisted that the only valid ground on which an ethical theory can stand is pleasure; when people claim that something is good, they mean that it gives them *pleasure*. He tried to demonstrate the possibility of being scientific about ethics or value by devising a *hedonic calculus* designed to calculate units of pleasure and pain. If you want to know how good something is, you measure how many units of pleasure it gives and if you want to know how bad something is, you measure the units of pain.

G. E. Moore, the great twentieth-century British representative of ethical nonnaturalism, maintained that any attempt to define an ethical term such as *good* by using natural properties as pleasure was an example of what he called the *naturalistic fallacy*. To see why this is a fallacy, notice that even if we define "good" as pleasure, we may still want to say that something is good but is not pleasant. When someone ponders whether pleasure is good he usually believes he is coming to grips with a serious question. He certainly is not pondering whether pleasure is pleasant. In other words, when anyone raises the question of whether pleasure, or for that matter any natural property, is good, he knows the good is something distinct from pleasure and is seeking the connection between the two.

Suppose the majority of people in the world became transformed into cannibals and experienced *intense pleasure* from eating members of minority groups. Even though this practice yielded such pleasure, might we not ask if such was good for the majority? Yet if the good were defined as pleasure it would not be meaningful to ask if that which gave pleasure were good, for by definition it would have to be. Moore believed it impossible to define good in terms of naturalistic properties because there would always be instances in which we could say something had the natural property but was still not good. If we had a proper definition, this would not be the case, because a proper definition is a tautology. For example, we could never say something is a square and then ask if it is a four-sided figure, because we know that by definition a square must always be a four-sided figure.

Moore's critique cut down the timber of more ethical theories than it was intended to, for it showed not only that naturalistic properties will not suffice to define good but also that good could not be defined at all, because there will always be some instance in which it would be possible to deny that something meeting the requirements of any particular definition was really good. Therefore, since it was not possible to define good, G. E. Moore reasoned that the property of good must be a very special kind of entity. But what kind?

The good, Moore answered, must be understood as that which is both *simple* and *nonnaturalistic*. It is impossible to define "yellow" to a blind man so that he can really grasp the meaning of it, for one must *see* what *yellow* is to really understand. Informing the blind man that yellow refers to light of a certain number of wave lengths does not give him any sense of what the color is. A color, such as yellow, can be defined simply by *pointing* to it. This is because it is *simple*. In the same way good is simple. It is a unique property. However, it is unlike a color in that it is also *nonnatural*. How can we distinguish a natural from a nonnatural property? Moore admitted that this was a tough question, but he came up with an easy answer. He said that if we can imagine a property *as existing by itself in time*, it is a natural property; if not, it is nonnatural. The problem with this definition, as philosopher C. D. Broad pointed out, is that *no* property or characteristic can be said to exist *in time by itself*. Thus there was no way to distinguish between natural and nonnatural properties. This criticism was so convincing that Moore himself was convinced and had to admit that his view was silly.

Nonetheless, historically Moore's conception of good as nonnatural had a curious influence on the ethical philosophy of logical empiricism or logical positivism. The logical positivists, who are empiricists, did an interesting thing. They agreed with Moore that no natural property can be used to define an ethical predicate. They could accept that much of Moore, but his validition of ethics in terms of intuition, as something that could simply be pointed to, was too much. Yet if they followed Moore in eliminating the empirical basis of ethics and then went on to eliminate his intuitional basis, then *nothing* would be left. Exactly! The logical positivists eliminated ethics as a valid field of knowledge.

The foundations of logical positivism were laid in the Vienna Circle, which originated in a seminar given by Moritz Schlick. Yet Schlick himself did not draw the conclusion that ethical statements are meaningless. As a matter of fact Schlick, in his *Problems of Ethics*, developed a normative ethical theory along hedonistic lines, holding that the morally good is that which brings the greatest happiness. One of the earliest statements of the *emotive theory*, which came to be the orthodox positivist theory of ethics, was set forth by Charles Ogden and I. A. Richards, who emphasized the importance of feeling in art. They made the point that language can be used either to describe an object or to express a feeling about it. If some-one tells us that a painting is excellent he conveys no information to us about the painting. In science such emotive language is not used; instead, science depends on symbolic language. In the former there is no reference to the object, but in the latter there is. This difference between emotive language used in art and the lack of it in science is at the heart of the fundamental cleavage between art and science. Early logical positivists adopted this Ogden-Richards approach and applied it to ethics. In 1935, in his *Philosophy and Logical Syntax,* Rudolf Carnap claimed that only mathematical-logical and empirical propositions are meaningful and that ethical propositions are neither of these two kinds. This is the theory that Alfred Jules Ayer elaborated and popularized, which has come to be known as the *emotive* theory of ethics. Ayer denied that ethics can be given a naturalistic interpretation and admitted ethical statements are nonnaturalistic, but he denied that the nonnatural had any cognitive validity —that is, he denied that it could be known. His conclusion was that there can be no hope for an empirical science of value. Value—or ethical— statements are not empirical and, as Moore had said, there cannot be a nonempirical or intuitive science of value. For this reason Ayer concluded that ethical statements are meaningless:

> The presence of an ethical symbol in a proposition adds nothing to its factual content. Thus if I say to someone, "You acted wrongly in stealing that money," I am not stating anything more than if I had simply said, "You stole that money." In adding that this action is wrong I am not making any further statement about it. I am simply evincing my moral disapproval of it. . . .[38]

Objectivists maintained that ethical statements provide us with infor-mation about the world; *subjectivists* claimed that they provide us with no information about the world but only with information about our own feelings. The logical positivists went one step further and claimed that ethical statements not only provide no information about the world but they do not even give meaningful expression to our feelings. According to Ayer, all they do is *vocalize* our feelings. They are excellent for clearing throats, but nothing more; they are just *excitants* of feelings, which "assert" nothing.

Ethical philosophies contend that ethical utterances provide us with knowledge, but, as Ayer pointed out, for a sentence to convey knowledge it must be an *assertion.* Any proposition about the empirical world must be capable of being *confirmed* or *disconfirmed*—that is, it can be *tested* by that world. If it cannot be confirmed or disconfirmed by comparison with the real world, then it must be sheer nonsense. The test of whether a sentence contains a proposition about the empirical world is whether it can be called true or false, and the only sentences we can characterize as being true or false are those that make *assertions.* The primary types of sentences are:

[38] Alfred Jules Ayer, *Language, Truth and Logic* (New York: Dover Publications, n.d.), p. 107.

1. DECLARATIVE: make assertions
2. EXCLAMATORY: make exclamations
3. IMPERATIVE: make commands
4. INTERROGATIVE: ask questions

We do not characterize exclamatory, imperative, or interrogative sentences as being *true* or *false*. Only declarative sentences may be judged true or false. The declarative sentence "It is raining" certainly may be determined to be either true or false. One may very well look out the window and see. However, if someone asked, "Is it raining?" and another person said, "Hm, that's true," we would say that the reply makes no sense, for there is obviously no way in which the question can be true or false. Similarly, if a person uttered the imperative sentence to another: "Shut the door," we would consider the other to be not very bright if he shook his head and said, "That's true."

There is a type of sentence that in form meets the requirements of a *declarative sentence* and yet provides problems that can be rather thorny. Consider the following sentence:

> *"The Sultan, the Chief Executive of the United States, is making a tour through Georgia, where he hopes to find a Sultana or a wife."*

Is this statement true or false? Obviously it is false. But in what sense is it false? If he had said that Richard Nixon is in Georgia looking for a wife we could say it was false on the grounds that Richard Nixon is not in Georgia looking for a wife. That is clear enough. But if we treated this sentence the same way we would have to say that the Sultan, the Chief Executive of the United States, is not in Georgia looking for a wife. We can recognize at once that this answer is quite misleading. The only conclusion we can reach is that it is not even possible to say the statement about the Sultan is false *because there is no Sultan of the United States* about whom a proposition could be either true or false. Sentences like this cannot be called true or false because they are based on *false assumptions*. Our example seems to be a declarative sentence, but that is deceptive. Technically it cannot be said such a sentence is true or false, because there is *no* Sultan of the United States. "The Sultan of the United States" is a false assumption.

According to the logical positivists, the situation is very similar with sentences containing *ethical predicates*, for ethical predicates have no basis in reality. They are false assumptions. Thus, for example, the sentence "This box is made of wood" may be true or false, because it is possible a box is or is not made of wood. "Wood" refers to a material that exists in the empirical world, and thus statements pertaining to it can be affirmed or denied. But what do words such as "right" or "wrong" refer to? Nothing. Think of the following sentence: "Shooting a man in the heart with a bullet from a high-powered rifle will kill him." This sentence can be affirmed or denied, because it is capable of being tested. We can check the records of every incident where someone has been shot in the heart to see if he dies. The sentence is therefore a declarative sentence and it makes an *assertion*, which can meaningfully be said to be true or false. It is quite different from a sentence of this type: "It is wrong to shoot a man and to kill him."

There is no way to *test* such a proposition, and hence there is no sense in even calling such a grouping of words a proposition. No amount of checking records or of observing cases of men being shot and killed will provide proof that behavior is either right or wrong. Many persons may not like to see others shot, but then again many others may indeed like it or there would not be so much of it going on. In any case, nothing can be proved about ethical terms because they do not refer to objective or empirical properties of the world. They are meaningless or, as A. J. Ayer said, they are nothing but *ejaculations*. As far as intellectual content is concerned, no more is achieved by saying that something is wrong than by groaning or moaning. If Ayer is correct, then the philosophers who have dedicated their lives to creating ethical theories could have done just as well by grunting.

To be sure, men and women get into very heated debates over ethical questions. We might well ask how people can argue about ethical statements if ethical predicates have no meaning. Ayer's answer was that they cannot. He admitted that people argue, but he claimed that they do not really argue about questions of value. According to him, if we look closely we will find that people are really arguing about questions of facts or about nothing. People who seem to be arguing about questions of value are really behaving in patterns dictated by certain habits that they call moral but in fact have nothing to do with morality. These patterns should be studied by social scientists, not by ethical philosophers. The moral habits of a group of people are of interest to social sciences, but they cannot be the basis of a moral science. As Ayer explains:

> There cannot be such a thing as ethical science, if by ethical science one means the elaboration of a "true" system of morals. For ... as ethical judgments are mere expressions of feeling, there can be no way of determining the validity of any ethical system. ...[39]

In evaluating Ayer's ethical theories we should note that his assumption (that his theory of ethics was *descriptive*) seems to be less than valid. Ayer claimed that he was not telling us how ethical statements *should* be used but how they *are* used. Yet his theory describes precisely how ethical statements are *not* used. Thus, while Ayer claimed that ethical statements cannot be true or false, the fact is that ordinary language does construe them as true or false. Far from reporting ordinary linguistic usage, Ayer's view is quite opposed to it. Today, when a great intellectual effort is needed to understand morality, it seems perverse to insist that we follow ordinary language in order to do it; but even if we accept this idea, it is not what Ayer did. In any event, it was early recognized, even by those in the positivist camp,

[39] Ayer, *Language, Truth, and Logic* (New York: Dover Publications, n.d.), p. 112.

that Ayer's emotivist theory had serious flaws. For this reason C. L. Stevenson's important modification of the emotivist position was welcomed by the positivists.

C. L. Stevenson saw that cognitive meaning plays a more important role in ethical judgments than positivists, such as Ayer, had allowed, According to him, there were two ways in which people could agree or disagree with each other. They could agree or disagree in *beliefs*, which is rational; or they could agree or disagree in *attitude*, which is not rational. Agreement or disagreement in science, Stevenson maintained, are matters of belief and therefore rational, whereas ethical disputes are disagreements in attitude, and therefore nonrational. As Stevenson explained:

> *The reasons which support or attack an ethical judgment ... are related to the judgment psychologically rather than logically. They do not strictly imply the judgment in the way that axioms imply theorems; nor are they related to the judgment inductively, as statements describing observations are related to scientific laws.*[40]

So far this sounds like Ayer, with its insistence on the noncognitive nature of ethical judgments. But unlike Ayer, Stevenson also saw an important descriptive component of ethical discourse. According to him, although the controversial aspects of ethics spring from disagreement in *attitude*, it must be remembered that these "irrational" attitudes are often shaped by "rational" beliefs. Stevenson developed his analysis of ethical judgment in terms of "working models." According to Stevenson's analysis, the following debate about good and bad:

A:
> *This is good.*

B:
> *No, it is bad.*

can be translated by a working model into the following form:

A:
> *I approve of this; do so as well.*

B:
> *No, I disapprove of it; do so as well.*[41]

This model illustrates the descriptive and emotive elements that are present in ethical judgments. The *declarative* part of the sentence—"I approve"—is descriptive of the attitude that the *imperative* clause—"do so as well"—expresses. The declarative part characterizes one's attitude as being one of approval or disapproval; the imperative part is basically an attempt

[40] Charles L. Stevenson, *Ethics and Language* (New Haven: Yale University Press, 1944), p. 113.

[41] *Ibid.*, p. 22.

to arouse emotion. It seeks to redirect attitudes. Thus the very essence of ethical terms such as "good" is their *emotive* meaning, which functions to alter attitudes by the mechanism of *suggestion*. In this sense ethical terms are basically *persuasive*. When we say that something is "good" we do not mean that it possesses some very noble property ("goodness") but that we want to persuade another to see things as we do. This is why Stevenson insisted that ethical judgments look mainly to the future, for they are made to encourage or discourage acts in the future. Stevenson believed that the emotive, persuasive aspect of ethical judgments is the main part. Rational methods are of no avail in bringing about *attitude* change; to cause a change in "beliefs" it is essential to adduce evidence that is logically relevant, but to change attitudes anything goes—one just has to make the hearer *believe* him. It does not matter if what one says is logical or makes sense, for in ethics anything is relevant that actually makes a person change his mind.

There are three basic difficulties with Stevenson's theory. The first concerns his distinction between belief and attitude; the second concerns his view that we make ethical judgments primarily to persuade others to our own cause; and the third has to do with his idea that anything is relevant in resolving ethical disagreement.

Stevenson denied there can be a science of value on the grounds that statements of value are based on attitudes, whereas statements of science are based on belief. However, this sharp distinction between belief and attitude is in fact not tenable. Ultimately belief itself is a certain kind of attitude; it is the attitude of being interested in matters of truth. The whole positivist ethical structure is based on a distinction between fact and value, science and ethics, but the basis of science is the search for truth, and truth itself is a value. Ultimately both ethics and science are founded on a faith. Thus the positivistic distinction between the cognitive and noncognitive types of discourse has its limitations.

The second inadequacy in Stevenson's thesis is his view that statements of morals are primarily intended to persuade. Actually the reasons why people make judgments of value are very complicated; there is no simple explanation such as persuasion. One thing we can be relatively sure of is that, inasmuch as values are real to people (if not to positivists), people do like to register their convictions about values even though they know that others will not be persuaded to accept them. Indeed some individuals may want others to know where they stand even though that will alienate rather than persuade them. Often people utter moral judgments in the hope of persuading others, but this is not always the case. Motivation is a complex psychological problem, and much more evidence would be needed than Stevenson has summoned. Yet I think we may safely assume that while ethical judgments are sometimes made in order to redirect attitudes, there are times when they are made simply as pronouncements about the world, which is, after all, believed by many to be in part moral.

Finally, it is not the case that anything goes in ethical disputes. If someone changes his mind about the communist party because he falls in love with a girl who belongs to it, I doubt that anyone would regard that as ethically relevant. There are many ways one can alter attitudes that would not be considered ethical.

Because the positivist theory allows no way to verify ethical pronouncements, most positivists are forced to take a radically subjectivistic interpretation of ethics. But in a very interesting book, *The Logic of Moral Discourse,* one logical positivist, Professor Paul Edwards, has shown how an emotivist can take an objectivist approach. As a positivist, Professor Edwards denied that ethical statements have any *ontological* status and also asserted that ethical statements function *emotively.* Nevertheless, he showed that when one says Mr. X is a good person one is referring to certain qualities in Mr. X and not necessarily to one's own approval.

As time went on, arguments such as this made it increasingly apparent that the early positivistic strictures on ethics went too far. In trying to stick to the facts the positivists missed the facts of moral life. It is simply unrealistic to say, for example, that when someone says a movie was good, he is merely commending it, grunting his approval, and attempting to guide the choices of others. We miss the whole point of his value statement if we do not ask why he wanted to commend the movie. Is it not because the movie possessed certain objective features or properties that are describable: good direction, acting, scenery, or plot? Similarly, when one says that a particular action is good, he may wish to convey his approval and convince others, but he is also referring to certain features of the act that make him want to commend it.

For these reasons it has been argued that the positivistic-analytic tradition, by its denial of objectivity or a substantial meaningfulness to value statements, impoverishes the moral world. In the fight for a better and more humane world something more is needed than the antinaturalistic debunking of ethical discourse. This something more has been provided by the ethical naturalists, who always insisted that ethical values are based on more than subjective feelings. In our own century the great American philosopher John Dewey (1858–1952), taking a naturalistic approach accepted the positivistic challenge and responded to it with vigor, dedicating his entire philosophy and life to building a science of value. As an answer to positivists like Ayer, who believed that only the empirically verifiable is meaningful and that ethical judgments therefore are not meaningful, Dewey developed a very ingenious analysis, which revealed that ethical statements are empirically verifiable.

Because Ayer had claimed that statements of value say nothing, Dewey decided to begin his analysis with a consideration of phenomena that admittedly say nothing. The first cries of a baby, for example, are purely ejaculatory. When a baby first cries he is certainly not expressing any theory of value; he is just manifesting facts of organic behavior. A mother will take the baby's cry as a sign that it is hungry or that a pin is pricking it, and she will act to change this organic condition. As time goes by the baby quickly recognizes that there is a connection between its crying and the mother's help. At this point the baby learns to cry, not just to make noise and express its discomfort but to recruit its mother's help. Thus cries that were at first ejaculatory become purposeful. What is more, the crying has become a *social activity,* for it is intended to evoke a response in another. This purposeful type of crying functions as a social sign. It has meaning, and propositions concerning it can be *empirically verified.*

According to Dewey then, even if valuations were ejaculations, like the baby's first cry, they could still be *meaningful.* For example, an ejaculation such as "Help!" taken in itself, certainly is not an explicit value expression; but if it is taken in connection with its existential context, then the ejaculation does amount to an affirmation, although not in so many words, that the situation with reference to which the cry was made is "bad" in the sense that it is objected to and that it can be made better with the aid of others. The significance of this is, Dewey found, that an empirical basis for asserting valuations can be shown to be meaningful. He found it by actually looking into the dynamics of the general behavior of men. Unlike the positivists, Dewey knew that an adequate theory of value must not merely account for the way people *talk,* but for their *general behavior.* He also knew that examining the *actual usage* of ethical terms could not solve our problems of value, for the positivistic-analytic had been simply naive when it assumes that logical analysis of the actual usage of ethical terms by plain people can serve as a model that will clarify all problems of value. The actual use of ethical terms is ambiguous, inconsistent, thoughtless, and variable. In physics, chemistry, biology, psychology, or sociology, we never think of appealing to common usage; on the contrary, there is a constant effort to achieve a precision of definition not found in common usage. What reason is there, then, to rely on common usage in ethics? Indeed, the positivists miss the dynamics of moral discourse precisely because they miss the dynamics of language— despite their great preoccupation with it. They abstract language from its living context and make of it something static. They take a nonhistorical and noncultural approach to language, seeing it in terms of language symbols (syntactics) and what the symbols refer to (semantics). Such an understanding of language omits the historical and cultural human being who connects the symbols with their referents.

Dewey was not preoccupied with language in the way the positivists were and yet he was aware, much more than they, of the great historical and cultural richness of language. As a result Dewey's contribution to the science of value was an aliveness to the actual data of moral experience.

Dewey did not claim that values are intrinsic properties of things; rather, he saw values as arising out of the problems of living. He expressed this by insisting that value be considered as a verb rather than as a noun. To conceive of value as a noun implies that values are static, whereas thinking of values as verbs emphasizes their dynamic nature. For Dewey, value means "valuing"—an activity. To understand values one has to get to the actual life situations in which they arise. In this sense values do not differ from other scientific data. For Dewey science is the process of *inquiry,* and all inquiry is born of a *problematic* or *indeterminate* situation and has for its purpose the transformation of that situation in a controlled manner into a *determinate* situation. Inquiry is a way to solve problems, and the process of inquiry is the same in solving problems of science, every-day problems, and problems of value. For this reason Dewey thought it was possible to deal scientifically with values. Where the positivists always took physics as their model whenever they talked about science, Dewey was more flexible. He did not think of science in terms of *one* particular science; rather, he thought of science in terms of the functions common to all sciences. As Dewey saw it, science is not basically a subject matter; it is a *procedure*. If science were a subject matter, then we would all have to agree that the subject matter of ethics is hopelessly different from that of physics. But if science is basically procedural in nature, then it can be applied to different fields—to both physics and ethics.

Dewey felt that if one were to test moral judgments scientifically, it would be necessary to see just how they function. In attempting to do this Dewey developed a theory of valuation that not only repudiates antinaturalistic ethical theories but also marks an advance beyond the prevailing naturalistic accounts, of which two—the "affective" and the "conative" were predominant. According to the *affective* account, values are related to *feelings*. Affective versions of value theory are based on the assumption that primary naturalistic properties are pleasures or enjoyments. In contrast, *conative* theories place emphasis on *strivings* rather than on feelings—on the grounds that feelings are too unreliable to serve as data for a science of value. The affective theory has an advantage over its rival inasmuch as feelings are obviously a very fundamental level of mental functioning, whereas strivings, which seem to derive from feelings, are not. Conversely, an advantage for the conative theory is that strivings can be openly observed by studying actions, whereas feelings cannot be observed. Which version of naturalism is more valid, the affective or the conative?

As Dewey understood it, neither is valid, for there is more to moral experience than *feeling* or *desiring* (affective theories) or than manifesting interest by striving (conative theories). Dewey wisely saw that there is another factor that is of utmost importance—*reflective thought*. Dewey interpreted value naturalistically, but he did so while insisting that intelligence is as natural to men as emotion. Thus for valuation to occur, mere *prizing* or holding dear—that is, mere *emotional esteem*—is not sufficient. There must also be *appraising*, or assigning a value to—there must be *intellectual estimation*. Dewey did not deny the importance of feeling and striving, but he knew that they do not tell the whole story about human values.

By adding the role of intellectual estimation to the study of ethics, Dewey made it possible to dismiss one of the chief arguments against the possibility of a science of ethics. The reason philosophers usually give for denying that ethics can be a science is that ethics deals with ends or goals, and we have no sound criteria in terms of which we can evaluate ends. But Dewey was convinced this did not present as great a problem as many believed. Dewey claimed that the intellectual estimation that goes on in the act of valuing is not so exclusively concerned with ends as is commonly imagined. After all, the values or ends we find are always *means* to other ends. It follows then that ends cannot be evaluated independently of means. Indeed, *valuing* an end invariably results from examining existing conditions to see what means are available to its realization. One must always consider what the consequences of the attainment of the end will be, and in terms of those consequences one can evaluate the worth of the end. This made it possible for Dewey to discuss ethics in less absolute terms than those used by earlier ethical philosophers. For example, where Kant had spoken of a good such as truth telling as though it were an end in itself, with the result that a person would be duty-bound to tell the Nazis where his mother was hiding rather than tell a lie, and where other philosophers had concluded that this idea was so repugnant that they preferred to think that the idea of good or bad must be meaningless as applied to human acting, Dewey was able to show that valuing can be meaningful as long as it is recognized that what we are evaluating are not ends (such as truth telling) but actions in the context of a never-ending sequence of results. One should not ask whether telling the truth is always a good end. Rather one should ask whether, in each particular case, telling the truth will produce desirable consequences. One would have to be quite depraved to say that it would be meaningless nonsense to value protecting one's mother over turning her in to the Nazis. When we speak of ethical values we must speak of the consequences of acts, not of the acts as ends in themselves.

Dewey's approach to ethics was a philosophical bombshell, considering that it had become virtually axiomatic in the social sciences that there is no rational way to appraise ends. It was widely supposed that it is possible to be rational about means, but not about ends. We can measure the effectiveness of means in terms of how they succeed in achieving given ends, but since an end is final, there is nothing in terms of which it can be judged. But Dewey maintained the end is not the end! He emphasized the necessity of understanding ends in the context of a means-end continuum in which an end is itself invariably a means to a further end. Dewey concluded that we must always consider means in relation to ends and ends in relation to means. Thus in a positivistic age, John Dewey showed that ethics need not be meaningless if we apply intelligence to the problems of value. He believed we could use the method of inquiry, which for him was tantamount to intelligence, to determine what is valuable. Dewey was firmly convinced that when *intelligent* investigation is made of a situation in which the choice of an end is a problem, it is possible to make meaningful conclusions about what course of action is right and what is wrong. The good end is the one that is most likely, as revealed by an intelligent appraisal, to resolve the problem in a satisfactory way.

The greatest plague upon the naturalist's house, of course, is the gap between the "is" and "ought." We have already discussed the fact that it is a logical fallacy to deduce the *normative* (what ought to be) from the *descriptive* (what is). Yet Dewey would answer that it simply is not true that making such a deduction is invariably fallacious. On the contrary, statements of what is can acquire a normative status in the context of actual problematic situations. That is, scientific propositions can attain a normative status when put in *use*. Because positivists (and idealists as well) have always abstracted from the rich, living, existential situation, they have always claimed that naturalists cannot come to *ought* conclusions, for the premises of naturalistic ethical arguments are factual, and the factual is not normative. Formally considered, this objection is perfectly true: it is invalid to come to an *ought* conclusion from premises that do not contain ought terms. But Dewey's whole point was that if we are to understand problems of value we must not consider them formally. We could spend from now to eternity pointing out that it is not good logic to derive "ought" conclusions from an "is" premise, but in the meantime men are faced with vital problems of value with which they must come to grips. Problems of value are not just logical problems. They are human problems. Because human problems of value arise in dynamic contexts of life, they must be understood in those contexts, and formal logic is not entirely adequate for this. Obligation does not depend upon a proper statement of a formal argument; rather, it arises from the urgency of a troubled situation.

Nonnaturalists insist that values cannot be deduced from facts because they assume that there is a natural bifurcation of fact and value in our world. In fact nature itself is *value-impregnated*. The facts of nature are not valueless, and normative implications are to be found in the very facts of life. Indeed the nature of man itself is normative, in the sense that man has certain needs the fulfillment of which is valuable to him because of the very nature of his being. To recognize this is to recognize how it came about that John Dewey, the philosopher who stood as a towering symbol of a relativistic or nonabsolutistic approach to life, actually planted the seeds from which there could grow an absolute basis for morality. Dewey had debunked the attempts of philosophers to find absolute standards of morality in such ends-in-themselves as pleasure, duty, power, nature, and God. But he himself provided such an absolute, for if ethical questions are problems of men, then what better standard might be found to regulate the conduct of men than the *nature of man?* Dewey believed there were certain fundamental and unchanging *needs* of man, and these can serve as a basis for moral evaluation.

Societies and cultures may have vastly different ways of realizing basic human needs, but through all those differences the basic human needs remain the same. It is fundamentally important to realize that cultural relativity does not imply ethical relativity. People may behave very differently, but this does not mean they do not have certain common needs. It only means there are various ways of serving those needs. These needs may be understood as the foundation for ethical norms. No matter how different cultures may be, in all cultures men experience needs for love, for affection, for ego satisfaction, and for intellectual and aesthetic expression. In many ways men may stand divided, but in these needs they are united. Does it not make sense to maintain that what man *needs*, which may be quite different from what he wants, is *good* for him? If we can discover these *basic human needs,* then we have a basis for morally evaluating cultures, institutions, policies, and behavior. All that which promotes, in whatever way, these basic human needs may be called good and may serve as the determinant of what should be done. All that which inhibits basic human needs may be regarded as wrong and may serve as the criterion for what should not be done.

Because Dewey was able to show the way to criticize cultures in terms of their ability to satisfy basic human needs, today social scientists are increasingly making themselves at home in the fortress of ethical absolutism, and cultural relativism, which dominated the intellectual scene a few years back, is now in retreat. Anthropological field research is confirming Dewey's claim that men have certain fundamental human needs, and it is becoming clear that a culture can be criticized by the degree to which it promotes these needs.

Erich Fromm developed a nonrelativistic position known as *Naturalistic Humanism*. Fromm sought to show that societies as well as individuals can be pathological. Social patterns that frustrate human growth, he argued, are in a very real sense unhealthy. If the social environment is hostile to the rights of men to freely express themselves and to find joy and pleasure in life, and if it is loveless, then it can make men sick. Social patterns that force men into bitter competition or condition them to prize things over human values distort humanity. Societies that repress human needs lack sane foundation and are in that sense immoral.

Fromm and many other social scientists are coming to see that the center of man's basic human needs is his need for *love*. To be raised without love is to be raised without humanity. The full life, the self-actualizing and self-realizing life, is the life filled with love. A society that frustrates the expression of human love is a sick society.

We can end our discussion of ethical theories then with the recognition that human values can be valid if they are based on human needs; and the paramount human need is the need for love. From the standpoint of ethics we can say the good life is the life of *love*. There is the wonderfully pregnant possibility that in *love* may be found a universal absolute, a basis for epistemology, metaphysics, and ethics, which can provide a unified vision of existence and can help unite a dangerously divided mankind.

Summary

1. Ethical issues emerge when men confront problems and must decide what to do—when they have to make a choice. Whereas the natural and social sciences provide us with information about what *is* the case, ethical statements tell us what *ought* to be. Thus the natural and social sciences have been designated *descriptive* or *factual* sciences but ethics has been called a *prescriptive* or *normative* study. The study of ethics involves consideration of what should be done, of what is good or evil, right or wrong. The student of ethics must undertake an examination of principles of value and of the meaning, function, and validity of such principles and of ethical predicates.

2. *Hedonism* is the thesis that pleasure is the good. Some hedonists claim only the pleasure of the moment matters but others insist that long-range pleasure must be decisive. In trying to be scientific about this question

Jeremy Bentham developed criteria that took into consideration long-term effects as well as immediate pleasure. Egoistic hedonism is the view that only "my" pleasure counts. It is the doctrine of selfishness. However, Bentham's utilitarianism assumes that since the pleasure of the individual is the good, the highest good would be the most pleasure for the greatest number of individuals. Bentham held that pleasure must be understood only in *quantitative* terms—how much and for how many—but his disciple J. S. Mill took the position that pleasure must be evaluated on the basis of qualitative standards. Mill believed there are higher and lower pleasures. The difficulty with this position is to develop the standard by which it can be shown that some pleasures are by their very nature higher or worth more than others. For example, if one maintains that mental pleasures are preferable to physical ones, he may have to appeal to a nonhedonistic standard to prove this is so.

3. The *ethics of duty* is the opposite view from that of hedonism. Immanuel Kant, one of its chief exponents, insisted that the only thing relevant to ethical evaluation is the state of the will. In making ethical evaluations it is never correct to consider consequences, for results or consequences are practical matters, not ethical ones. Whether or not an activity will yield pleasure is a psychological issue, not an ethical one. An act that is to be regarded as ethical must be based on *purely ethical* considerations. To Kant this meant that to be ethical, a person has to do his duty and not consider pleasure or any other consequences. Thus in ethical behavior there must be *no* consideration of consequences. Ethical commands then are absolute and must be taken as categorical imperatives—there can be no ifs, ands, or buts. Kant maintained the only good thing is a good will, and this means that one must act purely on the basis of duty and never on the basis of inclination.

4. It has been denied that people ever act purely out of a sense of duty or even purely out of motivations to obtain pleasure. What some philosophers, such as Friedrich Nietzsche, sought to show was that underlying all behavior is a fundamental drive for power. Nietzsche called for a transvaluation of all values based upon the basic *will to power*.

5. The metaphysical view that will is the ultimate reality has important ethical implications. If *will* is the basic force in existence, it may be concluded that in arriving at ethical decisions will, rather than reason, *ought* to be decisive. However, there is also a tradition of thought that, while admitting that "will" is a basic life force, denies that it should be the basis for ethical existence. Buddha and Arthur Schopenhauer thus asserted a need for renunciation as a fundamental ethic. Buddha showed how desire eternally frustrates man, and Schopenhauer carefully developed the thesis that the will to live is not only the basic reality but also that it drives man to a life of misery. Therefore Schopenhauer called for man to relinquish this force of will.

6. Of those who regarded emotional, volitional, or existential forces as more fundamental than rational ones, Schopenhauer taught that man had to seek escape from the suffering of the will to live; Nietzsche proclaimed that

the will to power was basic and that man should dare to "live dangerously"; and the Danish philosopher Sören Kierkegaard took still another approach, one that did not assume a basic will to power nor a need for ethical renunciation but called for a suspension of the ethical in favor of an existential leap into religion. Kierkegaard called for man to stand as a single one, a lonely individual with a deep existential and personal commitment to God.

7. In contemporary philosophy one can find three basic kinds of ethical theory explicitly defended—*Naturalism, Nonnaturalism,* and *Emotivism.* The naturalists maintain that value must be found in some natural property or state, such as pleasure, desire, human striving, or human nature. The nonnaturalists contend that value is intangible and therefore cannot be empirically described or even defined. Reacting to this view, the position of emotivism was formulated. Emotivism maintains that if value is not anything empirical and cannot be defined, then it cannot be anything at all. The emotivists argued that value, being incapable of empirical verification or of objective communication, had to be meaningless. Philosophers who were dissatisfied with this elimination of ethics attempted to develop other approaches. A particularly influential one in Anglo-American philosophical centers was the approach of *Ordinary Language,* in which philosophers did not return to the traditional approach of regarding value as some natural or nonnatural property nor dismiss the importance of ethics. Instead, they sought to locate actual ethical usage by concentrating upon the function of ethical words in ordinary language. Perhaps such an approach may keep ethics in business and give philosophers an excuse for working at teaching ethics, but it is not an approach that give ethics much substance. A more interesting and, one hopes, more promising approach involves a renewed interest in a form of naturalism. Increasing evidence is piling up to the effect that there are universal human needs, and based upon these there is the possibility of developing a science of ethics.

A Little Reflection
on Some Big Questions

5

The Big Questions

There are certain big questions about life and this universe that human beings ever have struggled with and to which they feel they must have some kind of satisfactory answer. Human beings have not only the obvious physiological and psychological needs but also philosophical needs. Simply put, these involve the desire to have some understanding of *what it is all about*, as Alfred North Whitehead said in defining philosophy. People want to know why they are here, why they suffer, where they are going, and whether there is any meaning and purpose in their lives and in this universe. Some fundamental questions human beings have raised and sought to answer in relation to these philosophical needs concern the existence of God, the freedom of man, and the nature of truth. Ideas men have held about God, freedom, and truth have mattered so much to them they have been willing not only to live for them but to die for them as well. Therefore, it is especially worthwhile to come to terms with the technical philosophical issues involving them.

Since questions about God, freedom, and truth are of such great import to men and since they cut across all the areas of philosophy studied—epistemology, metaphysics, and ethics—it should prove valuable to give some special attention to these crucial concerns in the hope that we will thus be able to promote at least a little reflection upon these big questions.

Does God Exist?

One day after I had finished presenting a lecture to my class I was making my may back to my office when I was confronted by an anxious student who insisted he had to see me in private, and right away! He seemed to be desperate. I beckoned him into my office, and there, somewhat fidgety, he furtively looked about my office and then blurted out the question, "Is there a God?" He added most emphatically, "I must know."

Throughout history that is a question to which people have felt they must have an answer; and philosophers have come forth to give them answers. Three classical and basic philosophical answers for the existence of God are known as the *ontological* argument, the *cosmological* argument, and the *teleological* argument.

It was in eleventh-century England that St. Anselm (1033–1109) gave explicit formulation to the *ontological* argument for the existence of God. Anselm was not trying to sell the idea of the existence of God to those who did not believe; rather, his object was to show those who did believe that there was a logical basis for their faith.

Anselm's tactic was to try to demonstrate that the very act of asserting there is no God involves an assumption that there is one. This can be easily understood when it is clearly seen what the meaning of God is. The term God refers to that being *than which none greater can be conceived*. If one accepts that definition, then one cannot reject the existence of God, for if God is that being who is greater than any of which we can conceive, it follows that as a very minimum He must be. For how could He be the greatest Being there is if He wasn't? That which exists in objective reality is surely greater than that which exists merely as an idea in the mind. If God is the greatest being, He must be; otherwise anything that *exists*, even a cockroach, would be greater. The greatest being is perfect, but it would be quite an imperfection if He did not even exist. Thus the very conception of the greatest conceivable being implies His existence.

Anselm lashed out at anyone who would admit he could conceive of God but who would fail to see that such a conception implied His existence. Such a person Anselm truly regarded as a fool. A very clever monk at the Monastery of Marmontiers, Gaunilo by name, responded to Anselm by writing his *Pro Insipiente* (*On Behalf of the Fool*). Gaunilo pointed out that he could conceive of the "Islands of the Blest" as greater than any isles that can be conceived. Yet Gaunilo did not plan to spend his vacation there for the very simple reason that even though he could conceive of these islands, they did not exist. His point, of course, was that merely having the idea of the greatest conceivable being does not mean that such an idea has objective reference or that such a being *actually* exists.

Anselm's answer to this criticism was that the ontological argument can *solely* be applied to God and surely not to islands. The greatest islands of which one could conceive would be greater than any other islands, but still islands are things that are only contingent and thus may or may not exist. It is only the greatest Being of which one can conceive that must exist, because such a being would have to be necessary as the greatest islands would not. The greatest islands of which one can conceive must be greater than any other, but they need not be absolutely perfect, as the greatest Being must be—and the greatest Being would not be absolutely perfect if He did not exist.

In modern times the German philosopher Immanuel Kant observed that he could conceive of a one-hundred-dollar bill in his pocket, but doing so did not make him any richer, because conceiving and actually being there are two different things. Kant's point was that *existence is not a predicate*. This means that actual existence can never be taken as a property of definition. One simply cannot define anything into existence. One cannot discover what exists by any analysis of terms. To find what exists one must explore objective reality.

Anselm could have responded to Kant, in the same way he had to Gaunilo, by claiming that the same rules that apply to all finite things simply do not apply to the infinite Being, but Kant clearly has the better argument here. Indeed, the weakness of Anselm's ontological argument was recognized long before Kant put the finishing touch to it in the eighteenth century, for medieval Christian philosophers, such as St. Thomas Aquinas (1225–1274), had felt the need to discover new logical proofs of the existence of God.

St. Thomas believed it was necessary to rely upon an analysis of the idea of God to show that He exists. The tracings of God are everywhere in the universe, and thus one need only look to find evidence for His existence. It is not necessary to turn to a word, as Anselm did; one can turn to the world. Indeed, St. Thomas argued that an assumption of God is required in order to adequately explain the world of sense experience. In the course of showing there are *five ways* to the existence of God, St. Thomas gave statement to the cosmological and teleological arguments.

The second way of St. Thomas to God is central. It is the way of causation. Things must be produced by something, for they do not cause themselves. For anything to cause itself, it would have to exist before itself to bring itself into being, and that makes no sense. All events have some cause, and that which causes an event must itself have a cause. One cannot regress infinitely, and that means there must be some point at which the entire series of cause and effect was specifically set into motion. To explain any simple thing before us now, ultimately we must be led back to a first cause. There are present things right here before us and intermediate things that caused the present things. These intermediate things, however, did not just pop out of the air; they had to have been caused themselves. If we trace these causes back far enough we will arrive at an uncaused cause, an absolute, which explains everything. Nothing could be happening in our universe now had not our universe at some point come into being. However, if we explain its origin in terms of any physicochemical elements or any finite forces, we would still have to explain what caused those elements or forces. Thus there must be an absolute, an ultimate force, which causes all else but is of such a nature that no cause is required to explain it. This St. Thomas understands as God.

Thus St. Thomas defended the Judaeo-Christian theory that the world was created out of nothing. What many find intellectually disturbing in this argument is the fact that it leaves unanswered the question of what was going on *before* creation. When one such disturbed person asked St. Augustine what was going on before the universe was created, the good saint answered that God was busy getting the fires of Hell good and hot for people who asked questions like that. That answer is not as facetious or evasive as it may sound, and St. Thomas would have given the same answer. Aquinas never pretended he could fill in empirical details about origins, and neither can anyone in present-day physics. The best thing to do with such questions is to turn them off, for they are meaningless and unanswerable. What Aquinas was saying was that the empirical world, being contingent, cannot explain itself, and thus there must be a noncontingent force that can explain it. This *cosmological* argument is a way of saying that the *cosmos* does not account for itself, and thus we must assume an absolute, which can account for it.

On the basis of the cosmological argument an adequate explanation for anything in this cosmos leads one back to the idea of a supreme being, or uncaused cause. The *teleological* argument for the existence of God, which was St. Thomas's fifth way, is based upon the idea that the universe is so harmoniously coordinated, so well planned, so designed that it must be the result of a planner or designer. Careful observation reveals that all things aim at some end or purpose, and the existence of such a grand cosmic order suggests that this is a purposeful universe. Such order and purpose as we find in the cosmos cannot be explained by chance. As Albert Einstein said, he could not believe that God plays dice with the universe, and biologist Lecomte du Nuoy argued that life could not have appeared as a result of chance. The elementary molecules of living organisms are all characterized by tremendous dissymmetry. "The probability for a single molecule of high dissymmetry to be formed by the action of chance and normal thermic agitation remains practically nil," du Nuoy concluded.[1]

The fact that so much in the universe is functionally interrelated suggests there was supreme conscious design. Not only theologians but great biologists such as Edmund Sinnott affirm that the whole universe is characterized by amazing patterning, orderly movement, and harmonious development. Upon some such understanding St. Thomas reasoned that there must be an ultimate Being who confers order upon the universe.

---

[1] Lecomte du Nuoy, *Human Destiny* (New York: New American Library, 1947), p. 35.

Not all have been convinced that the ways of St. Thomas really led to God. According to British empiricist David Hume, it is adequate to assign a cause to each particular event without having to seek a cause for an entire series itself. If one wishes to explain his ancestry he can do it quite adequately without needing to account for the origin of the universe. The parts can be explained even though the whole cannot.

There is no way to show there was a cause of the universe. We derive our idea of cause and effect by observing things appear in regular sequence. But the universe is unique. It could not be observed to appear in sequence with anything else. Thus we cannot say it has a cause, and even if we could, we could not say that cause is God. If we merely *infer* a cause of an entity without experience of it, we cannot ascribe to that cause anything beyond what would be required to produce that entity. If we put a body of twenty pounds on one side of a scale, and if that side goes up, we may infer a counterbalancing weight exceeding twenty pounds, but we cannot infer one exceeding ten thousand pounds. By the same token, we have no grounds upon which to infer some cause of the finite universe to be infinite.

Neither can we accept the contention that design (the teleological approach) in the universe implies an infinite or perfect God. In the first place the universe is not perfect, so why should we assume it was produced by a perfect being? Secondly, there is so much diversity in the universe that there is no reason to assume it was produced by only one being rather than by a team of gods. And if there is one God, why should we assume Him to be a divine intelligence? There is more in the universe analogous to vegetable or animal life than to human contrivance, so why not infer a god who is a supreme vegetable rather than a supreme intelligence? In this connection we should note that the most damaging development for the teleological argument, or argument from design, was Darwin's theory of evolution. *Natural selection* rather than theological purpose accounts for the amazing manner in which things are designed to achieve certain tasks.

Finally, there is the thesis that we must postulate the existence of God in order to explain the moral order in the universe. The problem with this argument is that there is more suffering, misery, ignorance, disease, famine, plague, catastrophe, war, and death than there is moral order. If God has the power to prevent people from slowly and painfully dying from cancer or if He can prevent the destruction wrought by earthquakes, and if He just idly stands by, it would seem less that He is an all-powerful and benevolent deity than that He is an all-powerful sadist. Some have contended God reveals Himself in history, but as philosopher Karl Popper has observed, history is nothing but a long chronicle of mass murder—not a very flattering place for God to be!

The trouble with formal proofs for the existence of God—or with disproofs for His existence, for that matter—is that the question of God is not a formal matter. The symbol of God has had tremendous psychosociological significance for mankind. Psychoanalyst Victor Frankl has made the point that man can endure any *how* if only he has a *why*, if only he has a sense of meaning or of something to live for. Frankl should know; he endured the *how* of a concentration camp. Where, however, is man to get that *why?* Man must have roots he can depend upon. Everything in this world is contingent, so that it cannot always be depended upon. It is only upon the assumption of an absolute, which we may call God, that man can find an ultimate *why*, which gives him the meaning to endure all life has to throw at him. This is a way of saying that man may need a God. If so, the basic philosophical question should not be whether or not one can prove God exists but whether or not one can live without assuming that there is a God, an absolute. The question of God may have to be approached from the standpoint of a logic of life rather than in terms of a formal logic.

To Biblical man God was not a proposition to be formally proved; he was encountered as a living reality. In the Bible we are informed that God is *He Who Is.* For the people of the Bible, knowing God was not a matter of listing attributes or defining Him; it was a matter of *experiencing* Him. Even St. Thomas was well aware that his rational proofs showed only *that* God is, not *what* God is. Logic can point the way to God, but only faith can enable one to *know* what God is. The faith of St. Thomas knew God as an existential reality, a living God encountered in faith, who gave men meaning and gave them a *why.* In our age when so many *hows* are failing, we may need greater understanding of this *why.*

Is Man Free?

It is written in the Rubáiyát of Omar Khayyám:

> *Tis all a Chequer-board of Nights and Days*
> *Where Destiny with Men for Pieces plays:*
> *Hither and thither moves, and mates, and slays,*
> *And one by one back in the Closet lays.*[2]

Some think that all of life is written in the stars while others assume it is secreted from the glands. That is, there are those who assume that behavior is a result of free choice, but there are others who presume we are but servants of cosmic destiny or that behavior is nothing but a reflex of heredity and environment. There are four basic types of answers to the question of whether man makes his own destiny or whether destiny just plays with men like pieces in a game of chess. The main answers to the question of man's freedom are: (1) *determinism*, (2) *fatalism*, (3) *indeterminism*, and (4) *libertarianism.* These positions may overlap in one way or another, and as we develop them they are not intended as exact descriptions of specific theories but as general descriptions of positions that have been historically defended.

The position of determinism is that every event is the necessary outcome of a cause or a set of causes. Some scientists presume that all that happens

---

[2] The *Rubáiyát of Omar Khayyám*, trans. Edward Fitzgerald (New York: Collier Books, 1962), p. 51.

can be explained by certain natural laws, whereas some theologians insist that all can be accounted for by supernatural laws. On either assumption we must conclude man is *determined* rather than *free*.

Two shades of determinism may be distinguished, and these are what the great American pragmatist William James called "hard" determinism and "soft" determinism. The *hard determinist* maintains that everything is a consequence of external forces, and such forces necessarily produce all that happens. Man is not free. *Soft determinists* go easier on freedom, for their argument defines being free simply as not being compelled or constrained. By this definition a man can be completely the product of his heredity and environment, and yet, since he is not forced to do a particular thing, he may thus be said to be free. The problem with this philosophical position is not that the soft determinist denies all that happens is a necessary outcome of antecedent conditions but that he *defines* being free in such a special sense that he can call man free even while man is being determined. A soft determinist thus might say a man who joins the army to avoid being drafted is free, and yet at the same time admit that he joined because of his whole past training, the way he was brought up, and because his girl left him for another. What sense does it make to call a man free if all he does is conditioned into him?

The hard determinist completely sweeps away freedom. Baron Holbach minced no words about it, saying, "Man's life is a line that nature commands him to describe upon the surface of the earth, without his ever being able to swerve from it, even for an instant."[3] As Schopenhauer put it, a man can do what he wills, but the catch is that he cannot *will* what he wills. What a man wills is determined by environmental and hereditary conditions. Inspired by the enormously successful mechanical explanations offered by Newtonian physics, the great French mathematician Laplace categorically denied that there can be any mystery in the universe and absolutely affirmed that everything can be explained scientifically. If there were a superintelligence, Laplace claimed, there is not anything in the universe he could not explain or predict.

If man can be explained by laws of nature just as physical objects can, why does he call himself free? Perhaps because it is flattering to do so. Having a consciousness, which is lacking in inanimate objects, man improperly assumes that the course he is following is of his own choice rather than a result of antecedent physical conditions. As Spinoza explains, "... Men believe themselves to be free simply because they are conscious of their own actions, knowing nothing of the causes by which they are determined."[4] According to Spinoza, if a stone that was hurled through the air by an external agency had consciousness and was aware of the

[3] Baron Holbach, "Of Man's Free Agency," in Robert E. Dewey, Francis W. Gramlich, Donald Loftsgordon, eds., *Problems of Ethics* (New York: The Macmillan Company, 1961), p. 51.

[4] J. Ratner, ed., *The Philosophy of Spinoza* (New York: Random House, Inc., 1927), p. 204.

course it was moving along but not of the forces that had set it into motion, the stone too would claim it was free.

In our own day Freudians have shown that men do things not because of free choice but because of deep unconscious forces and libidinal energy or sexual drives. Darwin described man as a product of evolution, as any animal is; Marx showed how man is shaped by economic forces over which he has no control; and behaviorist psychologists explained human behavior as conditioned by environmental forces. The point is there is a great weight of evidence in favor of a deterministic thesis. Psychologists and physiologists have long known that dogs can be conditioned to respond in specific ways. What seems to be more and more established is that men as well as dogs can be so conditioned, can be brainwashed. Dr. Joost A. Meerloo, a very distinguished student of brainwashing, has informed us in his book *The Rape of the Mind* that there actually exists such a thing as mass brainwashing, and that most of us could be its victims. There appear to be not only mechanical laws of nature but also principles of human behavior in accordance with which men can be conditioned or molded. The consequences of this for man are very great.

If we accept the determinist argument and understand human behavior as a consequence of external factors rather than of free choice, then it would seem we must recognize that our explanation of human behavior leaves no room for morality. If people do not choose their actions, then they are not really responsible for them, and there is no basis for praising or blaming them. Many philosophers strenuously object to the doctrine of determinism because it gives no basis for morality or punishment, but it is precisely for this reason many humanists find determinism appealing. The cause of crime, they maintain, is not the evil of men but hereditary and environmental conditions. The remedy, obviously, is not to punish men but to alter or remove those conditions. The great criminal attorney Clarence Darrow believed that men should not be punished precisely because behavior can be explained deterministically. The eminent criminologist, Negley Teeters, a determinist, contended that when we see a criminal, instead of condemning him, we should say, "There but for the grace of God go I." Of course, the thesis of hard determinism does not automatically entail the elimination of retributive punishment, for Professor Sidney Hook has reminded us that the Puritans piously observed "There but for the grace of God go I" whenever they watched a man they had sentenced to be hung being led to the gallows. Hook's point, however, is a non sequitur, for the fact remains that whenever hard determinists defend retributive punishment they are being inconsistent. Hard determinism as a doctrine, regardless of the erroneous conclusions one may draw from it, does not give a basis for punishment.

Determinism, we can see, tends to be a very humane doctrine inasmuch as it leads us to forget about punishing men for their failings and encourages us to ameliorate the conditions that gave rise to these failings. Philosophically considered, however, there does seem to be a general plague upon the house of determinism. If all that happens is a result of heredity and environment, as determinists claim, then it must follow that even those who defend determinism do so just because it makes sense but more fundamentally because their heredity and environment somehow impelled them to defend it; thus one could never be sure whether he was defending it because of its logical force or because he was forced to do so by conditioning influences.

If determinism runs into serious philosophical difficulties, there is even a worse collision with the doctrine of fatalism. Determinism implies that *given* certain conditions or states, certain other things must follow. Events do not occur in an arbitrary manner. The determinist maintains that certain things necessarily will follow from certain initial conditions, but he does not say what the initial conditions *must* be. The determinist says the past determines the present and the present determines the future. The *fatalist*, however, believes that all is moving in the direction of some divine or ultimate purpose or some final set of conditions. In this sense the fatalist might be said to maintain that the future determines the past. The fatalist contends not only that, given initial conditions, other things necessarily follow therefrom but also that, given the grand scheme of things, there necessarily had to have been certain initial conditions. There have been some influential defenses of fatalism.

Although not all of the teachings of Islam were fatalistic, some significant later doctrinal formulations rested upon the assumption that all that happens does so in accord with the will of God, so that not only what follows from the initial conditions but also the initial conditions themselves are determined. Everything that happens is thus predetermined by what God wills the outcome to be. In our own tradition a classic example of fatalism is to be discovered in the teachings of Calvin. Calvin's God allowed no free will and had absolute foreknowledge of everything that would ever occur. He preordained some people to eternal damnation and others to eternal life. There is nothing anyone on earth can do to alter that plan, and even good works are held to be of no avail.

The basic problem with fatalism is there really is no way of proving or disproving it. There is no way to test a proposition that affirms everything that happens must happen. In an ordinary experimental situation, we test a hypothesis by predicting what the outcome of the experiment will be; if a different outcome occurs, the hypothesis is disconfirmed. In the case of fatalistic determinism, however, it can be said that any outcome is what God willed. We can say of all fatalistic interpretations that until they are proved true we have no reason to believe them, and it does not seem possible that they can be proved true. Indeed, it is doubtful that even those who espouse some form of fatalism really can believe it. A friend of mine who ran a gas station said that when your time comes you go, and there's nothing at all you can do about it! Yet I noticed that whenever he walked across the street he looked very carefully both ways to see if all was clear. Apparently he was trying to prolong his time. Fatalism is not a rationally defensible position, and it is quite difficult to live consistently as if it were true.

There may be many difficulties with an ordinary deterministic theory, but at least one can defend it with empirical evidence, for it can be shown that from certain conditions other things necessarily follow. A determinist might argue that, given the sociohistoric set of conditions prior to 1914, World War I was inevitable. A fatalist, though, would say that World War I was inevitable regardless of the antecedent conditions. There is no way to validate this. The determinist maintains that *if* certain things are so, then other things must be. The fatalist assumes that what will be will be, *no matter what.*

The majority view of Western philosophy is neither determinist nor fatalist. In large part our philosophic tradition holds that man is free to make his own fate. All material things may be subject to natural laws, but the will of man is free from such causation. Despite the faith of the determinist that human behavior can be understood in the same way as the data of the natural sciences, there is far less precision in the social sciences than can be attained in physics or chemistry. Perhaps it is *will* that makes prediction far more difficult in the social sciences than in the natural sciences. The social scientist has to reckon with the choices of men, and there is naturally less certainty about where they will lead than there is about the outcome of the interactions of inanimate objects. Indeterminists in short have argued there is that in man, which we may call *will*, that is not determined by external factors.

A classic defense of indeterminism was developed by the great American pragmatist William James in his famous essay "The Dilemma of Determinism." James rejected both hard and soft determinism on the grounds both are based on the premise that there is no free choice. James appealed to direct experience to provide evidence of the existence of free choice. Feelings, which we all have such as regret or remorse, make no sense unless it is assumed there is free will, for people experience regret or sorrow only because they believe they could have done otherwise. If determinism were true, then people could never have done otherwise and thus there is no reason to feel any regret.

Suppose a determinist recognizes that experiencing regret is absurd but is unable to reject this feeling of regret because he is determined to experience it. Such a person would certainly be in a painful situation, but his hopelessness and pain do not prove that determinism is invalid. His dilemma does not mean that determinism is not an accurate description of reality, for it may just be that we are in the kind of universe that dooms us to feel remorse, regret, and guilt even though there is not the slightest logical basis for feeling them. James showed the effects of determinism are unfortunate, not that determinism is untrue.

What is interesting about William James's argument, however, is that in effect he was proposing we evaluate a thesis such as determinism on grounds other than pure logic or science. Moral experience of which regret is a key expression is enduring throughout history; there is a complex pattern of human action inextricably intertwined with assumptions such as free will and experiences such as regret. This way of experiencing is not arbitrary and is not an academic question; on the contrary, it is at the very heart of man's reality. Human beings come to terms with life and understand themselves as human through such experiences as regret, remorse, sorrow, and guilt. This entire mode of functioning cannot be simply discounted. Free will is a working assumption of human existence as it has evolved throughout history, and moral experience *is* an all-important aspect of that history. Percisely because human experience over the course of history does found itself upon a premise of freedom, we have an excellent working criterion on the basis of which we might *justify* free will.

According to the determinist, this is a world in which there are no real possibilities because what shall happen is irreversibly determined. To the indeterminist, this is the kind of universe in which there are real possibilities among which man can make choices, and our experience seems to confirm this to us. Since determinism itself is only a theory and not an established fact about the universe, why should we deny our experience of freedom?

There was a time when the scientific basis for determinism appeared far sounder that it does at present. Newtonian physics provided man with a perfect model for a deterministic explanation of the universe. A fundamental characteristic of classical mechanics is that its mechanical state at a given time completely determines what its mechanical state will be at any subsequent time. In terms of the Newtonian scheme, the result of the impact of any material particle with another could be predicted with exactitude. In recent decades, however, experimental findings in thermodynamics and electrodynamics have established that there cannot be precise prediction concerning individual particles. Prediction can be successful only in the case of aggregates or groups. Thus important domains of science can yield only statistical probability and not certainty. This discovery came as a crushing blow to the ideal of universal determinism.

The greatest setback to determinism, many believe, came as a result of developments in quantum mechanics. Of particular significance was Werner Heisenberg's formulation of the Principle of Uncertainty in 1927. On the subatomic level of reality, Heisenberg showed, there can be no certainty about the behavior of particles. When the position of an electron is located, its velocity cannot be determined, and when the velocity can be ascertained the position cannot be pinpointed. Classical mechanics had presented a deterministic image of nature, and building on that the argument was developed that man, as a part of nature, can be accounted for in deterministic categories. To those for whom quantum mechanics seemed to vindicate indeterminism, the results seemed perfectly applicable to man, and a new confidence in free will emerged.

A strong dissent to the view that quantum mechanics implies indeterminism was offered by Ernest Nagel, a contemporary philosopher. According to Nagel, it made most sense in terms of Newtonian physics to speak of a particle as having both position and momentum, and thus it was so *defined*. By the same token in the quantum model of explanation it makes sense to *define* a particle as not having an exact position and momentum. Thus it is Nagel's position that the main shift from Newton to Heisenberg is not from a deterministic to an indeterministic revelation of reality but simply from an intepretative scheme in which things are defined in one way to a scheme in which it is meaningful to define them in a different way. The point is that position and velocity do not mean in classical mechanics what they mean in quantum mechanics. The new physical theories do not offer a new discovery of what reality *is,* but a new way of *talking* about reality. Therefore Nagel concluded that we cannot contend that reality can no longer be understood as deterministic. (Strictly speaking, Nagel's thesis does not *imply* that it must be understood as deterministic either.)

Given this standoff between the hard determinists, who do not allow the possibility of free will, and the indeterminists, who allow for free will, perhaps we should pay a bit more attention to the *soft* determinists, who contend, in utter opposition to the majority view, that only if determinism is true can man be morally responsible. In assessing the validity of the indeterminist contention that the sole basis for free will is indeterminism, it will be highly instructive to view the arguments of soft determinists to see if they can make a case that free will is compatible with determinism.

David Hume maintained that there is what we called a liberty of spontaneity, which is completely compatible with determinism. There is also another kind of liberty, which Hume called liberty of indifference. People believe they are entirely at liberty to will or not to will certain actions to which they are generally indifferent. This kind of liberty, Hume pointed out, rests upon the indeterminist assumption that human conduct has no cause, but unless we can say human actions are *caused* by motives, moods, and the character of the agent there is no basis for praising or blaming him —no basis for moral responsibility. A soft determinist such as Hume maintains that a person can be free in the sense that he may choose between two possibilities—say, going to the movies or to the concert—and yet he can be determined in the sense there is a cause for his behavior.

The line taken by Hume was very fully developed by logical positivist Moritz Schlick, who went even further and maintained that the very problem of freedom of the will was a *pseudo* problem. Schlick believed that moral responsibility is supposed as being incompatible with determinism because of a general failure to distinguish two meanings of the term "law." There are *prescriptive* laws on one hand, and *descriptive* laws on the other. Prescriptive laws are rules that *compel* by imposing sanctions; descriptive laws are statements of how things in fact behave. Only "prescriptive" laws can interfere with freedom, for descriptive laws cannot compel anything. It would be absurd to say planets are forced to obey Kepler's laws and will be arrested if they fail to do so. Descriptive laws do not compel; they only express existing regularities. This applies to psychological laws as well as physical laws. A man's behavior may conform precisely to psychological laws, but such laws do not compel him, for the laws are valid only insofar as they accurately describe what their subject would be doing anyway, regardless of the law. Schlick's point is that freedom is not exemption from causality but that this does not entail compulsion. Although a man's character may be determined, we may call him free if he may come and go as he pleases.

Gilbert Ryle, the distinguished British philosopher, went further than Schlick and flatly denied there is such a thing as will to be free. The will is an occult quality we can never perceive. Volitions of other persons are never seen; they are only inferred from overt behavior. We can know about what the person overtly does, but we can know nothing about some unobservable inner quality. When a man frowns it would be ridiculous to assume he is doing something on his forehead and something else in some metaphysical place within himself. There cannot be a free will because there is no such thing as a will.

The soft determinists may not establish the case that determinism is a necessary presupposition of freedom, but their analysis does cast doubt on the indeterminist assumption that their position is the only one that is compatible with freedom.

The basic problem with soft determinists is that they want to have their cake and eat it too. They insist that a man is free if in a given situation he in fact does one thing when he might have done a different thing, and yet at the same time they assume that whatever he does is an outcome of his character, which has been determined. Thus the only real difference between soft determinists and hard determinists is that those of the "soft" school use the "word" freedom while the hard liners reject it. The burning question of freedom, however, has to do with the issue of whether man determines his own destiny, can make his character, or whether it is determined by external circumstances. The determinist maintains all that happens is *caused* by an unbreakable causal chain of antecedent factors; the indeterminist contends there is not necessarily a cause for every event, and thus there can be uncaused events. Between these two extreme positions lies the position of *libertarianism*, which avoids the pitfalls of both determinism and indeterminism. Libertarianism may be interpreted as taking the stand that although man's character may be formed by external influences, he can resist such forces by something within him and avoid being *completely* determined. Thus he can genuinely choose to do one thing rather than another. As C. Arthur Campbell, a champion of this view, puts it, the prime requirement of the libertarian view is that a person can be said to be free insofar as he is the sole cause of the act in question and is able to exert his causality in alternate ways. The *self* is thus held to be responsible for moral decision. A person's entire conditioning, his *character*, may dictate he should behave in one way, say as a criminal, and yet he may look into himself and behave in a way not consistent with his conditioning. It may seem that this character, his upbringing, and his environment are such that he should be unable to resist some temptation, and yet he does. This can easily be explained if we accept Campbell's assumption that man not only has an external dimension or *character*, but also an internal one that Campbell calls a *self*. This libertarian view seems to be given some verification whenever all our observations of a person lead us to conclusively predict he will act in a given way, but he defies all expectation and acts in a different way. If there is no further evidence to the contrary, may we not assume that something *in* him made it possible for him to resist his external conditioning and freely make a choice?

Most people do behave as if the doctrine of free will is true; at the very least they suppose that their choices do matter. This does not mean the thesis of free will is valid, but on the other hand, if the doctrine of determinism were obviously true why should it be so difficult for men to accept its truth? The point is that determinism has never been shown to be an incontrovertible explanation of human behavior, and under the circumstances there is justification for assuming that man is free, as such an assumption does illuminate human behavior.

It may be that the question of whether man is free is not really a *factual* question. It could be argued that factual evidence is not relevant to the determinism-free will controversy in the sense that no matter how much evidence was adduced in favor of determinism it could always be replied that it applies only to the *character* and not to the *self*. There are phenomena that can be best explained not by the discovery of empirical evidence but by the formulation of a theoretical and conceptual model, the function of which is to make the optimum sense of problems at hand. It may be that the most fruitful way of exploring the determinism-free will controversy is by considering which of these two doctrines is more compatible with an image of man in terms of which human beings can productively live. Thus, thinking of the position of determinism or of free will as models of explanation rather than as inductively established doctrines, the question is: Which makes most sense of and best illuminates the facts of human experience as we know them? If the issue is put in these terms, I think the position could be developed that the idea of freedom is an inherent part of the defining concept of man. The nature of human life may be such that man *must* understand himself as being free, for human life as we know it would not make much sense without the concept of freedom. The challenge and struggle, which so enrich life, usually emerge from situations in which individuals feel that their efforts can make a difference. Freedom seems to be a good working assumption for human life. If determinism were true, then there would be no basis for human effort, for why should man make an effort if what he does can make no difference? Indeed, understood in this way one can see that the doctrine of determinism can become a good psychological basis for irresponsibility. If what will be will be, then one has an excuse for doing nothing. I think a case can be made that life would not be very meaningful for human beings on deterministic grounds. Thus it may be necessary for us, insofar as we understand ourselves as human beings, to assume a view of man as free.

Freedom can be so real to men that it may be difficult for the most thoroughgoing determinist to escape presupposing freedom. Thus we find the great philosopher Spinoza telling us that "The mind has greater power over the emotions and is less subject thereto, insofar as it understands all things as necessary."[5] In effect Spinoza was saying here that if we recognize we are not free, we shall become free. All of his philosophy bore witness to the deterministic view that we are not free to change the world because we are all part of a grand causal chain, and yet his philosophy is also per-

[5] J. Ratner, ed., *The Philosophy of Spinoza* (New York: Random House, Inc., 1927), p. 256.

vaded by the idea that only if we accept determinism can we free ourselves of ignorance and emotional servitude. Now if we are completely determined it is not possible for us to listen to Spinoza unless we are determined to live in accord with his advice, and if we are so determined we do not need his advice. However, if it is within the capacity of man to free himself from the bondage of ignorance and emotional impulses and to come to see things under the aspect of eternity as Spinoza urged, then this seems to be a very significant type of freedom. If Spinoza believed the path of our lives to be as much determined as the course of a stone projected through the air, then his urging would be senseless. It seems we must conclude either that Spinoza was saying something absurd or that he very much understood the reality and value of freedom. The great French existentialist Jean Paul Sartre understood freedom as a negative reality, as a capacity in man to say "No" to that which would enslave him. Perhaps Spinoza's determinism was not so different from Sartre's defense of freedom, for Spinoza insisted that we cannot really change things but that we can say *no* to ignorance and to the pleadings of our emotions. It must be that he gives us this advice on the presupposition that we can take it. After all, why should one talk to a stone?

What Is Truth?

Socrates believed that philosophers are lovers of the vision of truth, but there have been philosophers who have supposed that it can be no more than an illusion. Protagoras, an astute Sophist thinker in the same era as Socrates, used his intellectual talents to utterly discredit the vision of truth. There is an amusing story about him that illustrates just how lightly he regarded it.

Protagoras made a contract with a student named Eulathus to teach him how to win cases in court. The contract stipulated very specifically that Eulathus would not have to pay Protagoras until and unless he won his first case in court. Protagoras discharged his obligation with the highest competence. There was one little problem: Eulathus refused to go into court. Since there was no case for him to win, poor Protagoras had no basis for collecting his teaching fee. Protagoras had no choice. He took Eulathus into court and sued him for his teaching fee. One might have expected Eulathus to have been most uneasy about being sued by the great master Protagoras, but Eulathus was convinced he could not lose. He reasoned that if he should win, the court verdict would be a decree not to pay Protagoras, and if he should lose then he would not have won his first case and therefore, in accordance with his agreement would not be obligated to pay Protagoras. The truth of the matter seems to be that Protagoras had been impaled on the horns of a dilemma by his own student. But what is truth? Protagoras could always play about with it. Protagoras calmly observed that if he would win the case the verdict would be that Eulathus would have to pay him, and that if he would lose then Eulathus would have won his first case and according to the agreement would have to pay him. The court's job was to get to the truth in this case. In face of the facts it did the best it could: it postponed decision for one hundred years.

Protagoras believed that since there are two sides to everything there can never be any one truthful version of anything, and thus truth must be relative. While the story about Protagoras in court was most entertaining, it would seem to support his serious philosophical contention that truth is relative. As a matter of fact however neither Protagoras nor any relativist has ever so much shown that truth is relative as that truth can be viewed from different angles. That there is more than one way to look at something does not mean that something both can and cannot be at one and the same time. In other words the truth is not relative, but our way of looking at it is. On this point it has often been averred that the history of science clearly demonstrates that truth is ever changing and therefore is relative. On the contrary what the history of science shows is that man's understanding of the truth changes. Once man believed the earth was the center of the universe, but with more complete understanding he came to see this earlier view was not true and thus changed his view. What changes in the history of science is not the truth but man's view of it. The truth was never that the earth was the center of the universe, and thus when the Copernican theory was formulated to show the earth could not be the center of the universe it was not the truth that changed but man's understanding of things.

A case has been made that it was not public enemy John Dillinger, as all the world believed, but a person who looked very much like him who was killed by the police. The fact is, however, that at 10:40 p.m., July 22, 1934 outside the Biograph Theater in Chicago either Dillinger was shot down by the police or he was not. While at first all the world believed Dillinger was gunned down by the police it may one day be established it was not he but instead ringer Jimmy Lawrence. If it ever is established Lawrence was the one who was killed that will not alter the truth but change our understanding of it. There is truth but we do not always know what it is. Before we get involved in knowing just *what* the truth is it would be well to clarify what we *mean* by truth. Theories of truth formulated by philosophers can be of valuable assistance here.

Basically there are three theories of truth: the correspondence theory, the coherence theory, and the pragmatic theory. The essence of the correspondence theory is that propositions must *agree* with facts to qualify as being true. Agreement is the key that opens the door to truth. The coherence theory involves the contention that in order for a proposition to be true it must be consistent with an entire system of judgments. Thus for this theory *consistency* rather than agreement is the key. The assumption of the pragmatic theory of truth is that a true proposition is one that is successful as an instrument of action. In terms of this theory *practical success* is the key.

Before undertaking an examination of these theories it should first be observed that there is one point in which all are in agreement, and that is that truth is not a property of things but of *propositions.* If someone mistakenly observed that a tree stump was a man crouching, one might correct him by saying, "That is a false statement because actually what you saw was not a man but a tree," but indeed it would be odd to correct him by saying "That's a false man." The point is that we make propositions about things, and it is not the *things* that are true or false but the *propositions.* It makes sense to say that the *statement* an object is a chair is true but it does not make sense to call something a "true" chair. Thus the various theories of truth are efforts at establishing criteria by which we can determine the truth of *propositions.*

The classic statement of the correspondence theory of truth is credited to Aristotle. According to Aristotle, to say of that which is that it is, or to say of that which is not that it is not is to utter the truth. This is quite simple and seems to make good common sense. If someone states that it is raining, then you look to see. If it *is,* the statement is true, and if rain is not coming down, the statement is false.

Although the correspondence theory of truth was given explicit formulation by Aristotle, its lasting appeal is testified to by the fact it has been given defense in rigorous logical form by contemporary philosopher Alfred Tarski. Tarski expressed the theory in the most careful logical language, but in doing so did not alter the general idea of it as understood by Aristotle: that is, that a proposition is true if the facts it designates actually obtain.

Certainly it is essential to make some use of the correspondence theory in verifying propositions, but it may be doubted the test of correspondence can lead us to truth. The catch in this theory is that on the assumption of it we are to understand that statements are true if they agree with some state of affairs that exists in reality, but we may not know what reality is. On the basis of the correspondence theory we are to match our propositions with the facts of reality, but what is reality? That's just what we must find and not what we can assume.

The test of *agreement* then has its pitfalls, and thus there are those who insist a far more reliable guide to truth can be found in the criterion of *consistency.* Advocates of the *coherence theory* of truth maintain that to be regarded as true a proposition must be consistent with the whole of our experience. We do not accept new ideas as true unless they do *fit* in, are *consistent* with, or *cohere* with the total system of our knowledge. If by long experience and accumulated understanding we accept certain things as being so, we generally and very naturally reject an idea or belief that is inconsistent with that experience and understanding.

The coherence theory is a useful one. In seeking to validate testimony we can easily determine the falsity of it if it in any way contradicts other information already established as correct. And in the history of science it is frequently the case that new theories are accepted and old ones rejected not simply upon the basis of agreement with the facts but more fundamentally in terms of *consistency* with an accepted corpus of knowledge.

When first accepted, the Copernican sun-centered theory of the universe did not better account for the facts scientifically than did the old Ptolemaic or earth-centered theory. The appeal of the Copernican theory was to a great extent aesthetic as well as scientific in that it was mathematically more simple and harmonious than the Ptolemaic. It can be said that in terms of logical structure the Copernican theory was more *beautiful*.

Thus science, which we think of as fact-oriented, involves conceptual, mathematical, and even aesthetic dimensions, which may be far removed from hard facts. Indeed, defenders of the coherence theory often observe that "facts" are not the simple hard and fast elements they are invariably assumed to be by "correspondence" theorists. The usual way of understanding facts is to suppose they are simply given. A fundamental distinction is drawn between *facts* and *judgments*. While facts are understood as hard evidence, judgments are understood as evaluations of such evidence. It is a presupposition of the correspondence theory that validation of judgments must proceed by a comparison of them with hard and fast facts. Correspondence theorists dispute the validity of this sharp distinction between facts and judgments. They contend that upon analysis it turns out that all facts actually are themselves forms of judgment. We might well suppose that a table is a brute fact that we can cast our eyes upon and put our hands on, whereas if someone claims, "That is a good table," we might say he has made a judgment about the table. But how much of a brute fact is the table itself as we perceive it? Actually the very solid object we perceive as a table can be shown by science to be no more in basic reality than a swarm of dancing molecules. It really cannot be said that a table is a brute fact and that judgments as to whether it is big or small, hard or soft, beautiful or plain, are of an entirely different order, for we never directly apprehend a table just as it exists in nature. Whenever we perceive some datum as being an object, such as a table, a whole complex of judgments are implicitly being made.

A defender of the correspondence theory would reply to this argument by pointing out that even if we do not encounter any brute facts as they are in nature, and even if we are actually making a judgment about sense data whenever we assert we are seeing a stone, nevertheless there is still a basic difference between the *kind* of judgment we make when we implicitly judge that certain sense data are such complexes as tables, chairs, and stones on the one hand, and the *kind* of judgment we make when we explicitly judge that something is a beautiful or good table on the other hand. Thus it can be said there are certain judgments human beings make about the world that it is convenient for us to label as "facts," and there is another variety of judgment, which we make about that which we label as facts, and these we call judgments.

Having developed this defense, an adherent of the correspondence theory might go further and attack the coherence theory by observing that a set of ideas can be perfectly *consistent* and also be perfectly *false*. The following propositions are perfectly consistent with one another:

All great scientists are men.

Madame Curie is a great scientist.

Therefore Madame Curie is a man.

The propositions are entirely consistent and the syllogism is valid, but it fails to provide us with the truth. The point is that consistency is the essential criterion in evaluating the validity of arguments rather than the truth of them. We must determine if the conclusions we arrive at are consistent with our premises in order to judge whether our arguments hold water, but such formal consistency does not guarantee factual accuracy. Surely we would want to think twice if we come up with an empirical finding that was inconsistent with some accepted body of knowledge, but if the whole system of knowledge is wrong, the consistency criterion would never help us realize it.

The coherence and correspondence theories have both positive and negative sides, but the pragmatist regards each of them as too immersed in abstract theorizing. Pragmatism repudiates both the coherence theory and the correspondence theory. The pragmatist simply advises us to observe what actually *works;* when we do what works, we shall have truth. In the realm of ethical theory the Utilitarians maintained that the good is that which has most utility and that which is socially most expedient. Apparently William James believed that what is good enough for the good is good enough for the truth, and so he applied the utilitarian approach to ethics to the theory of truth. In effect, James was telling us that if the good is what it is expedient for us to do, then the truth is what it is expedient for us to think. The simplest objection raised against this theory is that it might be expedient for us to think that all of our problems are caused by the communists, or that if we suffer from pain we need not undergo a medical examination because the pain will go away. The pragmatist, however, has an easy and very convincing answer to this objection: such thinking, he rightly points out, is not really expedient because if we fail to confront the real causes of our problem we will never be able to solve it.

There is another difficulty with the pragmatic theory, which is rather interesting. We all know that there are such things as expedient lies. But if expediency is understood as the criterion of truth, then such lies would be truths. This criticism has some validity, but I think it misses the deeper significance of the pragmatic theory, for the pragmatists are not asserting anything so simple as that truth is anything that satisfies anyone or is immediately expedient for him to believe. What the pragmatists maintain is that it is most meaningful to regard truth in terms of that which produces *verifiable* results. Truth, William James proclaimed, is the cash value of an idea. To critics of pragmatism this seemed like a cheap analogy taken from the business world. On its most serious levels, however, pragmatic theory means that what is true is what pays off in experimental fruitfulness. In this sense a hypothesis that pays off or works may be one quite contrary to what we personally desire or to what is simply expedient for us.

John Dewey, an American pragmatist like James, improved this theory by arguing that the correspondence theory was utterly inadequate as a basis for determining truth in the kind of world in which we live, for it assumes a world of stable and fixed facts—what William James had called a block universe. On the assumptions of the correspondence theory we are expected to compare our judgments with these facts. Dewey claimed man does not confront any such ready-made world of hard and fast facts. Man always interacts with his world, and in so doing he contributes to the making of truth. This is not a world of static things but of dynamic process. This is why Dewey so disliked the word "truth" itself; it suggests a world of fixed, unchanging facts. Dewey preferred the phrase "warranted assertibility." In the world of constant change it is more sensible to attempt to discover a warrant for our assertions in terms of empirical evidence than to attempt to discover anything as absolute as "truth." The real test of our ideas is that they *work*. If a person gets lost in the woods he does not want some absolute truth; he wants to find his way out.

Although Dewey did not like the word "truth," his position was that all that can be meant by speaking of an idea as being true is that the idea works in helping the person find his way out of the woods. Truth is not written into the very structure of the universe awaiting discovery by man. If man must hold onto the idea of truth, he should come to see that it is not something he finds but something he *makes*. This is the kind of world that is full of loose ends and problems. These are indeterminate situations. By the use of their intelligence or by a systematic process of inquiry, men must convert these indeterminate situations into determinate ones; and that means to tie the loose ends together and to solve the problems that confront them as best they can. Thus truth is not something eternal, which is lying about waiting to be found; rather, it is more something men *create* in the process of interacting with the world and of coming to terms with problematic situations.

In seeking to evaluate the pragmatic theory it may certainly be conceded that there are situations in which it can be said truth is made rather than found. Thus a baseball team or a football team *makes* the truth of its victory by actually winning. All life, however, is not like a baseball or football game. Indeed, it seems that in most situations it is not relevant to speak of man as making truth. For example, suppose someone tells you there are some trout in the stream. You go to the stream and look. If there are trout there it is not because you made the truth. It certainly makes sense to speak of *finding* the truth in such situations.

It might be maintained that the pragmatic theory is not a theory of truth at all; rather, it is a method for finding what is true. A person can make a verification and by doing so find out what is the truth of a given situation. The pragmatists seem to have confused the act of verifying with what is usually called truth. For pragmatists the act of verification is the same as making truth.

Furthermore, it seems to follow from the pragmatic theory that what is true today can be false tomorrow. Regarding this as a dynamic universe, pragmatists tend to insist that truth is ever changing. Of course, what was once true may at some time cease to be true, but that does not mean that truth itself changes. Thus it was once true that man was earthbound but now that he has set foot on the moon it is no longer true. But note that not only was it once true man was earthbound but it will always and forever be true that man *was once* earthbound. That man is not now earthbound does not change that truth; it creates a new situation for which there is a different truth.

Although the pragmatists have shown the correspondence theory to have limitations, they have not given us grounds for dismissing it. In effect, they say that we know a key is the true or right one when it actually works and opens the door. The correspondence philosophers, who also are not stopped at that door, maintain that the key opens the door only because it fits the *structure* of the lock. To this the pragmatists retort that one can suppose the key fits the structure of the lock only because it in fact works and opens the door. Yet this last retort is not entirely satisfactory because it presupposes there is a structure of the lock. Thus this returns us to that previously mentioned observation that the pragmatist theory is not really one of truth but is a means of *checking* what is true.

A satisfactory resolution of the matter seems to lie in none of the three theories taken separately. No one of the theories will yield the truth, but all do guide us to what we might regard as truth. There are times when we must compare a proposition with some factual state of affairs to test its adequacy. There are also times when we must ascertain whether a proposition is consistent with a whole set of established propositions. And, of course, we have to test to see if our hypotheses or ideas pay off by producing results for us. The road to truth is not a simple or easy one and may have to be paved with all three theories. Furthermore, it may be necessary to complement the three classical theories of truth with an existential approach to truth.

The correspondence, coherence, and pragmatic theories of truth are all *objective* in the sense, as we have already seen, that they maintain it is not things but propositions that are true; each of these theories prescribes definite objective procedures of ascertaining the truth. In many areas of living we find it adequate to rely upon an objective approach to truth. Generally speaking, this is the case in the field of law, in economic and political analysis, and in the natural sciences. However, in the matters of love, friendship, loyalty, or in the arts and literature, subjective feeling may prove more fruitful than formal objective procedure. If someone you felt quite strongly about exclaimed "I love you," and you thereupon requested a *logical proof,* not only might you not win your proof but you would be very likely to lose your beloved as well. Similarly in the case of religion, if someone insisted upon waiting for objective evidence or logical proofs before he would commit himself to a belief in God, his lack of faith could permanently alienate him from the possibility of experiencing a tie with the absolute. The point is that truth, if fully explored, may be found to lie, at least in part, in a heaven of direct experience beyond the earth of propositions.

Determination of truth may be more than a mere matter of the intelligence. Truth may have to be understood as that which *balances* in one's entire life. There are matters we cannot logically prove to be wrong, and yet somehow our whole life tells us they must be wrong. Sometimes a person will say, "I can't disprove what you are saying, but I know it is not so." If we wanted to be rigorous about it we might say that if he cannot disprove what we say, then he must accept it. In a logical vacuum our insistence would be rational, but such rigor may be out of place in a planet filled with life. It seems there are things that we can feel to be true or false, and that such feeling is more important in certain cases than logical reasoning. This is often the case when we feel that a person is lying. It may be that we cannot put our finger right on a logical point, and in so doing pinpoint a tissue of lie, and yet we cannot believe him. We may be mistaken in such a case, but the subtleties and rich complexities of life are such that often our feeling is a better guide in such matters than our logic. Of course, this argument should not be used as an excuse for letting our lives be ruled by unconfirmed intuition or imagining that we can get along reasonably well in life without a maximum effort to be as rational as possible in the various situations we face. There may well come a point at which our intuitive feelings will have to be confirmed by logic or subsequent experience. But by the same token the need for rationality and logic should not be taken as a denial of the fact that there may be an immediate apprehension that clicks in one's life.

There are some dangerous implications to the idea that truth has subjective dimensions. If it is to be admitted that the truth can be apprehended through feeling, then what must we say about the mob that feels it has the truth when it slips a noose around some poor wretch's neck and hangs him? Does not allowing truth a subjective validity give free rein to fanaticism? Perhaps. But perhaps not, for in this age of technology it is becoming a way of life for advanced technological powers to rationalize by logical means the most barbaric instincts. On the surface, what political leaders assert may be logically valid and yet existentially absurd. Power chooses its own axioms, and from these its think-tank experts draw theorems and postulates. They may be logical, but they are not adequate for human living. A nation can become fanatically committed to a logical proposition. Today's myths are not merely emotional bombs, for they are also rationally justified. One uses charts and graphs and logic to demonstrate that we must defend ourselves against the "monsters" out there. The charts and graphs and logic can be so dazzling that we forget to ask if there really *are* monsters out there. There is today a desperate need for the kind of human intuition that has difficulties with the logic of destruction, even though it may not be able to logically disprove its theorems. In this sense there is a human quality of truth, which surpasses logic, so that although we may say truth is subjective, it does not follow that this opens the door to fanaticism. The test of fanaticism does not depend upon whether we understand truth as subjective or objective, but upon whether we have human values to live by—and the test of our human values is subjective rather than objective.

The three major theories of truth—the correspondence theory, the coherence theory, and the pragmatic theory—all provide us with *standards* or criteria for determining truth and falsity, but what they fail to do is inform us what truth is. In this sense they may be less basic than an existential theory, which provides not just a way of verifying truth but also an analysis of the nature of truth. Just as in the field of ethics we saw that we have to understand value, good, and right in terms of the human being, so too in epistemology and metaphysics do we have to understand truth in terms of the human being. The philosophy of Heidegger is very relevant here, for he maintained that truth had to be understood as *disclosure*. The Greek word for truth originally meant *unhiddenness,* and we may say that he who lives in truth, or who *is* truth, does not hide anything. He discloses himself. I think this is an idea very well understood by people who know nothing at all about Greek etymology or about Martin Heidegger. For example, it is a common experience for people to find a speaker very convincing from a logical standpoint, and yet the harder he works at pushing his point, the less convinced his hearers become. What rings false is not to be found in his words or in his logic, but in himself. Every gesture, every grimace, every glance, every breath *discloses* something, and in the sum of those disclosures rather than in the words do we find the truth. This is particularly relevant in the instance of love. A girl may doubt a man's affection, and he will protest his love for her with great ardor in an attempt to assure her. And yet the more he tells her, the less she may believe him. This is because knowing the truth in such matters is not a question of logic or of words. His propositions may correspond to external facts ("Didn't I do such-and-such, and doesn't that show I love you?"), but if on a deeper level he does not disclose a commitment to what he is saying, she will not believe him. Propositional truth is less basic in this sense than objective truth.

To recognize truth as disclosure is to recognize that the essential ingredient of truth is oneself. People who are cut off from themselves by false emotions and artificial modes of behavior cannot really come to know themselves, and if they cannot know themselves they cannot know the truth. What Heidegger tells us is that if we cannot *be* the truth, we cannot know the truth. In a time when man is so engulfed by depersonalizing and dehumanizing forces, so bombarded with highly rationalized political and social myths, it may be a matter of human survival for him to find some answer to the question "What Is Truth?" To find this answer he will have to face the challenge offered by the proposition: to know the truth one must live it.

Summary

I. DOES GOD EXIST?

1. In classical philosophy there are three fundamental answers to the question of the existence of God. These are the *ontological* argument, the *cosmological* argument, and the *teleological* argument.

2. The *ontological* argument is constructed on the assumption that inherent in the very word *God* is proof of His existence. The premise is that one who knows the word God can only deny God's existence by contradicting himself. By definition God is the supreme and perfect Being, but a Being could not be understood as supreme or perfect unless he was understood

to exist. Kant's formidable criticism of this argument, in effect, was simply that you cannot define anything, even God, into existence.

3. The presupposition of the *cosmological* argument is that this contingent cosmos must have an absolute and ultimate foundation. In explaining the universe it is assumed that causes cannot be traced back infinitely. It is necessary to come to a starting point or a first cause. The first cause must itself be uncaused, for if the first cause itself needed a cause, all would still be in limbo, hanging in mid air as it were. This first cause is thus necessary and absolute. Another term for this first cause is God.

4. The thrust of the *teleological* argument is that everywhere in the universe there may be found evidence of design or plan, and this implies a designer or planner. A designer or planner of the whole universe must be God.

5. Formal arguments for the existence of God have been effectively controverted. It is not necessary for the universe to have had a first cause, but even assuming it did, it is not at all necessary to say that this is God. As for the teleological argument any design, which is found, can be explained in terms of the theory of evolution more adequately than in terms of the existence of God. However, if it cannot be proved there is a God, neither can it be proved there is not, and thus the whole question may be better resolved upon the level of faith or existential commitment.

II. IS MAN FREE?

6. Some of the main philosophical positions dealing with the question of whether or not there is freedom are *determinism, fatalism, indeterminism,* and *libertarianism.*

7. *Determinism* is the doctrine that all events are the *necessary* consequences of antecedent factors. Practically, this means everything that happens is the result of impersonal forces and laws rather than of personal choice or free will. Two forms of determinism may be distinguished. The first, *soft* determinism, permits us to speak as if we were free when we do one thing rather than another, although in fact what we have done is always explained as the inevitable outcome of an antecedent cause or set of causes. The second, *hard* determinism, is based upon the premise that there can be no freedom inasmuch as all is caused by necessary mechanical laws and forces. Since the hard determinist denies freedom, he also denies that man should even speak *as if* he could exercise free choice.

8. *Fatalism* is the view that what will be has been ordained by fate or God. While determinism views the future as a necessary outcome of the past, the fatalist seems to view the past as a necessary outcome of the future in the sense that all that happens *must* do so in order to fulfill some final purpose. The idea is that one must accept all that happens because it is written that it shall be.

9. *Indeterminism* is a defense of the view that the will can come to decisions and courses of action independently of antecedent physical and

psychological forces. On this view it is proper to speak of certain actions or events as not caused.

10. *Libertarianism* is the view that man has free will, on the basis of which he can resist external conditioning influences. Such behavior, however, is a result of inner motivations or ideals.

III. WHAT IS TRUTH?

11. There are three fundamental theories that are designed to show how man can find truth. They are the *correspondence* theory, the *coherence* theory, and the *pragmatic* theory.

12. The *correspondence* theory is the thesis that truth is that which corresponds with the facts. A statement is true if it describes a state of affairs that actually exists.

13. The *coherence* theory is the view that truth is that which coheres or fits in with an established corpus of knowledge. According to this theory, *consistency* with an accepted system of knowledge is the key to truth.

14. The *pragmatic* theory of truth assumes that whatever *works* for us or produces results is true.

15. One problem with the pragmatic theory is that we may never know what the facts really are. The trouble with the coherence theory is that something can be consistent and yet not be true, just as in the pragmatic theory things may seem to work for us and yet may not be true. Although each theory has weaknesses, each also has strengths. In seeking to understand truth one may need to make use of all these theories to some extent. Furthermore, it may also be necessary to accept the view that truth may be existential, in the sense that it is not a matter of propositions of statements but of something that can be known on some deep nonverbal level.

6

The Role of Philosophy in the Space Age

What Have We to Consider

The ultimate consequences of the scientific revolution in the modern world have been to place virtually unlimited power in man's hands. Can those frail hands hold it, or will it slip through them and blow mankind up? Man has now ascended to the moon, not because of his achievements in the area of philosophical speculation but because of his scientific and technical accomplishments.

We live in a time in which it seems we can push buttons to achieve most of our goals. The vast technological power of our civilization has resulted in the construction of an immense synthetic world. As things of the world become more technologically organized, however, human beings themselves become more spiritually and philosophically disorganized—and become more like things. As we enter the portals of outer space are we finding ourselves at the threshold of a great new human world, or a Brave New World? Instead of religion or philosophy to uplift us and give us joy, shall we take pills to create the desired mood? In this synthetic world shall we live artificially on a *soma*—the drug used in Huxley's *Brave New World* to provide men with a state of euphoria? Or shall we live naturally, enduring our problems with a human strength? Will science and technology set our purposes for us, or will we shape our own destiny by creating our own human philosophy? We may find it instructive to first answer the larger question of the meaning of science itself and its relation to philosophy.

To understand the meaning and nature of science and the significance of what it has for man, one must come to grips with problems of the philosophy of science. Science is an organized and systematic study of phenomena, an effort to render facts intelligible by providing explanations of them. Science is not just a random reporting of facts; rather, it is a conceptual system that provided answers to questions of why and how events take place. The job of science, then, is to illuminate the world for us by *explaining* things. This raises the question of what an explanation is. How does science explain what happens?

The classical account of what scientific explanation consists in is variously known as the Causal or Deterministic Theory, the Deductive Model, or the Covering Law Model. This model of explanation assumes that any particular phenomenon to be explained can be demonstrated to be logically covered by or deducible from certain general laws. In uncovering the connection between general laws and specific events, science reveals the essence of reality and gives us a description of the rational structure of the world. The causal or Deductive Model, which is very widely regarded as the most adequate account of the way science works, was given its clearest and most carefully defended statement by Carl G. Hempel and Paul Oppenheim in a classic essay called "The Logic of Explanation." The idea for this article was worked out by Hempel and Oppenheim with a common friend, Kurt Grelling, who along with his wife fell a victim to the Nazis in World War II. Grelling had hoped his work in this area would not be in vain, and thanks to Hempel and Oppenheim it was not.

Hempel and Oppenheim start out by observing that the fundamental goal of science is to make facts intelligible, to explain *why* things happen. To understand how science can accomplish this task we must first understand the structure of an explanation. All explanations consist of two basic elements: the *explanandum* and the *explanans*.[1] The *explanandum* is something that poses a question for us. It is some *specific occurrence*, which takes place in some definite space-time location. Thus, for example, suppose we wish to know why a book falls when dropped. The falling of the book is the *explanandum*, that which is to be explained. If the *explanandum* is that which is to be explained, the *explanans* is that which does the explaining. It is a statement or series of statements, which tells us *why* the event did occur. It does this by fulfilling two obligations: it states antecedent conditions and it states general laws.

---

[1] These expressions were taken from the Latin *explanare*, instead of customary *explicandum* and *explicans*, which are used in a different sense by Hemple and Oppenheim.

The *explanandum* describes phenomena to be explained, and the *explanans* explains phenomena by stating the antecedent conditions and by stating general laws. Stating antecedent conditions involves asserting the existence of certain facts, which are known independently of the facts to be explained. The antecedent conditions make it possible to link that which is to be explained with the relevant general laws in the form of a logical deduction. This takes the form of a syllogism in which the general law is the major premise, the antecedent conditions appear in the minor premise, and the thing to be explained falls into place as the conclusion. Thus in the case of our falling book, we have the following structure of explanation:

1. GENERAL LAW: (this says nothing whatever about the particular situation in question; rather, it asserts general principles): *All objects heavier than air fall if not supported.*

2. ANTECEDENT CONDITIONS: (must establish facts independently of the particular fact to be explained): *This book is an object heavier than air.*

3. FACT TO BE EXPLAINED: (the fact to be explained must be a logical consequence of the general theory and the known facts): *This book falls when dropped.*

We should note that when Hempel and Oppenheim maintained that an explanation in science answers the question *"why?"* they were going against a long tradition that has recognized that a golden achievement of scientific understanding came when Galileo stopped asking *why* things happened, as theologians had done, and started telling *how* things happened. Were Hempel and Oppenheim going backward in returning to the *why* questions Galileo had put to the wayside? In fact they were not, for when thinkers before Galileo had asked *why* things happened they were seeking an *ultimate purpose,* whereas when Hempel and Oppenheim asked *why* things happen they meant "according to what general laws, and by virtue of what antecedent conditions does the phenomenon occur?"[2]

There is always a gap between railway tracks. Why? It is necessary because tracks expand, and if there were no gap they would buckle. How do we know this? All steel expands when heated, and thus any particular tracks will expand. Then one may further ask *why* all steel expands. The answer is that all metal expands. Why? This process of questions and answers, it seems, can go on indefinitely, and we may as well stop here and ask how far can the question *why* be pushed? One may explain something has happened because it is an instance of a general law, and then one may show that this general law is itself covered by a more inclusive general law. First laws are derived directly from experience—for example, Kepler's three laws describing motion of the planets, or Galileo's law of free fall, and the law of the tides. These all explain certain known facts or tell *why* these facts occur.

[2] Carl G. Hempel and Paul Oppenheim, "The Logic of Explanation," in Feigl and Brodbeck, eds., *Readings in the Philosophy of Science* (New York: Appleton-Century Crofts, 1935), p. 320.

Then Newton went further and constructed a theory, which supplied a further why for all three previous theories. From Newton's laws and certain established facts it is possible to deduce all of the laws of Kepler, Galileo's law of free fall, and the law of tides. Then Einstein took another step and formulated an even more inclusive theory by which he could explain all of the previous theories and the facts they accounted for and much more. This process continues until the limit of the knowledge we possess is reached, which means, in effect, that it continues indefinitely.

Any explanation that can explain why something has happened can also be used to make predictions about what will happen. Indeed, prediction and explanation are so closely related that Hempel and Oppenheim maintained they are *symmetrical*. Explanations are directed toward past occurrences, and predictions are directed toward future ones. Reichenbach suggested this close relationship by calling explanation a type of "postdiction"—that is an explanation "predicts" what has already happened. The same laws that let me predict that if I leave a pot of water on a fire the water will boil, also let me "postdict" that if you left a pot of water on the fire yesterday it will have boiled, for explanation and prediction are logically similar.

The Hempel and Oppenheim theory of explanation is a most careful statement of what scientists do in accounting for the way things happen and it sums up what a great number of scientists take to be a description of their activity. If this model of scientific explanation is correct, it means we must view science as an accumulating of empirical data, a building up of laws out of such data, and a deducing of certain conclusions from those laws. Yet, despite the fact that many scientists accept the Hempel-Oppenheim model of scientific explanation, their deductive model does not have the field to itself. Another model, technically known as a *conventionalist* theory of science, views science as essentially nondeductive. One of the most outstanding advocates of this *conventionalist* theory was the great French mathematician Henri Poincairé, and one of the most illuminating contemporary statements of this approach has been offered by Stephen Toulmin, a teacher under whom I was fortunate enough to study the philosophy of science.

The crux of Toulmin's approach is that scientific explanation is not deductive, and that we do not derive explanations from factual laws. In some sciences and in the early stages of physics, facts may be central and can be verified by direct observation; on this level our knowledge can be enlarged by accumulating facts, and inference tends to proceed from facts to facts. Thus a naturalist studying the migration of swallows might plot the observed tracks of a large number of flocks, and by putting all these collected facts together, he might *discover* the new fact that all the swallows flew along great circles. Similarly, when calculations of the orbital motion of the planet Uranus kept producing discrepancies, the French astronomer Urbain Leverrier inferred that there must be a planet not known of at that time beyond the planet Uranus, which was disturbing its motion. As a consequence of this inference, this planet was discovered and named Neptune. This discovery resulted from the taking of facts already possessed and inferring to a new fact.

Toulmin, however, contended that this description of science as an endeavor that amasses facts and makes generalizations and predictions on the basis of them is not accurate except in the early stages of a science. On the contrary, this sort of deductive procedure is precisely what science is not involved in doing in its most important stages. As Toulmin saw it, science is not primarily engaged in the accumulation of facts. On its highest level science is engaged in discovering new rules of inference rather than new facts. A rule of inference is not itself a fact but a symbolic means for linking facts. The most important work done in a mature science is the novelty of a new scientific conclusion, which does not come from the factual data but from the *inference*. The deductive model claims that science consists in finding new phenomena and looking at them in a familiar way, but Toulmin turns this around and says that the essence of scientific discovery consists in looking at familiar phenomena in a new way. Science does not primarily give us new facts but new ways of looking at facts. Breakthroughs in science are really made when we gain a new perspective for understanding old problems.

Toulmin illustrated his view by examining the law of optics, which states "light travels in straight lines." Now just what did the scientific discovery that "light travels in straight lines" mean? One thing it does not mean is that light *always* travels in this way. It can be diffracted, refracted, or scattered, and these facts do not affect the validity of the principle that light travels in straight lines. The first thing we should notice if we want to understand the type of scientific explanation being offered in the generalization that light travels in straight lines is that the key words *light* and *travel* are given *novel* uses in the very statement of this discovery. The real discovery does not involve any new fact; rather, it makes us think of light patches and shadows in a *new way*, and "in consequence coming to ask new questions about them, questions like 'Where from?', 'Where to?' and 'How fast?', which are intelligible only if one thinks of the phenomena in this new way."[3] Until one has been introduced to the basic ideas of geometrical optics, one would not even know what a physicist meant when he talked about light "traveling." He surely does not mean "sending lanterns by rail." The principle of the rectilinear propagation of light was not a discovery of a new property—that is, it was not discovered *that light travels,* for no one has ever observed light traveling. Rather, it was discovered that it would be meaningful to describe light *as if it traveled.*

According to Toulmin's account, the value of scientific discovery lies in the fact that it provides *special ways* of looking at particular problems, which enable us to solve and make sense of them. Thus Toulmin understands the logical form of explanation in a very different way than do Hempel and Oppenheim. For him, it is not a matter of deduction from a general fact to a particular fact. Indeed, as Toulmin understands scientific explanation, the general premise is *never factual;* it is, rather, a more or less metaphorical

[3] Stephen Toulmin, *The Philosophy of Science* (London: Hutchinson's University Library, 1953), p. 21.

model that provides us with a way of looking at the phenomenon in question. Toulmin explains:

> *The discovery that light travels in straight lines—the transition from the state of affairs in which this was not known to that in which it was known—was a double one: it comprised the development of a technique for representing optical phenomena which was found to fit a wide variety of facts, and the adoption along with this technique of a new model, a new way of regarding these phenomena, and of understanding why they are as they are.*[4]

The law that light travels in straight lines does not imply that scientists had discovered light atomized into individual rays; it implies, rather, that they find it helpful to *represent* it as consisting of such rays. It is not what scientists find in the way of facts that counts, but the *ways* by which they *represent* facts. In this sense the major turning points in the history of science consist of major reconstructions of ways of thinking; they involve not so much the finding of new facts as the finding of new frameworks in terms of which facts can be understood or interpreted. Legitimate scientific theories are not constructed of facts or wrecked by them. According to Toulmin, the notion that old theories may have to be overthrown and new ones built whenever new facts are found is simply a popular misconception of the scientific method. Inadequate theories are dismantled only by the discovery of *new ways* of looking at facts, of *new conceptual* formulations.

Toulmin's emphasis on the way of looking at facts, rather than on facts themselves, certainly seems to be an advance over the simply deductive model of Hempel and Oppenheim. With its more sophisticated model of scientific explanations, his account of science recognizes the inescapable fact that there seems to be no such thing as a naked fact. Facts all come already clothed in theories. Terms are never purely phenomenological—that is, purely experiential or factual—never independent of interpretation. As the late Russell Hanson has made so clear, "There's more to seeing than meets the eyeball."[5] Hanson points out:

> *If only observers would restrict themselves to the color patches they see, the buzzes and tinkles they hear, the rough and smooth surfaces they touch, and the sweet or sour taste of things—only then could the strictly empirical basis of an observation be detached from the theoretical embroidery attached thereto; only then can the properties of nature be demarcated from the properties specified in the observers' theories about nature.*[6]

Of course, people do not restrict themselves to such fundamental observations, which is why we must recognize that it is conceptions of facts, not perceptions of facts, that we have to deal with. The statement "An apple is on the table" sounds like a simple enough statement of fact,

---

[4] *Ibid.*, p. 29.

[5] Norwood Russell Hanson, "Observation and Interpretation," in *Philosophy of Science Today,* ed. Sidney Morgenbesser (New York: Basic Books, Inc., 1967), p. 91.

[6] *Ibid.*, p. 90.

but actually it depends on the fact that our society conventionally interprets a certain array of facts—a certain range of colors, weights, shapes, sizes, textures, and tastes—as belonging to the same class: apple. Similarly, when we say that man is a mammal we are not stating a simple fact but are referring to our convention of agreeing to class together all vertebrate hairy animals that are viviparous and nurse their young. Why should it be considered a fact that man belongs to the same class as dogs, who have twice as many legs, and not a fact that man belongs to the same class as birds, who share the quality of two-leggedness with him? There is no reason; if early biologists had considered the number of legs more important than the way young are born, man would be a bird and not a mammal. If botanists considered taste and color more important than seed structure, then sour green apples and sweet red apples would not both be apples. The fact that the thing on the table is an apple and the fact that man is a mammal depend upon how we have agreed by convention to conceptualize these phenomena. If our conventional conceptions changed, then the "facts" would change—as indeed they did in the case of man, who was not considered an animal at all, let alone a mammal, until a relatively few centuries ago. For this reason, after studying the so-called facts that physicists attempt to understand, Hanson concluded:

> *Fundamental physics is primarily a search for intelligibility—it is philosophy of matter. Only secondarily is it a search for objects and facts. . . . Microphysicists seek new modes of conceptual organization. If that can be done the finding of new entities will follow. Gold is rarely discovered by one who has not got the lay of the land. . . .*
>
> *Physical science is not just a systematic exposure of the senses to the world; it is also a way of thinking about the world, a way of forming conceptions. The paradigm observer is not the man who sees and reports what all normal observers see and report, but the man who sees in physical objects what no one else has seen before.*[7]

Thus Toulmin and Hanson offer a creative, imaginative, and philosophical understanding of science. Their *conventionalist* or nondeductive understanding of scientific explanation results in a much less *mechanical* view of the world. Two particularly important consequences of their view are the rejection of the idea of *crucial experiment* and a new understanding of the nature and role of *scientific prediction*.

On traditional views of science, it is believed that a hypothesis is formed to explain some problem, and that this hypothesis should then be subjected to a crucial experiment. A hypothesis, theory, or law is always open to *empirical testing*, and it can always flunk the test: if we find a fact—just one fact—that is inconsistent with the theory, then the theory collapses. According to the conventionalists, however, there is no such thing as a crucial experiment in this sense. Because science is not primarily in the business of working with facts, the business of a scientific theory can never

[7] Norwood Russell Hanson, *Patterns of Discovery* (Cambridge: University Press, 1958), pp. 18f. and 30.

be shut down by facts. Phillip Frank, who has a great understanding of science, has pointed out that scientists never reject a theory because it disagrees with the facts unless a new theory is found to replace it. For example, scientists long held to the theory that plant and animal species were immutable—that is, each species had definite characteristics of its own that remained permanently unchangeable. Remarkably, they held this theory despite the fact that horticulturalists and animal breeders have been changing species for as long as men have been domesticating plants and animals and despite the fact that fossil evidence has been showing that species had been constantly changing over the course of natural history. No amount of contrary evidence could dislodge this theory. Yet Charles Darwin dislodged it. Did Darwin discover some new facts that proved the theory of the immutability of species was incorrect? No; he produced a new *theory*, which *explained* the mutability of species. This is a clear case of the fact that in science theories are refuted by other theories, not by facts. In a sense, then, science is exactly the opposite of what we generally suppose it to be: theories are not evaluated by facts; on the contrary, facts are evaluated in terms of theories. If a theory is accepted and if it accounts for things there is a need to explain, then facts conflicting with it will be reinterpreted. Facts can serve to displace a theory only when there is a new theory to replace the old.

Just as the nondeductive theory of explanation rejects the concept of the crucial experiment, so it also rejects the idea that prediction and explanation are symmetrical. Michael Scriven has pointed out that there are things we can explain very well but cannot predict. In the nice, neat, deductive world of science, explanation and prediction are always opposite sides of the same coin, so that if you turn one side over you will always see the other. However, Scriven has raised serious doubt about whether this is the case in the real world. Thus we can explain but we cannot predict that the *only* cause of X is Z. This is so because we may be able to show very clearly that Z is the cause of X, and yet Z may often occur without being followed by X. Indeed, it may not even be probable that if Z occurs, X will follow. What is more, although we can actually explain X by saying that it is caused by Z, there may be cases in which we can actually predict that when Z occurs it will *not* be followed by X; and *if* X does follow Z, we can say that Z explains its occurrences. This means that there are events that, although they may not be *predicted* by certain propositions, can be *explained* by those propositions. For example, sexual intercourse is the only cause of pregnancy, and one can explain every case of pregnancy by sexual intercourse. Yet one cannot predict that pregnancy will follow every intercourse, and, given the nature of female fertility, pregnancy is a less than probable outcome of an act of intercourse. If contraceptive methods are used, one can even predict that intercourse will not cause pregnancy; and yet if pregnancy does occur, it was caused by intercourse. In this last instance we can see clearly that explanation bears absolutely no relation to prediction.

These conventionalist and nondeductive arguments reveal that those who dismiss philosophy by comparing it to science and concluding that philosophy is not logically empirical enough and does not stick to the facts enough do not in fact have a valid point, for in science and in all life understanding is not a matter of fact gathering but of interpretation of fact, and for that a theoretical framework or model is required. Science provides models for understanding the universe and how it works, but man must also understand what meaning the universe has for him, what his place in it is, and what the point of things is. For this we must turn to philosophy for models. What is particularly needed in this highly technical age is not more information but more wisdom, more understanding of the information. We must understand what our knowledge *means*. Philosophical truths are ideas, conceptions, or theories which give us the best way of looking at or understanding facts. Philosophical ideas must be judged not as empirical formulations but as formulations that make sense of the empirical world with which science deals. They can equip us with a coherent explanation of existence, give us insights into the empirical conditions of our existence, and thus enable us to live more fruitfully.

Understanding the roles of science and philosophy this way opens the possibility that historically insoluble problems, such as whether man is *free*, what *justice* is, the nature of the *self*, the existence of *God*, or the meaning of truth, may not be insoluble if they are seen as *conceptual* rather than empirical questions. There may be no way to show *empirically* whether or not man is free, but that is because this is not an empirical question. We should not ask whether empirical facts verify the doctrine of free will or the doctrine of determinism. Rather, we should ask which of the two doctrines offers the more meaningful and adequate *concept* or model in terms of which we can make sense of life. Our study of the philosophy of science reveals that at all levels—that is, in science as well as in philosophy—we must always ask what views, beliefs, ideas, concepts, or modes of understanding make the most sense out of life and contribute the most to the full possibility of human development. Even the seemingly value-free world of science is permeated with value—with human meaning.

Summary

1. Because this is an age of science it is particularly important that man understand the meaning of science and its relation to philosophy and to human problems. This provides the discipline of the philosophy of science with a special importance, for it is this discipline that helps us understand the meaning and nature of science and clarify the implications of scientific findings.

2. Two basic approaches to philosophy of science may be distinguished. One approach we may call the Deductive or Covering Law Theory of science, and the other we may call the Conventionalist Theory of science.

3. According to the Deductive or Covering Law philosophy of science, scientific explanation consists in developing general laws and explaining specifics in terms of them. It is possible on this theory to deduce a specific

phenomena from general laws. When we have well-established general laws, we can explain what has happened and predict what will happen.

4. The Conventionalist school assumes that scientific explanation is not deductive and that we do not derive explanations from factual laws. Stephen Toulmin, a defender of this approach, claims that on its highest levels science is engaged in discovering new rules of inference rather than new facts. A rule of inference is not itself a fact but a symbolic device for linking facts. According to this approach, imaginative models must be formulated in terms of which we can understand facts. These models are not inductively built up from facts, and deductions are not made on the basis of them. A model in the conventionalist theory is a means of giving us a new perspective from which we can understand an old problem. A scientist must formulate some theory that will illuminate the facts. This means he is not looking for new facts but new devices for making sense of facts already available.

5. The importance of the conventionalist approach is that according to it science is not providing us with a description of reality but rather with a means of dealing with phenomena. This implies that creative genius is more significant than pure technical competence in the field of science. This in turn suggests the need for creative and imaginative ideas and theoretical or philosophical frameworks for dealing with them. Here the creative speculation of the philosopher may have urgent relevance.

PART III

THE PERSECUTION AND DEATH OF THE PHILOSOPHER

Philosophy, Human Freedom, and Tragedy

Philosophy As a Way of Life

The aim of a philosophy is to shape not only one's way of thinking but also one's way of life. Anyone who casts his bread into the waters of philosophy should find not only replenishment in the form of new ideas but also new meaning in his life. Ideally philosophical thinking should be balanced by a philosophical existence.

In our time—a time of widespread manipulation of opinion, of uncritical acceptance of official lines by vast multitudes throughout the world, and of growing perfection of thought control means—philosophical *criticism* becomes more than ever essential to the survival of truth and intellectual integrity; and *a fortiori*, in an age of increasing mechanization of mankind, of unprecedented technological development, and of the accompanying power to mold and control human behavior, the ability to live and function on a philosophical level becomes more than ever essential to the survival of humanity. We should not be able to separate the thought of a man from

345

346

THE
PERSECUTION
AND DEATH
OF THE
PHILOSOPHER

his life. Thinking and experiencing should blend into a continuum and provide a richly unified existence. The life of man should be unified through the integration of philosophical thought with philosophical behavior.

As life is actually lived, it may well be that a philosopher will think upon a philosophical level but will fail to live at that level. He may have a profound and full philosophical interpretation of the world even though his own life is shallow and empty. Kant did much more in his philosophy than in his life; in fact, he did not do much of anything in his life. Similarly, a philosophic interest in truth did not keep Sir Francis Bacon from being downright dishonest in his personal life. In his philosophy Seneca was a great Stoic who emphasized the need for man to live beyond all material circumstance, but in his private life he was a hardheaded businessman who knew how to pull off a fast deal.

Conversely, there have been many who have lived upon a philosophical level without thinking upon it. This has often been true of certain deeply religious persons or of persons not formally educated who lived very close to the earth, and it also seems to be more the case with people of the Orient than people of the Western world. If we had to choose, it would seem to be more valuable for men to live philosophically than for them to think philosophically, for living so puts them in touch with reality and gives them a satisfaction with life, which is very difficult to attain on an intellectual level. A man who does not have the wisdom that manifests itself in terms of elaborate thought patterns may be at no loss if he makes up for it with natural wisdom that expresses itself in his simple words and in his living. There is nothing artificial or contrived about such a person. He is mature, and knows how to accept life for what it is.

The most desirable situation is to both live and think upon a philosophical level. The philosophy of Socrates was so integrated into his life that he did not ever feel the need to write anything. There is a long list of philosophers who thought and lived beautifully—Epictetus, Marcus Aurelius, Giordano Bruno, Benedict Spinoza, Voltaire, and Henri Bergson. Such philosophers, as well as religious figures such as Buddha, Confucius, and Jesus, are beings in whom there was combined a wisdom of thinking and of feeling.

In this age of cybernetics man can put the computer to human use, or he can use himself as a computer and become an android. Man cannot substitute technical planning, mathematical projections, and organizational decrees for spontaneous human feeling and still remain human. When the logical is used in isolation from human purpose, man becomes pathological. Thus the philosophical way of life is especially important today because it involves an endeavor to make truth existential as well as intellectual. Once when a great religious teacher died, his disciple was asked to name the most important thing the late rabbi had ever done. "Whatever he happened to be doing," the disciple answered. A life of which this can be said is a life fully at one with itself. This is the type of life philosophy aims at, and it is a life supremely worth living.

If one will consider the creative possibilities in which a human being may live, it should become clear that one might think of a philosophy not merely in terms of theoretical formulations but also in terms of a man's life style. The writings of philosophers such as Plato, Aristotle, St. Thomas, Spinoza, Kant, and Hegel provide us with examples of philosophy, but the very lives of Socrates, Buddha, Jesus, St. Francis, Spinoza, and Gandhi may be understood as philosophies in themselves apart from whatever these men may have formally stated. They lived in very distinctive patterns and their lives themselves stand as arguments for truth, love, freedom, and peace. Indeed, the lives of such men may stand as such eloquent testimony to certain ideals that men of power may regard them as dangerously subversive to the routine order such power holders want. If philosophers may seem odd or eccentric to many people because they live differently from most of us, they may also seem dangerous because the truth in their lives exposes the lies by which many of us live.

Of course philosophy is profound thinking, but it is also—and more importantly—profound living. We can look for examples of the love of wisdom in profound lives as well as in profound ideas. Thus it may be most valuable to consider what we might regard as philosophical patterns of life, which, of course, can be lived by men other than professional philosophers. In the lives of such men we shall find great wisdom and in many of them great tragedy, which must result in a world still too much founded upon the folly of practicality and power.

No Harm Comes to Good Men

Philosophy is the love of wisdom. There are many who believe that for a red-blooded man there are better things to love than wisdom. It seems to be supposed by such persons that wisdom is an abstraction that one can best find when he manages to get lost from life. However, one cannot be on good terms with wisdom and on bad terms with life, for we would hardly call a man wise who did not get along well with life. If one really wishes to understand philosophy, it is not enough to learn to pass formal examinations in this subject; one must also learn to face the tests of living. If one has knowledge of the truth as an intellectual matter but does not live it, then this knowledge is shallow and incomplete; if a philosopher speaks about the truth and yet fails to make it a part of his existence, his words have a hollow ring.

When the philosopher seeks not only to know the truth but to live it, he is set free from enslaving needs to seek fame or fortune, pleasure or power. This makes it possible for him to belong to himself, to his beliefs, and to his ideals, and not to any power on earth. Of course, this makes philosophy a dangerous vocation, for the powers that be do not take lightly any man's effort to be free of them. History has been very much a flowing stream of blood, violence, and power, and those who have sought love, truth, and justice have often been drowned in its whirling currents. Those who have run the world have not offered philosophers a welcome home in it, and it is tragically true that the men who have devoted them-

348

THE
PERSECUTION
AND DEATH
OF THE
PHILOSCPHER

selves to the highest values not only have not been honored for their service but, on the contrary, have been treated as if they were criminals.

When we look at the life of Socrates we can see man at his very best, and the story of his life is one wonderful love affair with truth, justice, and virtue. Mankind paid him tribute for his unswerving dedication to goodness by casting him in prison, binding him in chains, and executing him with poison. Of course, had Socrates been willing to flirt with the attractive lady of injustice, to play politics, to make a compromise with those in power, he could easily have secured his freedom. To Socrates, however, that would have been the harshest and least acceptable condemnation. He had always taught that the unexamined life is not worth living, and his own existence was the most complete expression of the examined life. For such a man, accepting a compromise that would gain his freedom would have meant making his life a lie; by his own principles such a life would not be worth living. So Socrates chose death—chose to die for truth rather than live a lie. When his friends pleaded with him to renounce his beliefs and save his life, he patiently explained why he could not do so; and when they wept for his plight he comforted them. Socrates had once declared that no harm can come to a good man, and when his enemies killed him they did him a service, as he knew they would, for they brought his ideas fully to life.

French paintings XVIII–XIX Cent.
Jacques Louis David (1748–1825)
The Death of Socrates. *Oil on canvas. 51 × 77 1/4".*
The Metropolitan Museum of Art, Wolfe Fund.

With all of his heart and soul and his full being, Socrates so ardently loved the truth that his life revealed for us the meaning of loving truth, not as an abstract ideal but in the flesh and blood as a concrete reality. As the life of Socrates was so perfect an expression of the love of truth, so the life of Jesus was a beautiful expression of the truth of love. Socrates brought the world truth, and was poisoned for it; Jesus brought the world love and was crucified for it. When Pontius Pilate ordered Jesus to appear before him, Jesus declared to Pilate that he was born and came into the world to bear witness to the truth. The truth to which Jesus bore witness was the truth of love. Jesus was a simple and beautiful man who could do harm to no one and who brought love to everyone. For that he was despised and defiled as if he were the most depraved criminal. He was mocked, tortured, and crucified; yet he bore the malice and howling of the crowd with dignified silence. Though his body was tortured his soul could not be touched. Jesus asserted he was "free" to lay down his life; even when he was crucified his love was not harmed.

Just as Socrates was poisoned and Jesus was nailed to the cross, so Giordano Bruno, the man generally recognized as the first modern philosopher, was burned at the stake. Giordano Bruno formulated a brilliant image of an open universe, and in doing so he came into conflict with the closed minds of his world. Bruno sought to direct men to a new world and was punished by the old world. He was an honest and good man, dedicated to discovering the truth about the universe, and for this he "died, despised and suffering, after eight years of agony."[1]

Languishing in prison and suffering eight years of torment and abuse, Bruno was taken naked and bound to the stake, and at Campo di Fioro, the Square of Flowers, he was burned to death on February 17, 1600. The Church could not accept his views and so rejected them with fire. It was a horrendous ceremony, the burning of Bruno, and yet he faced it without fear. He said his soul would rise to paradise with the smoke and that he had nothing to fear here on earth. Those who had the power to put him in prison and to take his life did not have enough power to make him bow to their authority. Ironically, he had less to fear than they, and it was he who passed judgment on his judges: "Perchance you who pronounce my sentence are in greater fear than I who receive it."[2]

Benedict Spinoza, a giant even among the great philosophers, was greatly influenced by Bruno, and he too fell prey to the intolerance of man. Few men have lived so at peace with themselves and with the world as Spinoza, and yet this man was viciously rejected and condemned by his own people, cast aside by the woman he loved, and surrounded by a world of people torn with hatred; he died from tuberculosis at an early age. He asked very little of life and yet gave so much of it. This saint among men was not honored by his fellow men but "cursed and damned," according to the official declaration that excommunicated him from the Jewish religion. It

[1] Dorothea Waley Singer, *Giordano Bruno: His Life and Thought* (New York: Henry Schuman, 1950), p. 5.

[2] *Ibid.*, p. 179.

350

THE
PERSECUTION
AND DEATH
OF THE
PHILOSOPHER

was pronounced that he should be cursed day and night; people were ordered not to speak to him, not to stay under the same roof with him, and to remain a certain distance away from him. From the way in which he was treated it would seem he was a leper or a fiend rather than a simple man of truth. The Jews themselves were cut off from the rest of the world, and now Spinoza, a Jew, was further cut off from his own religion. His own father threw him out, and his friends refused to associate with him. Despite the hell of his existence, because of his internal calm, Spinoza lived a heavenly and a blessed life.

Just as the life of Spinoza is a beautiful expression of the tragic resignation of the philosopher, the life of Voltaire is a manifestation of the unconquerable laughter of wisdom. Voltaire did not have the same moving love of life one feels in Spinoza, and yet there was a great love in him—the love of freedom. His entire life was dedicated to a fight for freedom. Very early in his life Voltaire was taught that the price for his love of freedom might be his own liberty, as he was tossed into the bastille as a result of his free expression—but his stay in prison only intensified his concern for freedom. For the rest of his long life, wherever one found injustice, the deprivation of man's rights, or the loss of his freedom, one would be likely to find Voltaire there fighting against these.

In the nineteenth-century philosopher Sören Kierkegaard, the lonely Dane, can be found something of the Socratic love of truth, the truth of love, and the love of freedom. One finds in Kierkegaard not only the sense of the tragic but also the sense of the comic. Kierkegaard lived for Christ, and precisely for this reason he felt he had to live against the Christians. The Church as Kierkegaard knew it in his native Denmark had become too materialistic, too comfortable, and too corrupt. He lashed out against its iniquities, and in turn he himself was forced to feel its sting. He was but one man against the powerful establishment, and although truth was on his side virtually everyone else was against him. Kierkegaard was a sensitive soul who had a brilliant mind, the sharpest wit, and a keen sense of human dignity, and yet he was mocked and ridiculed as if he were a clown. Nonetheless, despite the personal consequences, he never relented in his effort to reveal inequities in the Church. In his efforts to bring the truth to the people, he took his case out into the streets. He gave all of his heart and soul and might to this mission and did so with such fervor that he finally collapsed in the streets. He was taken to the hospital and died not long after. Only after his death was it learned that he lived in dire poverty during his long struggle to bring new life to Christianity.

Kierkegaard was one of the last great philosophers whose lives are as exemplary as their works. One has a most difficult time finding this quality in contemporary philosophers, who have a tendency to blend into our technological and scientific environment and to become members of the academic community not noticeably different from academics in other fields. Yet even in this century the love of wisdom has not been entirely eroded and has remained strong in some of our great philosophers, such as the French philosopher Henri Bergson.

In an age of science Bergson was completely a man of science in the early part of his career; his only interest in nature was from an objective scientific point of view. He did not love life; rather, he dispassionately studied it. Then he moved into the country and began to take long walks until nature began to move into his soul and enlarge it with the warmth of a deep love for life. Bergson found a new vitality in himself, in life itself, and in his philosophy. The love of truth and the truth of love and freedom that more and more came to be part of his life were beautifully revealed in his latter days. Henri Bergson descended from a long line of strictly religious Jews, yet as he went on in life he found that Judaism did not give him the spiritual guidance and comfort he wanted. He then turned increasingly toward Catholicism until finally he decided to take the ultimate leap and become a Catholic. It was precisely at this time that fascism was really getting on the march, crushing Jews beneath its heals, on its way to world conquest. When the tentacles of the Nazi octopus entwined France in 1940 all Jewish professors were forced to resign from state universities. But under these conditions Bergson found that he could not renounce Judaism, even though the religion had lost its appeal to him. He stood strong and firm in the religion of his fathers, and renounced the Nazis instead. He resigned from his post and, instead of sitting back in the comfort his old age had earned, he stood in courage alongside the persecuted Jews. It was only discovered after his death that Bergson had already taken the step to Catholicism when the Nazis entered France. Although it would have given him satisfaction to reveal his conversion, he would not do so at a time when his fellow Jews found themselves in such trouble. He continued to serve his own religion even when it no longer served his spiritual yearnings.

Just as Bergson in France managed to love wisdom in this war-torn century, Bertrand Russell in England did so too. In Russell the love of wisdom manifested itself as an intense love of truth and freedom. When he took a moral stand against war during the first world war, Trinity College recognized his integrity by firing him. The War Office, acting as if he were an activist spy rather than a pacifist, prohibited Russell from certain areas lest he signal submarines or engage in some such acts of subversion. Finally after one particularly critical article about the war in a paper called the *Tribunal,* Bertrand Russell was put in prison. This was not the last time Russell came into conflict with authority as a direct consequence of his fervent commitment to free expression. In the United States he was denied his right to assume a teaching post he had been granted at the City College in New York. The Episcopal Church and various organizations of Catholics and Baptists were in terror that the moral order of the world would collapse if Russell were permitted to teach the philosophical foundations of mathematics at City College.

Yet, no matter what efforts were exerted to stop him, Russell never ceased in his personal fight to make this a better and more humane world. Indeed, as this philosopher grew older his zeal for justice grew younger and more vital. At the age of eighty-nine, when many who reach that age are being put safely away in an old-age home, Bertrand Russell was again jailed

352

THE
PERSECUTION
AND DEATH
OF THE
PHILOSOPHER

for his activities in a peace demonstration. When he died in 1970 at the age of ninety-eight, he was still actively engaged in the antiwar movement, after over half a century of vigorous work in pacifist causes.

Bertrand Russell's love of truth and freedom throughtout his life led him in a dedicated quest for peace. The love of wisdom embraces the love of peace, and perhaps no human being better exemplified this love than Mahatma Gandhi. If one were challenged to find one word with which to describe the philosophy of Mahatma Gandhi, he could not do better than with the word *Satyagraha*. It means *holding onto the truth,* or *soul force.* Gandhi had learned early in life that if one is to hold onto the truth one must absolutely renounce all violence. Gandhi was a small and frail person, but no amount of might upon this earth could deflect him from his course of truth and justice. In 1922 Gandhi was arrested for sedition and convicted. Before passing sentence, the judge provided Gandhi an opportunity to make a statement on his own behalf. Gandhi did not deny his guilt, ask for mercy, or plead for a lighter sentence; rather, he directly confronted the judge and informed him that he actually was even more guilty than the Advocate General realized in developing charges against him. Furthermore, Gandhi informed the judge, unless he were willing to step down and join Gandhi, it was his duty to impose the very stiffest sentence he could. Sentenced to six years in prison, Gandhi said that it was a light sentence and thanked the court for its courtesy; he was then led away to Sabarmati prison. When people came forth sobbing and fell at his feet, Gandhi, cheerful and smiling, sought to encourage them. In 1948 Gandhi, who always radiated the most beautiful love and sought for peace and unity in the world, was violently shot to death at a prayer meeting by a fanatic who could not stand Gandhi's tolerance of the Muslims. Thus Gandhi, who lived for nonviolence, died by violence. A man of hatred can always kill a man of love, but what he cannot kill is his love. To men such as Socrates, Jesus, and Gandhi, what matters is not how long a man lives but how he lives.

A philosopher can never resist a tyrant with force, for if he were to do so he would only become tyrannical himself. However, although the philosopher may not be able to summon armies, masses of wealth, or public support for what might be his unpopular ideas, his devotion to values provides him with the strength and courage to stand strong against all ill winds of tyranny. Indeed, he alone can always make totalitarianism imperfect by refusing to be a part of it.

Jean Paul Sartre expressed this idea and his love for freedom in his essay "The Republic of Silence." Sartre explained that those who resisted the Nazis were never more free than when they lost all of their rights. They were insulted and forced to take it in silence, but, just because an all-powerful police force tried to force them to hold their tongues, every single word assumed the importance of a declaration of principles. And because they were constantly hunted as beasts, every gesture took on the significance of a solemn commitment. Facing death, those in the French Resistance came to understand what was really important and because of that, they had the power to say "no" to the Nazis. In the end it is invariably the case that those who speak only with the voice of power or prestige never say so much as even the silence of a poisoned Socrates, a crucified Christ, or a bullet-riddled Gandhi.

In this age of technological and nuclear power, growing totalitarianism, and increasing dehumanization, men will have to learn more to say "no" and to stand alone. We must learn not only to say "no" to the violence of those in power but also to violent impulses within ourselves. An industrial age is an age of getting things done—an age of action. Lest we do the wrong things, however, we need to reflect upon our actions. If we are to have wisdom we shall have to look deeply into our world, our history, and ourselves.

When the judge pronounced sentence upon Gandhi, he solemnly observed that the law is no respecter of persons and that, therefore, Gandhi would have to be considered solely in the capacity of a criminal. When the civilization we have built looks upon men such as Socrates, Jesus, and Gandhi as criminals, we must ask if there is not something fundamentally wrong with it. The most noble among us have been treated with the greatest ignobility—have been tortured, tormented, beaten, imprisoned, and murdered—not by barbarians but by civilized men, not by criminals but by those entrusted with upholding the law. These men were acting in the name of civilized institutions that represented honor and justice, and their actions force us to ask if there is not something wrong with ourselves, for these are *our* institutions.

Conclusion

Of course, not all philosophers *love truth* so perfectly as Socrates, nor do they possess the *truth of love* so fully as Jesus, nor do they *love freedom* as completely as Voltaire or Bertrand Russell, nor do they *love peace* so profoundly as Gandhi, but these elements are found in some degree or in some balance in the love of wisdom. When we study philosophy we should see that behind what sometimes appears to be the eccentric lives of the philosophers or the impractical ideas that sometimes arise from their work is a love of wisdom, which gives them great personal power, meaning, and purpose. The student of philosophy should learn not only to know the ideas of philosophy but also to feel within himself a love for wisdom. Furthermore, if to love wisdom in some way or another involves loving truth, having the truth of love within oneself, and thus being set free so that one is able to find peace with oneself and the world, then to love wisdom is really to love life.

Before Gandhi was murdered in a sacred place, he was offered protection by police. He refused it, saying that the police could not protect him, that only God could protect him. He was shot, but that did not matter to him. He always lived as he wanted and died doing what he knew he must. No harm can come to a good man. Realizing this releases one from the

354

THE
PERSECUTION
AND DEATH
OF THE
PHILOSOPHER

fears that enslave so many and makes it possible to be open to all things with love. That is wisdom.

In the face of great opposition, persecution and even death, philosophers are men who love wisdom and have not altered their dedication to freedom. Voltaire who was ever harassed in his earlier life, nonetheless lived for the ideal of freedom, and as fate would have it he ended his life finding relative success and good fortune. To many philosophers and lovers of wisdom, fate however was not so kind and their lives were beset with tragedy, and yet in the end such tragedy conferred eloquence on their commitment to freedom. Harm does not really come to good men, at least not to their purpose in living.

There are men who pursue fame and fortune, pleasure and power, and in doing so they often step on those who get in their way. Such men bring to the world selfishness, greed, hatred, and injustice. That, however, is not all there is to human existence. There are also men who pursue truth and justice, and often they light the darkened world with a little love and touch man with a quality of goodness. They help make this, at least to some extent, a better place to live in. These men who love wisdom pursue these ideals and values with all their might in their lives, in their work, and even in their deaths.

A final thought may be communicated, as we reach the end of our philosophical journey. In an industrial civilization and world of pollution such as ours, all that is beautiful seems to become defiled, and there seems scant basis for the good and beautiful life. We have so long been rapt in science that the raptures of life have eluded us; and in a world of fragmentation nothing at all seems to hold together for man. Thus we simply seem to lack the philosophical basis for a noble existence. Yet there are possibilities. We saw in the work of Heidegger a monumental effort to provide us solid ground to walk upon in this space age. And if things in our universe seem too disconnected, we can find in the philosophy of Alfred North Whitehead a vision of a cosmos in which everything is connected. His is truly a cosmic philosophy that helps us "get it all together."

Whitehead was the first great philosopher to respond to the challenge of Einstein's new physics. With matter transformed into energy, Whitehead saw it as possible for us to understand this not as a universe of dead inert matter, but of pulsating energy. He saw it as a universe alive, and as one which could bring to life the spirit of wisdom. The new physics meant that this is not a universe in bits and pieces, not one of meaningless pushes and pulls, but one of unity. The scientist has to understand things in terms of formal patterns, not isolated cold facts. Living under the shadow of the Newtonian mechanical world view, man felt himself a displaced person in this world. At the very dawn of philosophy the Hindus saw the soul of man as one with the soul of the world, and thus could feel the deepest bonds with all existence. Now after thousands of years of philosophy and science Whitehead has contributed a poetic image of the universe, which is also scientific. Perhaps upon the basis of such a synoptic vision man shall again be able to smile upon the universe and regard it his home.

Glossary

Absolute: The self-complete and perfect, that which is not conditioned by or dependent upon anything else; that which is unchanging and ultimate, the ground of all existence and being.

Absolutism: The thesis there is absolute truth or value, that which is unchanging, necessary, and eternal.

Accident: That which exists only in another being, that which is qualified or contingent.

Agnosticism: The thesis that it is not possible to know God exists. Thus the agnostic does not categorically deny God exists but rather insists the only proper answer to the question of God's existence is, "I don't know."

Altruism: This is the position of benevolence. It is consideration of, or action on behalf of, the other even before oneself. It is the direct opposite of egoism. Egoism is the placing of one's own interests before all others'. Thus egoist Ayn Rand calls altruism "self-sacrifice" or "slavery."

Analytic judgment: An analytic judgment is one the truth of which is dependent upon formal analysis of its elements rather than upon factual verification. In such judgments the predicate term does not enlarge the subject but is contained within it. An example is the sentence, "The bachelor is an unmarried man." It would be a contradiction to assert one is a bachelor but married. We know when an analytic judgment is true, because to assert its opposite gives rise to contradiction.

Anthropomorphism: The attributing of human characteristics to that which is not human. A prime example in religion is the attributing of human qualities to gods.

Antinomy: Antinomy results when two contradictory ideas can be shown to be valid from the same premises.

Antithesis: The exact or polar opposite of a given idea, action, or event.

Apathia: The word that describes the Stoic's conception of the highest good. Apathia as used by the Stoic philosophers meant a willed indifference to their fate.

A posteriori: That which follows after. The philosophers known as the Empiricists insisted all knowledge is *a posteriori,* or derived from experience. To say knowledge is *a posteriori* is to say it is learned or comes only *after* man has experienced things. This view is directly opposed to the view of the rationalists that there can be innate or inborn ideas.

Ataraxia: The word which describes what the Epicurean philosophers took to be the highest good. Ataraxia is a state of imperturbable calm.

Atheism: The thesis that there is no God.

Atomism: The thesis that reality is composed of indivisible and indestructible mass particles ever in motion.

Attribute: In metaphysics an attribute is recognized as the essential property or characteristic of substance. An attribute is an indispensable quality of a substance but is not identical with a substance. This is so because a substance is that which exists in itself and is dependent upon nothing outside of itself whereas an attribute cannot exist by itself.

Aufklarung: The German word for Enlightenment. It implies liberation of man from dark superstition and ignorance, from prejudice and traditional thinking.

Axiology: The theory of value.

Becoming: In metaphysics this refers to the sphere or realm of change. It is a word that is used to refer to reality as process. By the use of the word Becoming there also may be reference to movement from a lower to a higher level, from potentiality to actualization.

Being: May be understood as all that exists, or as reality. Being may be understood as the realm of permanence, as that which is eternal and necessary.

Categorical imperative: The moral law of rational beings, which is absolute and unconditional. A categorical imperative is a command we *must* do something—and with no qualifications of that command.

Cogito, ergo sum: I think, therefore I am. One can doubt all things but it is impossible to doubt one is thinking because in the very process of doubting one must be thinking. Therefore, no matter what one does he cannot escape the fact he is thinking and so he exists as a thinking thing, a *res cogitans*. This was the line of argument developed by French philosopher René Descartes.

Coherence theory of truth: This is the thesis that the fundamental test of the truth of judgments is to be discovered in their mutual coherence or consistency in an established system of knowledge.

Conatus: The drive for self-preservation.

Correspondence theory of truth: The thesis

that the truth of propositions is to be found by matching them with facts or some state or states of affair in the external world.

Cosmogony: The theory of the origin of the world.

Cosmology: A theory of the meaning of the entire universe.

Cosmological argument for the existence of God: This is the line of reasoning that one cannot ultimately explain things if he gets involved in an infinite regress, and that means it is necessary to arrive at a first cause—that which is itself uncaused, unconditioned, absolute. God is then a first cause.

Cyrenaic School of Ethics: The school of ancient Greek philosophy founded by Aristippus. The primary tenet of the Cyrenaics is that the aim of life is pleasure of the moment. It is the view that one should get all the pleasure he can here and now.

Deism: The thesis that God exists separately from the universe he created and set into motion as a machine. Having set the machine in motion this God has no further personal interest in it.

Deontological ethics: The doctrine in ethics that actions can be known to be right no matter what their consequences.

Determinism: The thesis that all that happens in the universe does so inevitably as the result of fundamental laws. This implies that not only are all events lawful and predictable but that man has no free will and that his ideas and behavior are always an outcome of impersonal forces beyond his control.

Dialectic: In general this is the idea that *thought* or *ideas* are advanced through the development of contradictions and their resolution. Particularly since the nineteenth century, dialectic has been used to mean that all of *reality* develops through the conflict of opposites and their resolution.

Ding an sich: "Thing in itself." By this Kant meant reality as it is in itself, independent of man's perception or conception of it.

Dualism: From Latin *duo* meaning two. It is the thesis that reality is bifurcated; reality is divided into *two* fundamental substances or may be understood in terms of *two* basic forces.

Egoism: The teaching that one should seek his own good or welfare before that of all others. It is the opposite of altruism, which puts the good of others even before that of oneself.

Élan Vital: In the philosophy of Bergson this is the vital spark of life—that which resists any reduction to physicochemical elements. The élan vital is the source of creative growth and spontaneity in life.

Emotivism: The theory of ethics developed by the logical positivist school of philosophy and particularly associated with the teachings of A. J. Ayer of that school. The emotivist contention is that ethical words have emotive but no cognitive meaning. Cognitive meaning refers to that which is empirically verifiable and objectively communicable. Emotive meaning refers to the evocative power of words and has nothing to do with any rational meaning.

Empiricism: The school of philosophy that teaches all knowledge comes from, or has its base in, sense experience.

Entelechy: A self-fulfilling or self-realizing power.

Epiphenomenalism: The thesis that consciousness is nothing but a by-product of the physical nervous system.

Epistemology: The theory of knowledge.

Eros: Love in the sense of desire, physical love or love that is striving or ascending.

Eudaimonia: The basis of all classical Greek ethics. It means the state of well-being, satisfaction, or happiness.

Existentialism: Contemporary philosophy by which it is held that the individual's act of existence is more basic and real than any formal or abstract philosophical idea or set of ideas. The formula for existentialism has been expressed by the phrase "existence precedes essence," and by this it is meant that the concrete specific and actual experience of anything is more meaningful and real than any definition or intellectual explanation of it.

Fatalism: The attitude or view that whatever will be will be, and there is no possible altering or changing of that. As they say of television shows it may be said of all life that it has been prerecorded. God or Allah has predetermined all.

Felicific calculus: According to British philosopher Jeremy Bentham this was a scheme for calculating or measuring what is good by specifically showing what produces maximum pleasure.

Hedonism: From Greek *hedone,* the doctrine that pleasure is the good.

Hylozoism: The view that life and matter are inseparable and that nature is alive.

Idea: In Plato this refers to that which is ultimately real. The Idea is the Form or the universal pattern of reality. The Idea or Form in Plato is a universal, that which is spiritual, eternal, and necessary.

Idealism: In metaphysics, the general teachings that mind or spirit and the values thereof are dominant in the universe or are all that is real. In epistemology, the thesis that all that can be known are ideas or mental processes and the minds that are the cause of these.

Indeterminism: The thesis that the will can act independently of physical, psychological, and social factors and thus is free. Not all things can be explained by reference to causal laws as some acts elude these.

Innate ideas: Inborn truths, or that which we can know to be true because its source is from within rather than from without.

Intuition: The direct and immediate grasping of a truth; certain knowledge that is obtained by feeling rather than reasoning.

Logic: One of the main branches of philosophical study, which has to do with developing a way of thinking in accordance with the principles of valid inference; from the Greek word *Logos,* reason or discourse. In logic proper modes of reasoning from premises to conclusion are developed.

Logos: Reason or disclosure; sometimes understood as the cosmic reason or the Word, implying that there is rational order or that there is intelligibility in the very cosmic processes.

Materialism: The thesis that only matter or matter in motion is real and that matter in motion is the fundamental basis of all existence.

Mechanism: The thesis that everything can be accounted for on the basis of purely mechanical principles. All is explained as a consequence of matter in motion and the laws arising therefrom. Nature is taken as functioning automatically as a machine and without ultimate design or purpose.

Meliorism: The thesis that the world is not entirely good or evil but that there is good and evil in the world, and as a result of commitment and human effort things can be made better.

Metaphysics: One of the basic branches of philosophy; the study of Being or Reality.

Monad: In metaphysics refers to a basic

substance of reality. We may particularly think of the word monad as associated with the philosophy of Leibniz. Reality is made of a plurality of basic spiritual elements or units that he called *monads*, which according to him are not divisible, cannot be destroyed, and are immaterial and purposeful.

Monism: The thesis that there is only *one* basic reality.

Naturalism: Explaining the whole cosmos without any reference to the supernatural. The cosmos is understood as operating without any divine assistance on the basis of purposeless or mechanistic physical laws. The natural world is taken to be all there is, the whole of reality.

Naturalistic fallacy: This fallacy consists in the effort to define ethical terms by reference to natural properties. Since ethical terms are normative or "ought" statements and natural properties are factual or "is" statements, it is maintained that it is always a fallacy to identify ethical and natural properties in the form of a definition.

Nominalism: The thesis that abstract terms, general terms, or universals are only names and have no objective reference in reality. Reality is understood by the nominalist to consist purely of individual or particular entities or things.

Nous: Mind or Reason, the intellectual faculty.

Objective idealism: There is an objective reality independent of the knowledge subjects have of it. This objective reality is a spiritual and mental structure or pattern, intelligible and purposeful. Both the perceiver and the world are aspects of the spiritual absolute.

Occasionalism: A philosophical position concerning the mind-body problem. This is the thesis that mind and body are so utterly distinct that one can never have an effect upon the other, but God has so synchronized mind and body that they work in perfect harmony and coordination. It was held by Arnold Geulincx, the Dutch philosopher and follower of Descartes, that upon the occasion of a given bodily change there would occur the emergence of a sensation in the soul, and upon the *occasion* of a given volition in the soul there is a corresponding change in the nervous system of the body.

Ontological argument for the existence of God: The thesis that if one knows the word God he cannot deny His existence without contradiction. God is that Being than which none greater can be conceived. The greatest Being must be a perfect Being, and perfection includes existence. Hence it is a contradiction to say God is the greatest perfect Being but does not exist.

Ontology: The study of ultimate Being or ultimate reality.

Pantheism: The view that God is fully immanent in the universe or is identical with all of nature.

Philosophy: Literally, the love of wisdom. It has been called the most general science and in a sense is the most general study. It is systematic criticism of ultimate foundations. Historically philosophy has been the search for truth, goodness, and beauty.

Pluralism: The thesis that reality is constituted not of one substance (monism) nor even two (dualism), but of *many* substances.

Ponos: The highest virtue of cynic philosophers, meaning labor or pain.

Positivism: The view that the only legitimate kind of knowledge is scientific and that religious, metaphysical, and ethical modes of understanding are prescientific and devoid of any validity. Positivism is an effort to understand all of reality in categories of science. The philosophical founder of modern positivism was Frenchman Auguste Comte.

Pragmatism: The view that philosophy must be practical and assess questions in terms of concrete results—in terms of whatever works.

Psychophysical parallelism: The thesis that mind and body function in a way that they perfectly parallel each other. Mind and body, or the mental and physical, exactly correspond to each other.

Rationalism: The philosophy that understands knowledge as being based on reason rather than on perception. Rationalists place prime emphasis upon thought and deduction rather than upon experience or induction and often maintain that truth is *a priori* or innate.

Realism: In metaphysics, the teaching that universals, abstract ideas, or general terms are in themselves real. Plato held that universals are more real than particular things.

In epistemology, the teaching that the world perceived by our senses actually does exist externally to us or independently of us.

Right: The behavior that accords with ethical standards or principles. In this sense one does what is right when he acts in a way consistent with an ethical principle. A right is a claim one can make upon others. A legal right is a claim one can make against others that is recognized by law. A natural right is a claim one can make that may not be sanctioned by human law but is so by a higher law.

Skepticism: The thesis that no knowledge or truth or, at least, no absolute knowledge or truth is possible.

Solipsism: The view "I alone exist," or that the only thing one can really know is his own existence.

Substance: Literally, to stand under. Substance is the essence of what is real, or it may be understood as the ultimate principle.

Tabula rasa: A blank tablet. According to empiricist philosopher John Locke the mind at birth is a blank tablet and for knowledge to take place experience must write upon it.

Teleological: That which is purposeful or has a final goal. Mechanism accounts for present and future in terms of past but teleology accounts for present in terms of future as a fulfillment of purpose. A final end or goal is the cause of what happens.

Theism: The view that there is a supreme Being, a personal God.

Transcendent: That which goes beyond, that which is above, or that which is other than.

Universal: A general term or an abstract reality. A universal is that which is predicable of another. Thus we say the universal red is predicable of roses, fire engines, shirts, and all red things in the universe. A *universal* is the opposite of a *particular*. A particular is that which can be given a specific position in space and can be located in time. In other words, a particular is a definite thing whereas a universal is an abstract reality.

Utilitarianism: The ethical philosophy that defines good as the greatest happiness for the greatest number.

Vitalism: The thesis that there is that which cannot be reduced to physico-chemical terms, a basic life force, a vital spark.

Weltanschauung: The world view.

Index

hedonism, 228–48, 305
Hegel, Georg, W. F., 33, 51, 141, 146–55, 156, 183, 195, 196, 197, 347
Heidegger, Martin, 3, 4, 5, 207–16, 330
Heine, Heinrich, 9
Heisenberg, Werner, 64, 318
Heloise, 7, 8
Hempel, Carl G., 334–37
Heraclitus, 6, 34, 37, 155
Hesse, Hermann, 89
Hicks, R. D., 6n
Hippias, 38
history, 29
Hobbes, Thomas, 33, 56, 132, 217, 229–40, 287–89
d'Holbach, Baron, 136, 214
Holmes, Oliver Wendell, 151, 258
Holt, Edwin B., 105
homo mensura ("man is the measure" doctrine), 35
L'Homme Machine, 133
Hook, Sidney, 315
Hume, David, 33, 52, 70–90, 91, 94, 117, 118, 177, 249, 250, 312, 319
Hunza, The, 123, 124
hylozoism, 130, 358
hylozoists, 130
hypothetical imperative, 247

Idea, the (*see also* Form, eidos), 141–46, 197, 198, 210, 358
idealism, 53, 54, 104, 105, 106, 107, 108, 122, 140–55, 193, 216, 217, 236, 358
indeterminism, 313, 317–20, 331, 332, 358
induction, problem of, 80
intuition, 108–16, 118
Jacobson, Allan L., 128, 129
James, William, 120, 169, 314, 317, 326, 327
Jesus, 356, 349, 353
Johnson, Dr. Samuel, 61, 62
Journals, 194
Jung, Carl Gustav, 27

Kafka, Franz, 87
Kant, Immanuel, 9, 10, 90–102, 103, 118, 148, 248–68, 290, 303, 306, 310, 346, 347
Kaufmann, Walter, 4n
Kepler, Johannes, 335, 336
Kierkegaard, Søren, 15, 194–97, 214, 215, 276–82, 291, 307, 350

knowledge is perception, doctrine of (*see also* Empiricism), 34–37
Knox, Ronald, 66
Kornberg, Dr. Arthur, 115
Krikorian, Y. H., 153

Ladd, Bruce, 260n
Lalanne, Ludovic, 8
Landulf, Count, 8
Laplace, Pierre Simon, 136, 137, 314
Lapp, Ralph, 172
Laver, James, 30
Leahy, Admiral William D., 284
Leeuwenhoeck, Anton van, 133
Leibniz, Gottfried Wilhelm von, 33, 49, 51, 117, 173
Leighton, Dr. Joseph, 20
Lenin, Vladimir Illich Ulyanov, 68
Leucippus, 130, 217
Leviathan, 232
Leverrier, Urbain, 336
libertarianism, 313, 320–21, 332
Lincoln, Abraham, 233, 234
Locke, John, 33, 52–59, 60, 61, 71, 73, 105, 117
logical positivism, 89, 101, 103, 104, 181–93, 205, 218
"Logic of Explanation, The," 334
Logic of Moral Discourse, The, 300
Lucretius (Titus Lucretius Carus), 248

Machiavelli, Niccolò, 287, 288
Malebranche, Nicolas, 49
Malin Genie (Great Deceiver), 46
Marshall, George C., 288
Marvin, Walter T., 105
Marx, Karl, 14, 123, 138, 153, 155–62, 200, 217, 277, 315
materialism, 113, 115, 116, 122, 123–40, 193, 216, 217, 358
matters of fact, 73–73, 79
McMullin, Ernan, 137
mechanism, 113, 114, 115, 156, 162, 358
Meerloo, Joost, 315
Meinong, Alexius, 185, 186
Meno, 41
metaphysics, 119–216, 358
la Mettrie, Julien Offray, 133, 134, 135, 156, 172
Michelet, Jules, 13

Mill, John Stuart, 33, 68, 183, 229, 240, 246–48, 306
Milton, John, 132
mind-body problem (*see also* Dualism), 165–71
monism, 173–81, 183, 218
Montague, William Pepperell, 105
Moore, G. E., 103–07, 293–95

Nagel, Ernest, 135, 146n, 318–19
Napoleon, 137
naturalism, 122
Nausea, (*La Nausée*), 201
Neurath, Otto, 198, 192
New Realism, 105–106
Newton, Isaac, 78, 132, 133, 137, 318, 336
Neitzsche, Friederich, 5, 6, 15, 194, 203, 211, 278, 282, 287, 289–92, 306
noesis (rational intuition), 39
nominalism, 341, 359
Nostradamus, Michael, 30
noumena, 100, 101, 104
du Nuoy, Lecomte, 311

Occasionalism, 48, 49, 359
Ogden, Charles, 294, 295
Olson, Regine, 196, 282
ontological argument, 47, 309–10, 330, 359
Oppenheim, Paul, 334–37
Oppenheimer, Robert, 164
ordinary language, 169
Orelli, 8
Ortega y Gasset, José, 199

Parkes, Dr. A. S., 23
Paul, St., 48
Peirce, C. S., 169
People v. Beardsley, 254
People v. Hayner, 24
People v. Lewis, 82
Perkins, Rollin M., 24, 84
Perry, R. B., 69, 106, 106
Philosophical Investigations, 188
philosophy, 3–16
Philosophy and Logical Syntax, 295
Philosophy of Science, 42
Pickering, W. H., 172
Pitkin, Walter B., 105
Plato, 5, 8, 28, 33–42, 44, 50, 117, 141–46, 153, 183, 197, 210, 214, 217, 247, 290, 347
Poincare, Henri, 336